SOURCES

Notable Selections in *Education*

SECOND EDITION

About the Editor

FRED SCHULTZ has been a professor of education at the University of Akron in Akron, Ohio, since 1969. He received his B.S. in social science education in 1962, his M.S. in history and philosophy of education in 1966, and his Ph.D. in history and philosophy of education and American studies in 1969, all from Indiana University in Bloomington, Indiana. His B.A. degree in Spanish was conferred from the University of Akron in 1985. He also likes to study modern languages. Professor Schultz has been the editor of *Annual Editions: Education* (Dushkin/McGraw-Hill) since the 1978/79 edition of that volume, and he also edits *Annual Editions: Multicultural Education,* currently available in its 1997/98 edition. He is coauthor, with James Monroe Hughes, of *Education in America* (Harper & Row, 1976). He is a fellow of the Philosophy of Education Society in the United States and a member of the Philosophy of Education Society of Great Britain. His other professional memberships include the American Educational Research Association and the American Sociological Association. Professor Schultz was also president of the Ohio Valley Philosophy of Education Society in 1976. His articles and papers have appeared in numerous journals, including *Educational Theory, The Journal of Thought, Educational Considerations, Proceedings of the Philosophy of Education Society,* and *Proceedings of the Ohio Valley Philosophy of Education Society* (now *Philosophical Studies in Education*). In the 1970s Professor Schultz did freelance book manuscript editing for New York publishers, in addition to his primary work as a professor. He has also been a visiting professor at Kent State University in Kent, Ohio, and at Oberlin College.

SOURCES

Notable Selections in
Education

SECOND EDITION

Edited by
Fred Schultz
University of Akron

Dushkin/McGraw-Hill
A Division of The McGraw-Hill Companies

Manufactured in the United States of America

Second Edition

10 9 8 7 6 5 4 3

Library of Congress Cataloging-in-Publication Data
  Main entry under title:
    Sources: notable selections in education/edited by Fred Schultz.—2nd ed.
    Includes bibliographical references and index.
    1. Education—United States. I. Schultz, Fred, *comp.*

                                                                                                370′.973
  0-697-34333-2   ISSN: 1094-7620

 Printed on Recycled Paper

Preface

The study of education has been approached from several conflicting, and competing, perspectives. This has always been true, although the conflict has become even more pronounced in the past 100 years. The Greek philosopher Aristotle noted in his *Politics* that people in Athens in his time (about 2,350 years ago) could not come to a consensus over what the purposes and content of education should be. This is just as true in industrialized countries today. There are currently several competing ideological perspectives regarding the social and academic purposes of schooling. *Sources: Notable Selections in Education,* 2d ed., explores and samples some important perspectives and debates on the roles of schools, of teachers, and on the content of school curricula that have emerged over the past several decades. The book also samples important sources regarding the struggle of cultural minorities and women to attain equality of opportunity in the field of education.

The study of education has a rich and compelling legacy, and the 39 selections in this volume are from primary sources, both older and contemporary sources, that have greatly influenced American education since the 1890s. As we come to the end of the twentieth century, we can see that the literature on American education encompasses the classical humanist tradition in education, the revolutionary ideas concerning what education ought to be about that developed in the United States in the early and middle decades of the twentieth century, and the most current viewpoints and ideas on the psychology of learning that are emerging in the 1990s and that have already achieved the status of contemporary classics. I have attempted to bring together in one volume a collection of notable selections that uniquely summarizes the conflicting ideological and cultural perspectives that make up the literature in the field of education.

The reader will quickly be able to see the incredible magnitude of the differences between the competing perspectives placed side by side in this volume. For instance, the selections in Part 1 clearly demonstrate the differences in the points of view of the conservative tradition (seen in the selections by E. D. Hirsch, Jr., Diane Ravitch, and Mortimer Adler), the liberal-progressive tradition (represented by John Dewey and William Heard Kilpatrick), and the critical pedagogical perspective (evident in the writings of Henry A. Giroux, Michael W. Apple, Paulo Freire, and Ivan Illich) with regard to the ultimate aims of education. So it is throughout this volume, as competing perspectives on each of the areas of education examined are presented to the reader for his or her own judgment and evaluation.

There were several conceptual parameters that I tried to remain alert to as I went through the process of developing this book of readings. First, I wanted it to sample some highly important sources on education that either have, are, or are going to affect how people respond to the great debates now going on over how to improve the quality of what students learn in school as well as over proposals for new and different sorts of opportunities in the field of education. Second, I wanted the book to reflect the enormous struggle for human dignity and freedom of opportunity in the field of education in American society— in particular, the struggle of racial and ethnic minorities and the struggle of women to attain equal rights in the field of education. Third, I wanted the selections in this volume to accurately and fairly represent the conflicting ideological perspectives now competing for public acceptance in the recent literature on education. Fourth, I sought to sample some of the documentary sources on testing and assessment in American education in recent years. Finally, I wanted to include selections that reflect the great vein of literature that has developed on the inescapable interrelationships between formal educational institutions and the cultures that produce them, as well as the universe of discourse that governs differing conceptions of freedom and culture in the education of persons. I believe that this collection of notable selections does address all of these concerns.

Organization of the book.   The selections are organized topically around the major areas of study within education. Part 1 includes selections on the Foundations of Education; Part 2, Curriculum and Instruction; Part 3, Schools in a Multicultural Society; Part 4, The American Constitutional Tradition and Education; Part 5, Testing and Assessment of Learning; and Part 6, Society, Culture, and Education. Each selection is preceded by a short introductory headnote that places the selection in the context of its relevance to the literature in the field of education and that provides biographical information on the author.

Suggestions for reading the selections.   Student readers of this book are encouraged to read the introductory headnotes prior to reading the selections to which they refer. The headnotes will get you started in the right direction for reading the selections. It is also a good idea to keep in mind—and this is especially true in several of the older selections—that how language is used can and does change over time. The language used in some of the older selections is frequently sexist or nonstandard as compared to current usage. Until the middle of the twentieth century, writers commonly used the terms *he, him,* and *man,* among others, to make generic references to both males and females. Today we are much more sensitive to potentially sexist and racist language. Try to take into account the social contexts in which these older essays were written. Finally, keep in mind that all of the selections in this volume either had or are having notable impact on education and what takes place in the classroom.

On the Internet.   Each part in this book is preceded by an *On the Internet* page. This page provides a list of Internet site addresses that are relevant to the part as well as a description of each site.

A word to the instructor. An *Instructor's Manual With Test Questions* (multiple-choice and essay) is available through the publisher for instructors using *Sources: Notable Selections in Education,* 2d ed., in the classroom.

Acknowledgments. I was very pleased when I was first contacted about developing this volume. It has been a unique opportunity to place in the hands of readers notable sources that have had great impact on the directions of debate over the social purposes of education in American society. I would like to thank those who reviewed the first edition of *Sources* and responded with specific suggestions for the second edition:

Dorothy Engan-Barker
Mankato State University

Harry Morgan
State University of West Georgia

John C. Fischetti
University of Louisville

Christine Murray
SUNY College at Brockport

Jeffrey Kaplan
University of Central Florida

Jody A. Resko
Queens College

Judith Landrum
Northwestern College

Christopher F. Roellke
University of Richmond

Timothy Leonard
St. Xavier University

Patricia N. Toney
Boise State University

During the development of this edition, David Dean, list manager for the Sources series, provided enthusiastic, effective support and encouragement at each step of the publication process. I would also like to thank Mrs. Roberta Reese, word processing operator at the University of Akron, for her fast, accurate, and insightful work in the development of the support material for this volume. My thanks as well to David Brackley, developmental editor, and Tammy Ward, administrative assistant for the Sources series. There were many selections by other famous authors that I wanted to include in this volume. However, space limitations prevented inclusion of many equally important selections in this second edition of *Sources: Notable Selections in Education.* I welcome any comments or suggestions you may have about selections for the book. Please write to me in care of SOURCES, Dushkin/McGraw-Hill.

Fred Schultz
University of Akron

Contents

Preface   i

PART ONE   *Foundations of Education*   1

CHAPTER 1   The Conservative Tradition in Educational Thought   3

1.1   **E. D. HIRSCH, JR.,** from *Cultural Literacy: What Every American Needs to Know*   3

"We Americans have long accepted literacy as a paramount aim of schooling, but only recently have some of us who have done research in the field begun to realize that literacy is far more than a skill and that it requires large amounts of specific information."

1.2   **DIANE RAVITCH,** from *The Troubled Crusade: American Education, 1945–1980*   14

"In the crusade against ignorance, there have been no easy victories, but no lasting defeats."

1.3   **MORTIMER ADLER,** from "The Paideia Proposal: Rediscovering the Essence of Education," *The American School Board Journal*   22

"[F]or the health of science and scholarship, we need specialists who also are generalists—generally cultivated human beings, not just good plumbers. We need truly educated human beings who can perform their special tasks better precisely because they have general cultivation as well as intensely specialized training."

CHAPTER 2   The Progressive-Liberal Agenda   29

2.1   **JOHN DEWEY,** from *Democracy and Education: An Introduction to the Philosophy of Education*   29

"We thus reach a technical definition of education: It is that reconstruction or reorganization of experience which adds to the meaning of experience, and which increases ability to direct the course of subsequent experience."

2.2 **WILLIAM HEARD KILPATRICK,** from "The Project Method," *Teachers College Record* 35

"As the purposeful act is thus the typical unit of the worthy life in a democratic society, so also should it be made the typical unit of school procedure."

CHAPTER 3   The Critical Pedagogical Perspective 43

3.1 **HENRY A. GIROUX,** from "Culture, Power and Transformation in the Work of Paulo Freire: Toward a Politics of Education," in Henry A. Giroux, *Teachers as Intellectuals: Toward a Critical Pedagogy of Learning* 43

"Education in Freire's view becomes both an ideal and a referent for change in the service of a new kind of society. As an ideal, education 'speaks' to a form of cultural politics that transcends the theoretical boundaries of any one specific political doctrine, while simultaneously linking social theory and practice to the deepest aspects of emancipation."

3.2 **MICHAEL W. APPLE,** from *Ideology and Curriculum* 53

"A basic assumption seems to be that conflict among groups of people is *inherently* and fundamentally bad and we should strive to eliminate it *within* the established framework of institutions, rather than seeing conflict and contradiction as the basic 'driving forces' in society."

3.3 **PAULO FREIRE,** from *Pedagogy of the Oppressed,* trans. Myra Bergman Ramos 63

"Those truly committed to liberation must reject the banking concept in its entirety, adopting instead a concept of men as conscious beings, and consciousness as consciousness intent upon the world."

3.4 **IVAN ILLICH,** from *Deschooling Society* 71

"Institutional wisdom tells us that children need school. Institutional wisdom tells us that children learn in school. But this institutional wisdom is itself the product of schools because sound common sense tells us that only children can be taught in school."

PART TWO   *Curriculum and Instruction 79*

CHAPTER 4   Schooling 81

4.1 **MARIA MONTESSORI,** from *The Montessori Method* 81

"We call an individual disciplined when he is master of himself, and can, therefore, regulate his own conduct when it shall be necessary to follow some rule of life."

4.2   **KATHERINE CAMP MAYHEW AND ANNA CAMP EDWARDS,** from *The Dewey School: The Laboratory School of the University of Chicago, 1896–1903*   90

"The child's primary calling is growth."

4.3   **HAROLD RUGG AND ANN SHUMAKER,** from *The Child-Centered School: An Appraisal of the New Education*   100

"In the child-centered school... pupils are alive, active, working hard, inventing, organizing, contributing original ideas, assembling materials, carrying out enterprises. As individuals and as social groups pupils grow, and they grow in the capacity to govern themselves, to organize machinery for handling their collective affairs, as well as in individual capacity for creative self-expression."

CHAPTER 5   Curriculum Theory and Practice   110

5.1   HILDA TABA, from *Curriculum Development: Theory and Practice* 110

"Our society today has by no means agreed about what the central function of the school should be."

5.2   THEODORE R. SIZER, from *Horace's Hope: What Works for the American High School*   121

"Public education, then, is not at all or necessarily the same thing as our current system of schools. Other means to give the people access and intelligence—new configurations of educating institutions—may be better, more appropriate to our time, more respectful of current exigencies."

CHAPTER 6   Curriculum Development and the Language of Educational Debate   131

6.1   PETER McLAREN, from "Multiculturalism and the Postmodern Critique: Toward a Pedagogy of Resistance and Transformation," in Henry A. Giroux and Peter McLaren, eds., *Between Borders: Pedagogy and the Politics of Cultural Studies*   131

"I would like to pose an alternative analysis. I shall argue that, despite its limitations for constructing an emancipatory politics, postmodern criticism can offer educators and cultural workers a means of problematizing the issue of difference and diversity in ways that can deepen and extend existing debates over multiculturalism, pedagogy, and social transformation."

6.2   E. D. HIRSCH, JR., from *The Schools We Need and Why We Don't Have Them*   142

"People cannot effectively meet in the classroom or in the marketplace unless they can communicate with and learn from each another. It is the duty of a nation's educational system to create this domain of public communicability."

PART THREE *Schools in a Multicultural Society* 149

CHAPTER 7 The Struggle for Freedom in Education 151

7.1 **DIANE RAVITCH,** from *The Troubled Crusade: American Education, 1945–1980* 151

"Although racism was deeply embedded in American life and law, the experience of the war heightened the contradiction between the reality of racism and the ideals of American democracy."

7.2 **BOOKER T. WASHINGTON,** from a Speech During the Atlanta Exposition, Atlanta, Georgia, September 18, 1895 160

"There is no defense or security for any of us except in the highest intelligence and development of all."

7.3 **W. E. B. DU BOIS,** from *The Souls of Black Folk* 164

"But the hushing of the criticism of honest opponents is a dangerous thing. It leads some of the best of the critics to unfortunate silence and paralysis of effort, and others to burst into speech so passionately and intemperately as to lose listeners."

7.4 **JAMES BALDWIN,** from "A Talk to Teachers," *Saturday Review* 174

"The purpose of education, finally, is to create in a person the ability to look at the world for himself, to make his own decisions, to say to himself this is black or this is white, to decide for himself whether there is a God in heaven or not. To ask questions of the universe, and then learn to live with those questions, is the way he achieves his own identity. But no society is really anxious to have that kind of person around."

7.5 **MEYER WEINBERG,** from *A Chance to Learn: The History of Race and Education in the United States* 181

"Midcentury marked a turning point in the history of black America. The movement for equality came under black leadership, embraced unprecedented numbers of Negroes, and became national in scope. A persistent black initiative forced a reformulation of public policies in education."

CHAPTER 8 The Critical Perspective on the Struggle for Freedom in Education 193

8.1 **PAULO FREIRE AND DONALDO MACEDO,** from *Literacy: Reading the Word and the World* 193

"The students' voice should never be sacrificed, since it is the only means through which they make sense of their own experience in the world."

8.2   **BENJAMIN R. BARBER,** from *An Aristocracy of Everyone: The Politics of Education and the Future of America*   202

"Powerlessness is a justification for rebellion, but it is not a license for mindlessness. The reality of being without a voice can become part of a good argument, but it is not the same thing as a good argument; it certainly does not exempt the powerless and the voiceless from the obligation to offer good reasons. Indeed, this is precisely why there is both a need and a right to be heard—a right secured only through an education in liberty."

CHAPTER 9   Women and Education   212

9.1   **ELIZABETH CADY STANTON,** from *Eighty Years and More (1815–1897): Reminiscences of Elizabeth Cady Stanton*   212

"From the academy the boys of my class went to Union College at Schenectady. When those with whom I had studied and contended for prizes for five years came to bid me good-by, and I learned of the barrier that prevented me from following in their footsteps—'no girls admitted here'—my vexation and mortification knew no bounds. . . . I felt more keenly than ever the humiliation of the distinctions made on the ground of sex."

9.2   **AMERICAN ASSOCIATION OF UNIVERSITY WOMEN,** from *How Schools Shortchange Girls: A Study of Major Findings on Girls and Education*   221

"The AAUW Report presents a base for a new and enlightened education policy—a policy that will ensure that this nation will provide the best possible education for all of its children. It provides policymakers with impartial data on the ways in which our school system is failing to meet the needs of girls and with specific strategies that can be used to effect change."

9.3   **BELL HOOKS,** from *Teaching to Transgress: Education as the Practice of Freedom*   229

"After twenty years of teaching, I can confess that I am often most joyous in the classroom, brought closer here to the ecstatic than by most of life's experiences."

PART FOUR   *The American Constitutional Tradition and Education   233*

CHAPTER 10   The Struggle for Civil Liberty in the Schools   235

10.1   **U.S. SUPREME COURT,** from *Brown v. Board of Education of Topeka, Kansas* (1954)   235

"Does segregation of children in public schools solely on the basis of race, even though the physical facilities and other 'tangible' factors may be equal, deprive the children of the minority group of equal educational opportunities? We believe that it does."

10.2   **MARIAN WRIGHT EDELMAN,** from "Twenty Years After 'Brown': Where Are We Now?" *New York University Education Quarterly* 240

"As one who grew up in segregated and unequal schools, themselves the product of power inequities between whites and blacks grounded in the deep racism still pervasive in all America, I hold the strong view that real integration is the best goal and the best strategy for achieving nondiscriminatory, quality, and responsive education for black children and all children."

10.3   **UNITED STATES COMMISSION ON CIVIL RIGHTS,** from *A Better Chance to Learn: Bilingual-Bicultural Education*   252

"In *Lau v. Nichols*, the Supreme Court affirmed that interpretation of Title VI's scope, stating: 'Under these state-imposed standards there is no equality of treatment merely by providing students with the same facilities, text books, teachers, and curriculum; for students who do not understand English are effectively foreclosed from any meaningful education.'"

PART FIVE   *Testing and Assessment of Learning*   259

CHAPTER 11   Testing and the Critical Response Test   261

11.1   **BENJAMIN S. BLOOM ET AL.,** from *Taxonomy of Educational Objectives, Handbook I: Cognitive Domain*   261

"Our attempt to arrange educational behaviors from simple to complex was based on the idea that a particular simple behavior may become integrated with other equally simple behaviors to form a more complex behavior."

11.2   **DAVID R. KRATHWOHL, BENJAMIN S. BLOOM, AND BERTRAM B. MASIA,** from *Taxonomy of Educational Objectives, Handbook II: Affective Domain*   271

"The fact that we attempt to analyze the affective area separately from the cognitive is not intended to suggest that there is a fundamental separation. There is none."

11.3   GRANT P. WIGGINS, from *Assessing Student Performance: Exploring the Purpose and Limits of Testing*   286

"[T]ests are intrinsically prone to sacrifice validity to achieve reliability and to sacrifice the student's interests for the test maker's."

CHAPTER 12   The Cognitive Revolution in Learning   295

12.1   ANN L. BROWN ET AL., from "Learning, Remembering, and Understanding," in Paul H. Mussen, ed., *Handbook of Child Psychology, vol. 3: Cognitive Development,* 4th ed.   295

"At the end of the 1960s, a great deal of work was conducted on children's learning; during the 1970s, the main emphasis shifted to memory research. We will argue that, at the end of the 1970s and into the 1980s, the focus will again be on learning mechanisms, but this time guided by a cognitive theory of learning that draws its theoretical insights and empirical support from much wider domains than was previously the case."

12.2   JOHN BRANSFORD ET AL., from "Teaching Thinking and Problem Solving," *American Psychologist*   308

"Our goal in this article is to discuss some of the relevant research and to consider its implications for the issue of teaching thinking and problem solving."

12.3   HOWARD GARDNER AND JOSEPH WALTERS, from *Multiple Intelligences: The Theory in Practice*   315

"Multiple intelligences theory ... pluralizes the traditional concept. An intelligence entails the ability to solve problems or fashion products that are of consequence in a particular cultural setting or community. The problem-solving skill allows one to approach a situation in which a goal is to be obtained and to locate the appropriate route to that goal."

PART SIX   *Society, Culture, and Education   327*

CHAPTER 13   Social Change   329

13.1   JOHN DEWEY, from "Education and Social Change," *The Social Frontier: A Journal of Educational Criticism and Reconstruction*   329

"I shall do what I can, then, to indicate the factors that seem to me to enter into the problem, together with some of the reasons that prove that the schools do have a role—and an important one—in *production* of social change."

13.2   **I. L. KANDEL,** from *Conflicting Theories of Education*   338

"Education does not proceed in a vacuum; its character is determined by the group culture, and schools are institutions created by society to attain certain specific ends."

CHAPTER 14   Culture and Education   346

14.1   **HOWARD GARDNER,** from *Multiple Intelligences: The Theory in Practice*   346

"But there is an alternative vision that I would like to present—one based on a radically different view of the mind, and one that yields a very different view of school. It is a pluralistic view of mind, recognizing many different and discrete facets of cognition, acknowledging that people have different cognitive strengths and contrasting cognitive styles."

14.2   **JONATHAN KOZOL,** from *Amazing Grace: The Lives of Children and the Conscience of a Nation*   353

"Whatever good things may happen for the children of another generation are, in any case, of little solace to those who are children now and will not have their childhood to live a second time in the next century."

Acknowledgments   361

Index   364

PART ONE

Foundations of Education

Chapter 1 The Conservative Tradition in Educational Thought 3

Chapter 2 The Progressive-Liberal Agenda 29

Chapter 3 The Critical Pedagogical Perspective 43

On the Internet . . .

Sites appropriate to Part One

Between the late nineteenth and mid-twentieth centuries, many educational programs grew out of the American reform effort called the progressive movement.

```
http://www.ilt.columbia.edu/academic/
    digitexts/notes/prog_education.html
```

This edition of *Philanthropy, Culture and Society* is a condensation of the themes explored in Dr. Gene Edward Veith's new book on the renaissance of classical education. Here he gives a general background on classical education and cites three examples of their use in primary and secondary schools.

```
http://www.lead-inst.org/crc/pcs/
    pcs-0896.html
```

This is the home page of the National Paideia Center, the goal of which is to promote and support the efforts of educators who are implementing the long-term systemic school reform known as the Paideia Program.

```
http://www.unc.edu/depts/ed/
    cel-paideia.html
```

The Conservative Tradition in Educational Thought

1.1 E. D. HIRSCH, JR.

Literacy and Cultural Literacy

E. D. (Eric Donald) Hirsch, Jr., is a widely read, conservative scholar concerned with the purposes and content of school curricula. His views reflect a traditionalist consensus on what every student should learn or know.

In the selection that follows, he argues that the standard of literacy required of citizens of advanced modern states has risen in recent years and will continue to rise. He further argues that standards of literacy in American schools have not risen to meet world standards. He wishes to see as much emphasis placed on the information that students are taught as is currently placed on the skills that they are taught. He agrees that all students need higher levels of communications skills than ever before in order to enhance national and cultural unity. He provides some interesting examples to illustrate what he believes has been a major decline in standards of literacy in the United States.

Hirsch (b. 1928) is the Linden Kent Memorial Professor of English at the University of Virginia in Charlottesville, Virginia, and president of the Core Knowledge Foundation. He is coauthor, with Joseph F. Kett and James Trefil, of *The Dictionary of Cultural Literacy* (Houghton Mifflin, 1988) and coeditor,

4

*Chapter 1
The
Conservative
Tradition in
Educational
Thought*

with William G. Rowland, Jr., and Michael Stanford, of *First Dictionary of Cultural Literacy* (Houghton Mifflin, 1989). He is also the author of *The Schools We Need and Why We Don't Have Them* (Doubleday, 1996).

The following selection is from Hirsch's book *Cultural Literacy: What Every American Needs to Know* (Houghton Mifflin, 1987). At the end of that book is an appendix created with Joseph F. Kett and James Trefil that consists of a checklist of what every literate American ought to know.

Key Concept: cultural literacy

THE DECLINE OF LITERATE KNOWLEDGE

This [selection begins to] explain why we need to make some very specific educational changes in order to achieve a higher level of national literacy. It does not anatomize the literacy crisis or devote many pages to Scholastic Aptitude Test scores. It does not document at length what has already been established, that Americans do not read as well as they should. It takes no position about methods of initial reading instruction beyond insisting that content must receive as much emphasis as "skill." It does not discuss teacher training or educational funding or school governance. In fact, one of its major purposes is to break away entirely from what Jeanne S. Chall has called "the great debate" about methods of reading instruction. It focuses on what I conceive to be the great hidden problem in American education, and I hope that it reveals this problem so compellingly that anyone who is concerned about American education will be persuaded by [my] argument and act upon it.

The standard of literacy required by modern society has been rising throughout the developed world, but American literacy rates have not risen to meet this standard. What seemed an acceptable level in the 1950s is no longer acceptable in the late 1980s, when only highly literate societies can prosper economically. Much of Japan's industrial efficiency has been credited to its almost universally high level of literacy. But in the United States, only two thirds of our citizens are literate, and even among those the average level is too low and should be raised. The remaining third of our citizens need to be brought as close to true literacy as possible. Ultimately our aim should be to attain universal literacy at a very high level, to achieve not only greater economic prosperity but also greater social justice and more effective democracy. We Americans have long accepted literacy as a paramount aim of schooling, but only recently have some of us who have done research in the field begun to realize that literacy is far more than a skill and that it requires large amounts of specific information. . . .

Professor Chall is one of several reading specialists who have observed that "world knowledge" is essential to the development of reading and writing skills. What she calls world knowledge I call cultural literacy, namely, the network of information that all competent readers possess. It is the background information, stored in their minds, that enables them to take up a newspaper and read it with an adequate level of comprehension, getting the point, grasping the implications, relating what they read to the unstated context which alone gives meaning to what they read. In describing the contents of this neglected domain of background information, I try to direct attention to a new opening that can help our schools make the significant improvement in education that has so far eluded us. The achievement of high universal literacy is the key to all other fundamental improvements in American education.

Why is literacy so important in the modern world? Some of the reasons, like the need to fill out forms or get a good job, are so obvious that they needn't be discussed. But the chief reason is broader. The complex undertakings of modern life depend on the cooperation of many people with different specialties in different places. Where communications fail, so do the undertakings. (That is the moral of the story of the Tower of Babel.) The function of national literacy is to foster effective nationwide communications. Our chief instrument of communication over time and space is the standard national language, which is sustained by national literacy. Mature literacy alone enables the tower to be built, the business to be well managed, and the airplane to fly without crashing. All nationwide communications, whether by telephone, radio, TV, or writing are fundamentally dependent upon literacy, for the essence of literacy is not simply reading and writing but also the effective use of the standard literate language. In Spain and most of Latin America the literate language is standard written Spanish. In Japan it is standard written Japanese. In our country it is standard written English.

Linguists have used the term "standard written English" to describe both our written and spoken language, because they want to remind us that standard spoken English is based upon forms that have been fixed in dictionaries and grammars and are adhered to in books, magazines, and newspapers. Although standard written English has no intrinsic superiority to other languages and dialects, its stable written forms have now standardized the oral forms of the language spoken by educated Americans. The chief function of literacy is to make us masters of this standard instrument of knowledge and communication, thereby enabling us to give and receive complex information orally and in writing over time and space. Advancing technology, with its constant need for fast and complex communications, has made literacy ever more essential to commerce and domestic life. The literate language is more, not less, central in our society now than it was in the days before television and the silicon chip.

The recently rediscovered insight that literacy is more than a skill is based upon knowledge that all of us unconsciously have about language. We know instinctively that to understand what somebody is saying, we must understand more than the surface meanings of words; we have to understand the context as well. The need for background information applies all the more to reading and writing. To grasp the words on a page we have to know a lot of information that isn't set down on the page....

In the mid 1980s American business leaders have become alarmed by the lack of communication skills in the young people they employ. Recently, top executives of some large U.S. companies, including CBS and Exxon, met to discuss the fact that their younger middle-level executives could no longer communicate their ideas effectively in speech or writing. This group of companies has made a grant to the American Academy of Arts and Sciences to

6

*Chapter 1
The
Conservative
Tradition in
Educational
Thought*

analyze the causes of this growing problem. They want to know why, despite breathtaking advances in the technology of communication, the effectiveness of business communication has been slipping, to the detriment of our competitiveness in the world. The figures from NAEP [National Assessment of Educational Progress] surveys and the scores on the verbal SAT [Scholastic Aptitude Test] are solid evidence that literacy has been declining in this country just when our need for effective literacy has been sharply rising.

... [One] day my son asked his Latin class if they knew the name of an epic poem by Homer. One pupil shot up his hand and eagerly said, "The Alamo!" Was it just a slip for *The Iliad?* No, he didn't know what the Alamo was, either. To judge from other stories about information gaps in the young, many American schoolchildren are less well informed than this pupil. The following, by Benjamin J. Stein, is an excerpt from one of the most evocative recent accounts of youthful ignorance.

> I spend a lot of time with teen agers. Besides employing three of them part-time, I frequently conduct focus groups at Los Angeles area high schools to learn about teen agers' attitudes towards movies or television shows or nuclear arms or politicians....
>
> I have not yet found one single student in Los Angeles, in either college or high school, who could tell me the years when World War II was fought. Nor have I found one who could tell me the years when World War I was fought. Nor have I found one who knew when the American Civil War was fought....
>
> A few have known how many U.S. senators California has, but none has known how many Nevada or Oregon has. ("Really? Even though they're so small?")... Only two could tell me where Chicago is, even in the vaguest terms. (My particular favorite geography lesson was the junior at the University of California at Los Angeles who thought that Toronto must be in Italy. My second-favorite geography lesson is the junior at USC, a pre-law student, who thought that Washington, D.C. was in Washington State.)...
>
> Only two could even approximately identify Thomas Jefferson. Only one could place the date of the Declaration of Independence. None could name even one of the first ten amendments to the Constitution or connect them with the Bill of Rights....
>
> On and on it went. On and on it goes. I have mixed up episodes of ignorance of facts with ignorance of concepts because it seems to me that there is a connection.... The kids I saw (and there may be lots of others who are different) are not mentally prepared to continue the society because they basically do not understand the society well enough to value it.

My son assures me that his pupils are not ignorant. They know a great deal. Like every other human group they share a tremendous amount of knowledge among themselves, much of it learned in school. The trouble is that, from the standpoint of their literacy and their ability to communicate with others in our culture, what they know is ephemeral and narrowly confined to their own generation. Many young people strikingly lack the information that writers of American books and newspapers have traditionally taken for granted among their readers from all generations.... [O]ur children's lack of intergenerational information is a serious problem for the nation. The decline of literacy and the decline of shared knowledge are closely related, interdependent facts....

THE NATURE AND USE OF CULTURAL LITERACY

The documented decline in shared knowledge carries implications that go far beyond the shortcomings of executives and extend to larger questions of educational policy and social justice in our country. Mina Shaughnessy was a great English teacher who devoted her professional life to helping disadvantaged students become literate. At the 1980 conference dedicated to her memory, one of the speakers who followed me to the podium was the Harvard historian and sociologist Orlando Patterson. To my delight he departed from his prepared talk to mention mine. He seconded my argument that shared information is a necessary background to true literacy. Then he extended and deepened the ideas I had presented. Here is what Professor Patterson said, as recorded in the *Proceedings* of the conference.

> Industrialized civilization [imposes] a growing cultural and structural complexity which requires persons to have a broad grasp of what Professor Hirsch has called cultural literacy: a deep understanding of mainstream culture, which no longer has much to do with white Anglo-Saxon Protestants, but with the imperatives of industrial civilization. It is the need for cultural literacy, a profound conception of the whole civilization, which is often neglected in talk about literacy.

Patterson continued by drawing a connection between background information and the ability to hold positions of responsibility and power. He was particularly concerned with the importance for blacks and other minorities of possessing this information, which is essential for improving their social and economic status.

> The people who run society at the macro-level must be literate in this culture. For this reason, it is dangerous to overemphasize the problems of basic literacy or the relevancy of literacy to specific tasks, and more constructive to emphasize that blacks will be condemned in perpetuity to oversimplified, low-level tasks and will never gain their rightful place in controlling the levers of power unless they also acquire literacy in this wider cultural sense.

Although Patterson focused his remarks on the importance of cultural literacy for minorities, his observations hold for every culturally illiterate person in our nation. Indeed, as he observed, cultural literacy is not the property of any group or class.

> To assume that this wider culture is static is an error; in fact it is not. It's not a WASP culture; it doesn't belong to any group. It is essentially and constantly changing, and it is open. What is needed is recognition that the accurate metaphor or model for this wider literacy is not domination, but dialectic; each group participates and contributes, transforms and is transformed, as much as any other group.... The English language no longer belongs to any single group or nation. The same goes for any other area of the wider culture.

As Professor Patterson suggested, being taught to decode elementary reading materials and specific, job-related texts cannot constitute true literacy.

8

*Chapter 1
The
Conservative
Tradition in
Educational
Thought*

Such basic training does not make a person literate with respect to newspapers or other writings addressed to a general public. Moreover, a directly practical drawback of such narrow training is that it does not prepare anyone for technological change. Narrow vocational training in one state of a technology will not enable a person to read manuals that explain new developments in the same technology. In modern life we need general knowledge that enables us to deal with new ideas, events, and challenges. In today's world, general cultural literacy is more useful than what Professor Patterson terms "literacy to a specific task," because general literate information is the basis for many changing tasks.

Cultural literacy is even more important in the social sphere. The aim of universal literacy has never been a socially neutral mission in our country. Our traditional social goals were unforgettably renewed for us by Martin Luther King, Jr., in his "I Have a Dream" speech. King envisioned a country where the children of former slaves sit down at the table of equality with the children of former slave owners, where men and women deal with each other as equals and judge each other on their characters and achievements rather than their origins. Like Thomas Jefferson, he had a dream of a society founded not on race or class but on personal merit.

In the present day, that dream depends on mature literacy. No modern society can hope to become a just society without a high level of universal literacy. Putting aside for the moment the practical arguments about the economic uses of literacy, we can contemplate the even more basic principle that underlies our national system of education in the first place—that people in a democracy can be entrusted to decide all important matters for themselves because they can deliberate and communicate with one another. Universal literacy is inseparable from democracy and is the canvas for Martin Luther King's picture as well as for Thomas Jefferson's.

Both of these leaders understood that just having the right to vote is meaningless if a citizen is disenfranchised by illiteracy or semiliteracy. Illiterate and semiliterate Americans are condemned not only to poverty, but also to the powerlessness of incomprehension. Knowing that they do not understand the issues, and feeling prey to manipulative oversimplifications, they do not trust the system of which they are supposed to be the masters. They do not feel themselves to be active participants in our republic, and they often do not turn out to vote. The civic importance of cultural literacy lies in the fact that true enfranchisement depends upon knowledge, knowledge upon literacy, and literacy upon cultural literacy. . . .

Although nationalism may be regrettable in some of its worldwide political effects, a mastery of national culture is essential to mastery of the standard language in every modern nation. This point is important for educational policy, because educators often stress the virtues of multicultural education. Such study is indeed valuable in itself; it inculcates tolerance and provides a perspective on our own traditions and values. But however laudable it is, it should not be the primary focus of national education. It should not be allowed to supplant or interfere with our schools' responsibility to ensure our children's mastery of American literate culture. The acculturative responsibility of the schools is primary and fundamental. To teach the ways of one's own community has always been and still remains the essence of the education of our children, who enter neither a narrow tribal culture nor a transcendent world culture but a national literate culture. For profound historical reasons, this is the way of the modern world. It will not change soon, and it will certainly not be changed by educational policy alone.

E. D. Hirsch, Jr.

THE DECLINE OF TEACHING CULTURAL LITERACY

Why have our schools failed to fulfill their fundamental acculturative responsibility? In view of the immense importance of cultural literacy for speaking, listening, reading, and writing, why has the need for a definite, shared body of information been so rarely mentioned in discussions of education? In the educational writings of the past decade, I find almost nothing on this topic, which is not arcane. People who are introduced to the subject quickly understand why oral or written communication requires a lot of shared background knowledge. It's not the difficulty or novelty of the idea that has caused it to receive so little attention.

Let me hazard a guess about one reason for our neglect of the subject. We have ignored cultural literacy in thinking about education—certainly I as a researcher also ignored it until recently—precisely because it was something we have been able to take for granted. We ignore the air we breathe until it is thin or foul. Cultural literacy is the oxygen of social intercourse. Only when we run into cultural illiteracy are we shocked into recognizing the importance of the information that we had unconsciously assumed.

To be sure, a minimal level of information is possessed by any normal person who lives in the United States and speaks elementary English. Almost everybody knows what is meant by *dollar* and that cars must travel on the right-hand side of the road. But this elementary level of information is not sufficient for a modern democracy. It isn't sufficient to read newspapers (a sin against Jeffersonian democracy), and it isn't sufficient to achieve economic fairness and high productivity. Cultural literacy lies *above* the everyday levels of knowledge that everyone possesses and *below* the expert level known only to specialists. It is that middle ground of cultural knowledge possessed by the "common reader." It includes information that we have traditionally expected our children to receive in school, but which they no longer do.

During recent decades Americans have hesitated to make a decision about the specific knowledge that children need to learn in school. Our elementary schools are not only dominated by the content-neutral ideas of Rousseau and Dewey, they are also governed by approximately sixteen thousand independent school districts. We have viewed this dispersion of educational authority as an insurmountable obstacle to altering the fragmentation of the school curriculum even when we have questioned that fragmentation. We have permitted school policies that have shrunk the body of information that Americans share, and these policies have caused our national literacy to decline.

10

*Chapter 1
The
Conservative
Tradition in
Educational
Thought*

At the same time we have searched with some eagerness for causes such as television that lie outside the schools. But we should direct our attention undeviatingly toward what the schools teach rather than toward family structure, social class, or TV programming. No doubt, reforms outside the schools are important, but they are harder to accomplish. Moreover, we have accumulated a great deal of evidence that faulty policy in the schools is the chief cause of deficient literacy. Researchers who have studied the factors influencing educational outcomes have found that the school curriculum is the most important controllable influence on what our children know and don't know about our literate culture.

It will not do to blame television for the state of our literacy. Television watching does reduce reading and often encroaches on homework. Much of it is admittedly the intellectual equivalent of junk food. But in some respects, such as its use of standard written English, television watching is acculturative. Moreover, as Herbert Walberg points out, the schools themselves must be held partly responsible for excessive television watching, because they have not firmly insisted that students complete significant amounts of homework, an obvious way to increase time spent on reading and writing. Nor should our schools be excused by an appeal to the effects of the decline of the family or the vicious circle of poverty, important as these factors are. Schools have, or should have, children for six or seven hours a day, five days a week, nine months a year, for thirteen years or more. To assert that they are powerless to make a significant impact on what their students learn would be to make a claim about American education that few parents, teachers, or students would find it easy to accept.

Just how fragmented the American public school curriculum has become is described in *The Shopping Mall High School,* a report on five years of first-hand study inside public and private secondary schools. The authors report that our high schools offer courses of so many kinds that "the word 'curriculum' does not do justice to this astonishing variety." The offerings include not only academic courses of great diversity, but also courses in sports and hobbies and a "services curriculum" addressing emotional or social problems. All these courses are deemed "educationally valid" and carry course credit. Moreover, among academic offerings are numerous versions of each subject, corresponding to different levels of student interest and ability. Needless to say, the material covered in these "content area" courses is highly varied.

Cafeteria-style education, combined with the unwillingness of our schools to place demands on students, has resulted in a steady diminishment of commonly shared information between generations and between young people themselves. Those who graduate from the same school have often studied different subjects, and those who graduate from different schools have often studied different material even when their courses have carried the same titles. The inevitable consequence of the shopping mall high school is a lack of shared knowledge across and within schools. It would be hard to invent a more effective recipe for cultural fragmentation.

The formalistic educational theory behind the shopping mall school (the theory that any suitable content will inculcate reading, writing, and thinking skills) has had certain political advantages for school administrators. It has allowed them to stay scrupulously neutral with regard to content. Educational formalism enables them to regard the indiscriminate variety of school offerings as a positive virtue, on the grounds that such variety can accommodate the different interests and abilities of different students. Educational formalism has also conveniently allowed school administrators to meet objections to the traditional literate materials that used to be taught in the schools. Objectors have said that traditional materials are class-bound, white, Anglo-Saxon, and Protestant, not to mention racist, sexist, and excessively Western. Our schools have tried to offer enough diversity to meet these objections from liberals and enough Shakespeare to satisfy conservatives. Caught between ideological parties, the schools have been attracted irresistibly to a quantitative and formal approach to curriculum making rather than one based on sound judgments about what should be taught.

Some have objected that teaching the traditional literate culture means teaching conservative material. Orlando Patterson answered that objection when he pointed out that mainstream culture is not the province of any single social group and is constantly changing by assimilating new elements and expelling old ones. Although mainstream culture is tied to the written word and may therefore seem more formal and elitist than other elements of culture, that is an illusion. Literate culture is the most democratic culture in our land: it excludes nobody; it cuts across generations and social groups and classes; it is not usually one's first culture, but it should be everyone's second, existing as it does beyond the narrow spheres of family, neighborhood, and region.

As the universal second culture, literate culture has become the common currency for social and economic exchange in our democracy, and the only available ticket to full citizenship. Getting one's membership card is not tied to class or race. Membership is automatic if one learns the background information and the linguistic conventions that are needed to read, write, and speak effectively. Although everyone is literate in some local, regional, or ethnic culture, the connection between mainstream culture and the national written language justifies calling mainstream culture *the* basic culture of the nation.

The claim that universal cultural literacy would have the effect of preserving the political and social status quo is paradoxical because in fact the traditional forms of literate culture are precisely the most effective instruments for political and social change. All political discourse at the national level must use the stable forms of the national language and its associated culture. Take the example of *The Black Panther*, a radical and revolutionary newspaper if ever this country had one. Yet the *Panther* was highly conservative in its language and cultural assumptions, as it had to be in order to communicate effectively. What could be more radical in sentiment but more conservative in language and assumed knowledge than the following passages from that paper?

> The present period reveals the criminal growth of bourgeois democracy since the betrayal of those who died that this nation might live "free and indivisible." It exposes through the trial of the Chicago Seven, and its law and order edicts, its desperate turn toward the establishment of a police state. (January 17, 1970)

> In this land of "milk and honey," the "almighty dollar" rules supreme and is being upheld by the faithful troops who move without question in the name of

12

Chapter 1
The
Conservative
Tradition in
Educational
Thought

"law and order." Only in this garden of hypocrisy and inequality can a murderer not be considered a murderer—only here can innocent people be charged with a crime and be taken to court with the confessed criminal testifying against them. Incredible? (March 28, 1970)

In the United States, the world's most technologically advanced country, one million youths from 11 to 17 years of age are illiterate—unable to read as well as the average fourth grader, says a new government report. Why so much illiteracy in a land of so much knowledge? The answer is because there is racism. Blacks and other Nonwhites receive the worst education. (May 18, 1974)

The last item of the Black Panther Party platform, issued March 29, 1972, begins

> 10. WE WANT LAND, BREAD, HOUSING, EDUCATION, CLOTHING, JUSTICE, PEACE AND PEOPLE'S CONTROL OF MODERN TECHNOLOGY.
> When in the course of human events it becomes necessary for one people to dissolve the political bands which have connected them with another, and to assume among the powers of the earth the separate and equal station to which the laws of nature and nature's God entitle them, a decent respect to the opinions of mankind requires that they should declare the causes which impel them to the separation.

And so on for the first five hundred of Jefferson's words without the least hint, or need of one, that this is a verbatim repetition of an earlier revolutionary declaration. The writers for *The Black Panther* had clearly received a rigorous traditional education in American history, in the Declaration of Independence, the Pledge of Allegiance to the Flag, the Gettysburg Address, and the Bible, to mention only some of the direct quotations and allusions in these passages. They also received rigorous traditional instruction in reading, writing, and spelling. I have not found a single misspelled word in the many pages of radical sentiment I have examined in that newspaper. Radicalism in politics, but conservatism in literate knowledge and spelling: to be a conservative in the *means* of communication is the road to effectiveness in modern life, in whatever direction one wishes to be effective.

To withhold traditional culture from the school curriculum, and therefore from students, in the name of progressive ideas is in fact an unprogressive action that helps preserve the political and economic status quo. Middle-class children acquire mainstream literate culture by daily encounters with other literate persons. But less privileged children are denied consistent interchanges with literate persons and fail to receive this information in school. The most straightforward antidote to their deprivation is to make the essential information more readily available inside the schools.

Providing our children with traditional information by no means indoctrinates them in a conservative point of view. Conservatives who wish to preserve traditional values will find that these are not necessarily inculcated by a traditional education, which can in fact be subversive of the status quo. As a child of eleven, I turned against the conservative views of my family and the Southern community in which I grew up, precisely because I had been given a traditional education and was therefore literate enough to read Gunnar Myrdal's *An American Dilemma,* an epoch-making book in my life.

Although teaching children national mainstream culture doesn't mean forcing them to accept its values uncritically, it does enable them to understand those values in order to predict the typical attitudes of other Americans. The writers for *The Black Panther* clearly understood this when they quoted the Declaration of Independence. George Washington, for instance, is a name in our received culture that we associate with the truthfulness of the hero of the story of the cherry tree. Americans should be taught that value association, whether or not they believe the story. Far from accepting the cherry-tree tale or its implications, Oscar Wilde in "The Decay of Lying" used it ironically, in a way that is probably funnier to Americans than to the British audience he was addressing.

> [Truth telling is] vulgarizing mankind. The crude commercialism of America, its materializing spirit, its indifference to the poetical side of things, and its lack of imagination and of high unattainable ideals, are entirely due to that country having adopted for its national hero a man who, according to his own confession, was incapable of telling a lie, and it is not too much to say that the story of George Washington and the cherry tree has done more harm, and in a shorter space of time, than any other moral tale in the whole of literature.... And the amusing part of the whole thing is that the story of the cherry tree is an absolute myth.

For us no less than for Wilde, the values affirmed in traditional literate culture can serve a whole spectrum of value attitudes. Unquestionably, decisions about techniques of conveying traditions to our children are among the most sensitive and important decisions of a pluralistic nation. But the complex problem of how to teach values in American schools mustn't distract attention from our fundamental duty to teach shared content.

The failure of our schools to create a literate society is sometimes excused on the grounds that the schools have been asked to do too much. They are asked, for example, to pay due regard to the demands of both local and national acculturation. They are asked to teach not only American history but also state and city history, driving, cardiopulmonary resuscitation, consumerism, carpentry, cooking, and other special subjects. They are given the task of teaching information that is sometimes too rudimentary and sometimes too specialized. If the schools did not undertake this instruction, much of the information so provided would no doubt go unlearned. In some of our national moods we would like the schools to teach everything, but they cannot. There is a pressing need for clarity about our educational priorities.

From 1945 to 1980

Diane Ravitch is a historian of American education. In her book *The Troubled Crusade: American Education, 1945–1980* (Basic Books, 1983), she describes the educational situation in the United States in 1945 (at the end of World War II) and then records the transformation of American education through the ensuing 35 years, up to 1980. During these years efforts were made to end racial segregation in American schools in order to create greater educational opportunity for American youth and to obtain federal government aid for schooling in the states. Ravitch argues that the politics of schooling in America changed in these years. She documents the new social pressures on American school systems and universities in the decades immediately following the Second World War and describes the enormous demographic changes in the population and in the student body of the nation's schools. She also describes the crusade against ignorance in American society between 1945 and 1980 and portrays an American faith that education will provide the basis for social improvement.

The following selection is from the epilogue to *The Troubled Crusade.* In it, Ravitch synthesizes her major findings regarding the great cultural changes that affected schooling in America from 1945 to 1980.

Ravitch has been an important commentator on education and society since 1974, when she published *The Great School Wars: New York City, 1805–1973* (Basic Books, 1974). She has been a senior research fellow with the Brookings Institution and a senior research professor at New York University. Ravitch has contributed many important essays to scholarly journals, including *The American Scholar,* and she has written or edited several important books, including *Against Mediocrity: The Humanities in America's High Schools* (Holmes & Meier, 1984), edited with Chester E. Finn, Jr., and Robert T. Fancher. She is also the editor of *The American Reader: Words That Moved a Nation* (Harper Collins, 1990) and *Debating the Future of American Education: Do We Need National Standards and Assessments?* (Brookings Institution, 1995). And she coauthored, with Chester E. Finn, Jr., *What Do Our 17-Year-Olds Know? A Report on the First National Assessment of History and Literature* (Harper & Row, 1987).

Key Concept: the crusade against ignorance

When hearings on federal aid to education were held in 1945 and teachers came from around the nation to tell the Congress about the needs of their schools, the problems of American education seemed nearly insoluble. It was no accident that the teachers who testified came from rural districts, because it was there that the schools were in the direst financial straits. Urban districts were conspicuous by their absence from these hearings, because they were considered relatively privileged, well staffed, and well financed. Rural schools, however, suffered from low funding, poor facilities, obsolete teaching materials, and a critical teacher shortage.

Inequitable funding was only the most immediate problem, however. Whether urban or rural, privileged or poor, American schools reflected the racial bias that was common in the larger society. In many states, this bias was institutionalized in racially separate schools where black students received fewer months of schooling and had teachers who had less training and lower pay than their white peers. So deeply imbedded was the practice of racial segregation that there seemed little reason to believe, at war's end, that any political change might be seismic enough to destroy the power of state-enforced racial segregation. Furthermore, access to higher education—though by no means narrow when compared to other nations—was available to fewer than one of every six college-age youths. For black youths, the opportunity for higher education was far less, since they suffered the double burden of an inadequate preparation and exclusion from many "white" colleges and universities. The schools were part of a vicious circle, because exclusion from educational opportunity guaranteed exclusion from economic opportunity.

In the thirty-five years after the Second World War, American education was transformed, though not always in ways that were predictable or intended. Through the course of the fight for federal aid to education and the struggle to abolish racial segregation, the politics of American education changed substantially. In 1949, when Senator Taft's proposal for federal aid came close to passing, everyone agreed—Republican and Democrat, Catholic, Protestant, and Jew, black and white, representatives of labor and business—that there should be no federal control of education. Taft's bill stipulated that "nothing contained in this Act shall be construed to authorize any department, agency, officer, or employee of the United States to exercise any direction, supervision, or control over, or to prescribe any requirements with respect to any school, or any State educational institution or agency" which received federal funds. In 1965, when Congress was concerned above all about racial injustice, the issue of federal control was seen as a "red herring" thrown up by recalcitrant southern congressmen. Regardless of declarations, once federal dollars were involved, there was no quarantining the activities of school districts from the watchful eye of the courts, the Congress, and the federal civil rights agencies.

Over these thirty-five years, educational decision making expanded beyond the traditional state-local district connection. What a given school decided to do regarding its curriculum, its personnel policy, its disciplinary procedures, and its allocation of resources was no longer a local matter. Not every wrong would be righted, but a serious misstep invited the attention of federal officials, state officials, the national press, civil rights organizations, powerful teachers' unions, and professional associations. The rhetoric changed: in the new situation, it seemed archaic to speak about keeping the schools "out of politics." Of course, the schools had always been "in politics," in the sense that they had

16

*Chapter 1
The
Conservative
Tradition in
Educational
Thought*

to compete with other public agencies for funds, they awarded contracts for services, they selected teachers and administrators, and they made their peace with the mores of the surrounding community.

But the new politics of the schools rotated about a state-federal axis rather than a local-state axis. The good superintendent or principal in 1945 maintained good relations with the mayor, the city council, and the school board. By 1980, the alert school administrator had to stay informed about the activities of Congress, the Department of Education, federal regulatory agencies, the courts, and the state legislature in order to see whether some new program had been developed that might provide new funds or whether some current activity had been proscribed or curtailed. School politics became more like American politics in general, in which different interest groups lobbied for funds, sought special relationships with congressional committees, and fought off rival claimants.

Relations between the lay public and the teaching profession also changed in significant ways. In the 1940s, few teachers belonged to a union; strikes were uncommon; administrators were powerful within their school building or their district in hiring, promoting, and assigning teachers. Though their pay was low, teachers had more education than did the parents of their students and commanded the respect that went with the authority they wielded. Teaching attracted a number of gifted women, for whom other career opportunities were limited. In some communities, there were substantial restrictions placed on teachers' behavior; as models for the community's youth, teachers were expected not to smoke or drink or otherwise set a bad example.

The growth of higher education, and especially of community colleges, drew away from the high schools those teachers who preferred the higher status and higher pay associated with being a professor and the chance to teach without discipline problems. The growth of new opportunities for women in law, medicine, and business drew away many of the bright female college graduates who would have previously entered elementary and secondary teaching. The increased educational attainment of the population as a whole meant that teachers were no longer more educated than were parents and could not automatically count on the respect of parents; nor, after the rise of the youth culture in the 1960s, with its antiauthority attitudes, could teachers count on the respect of their adolescent students. These were part of the background conditions within which teacher unionism spread, giving teacher organizations more political power than any of the school boards they negotiated with and making teachers nearly invulnerable to the discontents of the lay public which previously had both admired and disciplined them.

So customary was it to criticize the public schools, whether in the 1940s, the 1950s, the 1960s, or the 1970s, that it was easy to forget the ways in which the schools had been amazingly successful. Americans had long ago decided, without too much discussion of the matter, that education would be the best vehicle through which to change society. The attack against racial segregation, characteristically, was fought out in the schools, and the dismantling of the racial caste system began in the schools and spread to other areas of American life. More than any other institution in American society, the schools became the means through which the goal of equity was pursued. The battle took place around the schools because they provided the setting in which children learned to get along with others beyond their immediate families and in which children and young people developed (or failed to develop) the skills, knowledge, and intelligence to realize their aspirations.

The goal of access to higher education was realized far beyond the most optimistic predictions of President Truman's Commission on Higher Education. The commission's hope that the state might establish extensive community college systems was fully realized by 1980. Its wish that 4.6 million students might attend college by 1960 was derided by many in higher education as both impossible because of the limited number of able students and undesirable because of the certainty that it would degrade the standards of higher education. But fantastic as its prediction sounded in 1947, by 1980 more than 12 million students were enrolled in institutions of higher education. And so fully engaged were colleges and universities in the life of the American people, that fully 38 percent of all their students in 1980 were over the age of twenty-five, returning to improve their minds, their skills, their credentials, or their hobbies. After 1972, college-going was substantially subsidized by a massive federal program of grants and loans, which amounted to more than $5 billion annually by 1980.

Higher levels of participation in the colleges and universities reflected the rising level of educational attainment for the population as a whole. At the end of the war, about 40 of every 100 young people remained in high school long enough to graduate, and about 16 then entered college. By 1980, 75 of every 100 youths graduated from high school, and about 45 then entered college. The gap in educational attainment between whites and blacks was narrowed substantially in the 1960s and 1970s. In 1960, about 40 percent of black youngsters finished high school, compared to some 67 percent of whites; by 1980, 70 percent of blacks did so, compared to 82.5 percent of whites. The gap remained, but the progress in reducing it was remarkable.

The democratization of access to higher education did not, as the critics feared, destroy it. Although some public institutions (like the City College of New York) were transformed from elite liberal arts colleges to open-admissions institutions, in response to egalitarian pressures, the occurrence was atypical. American higher education responded to the onrushing tide of students by adopting what one observer has called a "division of labor between and within institutions." Some colleges and universities remained elite in their admissions standards and in their commitment to teaching and research; some other institutions were or became "service institutions," dedicated to preparing young men and women for technical, vocational, and semiprofessional careers. And many big state universities combined both functions within the same institution, providing both high-quality academic departments for those who sought a liberal education and service programs for the career-oriented. This adaptation enabled higher education both to expand to meet the new demand for higher education and to protect the pre-eminence of its research and scholarship functions.

Other seemingly intractable problems were alleviated or dissipated as American society became more educated and more homogeneous. The bitter religious tensions that had long blocked federal aid to education had eased by 1980; Catholics, Protestants, and Jews had become accustomed to working together in an ecumenical spirit on common problems. Although covert anti-

18

Chapter 1
The
Conservative
Tradition in
Educational
Thought

Catholicism and anti-Semitism lingered, they had lost their respectability. In the rapid advance of urbanization and modernization, American society had become so secularized that the religious groups most likely to encounter bigotry were Fundamentalists, particularly Protestant and Jewish denominations that clung to biblical commands.

The rising levels of educational attainment resulted from and contributed to a fast-rising standard of living. State and federal governments supported the expansion of educational opportunity because they believed that education was an appropriate way to develop human resources and that it made sense to invest public funds in raising the population's literacy and skills. Broad participation in educational opportunities throughout the nation was both a cause and an effect of the nation's scientific and technological progress.

Yet all was not well. Absolute social progress was accompanied by a rising sense of relative deprivation. In the midst of an affluent society, the persistence of poverty was a reproach to national ideals, even if the actual condition of the poor had improved over time. The shifting demography of the postwar era created new problems. The desire for increased opportunity and the decline of agricultural employment propelled large numbers of poor blacks and Hispanics to the urban centers in the 1950s and 1960s, and the cities developed vast slum areas, where the poor concentrated, dependent on impersonal public institutions, bereft of the sense of family and community that had sustained their counterparts in rural areas. By 1980, most large cities had a black and Hispanic majority in their public schools, reflecting the flight of whites to the suburbs and private schools. Many of these big-city school systems, having staggered through conflict after conflict, over such issues as desegregation, community control, and fiscal crises, suffered from severe demoralization. For decades they had thought of themselves as the nation's pace-setting school districts, but by the 1960s their middle-class student population was leaving, achievement scores were sinking, disciplinary problems soared, vandalism became common, and the teaching staff became defensive and insulated. More and more children were staying in school longer than ever, but it was not clear to the students, the teachers, or the parents that the quality of education was as good as it had been in less complicated times.

Concern about educational quality was not limited to big-city schools. Once it had become certain that universal access to education at all levels had been largely secured, educators began to turn their attention to the state of learning, which was far from secure. The debate about standards that had been initiated as a result of the decline in SAT scores produced evidence that other standardized test scores had been dropping, beginning in about the fifth grade; that enrollments in advanced courses in mathematics and science in high school had fallen steadily since the mid-1960s; that widely-used textbooks had reduced their reading levels in order to adjust to falling verbal abilities; that homework assignments had been sharply curtailed and that grade inflation was common; that large numbers of easy or nonverbal electives had been added to the schools' curricula as substitute for demanding courses; that writing skills had declined, at least in part because writing was not systematically emphasized as a part of learning and thinking, and because short-answer quizzes and standardized tests had gained a place alongside of, or in place of, the essay.

The pervasive influence of television, that highly entertaining but passivity-inducing medium of communication, was an important element in the new situation. But also part of the heightened criticism was a question about the fate of humane culture. The issue, which echoed complaints about the permissive aspects of progressive education and open education, was whether a democratic education system best served its students by letting them choose what they wanted to study, if they wanted to study; or whether it served them best by seeing that each and every one of them received a liberal education—including literature and language, science and mathematics, history and the arts. The debate reiterated the old arguments: one side claimed that a democratic school system had to proceed through the willing consent of the governed; the other insisted that a democratic school system had to assure everyone a sound education or suffer the creation of differential elites and of intolerable popular ignorance.

Beyond the obvious gains and losses that had been registered in the course of thirty-five years was a change in climate so basic and yet so elusive that it was difficult to measure or even describe. Although some few big-city high schools were vast educational factories in 1945, most schools, colleges, and even universities were small compared to what was to come. In some communities, teachers "boarded" with families, not because of choice but because of low pay; not a situation they might have chosen, but one that assured intimate familiarity with the community and the children. Even where teachers led independent lives, they were expected to spend after-school hours as supervisors of extracurricular activities and to know their students; they, in turn, could count on parents to support and reinforce the demands made by the school. Colleges and universities never questioned their role *in loco parentis:* they were responsible for the young men and women in their care, as if the institution itself were their parents. Alcohol was seldom permitted on campus, drugs were unheard of, and even the social lives of the students were regulated; infractions of the rules of behavior might be punished by suspension or expulsion.

Much had changed by 1980. The drive to consolidate small schools and small school districts had largely succeeded, helped along by the vast expansion of enrollments in the 1950s and 1960s. Big schools became the rule, not the exception. In a society where bigger was considered better, small districts and small schools were described as backward and inefficient. The number of school districts shrank dramatically, from one hundred thousand at war's end to sixteen thousand in 1980. While total enrollment in elementary and secondary schools nearly doubled during the thirty-five-year span (from 23 million to 40 million), the number of schools dropped from one hundred and eighty-five thousand to eighty-six thousand. More and more students went to larger schools. In higher education, institutions enrolling more than twenty thousand students increased from ten in 1948 to one hundred and fifteen by 1980. Growth had many benefits: efficiency of scale, diversity of curriculum, differentiation of types of students and teachers. Enlargement meant exposure to a more varied setting and interaction with a broader variety of ideas and people than was possible in a small school or college.

The trade-off, of course, was that bigness meant impersonality, bureaucratization, diminished contact between faculty and students, formalization of

20

*Chapter 1
The
Conservative
Tradition in
Educational
Thought*

relationships among colleagues, a weakening of the bonds of community. Colleges and universities withdrew from the *in loco parentis* role that they had previously exercised. No longer part of a community of values shared with students and parents, teachers and administrators found it difficult to administer discipline or even to establish rules that everyone found acceptable. Teachers and professors defended themselves against the new anonymity by joining unions. Students, complaining that no one knew their names, wrote them vividly in the bathrooms and hallways of their schools. The invasion of drugs, first in college in the 1960s, then in high schools and even junior high schools in the 1970s, dulled students' senses and insulated a portion of the student body from adult standards. The lingering influence of the counterculture, that remnant of the 1960s youth rebellion, left many adults wondering whether there were any standards of learning or effort or behavior worth defending.

American education had succeeded in so many ways that were real, tangible, and important—in providing modern buildings, larger enrollment, better materials, better trained teachers, more courses, more departments, and more graduates—that it sometimes seemed difficult for educators to remember what they had accomplished or why they had struggled so hard, or not to wonder whether they had gone wrong somewhere or why so many people criticized the nation's schools, colleges, and universities.

The following vignette, not necessarily representative, is nonetheless true. In 1945, at the beginning of this account, Mrs. Florence Christmas traveled to Washington, D.C., to tell the Senate Committee on Education about the Antioch School, where she was principal. She told them that there were three teachers for 190 children; that she was not only the principal but taught all subjects in four grades. It was a moving story, not just because of the difference between the salaries of the white and black teachers or between the number of months of schooling for white and black students, but because her dedication shone through her testimony. Even more than that, what was apparent was the evident commitment of the parents to the survival of the school and the education of their children, no matter how meager their present chances. Mrs. Christmas died in 1957, not living to see the Antioch School consolidated two years later, along with other small black schools into the Hazlehurst, Mississippi, city school district. The new, all-black, elementary school was much larger; Mrs. Christmas' sister became its principal, and there were six teachers in the first grade alone.

In the late 1960s, under pressure from the federal government, the Hazlehurst district offered its black and white students "free choice" to go to whichever school they wanted. A few black students went to the white school, but most students stayed with their friends. Rowan Torrey, a nephew of Mrs. Christmas, was one of those who chose to stay in the black school; he thought it was better. He liked the school spirit; he liked the way several busloads of kids followed the football team to their matches and cheered them on, and he was proud of the seventy-member band and the school choir. Torrey graduated in 1969 and went to Millsaps College, a small, previously all-white liberal arts college in Jackson. The next year the federal government lowered the boom on Hazlehurst and required the integration of the white and black schools.

The town whites promptly opened Copiah Academy, a private school, and abandoned the public schools.

When Rowan Torrey moved back to Hazlehurst in 1980 after serving in the Marines, he went to work for the federal Job Corps, helping young people acquire basic skills and vocational training. Most of his enrollees, including some with high school diplomas, were barely literate. He began to take a close look at the schools. What he saw was a small system that was more than 90 percent black, an integrated staff with white administrators who had suffered "culture shock" after integration and who were "afraid to discipline black kids." Graduation requirements had dropped precipitously during the decade after desegregation, the college preparatory courses had been substantially reduced, students were choosing their own courses, and discipline was lax. But that was not all: the buildings needed repairs, the band instruments had largely disappeared, the choir was a sometime thing, and the football team had a season of 0 and 10.

Born and bred in Mississippi, but college educated and toughened in the Marines, Rowan Torrey decided to fight. As a lay citizen, he took up the family tradition of commitment to public education and agitated for better schools. A new superintendent (a white, third-generation Mississippian who enrolled his daughter in the elementary school) was hired, a strict disciplinarian. Graduation requirements went up, and the district began eliminating options and telling students which academic courses they would have to take. Class size in the district averaged about twenty, though it was smaller in advanced science classes. Even as it tried to right itself, the district weathered a fiscal crisis; only the steady flow of federal funds enabled it to maintain kindergartens, teachers' aides, and special reading and math programs in the early grades.

In Hazlehurst, where there is a black public school system and a white private academy, the schools are not building a new social order but they are making their contribution. In the past decade, new employment opportunities have opened up for educated blacks, as tellers and accountants in local banks, as operators of nationally franchised businesses, as administrators in public agencies. "We had a tremendous opportunity to unite our community, black and white," Rowan Torrey laments, "and we wasted it." It was not the blacks who wasted it, but the whites who fled.

Yet if one had the courage of those who served on the President's Committee on Civil Rights in 1947 and the vision of those who projected the growth of American higher education in the same year, it would be possible to counsel against despair. In the crusade against ignorance, there have been no easy victories, but no lasting defeats. Those who have labored on behalf of American education have seen so many barriers scaled, so much hatred dispelled, so many possibilities remaining to provide the basis for future reconciliation. To believe in education is to believe in the future, to believe in what may be accomplished through the disciplined use of intelligence, allied with cooperation and good will. If it seems naïvely American to put so much stock in schools, colleges, universities, and the endless prospect of self-improvement and social improvement, it is an admirable, and perhaps even a noble, flaw.

The Paideia Proposal: Rediscovering the Essence of Education

Mortimer Adler (b. 1902) is an advocate of freedom and individual responsibility who champions classical humanist educational ideals. An American philosopher and educator, Adler developed the "great books" seminars and curricula with Robert M. Hutchins. Rooted in the belief that education should be universal, the great books curricula were based on more than 400 works of major Western authors (classical and modern). Adler and Hutchins identified many of these great works in a 54-volume set of books entitled *Great Books of the Western World Between 1945 and 1952*.

Adler has many other publications to his credit, including *The American Testament* (Praeger, 1975); *Aristotle for Everybody* (Macmillan, 1978); *The Conditions of Philosophy* (Atheneum, 1965); and *The Great Ideas: A Lexicon of Western Thought* (Maxwell Macmillan International, 1992).

In the selection that follows, which is from "The Paideia Proposal: Rediscovering the Essence of Education," *The American School Board Journal* (July 1982), Adler sets down what he believes are the basic aims of education. He argues that there should be a common school curriculum for everyone to follow at some level. Adler then explores some of the basic essential characteristics upon which a common curriculum would focus.

Key Concept: the Paideia Proposal

*I*n the first 80 years of this century, we have met the obligation imposed on us by the principle of equal educational opportunity, but only in a quantitative sense. Now, as we approach the end of the century, we must achieve equality in qualitative terms.

This means a completely one-track system of schooling. It means, at the basic level, giving all the young the same kind of schooling, whether or not they are college bound.

We are aware that children, although equal in their common humanity and fundamental human rights, are unequal as individuals, differing in their capacity to learn. In addition, the homes and environments from which they come to school are unequal—either predisposing the child for schooling or doing the opposite.

Consequently, the Paideia Proposal, faithful to the principle of equal educational opportunity, includes the suggestion that inequalities due to environmental factors must be overcome by some form of preschool preparation—at least one year for all and two or even three for some. We know that to make such preschool tutelage compulsory at the public expense would be tantamount to increasing the duration of compulsory schooling from 12 years to 13, 14, or 15 years. Nevertheless, we think that this preschool adjunct to the 12 years of compulsory basic schooling is so important that some way must be found to make it available for all and to see that all use it to advantage.

THE ESSENTIALS OF BASIC SCHOOLING

The objectives of basic schooling should be the same for the whole school population. In our current two-track or multitrack system, the learning objectives are not the same for all. And even when the objectives aimed at those on the upper track are correct, the course of study now provided does not adequately realize these correct objectives. On all tracks in our current system, we fail to cultivate proficiency in the common tasks of learning, and we especially fail to develop sufficiently the indispensable skills of learning.

The uniform objectives of basic schooling should be threefold. They should correspond to three aspects of the common future to which all the children are destined: (1) Our society provides all children ample opportunity for personal development. Given such opportunity, each individual is under a moral obligation to make the most of himself and his life. Basic schooling must facilitate this accomplishment. (2) All the children will become, when of age, full-fledged citizens with suffrage and other political responsibilities. Basic schooling must do everything it can to make them good citizens, able to perform the duties of citizenship with all the trained intelligence that each is able to achieve. (3) When they are grown, all (or certainly most) of the children will engage in some form of work to earn a living. Basic schooling must prepare them for earning a living, but not by training them for this or that specific job while they are still in school.

To achieve these three objectives, the character of basic schooling must be general and liberal. It should have a single, required, 12-year course of study for all, with no electives except one—an elective choice with regard to a second language, to be selected from such modern languages as French, German, Italian, Spanish, Russian, and Chinese. The elimination of all electives, with this one exception, excludes what *should* be excluded—all forms of specialization, including particularized job training.

In its final form, the Paideia Proposal will detail this required course of study, but I will summarize the curriculum here in its bare outline. It consists

24

*Chapter 1
The
Conservative
Tradition in
Educational
Thought*

of three main columns of teaching and learning, running through the 12 years and progressing, of course, from the simple to the more complex, from the less difficult to the more difficult, as the students grow older. Understand: The three columns represent three distinct modes of teaching and learning. They do not represent a series of courses. A specific course or class may employ more than one mode of teaching and learning, but all three modes are essential to the overall course of study.

The first column is devoted to acquiring knowledge in three subject areas: (A) language, literature, and the fine arts; (B) mathematics and natural science; (C) history, geography, and social studies.

The second column is devoted to developing the intellectual skills of learning. These include all the language skills necessary for thought and communication—the skills of reading, writing, speaking, listening. They also include mathematical and scientific skills; the skills of observing, measuring, estimating, and calculating; and skills in the use of the computer and of other scientific instruments. Together, these skills make it possible to think clearly and critically. They once were called the liberal arts—the intellectual skills indispensable to being competent as a learner.

The third column is devoted to enlarging the understanding of ideas and values. The materials of the third column are books (*not* textbooks), and other products of human artistry. These materials include books of every variety—historical, scientific, and philosophical as well as poems, stories, and essays—and also individual pieces of music, visual art, dramatic productions, dance productions, film or television productions. Music and works of visual art can be used in seminars in which ideas are discussed; but as with poetry and fiction, they also are to be experienced aesthetically, to be enjoyed and admired for their excellence. In this connection, exercises in the composition of poetry, music, and visual works and in the production of dramatic works should be used to develop the appreciation of excellence.

The three columns represent three different kinds of learning on the part of the student and three different kinds of instruction on the part of teachers.

In the first column, the students are engaged in acquiring information and organized knowledge about nature, man, and human society. The method of instruction here, using textbooks and manuals, is didactic. The teacher lectures, invites responses from the students, monitors the acquisition of knowledge, and tests that acquisition in various ways.

In the second column, the students are engaged in developing habits of performance, which is all that is involved in the development of an art of skill. Art, skill, or technique is nothing more than a cultivated, habitual ability to do a certain kind of thing well, whether that is swimming and dancing or reading and writing. Here, students are acquiring linguistic, mathematical, scientific, and historical *know-how* in contrast to what they acquire in the first column, which is *know-that* with respect to language, literature, and the fine arts, mathematics and science, history, geography, and social studies. Here, the method of instruction cannot be didactic or monitorial; it cannot be dependent on textbooks. It must be coaching, the same kind used in the gym to develop bodily skills; only here it is used by a different kind of coach in the classroom to develop intellectual skills.

In the third column, students are engaged in a process of enlightenment, the process whereby they develop their understanding of the basic and controlling ideas in all fields of subject matter and come to appreciate better all the human values embodied in works of art. Here, students move progressively from understanding less to understanding more—understanding better what they already know and appreciating more what they already have experienced. Here, the method of instruction cannot be either didactic or coaching. It must be the Socratic, or maieutic, method of questioning and discussing. It should not occur in an ordinary classroom with the students sitting in rows and the teacher in front of the class, but in a seminar room, with the students sitting around a table and the teacher sitting with them as an equal, even though a little older and wiser.

Of these three main elements in the required curriculum, the third column is completely innovative. Nothing like this is done in our schools, and because it is completely absent from the ordinary curriculum of basic schooling, the students never have the experience of having their minds addressed in a challenging way or of being asked to think about important ideas, to express their thoughts, to defend their opinions in a reasonable fashion.

The only thing that is innovative about the second column is the insistence that the method of instruction here must be coaching carried on either with one student at a time or with very small groups of students. Nothing else can be effective in the development of a skill, be it bodily or intellectual. The absence of such individualized coaching in our schools explains why most of the students cannot read well, write well, speak well, listen well, or perform well any of the other basic intellectual operations.

The three columns are closely interconnected and integrated, but the middle column—the one concerned with linguistic, mathematical, and scientific skills—is central. It both supports and is supported by the other two columns. All the intellectual skills with which it is concerned must be exercised in the study of the three basic subject-matters and in acquiring knowledge about them, and these intellectual skills must be exercised in the seminars devoted to the discussion of books and other things.

In addition to the three main columns in the curriculum, ascending through the 12 years of basic schooling, there are three adjuncts: One is 12 years of physical training, accompanied by instruction in bodily care and hygiene. The second, running through something less than 12 years, is the development of basic manual skills, such as cooking, sewing, carpentry, and the operation of all kinds of machines. The third, reserved for the last year or two, is an introduction to the whole world of work—the range of occupations in which human beings earn their livings. This is not particularized job training. It is the very opposite. It aims at a broad understanding of what is involved in working for a living and of the various ways in which that can be done. If, at the end of 12 years, students wish training for specific jobs, they should get that in two-year community or junior colleges, or on the job itself, or in technical institutes of one sort or another.

Everything that has not been specifically mentioned as occupying the time of the school day should be reserved for after-hours and have the status of extracurricular activities.

26

*Chapter 1
The
Conservative
Tradition in
Educational
Thought*

Please, note: The required course of study just described is as important for what it *displaces* as for what it introduces. It displaces a multitude of elective courses, especially those offered in our secondary schools, most of which make little or no contribution to general, liberal education. It eliminates all narrowly specialized job training, which now abounds in our schools. It throws out of the curriculum and into the category of optional extracurricular activities a variety of things that have little or no educational value.

If it did not call for all these displacements, there would not be enough time in the school day or year to accomplish everything that is essential to the general, liberal learning that must be the content of basic schooling.

THE QUINTESSENTIAL ELEMENT

So far, I have set forth the bare essentials of the Paideia Proposal with regard to basic schooling. I have not yet mentioned the quintessential element—the *sine qua non*—without which nothing else can possibly come to fruition, no matter how sound it might be in principle. The heart of the matter is the quality of learning and the quality of teaching that occupies the school day, not to mention the quality of the homework after school.

First, the learning must be active. It must use the whole mind, not just the memory. It must be learning by discovery, in which the student, never the teacher, is the primary agent. Learning by discovery, which is the only genuine learning, may be either unaided or aided. It is unaided only for geniuses. For most students, discovery must be aided.

Here is where teachers come in—as aids in the process of learning by discovery, not as knowers who attempt to put the knowledge they have into the minds of their students. The quality of the teaching, in short, depends crucially upon how the teacher conceives his role in the process of learning, and that must be as an aid to the student's process of discovery.

I am prepared for the questions that must be agitating you by now: How and where will we get the teachers who can perform as teachers should? How will we be able to staff the program with teachers so trained that they will be competent to provide the quality of instruction required for the quality of learning desired?

The first part of our answer to these questions is negative: We *cannot* get the teachers we need for the Paideia program from schools of education *as they are now constituted*. As teachers are now trained for teaching, they simply will not do. The ideal—an impracticable ideal—would be to ask for teachers who are, themselves, truly educated human beings. But truly educated human beings are too rare. Even if we could draft all who are now alive, there still would be far too few to staff our schools.

Well, then, what can we look for? Look for teachers who are actively engaged in the process of *becoming* educated human beings, who are themselves deeply motivated to develop their own minds. Assuming this is not too much to ask for the present, how should teachers be schooled and trained in the future? First, they should have the same kind of basic schooling that is recommended in the Paideia Proposal. Second, they should have additional schooling, at the college and even the university level, in which the same kind of general, liberal learning is carried on at advanced levels—more deeply, broadly, and intensively than it can be done in the first 12 years of schooling. Third, they must be given something analogous to the clinical experience in the training of physicians. They must engage in practice-teaching under supervision, which is another way of saying that they must be *coached* in the arts of teaching, not just given didactic instruction in educational psychology and in pedagogy. Finally, and most important of all, they must learn how to teach well by being exposed to the performances of those who are masters of the arts involved in teaching.

It is by watching a good teacher at work that they will be able to perceive what is involved in the process of assisting others to learn by discovery. Perceiving it, they must then try to emulate what they observe, and through this process, they slowly will become good teachers themselves.

The Paideia Proposal recognizes the need for three different kinds of institutions at the collegiate level: The two-year community or junior college should offer a wide choice of electives that give students some training in one or another specialized field, mainly those fields of study that have something to do with earning a living. The four-year college also should offer a wide variety of electives, to be chosen by students who aim at the various professional or technical occupations that require advanced study. Those elective majors chosen by students should be accompanied, for all students, by one required minor, in which the kind of general and liberal learning that was begun at the level of basic schooling is continued at a higher level in the four years of college. And we should have still a third type of collegiate institution—a four-year college in which general, liberal learning at a higher level constitutes a required course of study that is to be taken by all students. *It is this third type of college, by the way, that should be attended by all who plan to become teachers in our basic schools.*

At the university level, there should be a continuation of general, liberal learning at a still higher level to accompany intensive specialization in this or that field of science or scholarship, this or that learned profession. Our insistence on the continuation of general, liberal learning at all the higher levels of schooling stems from our concern with the worst cultural disease that is rampant in our society—*the barbarism of specialization.*

There is no question that our technologically advanced industrial society needs specialists of all sorts. There is no question that the advancement of knowledge in all fields of science and scholarship, and in all the learned professions, needs intense specialization. But for the sake of preserving and enhancing our cultural traditions, as well as for the health of science and scholarship, we need specialists who also are generalists—generally cultivated human beings, not just good plumbers. We need truly educated human beings who can perform their special tasks better precisely because they have general cultivation as well as intensely specialized training.

Changes indeed are needed in higher education, but those improvements cannot reasonably be expected unless improvement in basic schooling makes that possible.

THE FUTURE OF OUR FREE INSTITUTIONS

I already have declared as emphatically as I know how that the quality of human life in our society depends on the quality of the schooling we give our young people, both basic and advanced. But a marked elevation in the quality of human life is not the only reason improving the quality of schooling is so necessary—not the only reason we must move heaven and earth to stop the deterioration of our schools and turn them in the opposite direction. The other reason is to safeguard the future of our free institutions.

They cannot prosper, they may not even survive, unless we do something to rescue our schools from their current deplorable deterioration. Democracy, in the full sense of that term, came into existence only in this century and only in a few countries on earth, among which the United States is an outstanding example. But democracy came into existence in this century only in its initial conditions, all of which hold out promises for the future that remain to be fulfilled. Unless we do something about improving the quality of basic schooling for all and the quality of advanced schooling for some, there is little chance that those promises ever will be fulfilled. And if they are not, our free institutions are doomed to decay and wither away.

We face many insistently urgent problems. Our prosperity and even our survival depend on the solution of those problems—the threat of nuclear war, the exhaustion of essential resources and of supplies of energy, the pollution or spoilage of the environment, the spiraling of inflation accompanied by the spread of unemployment.

To solve these problems, we need resourceful and innovative leadership. For that to arise and be effective, an educated populace is needed. Trained intelligence—not only on the part of leaders, but also on the part of followers—holds the key to the solution of the problems our society faces. Achieving peace, prosperity, and plenty could put us on the threshold of an early paradise. But a much better educational system than now exists also is needed, for that alone can carry us across the threshold. Without it, a poorly schooled population will not be able to put to good use the opportunities afforded by the achievement of the general welfare. Those who are not schooled to enjoy society can only despoil its institutions and corrupt themselves.

CHAPTER 2 The Progressive-Liberal Agenda

2.1 JOHN DEWEY

Democracy and Education: An Introduction to the Philosophy of Education

In 1916 John Dewey published what was to become one of the most influential and debated works on the philosophy of education. *Democracy and Education: An Introduction to the Philosophy of Education* (Macmillan, 1916), from which the following selection has been excerpted, is a comprehensive textbook on the philosophy of education and a sharp, progressive-liberal pedagogical response to the rhetoric of classical humanist scholars. The book became a major focus of controversy because there was a spirited classical humanist opposition to Dewey's pragmatic-progressive theory of education.

At the time that *Democracy and Education* was published, Dewey (1859–1952) was in his 12th year as a professor of philosophy at Columbia University and his 32d year as a university professor. Dewey taught a total of 33 years at Columbia before retiring from teaching in 1937. He then became a world traveler and a highly acclaimed commentator on the challenges facing democratic societies in the 1930s. He continued to write and publish right up to his death at almost 93 years of age. In addition to *Democracy and Education,* Dewey is also the author of *Essays in Experimental Logic* and *Reconstruction in Philosophy,* both of which were published in 1916.

Key Concept: education as a reconstruction or reorganization of experience

Education as Reconstruction

In its contrast with the ideas both of unfolding of latent powers from within, and of formation from without, whether by physical nature or by the cultural products of the past, the ideal of growth results in the conception that education is a constant reorganizing or reconstructing of experience. It has all the time an immediate end, and so far as activity is educative, it reaches that end —the direct transformation of the quality of experience. Infancy, youth, adult life—all stand on the same educative level in the sense that what is really *learned* at any and every stage of experience constitutes the value of that experience, and in the sense that it is the chief business of life at every point to make living thus contribute to an enrichment of its own perceptible meaning.

We thus reach a technical definition of education: It is that reconstruction or reorganization of experience which adds to the meaning of experience, and which increases ability to direct the course of subsequent experience. (1) The increment of meaning corresponds to the increased perception of the connections and continuities of the activities in which we are engaged. The activity begins in an impulsive form; that is, it is blind. It does not know what it is about; that is to say, what are its interactions with other activities. An activity which brings education or instruction with it makes one aware of some of the connections which had been imperceptible.... [A] child who reaches for a bright light gets burned. Henceforth he *knows* that a certain act of touching in connection with a certain act of vision (and *vice-versa*) means heat and pain; or, a certain light means a source of heat. The acts by which a scientific man in his laboratory learns more about flame differ no whit in principle. By doing certain things, he makes perceptible certain connections of heat with other things, which had been previously ignored. Thus his acts in relation to these things get more meaning; he knows better what he is doing or 'is about' when he has to do with them; he can *intend* consequences instead of just letting them happen —all synonymous ways of saying the same thing. At the same stroke, the flame has gained in meaning; all that is known about combustion, oxidation, about light and temperature, may become an intrinsic part of its intellectual content.

(2) The other side of an educative experience is an added power of subsequent direction or control. To say that one knows what he is about, or can intend certain consequences, is to say, of course, that he can better anticipate what is going to happen; that he can, therefore, get ready or prepare in advance so as to secure beneficial consequences and avert undesirable ones. A genuinely educative experience, then, one in which instruction is conveyed and ability increased, is contradistinguished from a routine activity on one hand, and a

capricious activity on the other. (*a*) In the latter one 'does not care what happens'; one just lets himself go and avoids connecting the consequences of one's act (the evidences of its connections with other things) with the act. It is customary to frown upon such aimless random activity, treating it as willful mischief or carelessness or lawlessness. But there is a tendency to seek the cause of such aimless activities in the youth's own disposition, isolated from everything else. But in fact such activity is explosive, and due to maladjustment with surroundings. Individuals act capriciously whenever they act under external dictation, or from being told, without having a purpose of their own or perceiving the bearing of the deed upon other acts. One may learn by doing something which he does not understand; even in the most intelligent action, we do much which we do not mean, because the largest portion of the connections of the act we consciously intend are not perceived or anticipated. But we learn only because after the act is performed we note results which we had not noted before. But much work in school consists in setting up rules by which pupils are to act of such a sort that even after pupils have acted, they are not led to see the connection between the result—say the answer—and the method pursued. So far as they are concerned, the whole thing is a trick and a kind of miracle. Such action is essentially capricious, and leads to capricious habits. (*b*) Routine, action, action which is automatic, may increase skill to do a *particular* thing. In so far, it might be said to have an educative effect. But it does not lead to new perceptions of bearings and connections; it limits rather than widens the meaning-horizon. And since the environment changes and our way of acting has to be modified in order successfully to keep a balanced connection with things, an isolated uniform way of acting becomes disastrous at some critical moment. The vaunted 'skill' turns out gross ineptitude.

The essential contrast of the idea of education as continuous reconstruction with... other one-sided conceptions... is that it identifies the end (the result) and the process. This is verbally self-contradictory, but only verbally. It means that experience as an active process occupies time and that its later period completes its earlier portion; it brings to light connections involved, but hitherto unperceived. The later outcome thus reveals the meaning of the earlier, while the experience as a whole establishes a bent or disposition toward the things possessing this meaning. Every such continuous experience or activity is educative, and all education resides in having such experiences.

It remains only to point out (what will receive more ample attention later) that the reconstruction of experience may be social as well as personal. For purposes of simplification we have spoken... somewhat as if the education of the immature which fills them with the spirit of the social group to which they belong, were a sort of catching up of the child with the aptitudes and resources of the adult group. In static societies, societies which make the maintenance of established custom their measure of value, this conception applies in the main. But not in progressive communities. They endeavor to shape the experiences of the young so that instead of reproducing current habits, better habits shall be formed, and thus the future adult society be an improvement on their own. Men have long had some intimation of the extent to which education may be consciously used to eliminate obvious social evils through starting the young on paths which shall not produce these ills, and some idea of the extent in which education may be made an instrument of realizing the better hopes of men. But we are doubtless far from realizing the potential efficacy of education as a constructive agency of improving society, from realizing that it represents not only a development of children and youth but also of the future society of which they will be the constituents. . . .

THE DEMOCRATIC CONCEPTION
IN EDUCATION

For the most part, save incidentally, we have hitherto been concerned with education as it may exist in any social group. We have now to make explicit the differences in the spirit, material, and method of education as it operates in different types of community life. To say that education is a social function, securing direction and development in the immature through their participation in the life of the group to which they belong, is to say in effect that education will vary with the quality of life which prevails in a group. Particularly is it true that a society which not only changes but which has the ideal of such change as will improve it, will have different standards and methods of education from one which aims simply at the perpetuation of its own customs. To make the general ideas set forth applicable to our own educational practice, it is, therefore, necessary to come to closer quarters with the nature of present social life.

The Implications of Human Association

Society is one word, but many things. Men associate together in all kinds of ways and for all kinds of purposes. One man is concerned in a multitude of diverse groups, in which his associates may be quite different. It often seems as if they had nothing in common except that they are modes of associated life. Within every larger social organization there are numerous minor groups: not only political subdivisions, but industrial, scientific, religious, associations. There are political parties with differing aims, social sets, cliques, gangs, corporations, partnerships, groups bound closely together by ties of blood, and so in endless variety. In many modern states, and in some ancient, there is great diversity of populations, of varying languages, religions, moral codes, and traditions. From this standpoint, many a minor political unit, one of our large cities, for example, is a congeries of loosely associated societies, rather than an inclusive and permeating community of action and thought.

The terms society, community, are thus ambiguous. They have both a eulogistic or normative sense, and a descriptive sense; a meaning *de jure* and a meaning *de facto*. In social philosophy, the former connotation is almost always uppermost. Society is conceived as one by its very nature. The qualities which accompany this unity, praiseworthy community of purpose and welfare, loyalty to public ends, mutuality of sympathy, are emphasized. But when we look at the facts which the term *denotes* instead of confining our attention to its intrinsic *connotation,* we find not unity, but a plurality of societies, good and bad.

Men banded together in a criminal conspiracy, business aggregations that prey upon the public while serving it, political machines held together by the interest of plunder, are included. If it is said that such organizations are not societies because they do not meet the ideal requirements of the notion of society, the answer, in part, is that the conception of society is then made so "ideal" as to be of no use, having no reference to facts; and in part, that each of these organizations, no matter how opposed to the interests of other groups, has something of the praiseworthy qualities of "Society" which hold it together. There is honor among thieves, and a band of robbers has a common interest as respects its members. Gangs are marked by fraternal feeling, and narrow cliques by intense loyalty to their own codes. Family life may be marked by exclusiveness, suspicion, and jealousy as to those without, and yet be a model of amity and mutual aid within. Any education given by a group tends to socialize its members, but the quality and value of the socialization depends upon the habits and aims of the group.

Hence, once more, the need of a measure for the worth of any given mode of social life. In seeking this measure, we have to avoid two extremes. We cannot set up, out of our heads, something we regard as an ideal society. We must base our conception upon societies which actually exist, in order to have any assurance that our ideal is a practicable one. But, as we have just seen, the ideal cannot simply repeat the traits which are actually found. The problem is to extract the desirable traits of forms of community life which actually exist, and employ them to criticize undesirable features and suggest improvement. Now in any social group whatever, even in a gang of thieves, we find some interest held in common, and we find a certain amount of interaction and coöperative intercourse with other groups. From these two traits we derive our standard. How numerous and varied are the interests which are consciously shared? How full and free is the interplay with other forms of association? If we apply these considerations to, say, a criminal band, we find that the ties which consciously hold the members together are few in number, reducible almost to a common interest in plunder; and that they are of such a nature as to isolate the group from other groups with respect to give and take of the values of life. Hence, the education such a society gives is partial and distorted. If we take, on the other hand, the kind of family life which illustrates the standard, we find that there are material, intellectual, aesthetic interests in which all participate and that the progress of one member has worth for the experience of other members—it is readily communicable—and that the family is not an isolated whole, but enters intimately into relationships with business groups, with schools, with all the agencies of culture, as well as with other similar groups, and that it plays a due part in the political organization and in return receives support from it. In short, there are many interests consciously communicated and shared; and there are varied and free points of contact with other modes of association.

... The two elements in our criterion both point to democracy. The first signifies not only more numerous and more varied points of shared common interest, but greater reliance upon the recognition of mutual interests as a factor in social control. The second means not only freer interaction between social groups (once isolated so far as intention could keep up a separation) but change in social habit—its continuous readjustment through meeting the new situations produced by varied intercourse. And these two traits are precisely what characterize the democratically constituted society.

Upon the educational side, we note first that the realization of a form of social life in which interests are mutually interpenetrating, and where progress, or readjustment, is an important consideration, makes a democratic community more interested than other communities have cause to be in deliberate and systematic education. The devotion of democracy to education is a familiar fact. The superficial explanation is that a government resting upon popular suffrage cannot be successful unless those who elect and who obey their governors are educated. Since a democratic society repudiates the principle of external authority, it must find a substitute in voluntary disposition and interest; these can be created only by education. But there is a deeper explanation. A democracy is more than a form of government; it is primarily a mode of associated living, of conjoint communicated experience. The extension in space of the number of individuals who participate in an interest so that each has to refer his own action to that of others, and to consider the action of others to give point and direction to his own, is equivalent to the breaking down of those barriers of class, race, and national territory which kept men from perceiving the full import of their activity. These more numerous and more varied points of contact denote a greater diversity of stimuli to which an individual has to respond; they consequently put a premium on variation in his action. They secure a liberation of powers which remain suppressed as long as the incitations to action are partial, as they must be in a group which in its exclusiveness shuts out many interests.

The widening of the area of shared concerns, and the liberation of a greater diversity of personal capacities which characterize a democracy, are not of course the product of deliberation and conscious effort. On the contrary, they were caused by the development of modes of manufacture and commerce, travel, migration, and intercommunication which flowed from the command of science over natural energy. But after greater individualization on one hand, and a broader community of interest on the other have come into existence, it is a matter of deliberate effort to sustain and extend them. Obviously a society to which stratification into separate classes would be fatal, must see to it that intellectual opportunities are accessible to all on equable and easy terms. A society marked off into classes need be specially attentive only to the education of its ruling elements. A society which is mobile, which is full of channels for the distribution of a change occurring anywhere, must see to it that its members are educated to personal initiative and adaptability. Otherwise, they will be overwhelmed by the changes in which they are caught and whose significance or connections they do not perceive. The result will be a confusion in which a few will appropriate to themselves the results of the blind and externally directed activities of others.

2.2 WILLIAM HEARD KILPATRICK

The Project Method

William Heard Kilpatrick (1871–1965) is regarded as one of the principal founders of progressive, experience-based education. He attended Mercer University in Macon, Georgia, and did his graduate studies at Johns Hopkins University in Baltimore, Maryland. He was a teacher in the Mercer public schools and at Mercer University, and he was appointed to the faculty of Teachers College, Columbia University, as a professor of the philosophy of education in 1909. This appointment allowed Kilpatrick to develop a close working relationship with fellow progressive educator John Dewey, a faculty member in the Department of Philosophy at Columbia. Kilpatrick became one of the leading exponents of child-centered, experience-based schooling in the early decades of the twentieth century, and his long, active career at Teachers College continued until 1938. Kilpatrick was a major interpreter of the early writings of John Dewey, and he had many works published, including *Education for a Changing Civilization* (1926). The following selection is from "The Project Method," which was published in Columbia University's *Teachers College Record* in September 1918. In it, Kilpatrick describes his "project method" of teaching, emphasizing the use of purposeful activity as the basis of education.

Key Concept: the project method

My whole philosophic outlook had made me suspicious of so-called 'fundamental principles'. Was there yet another way of attaining unity? I do not mean to say that I asked these questions, either in these words or in this order. Rather is this a retrospective ordering of the more important outcomes. As the desired unification lay specifically in the field of method, might not some typical unit of concrete procedure supply the need—some unit of conduct that should be, as it were, a sample of life, a fair sample of the worthy life and consequently of education? As these questionings rose more definitely to mind, there came increasingly a belief—corroborated on many sides—that the unifying idea I sought was to be found in the conception of wholehearted purposeful activity proceeding in a social environment, or more briefly, in the unit element of such activity, the hearty purposeful act.

It is to this purposeful act with the emphasis on the word purpose that I myself apply the term 'project'. I did not invent the term nor did I start it on its educational career. Indeed, I do not know how long it had already been in use. I did, however, consciously appropriate the word to designate to myself and for my classes the typical unit of the worthy life described above. Others who were using the term seemed to me either to use it in a mechanical and partial sense or to be intending in a general way what I tried to define more exactly. The purpose of this article is to attempt to clarify the concept underlying the term as much as it is to defend the claim of the concept to a place in our educational thinking. The actual terminology with which to designate the concept is, as was said before, to my mind a matter of relatively small moment. If, however, we think of a project as a pro-ject, something pro-jected, the reason for adopting the term may better appear.

Postponing yet a little further the more systematic presentation of the matter, let us from some typical instances see more concretely what is contemplated under the term project or hearty purposeful act. Suppose a girl has made a dress. If she did in hearty fashion purpose to make the dress, if she planned it, if she made it herself, then I should say the instance is that of a typical project. We have in it a wholehearted purposeful act carried on amid social surroundings. That the dressmaking was purposeful is clear; and the purpose once formed dominated each succeeding step in the process and gave unity to the whole. That the girl was wholehearted in the work was assured in the illustration. That the activity proceeded in a social environment is clear; other girls at least are to see the dress. As another instance, suppose a boy undertakes to get out a school newspaper. If he is in earnest about it, we again have an effective purpose as the essence of a project. So we may instance a pupil writing a letter (if the hearty purpose is present), a child listening absorbedly to a story, Newton explaining the motion of the moon on the principles of terrestrial dynamics, Demosthenes trying to arouse the Greeks against Philip, Da Vinci painting the *Last Supper*, my writing this article, a boy solving with felt purpose an 'original' in geometry. All of the foregoing have been acts of individual purposing, but there are just as truly group projects: a class presents a play, a group of boys organize a base-ball nine, three pupils prepare to read a story to their comrades. It is clear then that projects may present every variety that purposes present in life. It is also clear that a mere description of outwardly observable facts might not disclose the essential factor, namely the presence of a dominating purpose. It is equally true that there can be every degree of approximation to full projects according as the animating purpose varies in clearness and strength. If we conceive activities as ranging on a scale from those performed under dire compulsion up to those into which one puts his 'whole heart', the argument herein made restricts the term 'project' or purposeful act to the upper portions of the scale. An exact dividing line is hard to draw, and yields indeed in importance to the notion that psychological value increases with the degree of approximation to 'wholeheartedness'. As to the social environment element, some may feel that, however important this is to the fullest educative experience, it is still not essential to the conception of the purposeful act as here presented. These might, therefore, wish to leave this element out of the defining discussion. To this I should not object if it were clearly understood that the resulting concept—now essentially psychological in character—demands, generally speaking, the social situation both for its practical working and for the comparative valuation of proffered projects.

With this general introduction, we may, in the first place, say that the purposeful act is the typical unit of the worthy life. Not that all purposes are good, but that the worthy life consists of purposive activity and not mere drifting. We scorn the man who passively accepts what 'fate' or mere chance brings to him. We admire the man who is master of his fate, who with deliberate regard for a total situation forms clear and far-reaching purposes, who plans and executes with nice care the purposes so formed. A man who habitually so regulates his life with reference to worthy social aims meets at once the demands for practical efficiency and of moral responsibility. Such a one presents the ideal of democratic citizenship. It is equally true that the purposeful act is not the unit of life for the serf or the slave. . . .

As the purposeful act is thus the typical unit of the worthy life in a democratic society, so also should it be made the typical unit of school procedure. We of America have for years increasingly desired that education be considered as life itself and not as a mere preparation for later living. The conception before us promises a definite step toward the attainment of this end. If the purposeful act be in reality the typical unit of the worthy life, then it follows that to base education on purposeful acts is exactly to identify the process of education with worthy living itself. The two become then the same. All the arguments for placing education on a life basis seem, to me at any rate, to concur in support of this thesis. On this basis education has become life. And if the purposeful act thus makes of education life itself, could we reasoning in advance expect to find a better preparation for later life than practice in living now? We have heard of old that "we learn to do by doing," and much wisdom resides in the saying. If the worthy life of the coming day is to consist of well-chosen purposeful acts, what preparation for that time could promise more than practice now, under discriminating guidance, in forming and executing worthy purposes? To this end must the child have within rather large limits the opportunity to purpose. For the issues of his act he must—in like limits—be held accountable. That the child may properly progress, the total situation—all the factors of life, including comrades—speaking, if need be through the teacher, must make clear its selective judgment upon what is done, approving the better, rejecting the worse. In a true sense the whole remaining discussion is but to support the contention here argued in advance that education based on the purposeful act prepares best for life while at the same time it constitutes the present worthy life itself. . . .

How then does the purposeful act utilize the laws of learning? A boy is intent upon making a kite that will fly. Hitherto he has not succeeded. His purpose is clear. This purpose is but the 'set' consciously and volitionally bent on its end. As set the purpose is the inner urge that carries the boy on in the face of hindrance and difficulty. It brings 'readiness' to pertinent inner resources of knowledge and thought. Eye and hand are made alert. The purpose acting as aim guides the boy's thinking, directs his examination of plan and material, elicits from within appropriate suggestions, and tests these several suggestions by their pertinency to the end in view. The purpose in that it contemplates a specific end defines success: the kite must fly or he has failed. The progressive attaining of success with reference to subordinate aims brings satisfaction at the successive stages of completion. . . . The purpose thus supplies the motive power, makes available inner resources, guides the process to its preconceived end, and by this satisfying success fixes in the boy's mind and character the successful steps as part and parcel of one whole. The purposeful act does utilize the laws of learning.

But this account does not yet exhaust the influence of the purpose on the resulting learning. Suppose as extreme cases two boys making kites, the one with wholeheartedness of purpose, as we have just described, the other under direct compulsion as a most unwelcome task. For simplicity's sake suppose the latter under enforced directions makes a kite identical with the other. The steps that in either case actually produced the kite let us call the *primary* responses for that case. Evidently these will, in the two cases, in part agree, and in part differ. The respects in which they agree furnish the kind of responses that we can and customarily do assign as tasks—the external irreducible minimum for the matter at hand. Upon such we can feasibly insist, even to the point of punishment if we do so decide. Additional to the primary responses which produced the respective kites, there will be yet other responses that accompany the kitemaking, not so much by way of outward doing as of inward thought and feeling. These additional responses may be divided into *associate* and *concomitant* responses. By associate responses we refer to those thoughts which are suggested in rather close connection with the primary responses and with the materials used and the ends sought.[1] By the term concomitant reference is made to certain responses yet a little further off from the immediate operation of kitemaking, which result ultimately in attitudes and generalizations. It is in this way that such attitudes are produced as self-respect or the contrary, and such relatively abstract ideals as accuracy or neatness. These words, primary, associate, and concomitant, will be used as well of the resulting learning as of the responses that bring the learning. The terminology is not entirely happy, and exact lines of division are not easy to draw; but the distinctions may perhaps help us to see a further function of purpose.

... The factor of 'set' conditions the learning process. A strong set acting through the satisfaction which attends success fixes quickly and strongly the bonds which brought success. In the case of coercion, however, a different state of affairs holds. There are in effect two sets operating: one set, kept in existence solely through coercion, is concerned to make a kite that will pass muster; the other set has a different end and would pursue a different course were the coercion removed. Each set in so far as it actually exists means a possible satisfaction and in that degree a possible learning. But the two sets, being opposed, mean at times a confusion as to the object of success; and in every case each set destroys a part of the other's satisfaction and so hampers the primary learning. Moreover, for the wholehearted act the several steps of the primary responses are welded together, as it were, at the forge of conscious purpose, and so have not only a stronger connection of part with part but greater flexibility of the whole to thought. So far then as concerns even the barest mechanics of kitemaking, the boy of wholehearted purpose will emerge with a higher degree of skill and knowledge and his learning will longer abide with him.

In the case of the associate responses, the difference is equally noticeable. The unified set of wholeheartedness will render available all the pertinent connected inner resources. A wealth of marginal responses will be ready to come forward at every opportunity. Thoughts will be turned over and over, and each step will be connected in may ways with other experiences. Alluring leads in various allied directions will open before the boy, which only the dominant present purpose could suffice to postpone. The element of satisfaction will attend connections seen, so that the complex of allied thinking will the longer remain as a mental possession. All of this is exactly not so with the other boy. The forbidden 'set', so long as it persists, will pretty effectually quench the glow of thought. Unreadiness will rather characterize his attitude. Responses accessory to the work at hand will be few in number, and the few that come will lack the element of satisfaction to fix them. Where the one boy has a wealth of associated ideas, the other has poverty. What abides with the one, is fleeting with the other. Even more pronounced is the difference in the by-products or concomitants from these contrasted activities. The one boy looks upon his school activity with joy and confidence and plans yet other projects; the other counts his school a bore and begins to look elsewhere for the expression there denied. To the one the teacher is a friend and comrade; to the other, a taskmaster and enemy. The one easily feels himself on the side of the school and other social agencies, the other with equal ease considers them all instruments of suppression. Furthermore, under the allied readiness which follows purpose, attention is more easily led to helpful generalizations of method and to such ideals as exactness or fairness. Desirable concomitants are more likely with the hearty purposeful act.

The contrasts here made are consciously of extremes. Most children live between the two. The question is whether we shall not consciously put before us as an ideal the one type of activity and approximate it as closely as we can rather than supinely rest content to live as close to the other type as do the general run of our American schools. Does not the ordinary school among us put its almost exclusive attention on the primary responses and the learning of these in the second fashion here described? Do we not too often reduce the subject matter of instruction to the level of this type alone? Does not our examination system —even our scientific tests at times—tend to carry us in the same direction? How many children at the close of a course decisively shut the book and say, "Thank gracious, I am through with that!" How many people 'get an education' and yet hate books and hate to think?

The thought suggested at the close of the preceding paragraph may be generalized into a criterion more widely applicable. The richness of life is seen upon reflection to depend, in large measure at least, upon the tendency of what one does to suggest and prepare for succeeding activities. Any activity —beyond the barest physical want—which does not thus 'lead on' becomes in time stale and flat. Such 'leading on' means that the individual has been modified so that he sees what before he did not see or does what before he could not do. But this is exactly to say that the activity has had an educative effect. Not to elaborate the argument, we may assert that the richness of life depends exactly on its tendency to lead one on to other like fruitful activity; that the degree of this tendency consists exactly in the educative effect of the activity involved; and that we may therefore take as the criterion of the value of any activity— whether intentionally educative or not—its tendency directly or indirectly to lead the individual and others whom he touches on to other like fruitful activity. If we apply this criterion to the common run of American schools we find exactly the discouraging results indicated above. It is the thesis of this paper that these evil results must inevitably follow the effort to found our educational procedure on an unending round of set tasks in conscious disregard of the element of dominant purpose in those who perform the tasks. This again is not to say that every purpose is good nor that the child is a suitable judge as between purposes nor that he is never to be forced to act against a purpose which he entertains. We contemplate no scheme of subordination of teacher or school to childish whim; but we do mean that any plan of educational procedure which does not aim consciously and insistently at securing and utilizing vigorous purposing on the part of the pupils is founded essentially on an ineffective and unfruitful basis. Nor is the quest for desirable purposes hopeless. There is no necessary conflict in kind between the social demands and the child's interests.... It is the special duty and opportunity of the teacher to guide the pupil through his present interests and achievement into the wider interests and achievement demanded by the wider social life of the older world.

The question of moral education was implicitly raised in the preceding paragraph. What is the effect on morals of the plan herein advocated? A full discussion is unfortunately impossible. Speaking for myself, however, I consider the possibilities for building moral character in a régime of purposeful activity one of the strongest points in its favor; and contrariwise the tendency toward a selfish individualism one of the strongest counts against our customary set-task sit-alone-at-your-own-desk procedure. Moral character is primarily an affair of shared social relationships, the disposition to determine one's conduct and attitudes with reference to the welfare of the group. This means, psychologically, building stimulus-response bonds such that when certain ideas are present as stimuli certain approved responses will follow. We are then concerned that children get a goodly stock of ideas to serve as stimuli for conduct, that they develop good judgment for selecting the idea appropriate in a given case, and that they have firmly built such response bonds as will bring—as inevitably as possible—the appropriate conduct once the proper idea has been chosen. In terms of this (necessarily simplified) analysis we wish such school procedure as will most probably result in the requisite body of ideas, in the needed skill in judging a moral situation, and in unfailing appropriate response bonds. To get these three can we conceive of a better way than by living in a social *milieu* which provides, under competent supervision, for shared coping with a variety of social situations? In the school procedure here advocated children are living together in the pursuit of a rich variety of purposes, some individually sought, many conjointly. As must happen in social commingling, occasions of moral stress will arise, but here—fortunately—under conditions that exclude extreme and especially harmful cases. Under the eye of the skillful teacher the children as an embryonic society will make increasingly finer discriminations as to what is right and proper. Ideas and judgment come thus. Motive and occasion arise together; the teacher has but to steer the process of evaluating the situation. The teacher's success—if we believe in democracy—will consist in gradually eliminating himself or herself from the success of the procedure....

The question of the growth or building of interests is important in the theory of the plan here discussed. Many points still prove difficult, but some things can be said. Most obvious is the fact of 'maturing' (itself a difficult topic).

At first an infant responds automatically to his environment. Only later, after many experiences have been organized, can he, properly speaking, entertain purposes; and in this there are many gradations. Similarly, the earliest steps involved in working out a 'set' are those that have been instinctively joined with the process. Later on, steps may be taken by 'suggestion' (the relatively automatic working of acquired associations). Only comparatively late do we find true adaptation of means to end, the conscious choice of steps to the attainment of deliberately formed purposes. These considerations must qualify any statements made regarding child purposes. One result of the growth here discussed is the 'leading on' it affords. A skill acquired as end can be applied as means to new purposes. Skill or idea arising first in connection with means may be singled out for special consideration and so form new ends. This last is one of the most fruitful sources of new interests, particularly of the intellectual kind.

In connection with this 'maturing' goes a general increase in the 'interest span', the length of time during which a set will remain active, the time within which a child will—if allowed—work at any given project. What part of this increase is due to nature and physical maturing, what part to nurture, why the span is long for some activities and short for others, how we can increase the span in any given cases, are questions of the greatest moment for the educator. It is a matter of common knowledge that within limits 'interests' may be built up, the correlative interest spans appreciably increased....

It may be well to come closer to the customary subject matter of the school. Let us consider the classification of the different types of projects: Type I, where the purpose is to embody some idea or plan in external form, as building a boat, writing a letter, presenting a play; type 2, where the purpose is to enjoy some (esthetic) experience, as listening to a story, hearing a symphony, appreciating a picture; type 3, where the purpose is to straighten out some intellectual difficulty, to solve some problem, as to find out whether or not dew falls, to ascertain how New York outgrew Philadelphia; type 4, where the purpose is to obtain some item or degree of skill or knowledge, as learning to write grade 14 on the Thorndike Scale, learning the irregular verbs in French. It is at once evident that these groupings more or less overlap and that one type may be used as means to another as end. It may be of interest to note that with these definitions the project method logically includes the problem method as a special case. The value of such a classification as that here given seems to me to lie in the light it should throw on the kind of projects teachers may expect and on the procedure that normally prevails in the several types. For type I the following steps have been suggested: purposing, planning, executing, and judging. It is in accord with the general theory here advocated that the child as far as possible take each step himself. Total failure, however, may hurt more than assistance. The opposed dangers seem to be on the one hand that the child may not come out master of the process, on the other, that he may waste time. The teacher must steer the child through these narrows, taking care meanwhile to avoid the other dangers previously discussed. The function of the purpose and the place of thinking in the process need but be mentioned. Attention may be called to the fourth step, that the child as he grows older may increasingly judge the result in terms of the aim and with increasing care and success draw from the process its lessons for the future.

41

*William Heard
Kilpatrick*

Type 2, enjoying an esthetic experience, may seem to some hardly to belong in the list of projects. But the factor of purpose undoubtedly guides the process and—I must think—influences the growth of appreciation. I have, however, as yet no definite procedure steps to point out.

Type 3, that of the problem, is of all the best known, owing to the work of Professors Dewey and McMurry. The steps that have been used are those of the Dewey analysis of thought.[2] The type lends itself, next to type 4, best of all to our ordinary schoolroom work. For this reason I have myself feared its overemphasis. Our schools—at least in my judgment—do emphatically need a great increase in the social activity possible in type I. Type 4, where the purpose has to do with specific items of knowledge or skill, would seem to call for the same steps as type I—purposing, planning, executing, and judging. Only here, the planning had perhaps best come from the psychologist. In this type also there is danger of over-emphasis. Some teachers indeed may not closely discriminate between drill as a project and a drill as a set task, although the results will be markedly different....

In conclusion, then, we may say that the child is naturally active, especially along social lines. Heretofore a régime of coercion has only too often reduced our schools to aimless dawdling and our pupils to selfish individualists. Some in reaction have resorted to foolish humoring of childish whims. The contention of this paper is that wholehearted purposeful activity in a social situation as the typical unit of school procedure is the best guarantee of the utilization of the child's native capacities now too frequently wasted. Under proper guidance purpose means efficiency, not only in reaching the projected end of the activity immediately at hand, but even more in securing from the activity the learning which it potentially contains. Learning of all kinds and in its all desirable ramifications best proceeds in proportion as wholeheartedness of purpose is present. With the child naturally social and with the skillful teacher to stimulate and guide his purposing, we can especially expect that kind of learning we call character building. The necessary reconstruction consequent upon these considerations offers a most alluring 'project' to the teacher who but dares to purpose.

NOTES

1. The term accessory was used in the original article where the word associate is now used with a slight difference of meaning, however.
2. Dewey, *How We Think,* Chap. VI.

CHAPTER 3 The Critical Pedagogical Perspective

3.1 HENRY A. GIROUX

Culture, Power and Transformation in the Work of Paulo Freire

Henry A. Giroux, a scholar in critical theory of education, is considered one of the most important writers on critical pedagogy. Formerly a professor at Miami University in Oxford, Ohio, he presently holds an endowed professorial chair at Pennsylvania State University in University Park, Pennsylvania. His many publications, including *Theory and Resistance: A Pedagogy for the Opposition* (Bergin & Garvey, 1983), have been widely read and cited. Among his most recent books are *Border Crossings* (Routledge, 1992) and *Living Dangerously* (Peter Lang, 1993). He is also coeditor, with Paulo Freire, of the Critical Studies in Education series (Bergin & Garvey).

In the selection that follows, which is from *Teachers as Intellectuals: Toward a Critical Pedagogy of Learning* (Bergin & Garvey, 1988), Professor Giroux discusses the ideas of culture, power, and transformation in the work of educator Paulo Freire. He points out that Freire sees education as an empowering force for people, that education necessarily addresses a kind of cultural politics. Giroux agrees with Freire that cultural politics is a broader concept than any particular political doctrine. Giroux concludes that the liberation of persons through education must necessarily involve critical engagement with and evaluation of the dominant cultural and political forces in any society.

Key Concept: education and cultural politics

Paulo Freire's work continues to represent a theoretically refreshing and politically viable alternative to the current impasse in educational theory and practice in North America. Freire has appropriated the unclaimed heritage of emancipatory ideas in those versions of secular and religious philosophy located within the corpus of bourgeois thought. He has also critically integrated into his work a heritage of radical thought without assimilating many of the problems that have plagued it historically. In effect, Freire combines what I have called the "language of critique" with the "language of possibility."

Utilizing the language of critique, Freire has fashioned a theory of education that takes seriously the relationship between radical critical theory and the imperatives of radical commitment and struggle. Drawing upon his experiences in Latin America, Africa, and North America, he has generated a discourse that deepens our understanding of the dynamics and complexity of domination. In this instance, Freire rightly argues that domination cannot be reduced exclusively to a form of class domination. With the notion of difference as a guiding theoretical thread, Freire rejects the idea that there is a universalized form of oppression. Instead, he acknowledges and locates within different social fields forms of suffering that speak to particular modes of domination and, consequently, diverse forms of collective struggle and resistance. By recognizing that certain forms of oppression are not reducible to class oppression, Freire steps outside standard Marxist Analyses; he argues that society contains a multiplicity of contradictory social relations, over which social groups can struggle and organize themselves. This is manifest in those social relations in which the ideological and material conditions of gender, racial, and age discrimination are at work.

Equally important is the insight that domination is more than the simple imposition of arbitrary power by one group over another. Instead, for Freire, the logic of domination represents a combination of historical and contemporary ideological and material practices that are never completely successful, always embody contradictions, and are constantly being fought over within asymmetrical relations of power. Underlying Freire's language of critique, in this case, is the insight that history is never foreclosed. Just as the actions of men and women are limited by the specific constraints in which they find themselves, they also make those constraints and the possibilities that may follow from challenging them.

Within this theoretical juncture Freire introduces a new dimension to radical educational theory and practice. I say new because he links the process of struggle to the particularities of people's lives while simultaneously arguing for a faith in the power of the oppressed to struggle in the interests of their own liberation. This is a notion of education fashioned in more than critique and Orwellian pessimism; it is a discourse that creates a new starting point by trying to make hope realizable and despair unconvincing.

Education in Freire's view becomes both an ideal and a referent for change in the service of a new kind of society. As an ideal, education "speaks" to a form of cultural politics that transcends the theoretical boundaries of any one specific political doctrine, while simultaneously linking social theory and practice to the deepest aspects of emancipation. Thus, as an expression of radical social theory, Freire's cultural politics is broader and more fundamental than any one specific political discourse such as classical Marxist theory, a point that often confuses his critics. In fact, his represents a theoretical discourse whose underlying interests are fashioned around a struggle against all forms of subjective and objective domination as well as a struggle for forms of knowledge, skills, and social relations that provide the conditions for social and, hence, self-emancipation.

As a referent for change, education represents both a site and a particular type of engagement with the dominant society. For Freire, education includes and moves beyond the notion of schooling. Schools are only one important site where education takes place, where men and women both produce and are the product of specific social and pedagogical relations. Education represents, in Freire's view, both a struggle for meaning and a struggle over power relations. Its dynamic springs from the dialectical relation between individuals and groups who live out their lives within specific historical conditions and structural constraints, on the one hand, and those cultural forms and ideologies that give rise to the contradictions and struggles that define the lived realities of various societies on the other. Education is that terrain where power and politics are given a fundamental expression, where the production of meaning, desire, language, and values engage and respond to the deeper beliefs about what it means to be human, to dream, and to name and struggle for a particular future and form of social life. Education becomes a form of action that joins the languages of critique and possibility. It represents, finally, the need for a passionate commitment by educators to make the political more pedagogical, that is, to make critical reflection and action fundamental parts of a social project that not only engages forms of oppression but develops a deep and abiding faith in the struggle to humanize life itself. It is the particular nature of this social project that gives Freire's work its theoretical distinctiveness.

The theoretical distinctiveness of Freire's work can best be understood by examining briefly how his discourse stands between two radical traditions. On the one hand, the language of critique as it is expressed in Freire's work embodies many of the analyses that characterize what has been called the new sociology of education. On the other hand, Freire's philosophy of hope and struggle is rooted in a language of possibility that draws extensively from the tradition of liberation theology. It is from the merging of these two traditions that Freire has produced a discourse that not only gives meaning and theoretical coherence to his work, but also provides the basis for a more comprehensive and critical theory of pedagogical struggle.

THE NEW SOCIOLOGY OF EDUCATION AND
THE LANGUAGE OF CRITIQUE

The new sociology of education emerged in full strength in England and the United States over a decade ago as a critical response to what can be loosely termed the discourse of traditional educational theory and practice. The central question, against which it developed its criticism of traditional schooling as well as its own theoretical discourse, is typically Freirean: How does one make education meaningful so as to make it critical and, one hopes, emancipatory.

Radical critics, for the most part, agree that educational traditionalists generally ignore the question. They elude the issue through the paradoxical depoliticizing [of] the language of schooling while reproducing and legitimating capitalist ideologies. The most obvious expression of this approach can be seen in the positivist discourse used by traditional educational theorists. A positivist discourse, in this case, takes as its most important concerns the mastery of pedagogical techniques and the transmission of knowledge instrumental to the existing society. In the traditional world view, schools are merely instructional sites.

Critical educational theorists argue that traditional educational theory suppresses important questions regarding knowledge, power, and domination. Furthermore, schools do not provide opportunities in the broad western humanist tradition for self- and social empowerment in the society at large. In contrast, critical educators provide theoretical arguments and enormous amounts of empirical evidence to suggest that schools are in fact, agencies of social, economic and cultural reproduction. At best, public schooling offers limited individual mobility to members of the working class and other oppressed groups, but, in the final analysis, public schools are powerful instruments for the reproduction of capitalist relations of production and the legitimating ideologies of everyday life.

For the new sociology of education, schools are analyzed primarily within the language of critique and domination. Yet, since schools are viewed primarily as reproductive in nature, left critics fail to provide a programmatic discourse through which the opportunity for counterhegemonic practices could be established. The agony of the left in this case is that its language of critique offered no hope for teachers, parents, or students to wage a political struggle within the schools themselves. Consequently, the language of critique is subsumed within the discourse of despair.

Freire's earlier work shares a remarkable similarity with some of the major theoretical tenets found in the new sociology of education. By redefining and politicizing the notion of literacy, Freire develops a similar type of critical analysis in which he claims that traditional forms of education function primarily to objectify and alienate oppressed groups. Moreover, Freire explores in great depth the reproductive nature of dominant culture and systematically analyzed how it functions through specific social practices and texts to produce and maintain a "culture of silence" among the Brazilian peasants with whom he worked. Though Freire does not use the term "hidden curriculum" as part of his discourse, he demonstrates pedagogical approaches through which groups of learners can decode ideological and material practices whose form, content, and selective omissions contain the logic of domination and oppression. In addition, Freire links the selection, discussion, and evaluation of knowledge to the pedagogical processes that provide a context for such activity. In his view, it is impossible to separate one from the other, and any viable pedagogical practice has to link radical forms of knowledge with corresponding radical social practices.

The major difference between Freire's work and the new sociology of education is that the latter appears to start and end with the logic of political, economic, and cultural reproduction, whereas Freire's analysis begins with the process of production, that is, the various ways human beings construct their own voices and validate their contradictory experiences within specific historical settings and constraints. The reproduction of capitalist rationality and other forms of oppression is only one political and theoretical moment in the process of domination, rather than an all-encompassing aspect of human existence. It is something to be decoded, challenged, and transformed but only within the ongoing discourse, experiences, and histories of the oppressed themselves. It is in this shift from the discourse of reproduction and critique to the language of possibility and engagement that Freire draws from other traditions and fashions a more comprehensive and radical pedagogy.

LIBERATION THEOLOGY AND THE LANGUAGE OF POSSIBILITY

Central to Freire's politics and pedagogy is a philosophical vision of a liberated humanity. The nature of this vision is rooted in a respect for life. The hope and vision of the future that it inspires are not meant to provide consolation for the oppressed as much as to promote ongoing forms of critique and a struggle against objective forces of oppression. By combining the dynamics of critique and collective struggle with a philosophy of hope, Freire has created a language of possibility, what he calls a permanent prophetic vision. Underlying this prophetic vision is a faith, which Dorothée Soelle argues in *Choosing Life*, "makes life present to us and so makes it possible.... It is a great 'Yes' to life ... [one that] presupposes our power to struggle."

Freire's opposition to all forms of oppression, his call to link ideology critique with collective action, and the prophetic vision central to his politics are heavily indebted to the spirit and ideological dynamics that have both informed and characterized the Liberation Theology Movement that has emerged primarily out of Latin America in the last decade. In truly dialectical fashion, Freire has both criticized and rescued the radical underside of revolutionary Christianity. As the reader will discover, Freire is a harsh critic of the reactionary church. At the same time, he situates his faith and sense of hope in the God of history and the oppressed whose teachings make it impossible, in Freire's words, to "reconcile Christian love with the exploitation of human beings."

Within the discourse of liberation theology, Freire fashions a powerful antidote to the cynicism and despair of many left radical critics. Though utopian, his analysis is concrete in its nature and appeal, taking as its starting point collective actors in their various historical settings and the particularity of their problems and forms of oppression. It is utopian only in its refusal to surrender to the risks and dangers that face all challenges to dominant power structures. It is prophetic in that it views the Kingdom of God as something to be created on earth but only through a faith in both other human beings and the necessity of permanent struggle. The notion of faith that emerges in Freire's work is informed by the memory of the oppressed, the suffering that must not be allowed to continue, and the need never to forget that the prophetic vision is an ongoing process, a vital aspect of the very nature of human life. By combining the discourses of critique and possibility Freire joins history and theology so as to provide the theoretical basis for a radical pedagogy that expresses hope, critical reflection, and collective struggle.

It is at this juncture that the work of Paulo Freire becomes crucial to the development of a radical pedagogy. For in Freire we find the dialectician of contradictions and emancipation. His discourse bridges the relationship between agency and structure, situates human action in constraints forged in historical and contemporary practices, while simultaneously pointing to the spaces, contradictions, and forms of resistance that raise the possibility for social struggle. I will conclude by turning briefly to those theoretical elements in Freire's work that seem vital to developing a new language and theoretical foundation for a radical theory of pedagogy, particularly in a North American context.

Two qualifications must be made before I begin. First, Freire's mode of analysis cannot be dismissed as irrelevant to a North American context. Although critics have argued that his experiences with Brazilian peasants do not translate adequately for educators in the advanced industrial countries of the West, Freire makes it clear through the force of his examples and the variety of pedagogical experiences he provides that the context for his work is international in scope. Not only does he capitalize on his experiences in Brazil, he also draws on his work in Chile, Africa, and the United States. Furthermore, he not only takes as the object of his criticism adult education, but also the pedagogical practices of the Catholic Church, social workers, and public education. As he has pointed out repeatedly, the object of his analysis and the language he uses is for the oppressed everywhere; his concept of the Third World is ideological and political rather than merely geographic.

This leads to the second qualification. In order to be true to the spirit of Freire's most profound pedagogical beliefs, it must be stated that he would never argue that his work is meant to be adopted unproblematically to any site or pedagogical context. What Freire does provide is a metalanguage that generates a set of categories and social practices. Freire's work is not meant to offer radical recipes for instant forms of critical pedagogy, it is a series of theoretical signposts that need to be decoded and critically appropriated within the specific contexts in which they might be useful.

Power, for Freire, both a negative and a positive force, its character is dialectical, and its mode of operation is always more than simply repressive. Power works on and through people. Domination is never so complete that power is experienced exclusively as a negative force, yet power is at the basis of all forms of behavior in which people resist, struggle, and fight for a better world. In a general sense, Freire's theory of power and his demonstration of its dialectical character serve the important function of broadening the spheres and terrains on which power operates. Power, in this instance, is not exhausted in those public and private spheres by governments, ruling classes, and other dominant groups. It is more ubiquitous and is expressed in a range of oppositional public spaces and spheres that traditionally have been characterized by the *absence* of power and thus any form of resistance.

Freire's view of power suggests not only an alternative perspective to those radical theorists trapped in the straitjacket of despair and cynicism, it also stresses that there are always cracks, tensions, and contradictions in various social spheres such as schools where power can be exercised as a positive force in the name of resistance. Furthermore, Freire understands that power—domination—is not simply imposed by the state through agencies such as the police, the army, and the courts. Domination is also expressed in the way in which power, technology, and ideology come together to produce knowledge, social relations, and other concrete cultural forms that indirectly silence people. It is also found in the way in which the oppressed internalize and thus participate in their own oppression. This is an important point in Freire's work and directs us to the ways in which domination is subjectively experienced through its internalization and sedimentation in the very needs of the personality. What is at work here is an important attempt to examine the psychically repressive aspects of domination and the internal obstacles to self-knowledge and, thus, to forms of social and self emancipation.

Freire broadens the notion of learning to include how the body learns tacitly, how habit translates into sedimented history, and, most importantly, how knowledge itself may block the development of certain subjectivities and ways of experiencing the world. Ironically, emancipatory forms of knowledge may be refused by those who could most benefit from such knowledge. In this case, accommodation to the logic domination by the oppressed may take the form of actively resisting forms of knowledge that pose a challenge to their world view. Rather than a passive acceptance of domination, knowledge becomes instead an active dynamic of negation, an active refusal to listen, to hear, or to affirm one's own possibilities. The pedagogical questions that emerge from this view of domination are: How do radical educators assess and address the elements of repression and forgetting at the heart of this domination? What accounts for the conditions that sustain an active refusal to know or to learn in the face of knowledge that may challenge the nature of domination itself?

The message that emerges from Freire's pedagogy is relatively clear. If radical educators are to understand the meaning of liberation, they must first be aware of the form that domination takes, the nature of its location, and the problems it poses to those who experience it as both a subjective and objective force. But such a project would be impossible unless one took the historical and cultural particularities, the forms of social life, of subordinate and oppressed groups as a starting point for such an analysis. It is to this issue in Freire's work that I now turn.

FREIRE'S PHILOSOPHY OF EXPERIENCE AND CULTURAL PRODUCTION

One of the most important theoretical elements for a radical pedagogy that Freire provides is his view of experience and cultural production. Freire's notion of culture is at odds with both conservative and progressive positions. In the first instance, he rejects the notion that culture can be divided easily into high, popular, and low forms, with high culture representing the most advanced heritage of a nation. Culture, in this view, hides the ideologies that legitimate and distribute specific forms of culture as if they were unrelated to ruling class interests and existing configurations of power. In the second instance, he rejects the notion that the moment of cultural creation rests solely with ruling groups and that dominant cultural forms harbor merely the seeds of domination. Related to this position, and also rejected by Freire, is the assumption that oppressed groups possess by their very location in the apparatus of domination a progressive and revolutionary culture waiting only to be released from the fetters of ruling class domination.

For Freire, culture is the representation of lived experiences, material artifacts, and practices forged within the unequal and dialectical relations that different groups establish in a given society at a particular historical point. Culture is a form of production whose processes are intimately connected with the structuring of different social formations, particularly those that are gender, age, racial, and class related. It is also a form of production that helps human agents, through their use of language and other material resources, to transform society. In this case, culture is closely related to the dynamics of power and produces asymmetries in the ability of individuals and groups to define and achieve their goals. Furthermore, culture is also an arena of struggle and contradiction, and there is no one culture in the homogeneous sense. On the contrary, there are dominant and subordinate cultures that express different interests and operate from different and unequal terrains of power.

Freire argues for a notion of cultural power that takes as its staring point the social and historical particularities that constitute the problems, sufferings, visions, and acts of resistance that comprise the cultural forms of subordinate groups. Cultural power then has a dual focus as part of his strategy to make the political more pedagogical. First, educators will have to work with the experiences that students bring to schools and other educational sites. This means making these experiences, public and private, the object of debate and confirmation; it means legitimating such experiences in order to give those who live and move within them a sense of affirmation and to provide the conditions for students and others to display an active voice and presence. The pedagogical experience here becomes an invitation to make visible the languages, dreams, values, and encounters that constitute the lives of those whose histories are often actively silenced. But Freire does more than argue for the legitimation of the culture of the oppressed. He also recognizes that such experiences are contradictory in nature and harbor not only radical potentialities but also the sedimentations of domination. Cultural power takes a twist in this instance and refers to the need to *work on* the experiences that make up the lives of the oppressed. Such experiences in their varied cultural forms have to be recovered critically so as to reveal both their strengths and weaknesses. Moreover, self-critique is complimented in the name of a radical pedagogy designed to unearth and critically appropriate those unclaimed emancipatory moments in bourgeois knowledge and experience that further provide the skills the oppressed will need to exercise leadership in the dominant society.

What is striking in this presentation is that Freire has fashioned a theory of cultural power and production that begins with popular education. Instead of offering abstract generalities about human nature, he rightly argues for pedagogical principles that arise from the concrete practices—the terrains on which people live out their everyday experiences. All of this suggests taking seriously the cultural capital of the oppressed, developing critical and analytical tools to interrogate it, and staying in touch with dominant definitions of knowledge so we can analyze them for their usefulness and for the ways in which they bear the logic of domination.

FREIRE, TRANSFORMATIVE INTELLECTUALS, AND THE THEORY-PRACTICE RELATIONSHIP

Radical social theory has been plagued historically by the development of the relationship between intellectuals and the masses, on the one hand, and the relationship between theory and practice. Under the call for the unity of theory and practice, the possibility for emancipatory practice has often been negated through forms of vanguardism in which intellectuals effectively removed from the popular forces the ability to define for themselves the limits of their aims and practice. By assuming a virtual monopoly in the exercise of theoretical leadership, intellectuals unknowingly reproduced the division of mental and manual labor that was at the core of most forms of domination. Instead of developing theories of practice, which were rooted in the concrete experience of listening and learning with the oppressed, Marxist intellectuals developed theories for practice or technical instruments for change that ignored the necessity for a dialectical reflection on the everyday dynamics and problems of the oppressed within the context of radical social transformation.

Freire refutes this approach to the theory-practice relationship and redefines the very idea of the intellectual. Like the Italian social theorist, Antonio Gramsci, Freire redefines the category of intellectual and argues that all men and women are intellectuals. That is, regardless of social and economic function all human beings perform as intellectuals by constantly interpreting and giving meaning to the world and by participating in a particular conception of the world. Moreover, the oppressed need to develop their own organic and transformative intellectuals who can learn with such groups while simultaneously helping to foster modes of self-education and struggle against various forms of oppression. In this case, intellectuals are organic in that they are *not* outsiders bringing theory to the masses. On the contrary, they are theorists fused organically with the culture and practical activities of the oppressed. Rather than casually dispense knowledge to the grateful masses, intellectuals fuse with the oppressed in order to make and remake the conditions necessary for a radical social project.

This position is crucial in highlighting the political function and importance of intellectuals. Equally significant is the way it redefines the notion of political struggle by emphasizing its pedagogical nature and the centrality of the popular and democratic nature of such a struggle. This raises the important question of how Freire defines the relation between theory and practice.

For Freire, "there is no theoretic context if it is not in a dialectical unity with the concrete context." Rather than call for the collapse of theory into practice, Freire argues for a certain distance between theory and practice. He views theory as anticipatory in its nature and posits that it must take the concepts of understanding and possibility as its central moments. Theory is informed by an oppositional discourse that preserves its critical distance from the "facts" and experiences of the given society. The tension, indeed, the conflict with practice belongs to the essence of theory and is grounded in its very structure. Theory does not dictate practice; rather, it serves to hold practice at arm's length so as to mediate and critically comprehend the type of praxis needed within a specific setting at a particular time. There is no appeal to universal laws or historical necessity here; theory emerges within specific contexts and forms of experience in order to examine such contexts critically and then to intervene on the basis of an informed praxis.

But Freire's contribution to the nature of theory and practice and the role of the intellectual in the process of social transformation contains another important dimension. Theory must be seen as the production of forms of discourse that arise from various specific social sites. Such a discourse may arise from the universities, from peasant communities, from workers councils, or from within various social movements. The issue here is that radical educators recognize that these different sites give rise to various forms of theoretical production and practice. Each of these sites provides diverse and critical insights into the nature of domination and the possibilities for social and self-emancipation, and they do so from the historical and social particularities that give them meaning. What brings them together is a mutual respect forged in criticism and the need to struggle against all forms of domination.

3.2 MICHAEL W. APPLE

The Hidden Curriculum and the Nature of Conflict

Michael W. Apple is a distinguished scholar in the critical theory of education and one of the major writers in the new sociology of education. His books have received widespread attention in England and America.

The selection that follows is from chapter 5, "The Hidden Curriculum and the Nature of Conflict," of Apple's book *Ideology and Curriculum* (Routledge & Kegan Paul, 1979). In it, Apple argues that public school curricula tend to stress hegemonic (dominant) social values. Furthermore, these curricula are designed to get students to accept existing social values, rules, and institutions as predetermined, "neutral," and unchangeable, rather than as changing, fluid, and open to dialectic challenge by students or their teachers. The "hidden curriculum" of most schools, Apple says, is composed of "consensus" values and attitudes that dominant social groups wish to impose on all others. Tacit (silent) rules as to what behaviors and attitudes are acceptable are embedded in all school curricula. Students are encouraged to conform to and accept rather than enter into conflict with the dominant social values. Apple concludes that students need to be taught how to counter hegemonic social values in school curricula.

Key Concept: the "hidden curriculum"

*B*efore proceeding, . . . it is important to note that in order for the school to continue to perform in a relatively smooth manner its complex historical roles in the maximization of the production of technical knowledge and in the socialization of students into the normative structure required by our society, it has to do something else which is related to and helps underpin both roles. It has to make legitimate a basically technical perspective, a tension of consciousness that responds to the social and intellectual world in an acritical fashion. That is, the school needs to make all this seem natural. A society based on technical cultural capital and individual accumulation of economic capital needs to seem as if it were the only possible world. Part of the school's role, in other words, is to contribute to the distribution of what the critical theorists of the Frankfurt School might call purposive-rational patterns of rationality and action.

This is an important element in ideological hegemony, for,... in order for students' definitions of situations (like those taught in their initial school experience) to be maintained, these definitions must be ongoingly confirmed. This confirmation must entail a continuation of the patterns of interaction that dominated kindergarten, of course. But, since students, as they get older, now verbally reason with some facility, and can think through aspects of their social and cultural conditions, the curriculum content itself becomes even more important. There needs to be continuous and increasingly sophisticated *justification* for acceptance of the distinctions and social rules they learned earlier. This justification needs to *set the ideological limits* of such thinking by embodying 'appropriate' ways in which students can begin to reason through the logic of why the institutions and the culture they interact with everyday are in fact legitimate. This requires that institutions, commonsense rules, and knowledge be seen as relatively pregiven, neutral, and basically unchanging because they all continue to exist by 'consensus.' Thus, the curriculum should stress hegemonic assumptions, ones which ignore the actual working of power in cultural and social life and which point to the naturalness of acceptance, institutional beneficence, and a positivistic vision in which knowledge is divorced from the real human actors who created it. The key to uncovering this, I believe, is the treatment of *conflict* in the curriculum.

CONFLICT AND THE HIDDEN CURRICULUM

The fact that schools normally seem neutral and are usually *overtly* insulated from political processes and ideological argumentation has both positive and negative qualities. The insulation has served to defend the school against whims and fads that can often have a destructive effect upon educational practice. It also, however, can make the school rather unresponsive to the needs of local communities and a changing social order. The pros and cons of the schools as a 'conservative' institution have been argued fervently for the last ten years or so, at least. Among the most articulate of the spokespeople have been Edgar Z. Friedenberg and the late Jules Henry. Aside from the discussions of the teaching of work related norms, the covert teaching of an achievement and marketplace ethic and the probable substitution of a 'middle class' and often 'schizophrenic' value system for a student's own biographical meanings have been some of the topics most usually subject to analysis. As we saw, a good deal of the focus has been on what Jackson has so felicitously labeled the 'hidden curriculum'—that is, on the norms and values that are implicitly, but effectively, taught in schools and that are not usually talked about in teachers' statements of end or goals....

It has become increasingly evident that the formal corpus of school knowledge found in, say, most history books and social studies texts and materials has, over the years, presented a somewhat biased view of the true nature of the amount and possible use of internecine strife in which groups in this country and others have engaged. Our side is good; their side is bad. 'We' are peace loving and want an end to strife; 'they' are warlike and aim to dominate. The list could be extended considerably especially in racial and class matters.[1] Yet, we must go beyond this type of analysis, often even beyond the work of the revisionist historians, political scientists, students of political socialization, and educators to get at many of the roots of the teaching of this dominant orientation. I shall examine here two specific areas—social studies and science. In so doing, I shall point out that the presentation of these two areas (among others) in schools both mirrors and fosters an ideology that is oriented to a static perspective: in the social studies, on the positive and even essential functions of social conflict; and in science, on the nature of scientific work and argumentation and on what has been called 'revolutionary' science. The view presented of science, especially, in the schools is particularly interesting since it is essentially an archetype of the ideological position on conflict I wish to illuminate.

Two tacit assumptions seem to be prominent in teaching and in curricular materials. The first centers around a negative position on the nature and uses of conflict. The second focuses on men and women as recipients of values and institutions, not on men and women as creators and recreators of values and institutions. These assumptions act as basic guidelines that order experiences.

BASIC RULES AND TACIT ASSUMPTIONS

The concept of hegemony implies that fundamental patterns in society are held together by tacit ideological assumptions, rules if you will, which are not usually conscious, as well as economic control and power. These rules serve to organize and legitimate the activity of the many individuals whose interaction makes up a social order. Analytically it is helpful to distinguish two types of rules—constitutive or basic rules and preference rules.[2] Basic rules are like the rules of a game; they are broad parameters in which action takes place. Preference rules, as the name suggests, are the choices one has within the rules of the game. Take chess, for instance. There are basic ground rules (which are not usually brought to a level of awareness) that make chess different from, say, checkers or other board games or even nonboard games. And within the game of chess, one has choices of the moves to make within this constitutive framework. Pawn's choices involve moving forward (except in 'taking' an opponent), rooks move forward or side to side, and so forth. If an opponent's pawn were to jump over three men to put you in check, then he obviously would not be following the 'rules of the game;' nor would he be following the tacitly accepted rules if he, say, swept all your men from the board and shouted 'I win!'

On the very broadest level, one of the constitutive rules most predominant in our society involves the notion of trust. When we drive down the street, we trust that the car approaching from the opposite direction will stay in its lane. Unless there is some outward manifestation of deviance from this rule, we never even bring to a level of conscious awareness how this basic rule of activity organizes our lives.[3] A similar rule is the one that posits the legitimate bounds of conflict. The rules of the game implicitly set out the boundaries of the activities people are to engage or not to engage in, the types of questions to ask, and the acceptance or rejection of other people's activities.[4] Within these boundaries, there are choices among a range of activities. We can use the courts, but not bomb; we can argue, but not duel; and so forth. A basic assumption seems to be that conflict among groups of people is *inherently* and fundamentally bad and we should strive to eliminate it *within* the established framework of institutions, rather than seeing conflict and contradiction as the basic 'driving forces' in society.

While some of the better schools and classrooms are alive with issues and controversy, the controversies usually exhibited in schools concern choices *within* the parameters of implicitly held rules of activity. Little attempt is made to focus on the parameters themselves.

The hidden curriculum in schools serves to reinforce basic rules surrounding the nature of conflict and its uses. It posits a network of assumptions that, when internalized by students, establishes the boundaries of legitimacy. This process is accomplished not so much by explicit instances showing the negative value of conflict, but by nearly the total absence of instances showing the importance of intellectual and normative conflict in subject areas. The fact is that these assumptions are obligatory for the students, since at no time are the assumptions articulated or questioned. By the very fact that they are tacit, that they reside not at the roof but the root of our brains, their potency as aspects of hegemony is enlarged. . . .

Social studies and science as they are taught in the large majority of schools provide some of the most explicit instances of the hidden teaching. I have chosen these areas for two reasons. First, there has been built up a rather extensive and important literature concerned with the sociology of the disciplines of scientific endeavor. This literature deals rather insightfully with the 'logic in use' of scientists (that is, what scientists seem actually to do) as opposed to the 'reconstructed logic' of scientists (that is, what philosophers of science and other observers say scientists do) that is normally taught in schools.[5] Second, in social studies the problems we discuss can be illuminated rather clearly by drawing upon selected Marxian notions to show that the commonsense views of social life often found in the teaching of social studies are not inevitable. Let us examine science initially. In so doing, I also want to propose, . . . an alternate or, rather, a broader view of scientific endeavor that should be considered by educators and, especially, curriculum workers, if they are, at the very least, to focus on the ideological assumptions inherent in much that is taught in our educational institutions. . . .

What is intriguing is the nearly complete lack of treatment of or even reference to conflict as a social concern or as a category of thought in most available social studies curricula or in most classrooms observed. Of the more popular materials, only those developed under the aegis of the late Hilda Taba refer to it as a key concept. However, while the Taba Social Studies Curriculum overtly focuses on conflict, and while this focus in itself is a welcome sight, its orientation is on the serious consequences of sustained conflict rather than on the many positive aspects also associated with conflict itself. Conflict again is viewed as 'dysfunctional,' even though it is pictured as being ever present.[6]

As was noted previously, to a large extent society as it exists, in *both* its positive and negative aspects, is held together by implicit commonsense rules and paradigms of thought, by hegemony as well as by overt power. Social studies materials such as this (and there are many others to which I have not referred) can contribute to the reinforcing and tacit teaching of certain dominant basic assumptions and, hence, a pro-consensus and anti-dissension belief structure.

This view is being countered somewhat by a portion of the content now being taught under the rubric of Black and Women's Studies. Here, struggle and conflict on a communal basis are often explicitly and positively focused upon.[7] While many curriculists may find such overt espousal of community goals somewhat antithetical to their own inclinations, the fact that there has been an attempt to present a comparatively realistic outlook on the significant history and uses of conflict in the progress of social classes and groups, through the civil rights and black power movements for instance, must be recognized. Even those who would not applaud or would applaud only a rather safe or conservative view on this subject should realize the potency and positive value of just such a perspective for developing a group consciousness and a cohesiveness not heretofore possible. This point will be made again in my more general discussion of the uses of conflict in social groups.

To say, however, that most Black Studies curricula exhibit this same perspective would be less than accurate. One could also point to the by now apparent presentation of Black historical material where those Blacks are presented who stayed within what were considered to be the legitimate boundaries (constitutive rules) of protest or progressed in accepted economic, athletic, scholarly, or artistic fields. Usually, one does not find reference to Malcolm X, Marcus Garvey, or others who offered a potent critique of existing modes of economic and cultural control and activity. However, it is the *massiveness* of the tacit presentation of the consensus perspective that must be stressed, as well as its occurrence in the two areas examined in this chapter.

It is not sufficient, though, for our purposes to 'merely' illuminate how the hidden currriculum obligates students to experience certain encounters with basic rules. It is essential that an alternative view be posited and that the uses of social conflict that I have been mentioning be documented.

It is possible to counter the consensus orientation with a somewhat less consensus bound set of assumptions, assumptions that seem to be as empirically warranted, if not more so, as those to which I have raised objections. For instance, some social theorists have taken the position that 'society is not primarily a smoothly functioning order of the form of a social organism, a social system, or a static social fabric.' Rather, continuous change in the elements *and* basic structural form of society is a dominant characteristic. Conflicts are the systematic products of the changing structure of a society and by their very nature tend to lead to progress. The 'order' of society, hence, becomes the regularity of change. The 'reality' of society is conflict and flux, not a 'closed functional system.'[8] It has been stated that the most significant contribution to the understanding of society made by Marx was his insight that a major source of change and innovation is internal conflict.[9] In essence, therefore, conflicts must be looked at as a basic and often beneficial dimension of the dialectic of activity we label society. . . .

I have been proposing an alternative outlook on the presence and uses of conflict in social groups. It is feasible for it to be used as a more objective foundation for designing curricula and guiding teaching so that the more static hidden curriculum students encounter can be counterbalanced to some extent. The explicit focusing on conflict as a legitimate category of conceptualization and as a valid and essential dimension of collective life could enable the development by students of a more viable and potent political and intellectual perspective from which to perceive their relation to existing economic and political institutions. At the least, such a perspective gives them a better understanding of the tacit ideological assumptions that act to structure their own activity.

PROGRAMMATIC CONSIDERATIONS

There are a number of programmatic suggestions that can be made that could at least partially serve to counterbalance the hidden curriculum and selective tradition most evident in science and social studies as representatives of the formal corpus of school knowledge. While these are by their very nature still rather tentative and only partial, they may prove important.

A more balanced presentation of some of the espoused values of science is essential, especially that relating to organized skepticism. The historical importance to the scientific communities of the overriding skeptical outlook needs to be recognized and focused upon.

The history of science can be seen as a continuing dialectic of controversy and conflict between advocates of competing research programs and paradigms, between accepted answers and challenges to these 'truths.' As such, science itself could be presented with a greater historical orientation documenting the conceptual revolutions necessary for significant breakthroughs to occur.

Rather than adhering to a view of science as truth, the balanced presentation of science as truth-until-further-notice, as a process of continual change, could prevent the crystallization of attitude. In this connection also, the study of how conceptual revolutions in science have proceeded would contribute to a less positive perspective on consensus as the only mode of progress.

To this point can be added a focus upon the moral uses and dilemmas of science. For example, personalizing the history of science through cases such as Oppenheimer, Watson, and, intriguingly, the controversy surrounding the Velikovsky case, would indeed be helpful.[10] When taken together with a serious analysis of, say, the role of women in science and medicine, these suggestions would help to eliminate the bias of present curricula by introducing the idea of personal and interpersonal controversy and conflict.[11]

In the social studies, a number of suggestions can be made. The comparative study of revolution, say the American, French, Russian, Portuguese, and Chinese, would serve to focus upon the properties of the human condition that cause and are ameliorated by interpersonal conflict. This suggestion is made more appropriate when coupled with the fact that in many countries revolution is the legitimate (in a quite real sense of the word) mode of procedure for redressing grievances. To this could be added studies of economic and cultural imperialism.[12]

A more realistic appraisal and presentation of the uses of conflict in the legal and economic rights movement of Blacks, Indians, women, workers, and others would no doubt assist in the formation of a perspective that perceives these and similar activities as legitimate models of action. The fact that laws *had* to be broken and were then struck down by the courts later is not usually focused upon in social studies curricula. Yet, it was through these types of activities that a good deal of progress was and is made. Here community and 'movement' studies of how changes have been effected is an interesting process, one that should prove of considerable moment. This points to how critical it is that things like serious labor history be taught in schools. All too often we minimize the history of the concrete struggles workers had to engage in and the sacrifices they made. At the same time, students can be led to ground their own family and personal experiences in the history of class and ethnic group as well. Numerous bibliographies on topics such as labor history, the struggles of women, Blacks, and others are available to assist us in countering the selective tradition here.[13]

Beyond these suggestions for specific programmatic changes, one further area should be noted. Sociological 'paradigms' also attempt to account for the commonsense reality in which students and teachers dwell. Schools are integrally involved in this reality and its internalization. It might be wise to consider engaging students in the articulation and development of paradigms of activity within their everyday lives at school. Such involvement could enable students to come to grips with and amplify crucial insights into their own conditionedness and freedom. Such insights could potentially alter the original paradigm and the commonsense reality itself. It would also make possible to a greater degree a concrete and meaningful educational encounter for students with the process of value and institutional recreation. Social action curricula and student rights struggles, though limited in their usefulness because of the serious danger of 'incorporation,' could be quite helpful here in giving students a sense of their own possible competence in challenging hegemonic conditions in certain areas.[14]

CONCLUSIONS

Research on political socialization of children seems to indicate the importance of the president and the police as points of contact between children and the structures of authority and legitimacy in a society.[15] For instance, there is a strongly personal initial bond between the child and these representatives of the structures of authority. As the child matures, these very personal ties are transferred to more anonymous institutions such as Congress or to political activities such as voting. The tendency to lift impersonal institutions to high esteem may be quite an important source of the relative stability and durability of the structures of authority in industrial societies.[16]

Yet it is not quite certain that this formulation really answers the questions one could raise concerning political and social stability. The foundation of political (broadly conceived) leanings and relations to political and social structures is in a belief system that itself rests upon basic patterns of assumptions 'determined' by social and economic activity. Such rules for activity (and thought as a fundamental form of this activity) are probably more important to a person's relation to his or her life-world than we realize. We have been examining one of these constitutive ideological assumptions.

It has been my contention that the schools systematically distort the functions of social conflict in collectivities. The social, intellectual, and political manifestations of this distortion are manifold. They may contribute significantly to the ideological underpinnings that serve to fundamentally orient individuals toward an unequal society.

Students in most schools and in urban centers in particular are presented with a view that serves to legitimate the existing social order since change, conflict, and men and women as creators as well as receivers of values and institutions are systematically neglected. I have pointed to the massiveness of the presentation. Now something else must be stressed once again—the fact that these meaning structures are obligatory. Students receive them from persons who are 'significant others' in their lives, through their teachers, other role models in books and elsewhere. To change this situation, students' perceptions of to whom they are to look as holders of 'expert knowledge' must be radically altered. In ghetto areas, a partial answer is, perhaps, instituting a more radical perspective in the schools. This change can be carried out only by political activity. As has been mentioned before, it may very well be that to divorce an educator's educational existence from his or her other political existence is to forget that as an act of influence, education is also an inherently political act. Yet with this political sensitivity must also come a fair measure of economic and cultural understanding that speaks to the power of these ideological meanings, that situates them back into the actual social processes which generated them.

Thus, that these assumptions exist should not surprise us given the argument about the 'inner logic' of a particular economic and ideological form. The selective tradition I have analyzed... is a 'natural' outgrowth of the relations between our extant cultural and economic institutions. When a society 'requires,' at both an economic and a cultural level, the maximization (not distribution) of the production of technical knowledge, then the science that is taught will be divorced from the concrete human practices that sustain it. When a society 'requires,' at an economic level, the 'production' of agents who have internalized norms which stress engaging in often personally meaningless work, acceptance of our basic political and economic institutions as stable and always beneficient, a belief structure resting on consensus, and a positivistic and technical logic, then we would expect that the formal and informal curricula, the cultural capital, in schools will become aspects of hegemony. The inner logic of these tensions and expectations will set the limits, the constitutive rules, that will become our common sense. Any other response will seem unnatural, which is exactly the point both Williams and Gramsci have maintained.

The overt and covert teaching of these views of science and social life combine with and justify earlier socialization. Both make it quite difficult for one to be at all aware of the ideological saturation that goes on. For if the 'facts' of the world do rest on our theories of them, then the world people see, the economic and cultural meanings they give to it, will be defined in such a way as to be self-justifying. Meanings are given about the way the world 'really is' and the economic and cultural interests that determine *why* it is this way are legitimated as well. The ideological function is circular. Power and knowledge are here again intimately and subtly linked through the roots of our common sense, through hegemony.

One of the primary tasks ... has been to present lenses that are alternative to those that normally legitimate many of the activities and encounters curriculists design for students. It will become clearer as this volume progresses that the curriculum field itself has limited its own forms of consciousness so that the political and ideological assumptions that undergird a good deal of its normal patterns of activity are as hidden as those that students encounter in schools.[17] I have pointed to the possibilities inherent in a more realistic approach to the nature of conflict as one alternative 'form of consciousness.' ...

Without an analysis and greater understanding of these latent assumptions, educators run the very real risk of continuing to let ideological values work through them. A conscious advocacy of a more realistic outlook on and teaching of the dialectic of social change would, no doubt, contribute to preparing students with the political and conceptual tools necessary to deal with the dense reality they must face. However, can we accomplish the same for curriculists and other educators? Can we illuminate the political and conceptual tools needed to face the unequal society in which they also live? The most fruitful way to begin this task is to document what their conceptual and political tools do *now:* Do they again maintain a false consensus? How do they act as aspects of hegemony? What are their latent ideological functions? With a firmer grasp on the way schools assist in the creation of hegemony through the 'socialization' of students, it is this task—how hegemony operates in the heads of educators—to which we shall now turn.

NOTES

1. See, for example, Edith F. Gibson, 'The Three D's: Distortion, Deletion, Denial,' *Social Education,* XXXIII (April, 1969), 405–9 and Sidney M. Willhelm, *Who Needs the Negro?* (Cambridge, Mass.: Schenkman, 1970).
2. Helen McClure and George Fischer, 'Ideology and Opinion Making: General Problems of Analysis' (New York: Columbia University Bureau of Applied Social Research, July, 1969, mimeographed).
3. The language of 'rules of activity' is less analytically troublesome than the distinction often made between thought and action, since it implies that the distinction is somewhat naive and enables action—perceptual, conceptual, and bodily—to be the fundamental category of an individual's response to his or her situation. While we often use rules of activity and assumptions interchangeably, the point should be made that assumptions usually connote a less inclusive category of phenomena and are actually indicative of the existence of these socially sedimented rules and boundaries that seem to affect even our very perceptions. Further work on such rules can be found in the ethnomethodological literature and, of course, in the later Wittgenstein. See, for example, Harold Garfinkel, *Studies in Ethnomethodology* (Englewood Cliffs,

N.J.: Prentice-Hall, 1967) and Ludwig Wittgenstein, *Philosophical Investigations* (New York: Macmillan, 1953).

4. In essence, the 'system' that many individuals decry is *not only* an ordered interrelationship of institutions, but a framework of fundamental assumptions that act in a dialectical relationship with these institutions.

5. Michael W. Apple, 'Community, Knowledge and the Structure of Disciplines,' *The Educational Forum,* XXXVII (November, 1972), 75–82.

6. Maxine Durkin, *et al., The Taba Social Studies Curriculum: Communities Around Us* (Reading, Mass.: Addison-Wesley, 1969), p. v.

7. Nathan Hare, 'The Teaching of Black History and Culture in the Secondary Schools,' *Social Education,* XXXIII (April, 1969), 385–8, and Preston Wilcox, 'Education for Black Liberation,' *New Generation,* L1 (Winter 1969), 20–1.

8. Ralf Dahrendorf, *Class and Class Conflict in Industrial Societies* (Stanford: Stanford University Press, 1959), p. 27. For concrete studies of conflict both within and among classes in corporate society, see R. W. Connell, *Ruling Class, Ruling Culture* (Cambridge University Press, 1977) and Nicos Poulantzas, *Classes in Contemporary Capitalism* (London: New Left Books, 1975).

9. Jack Walker, 'A Critique of the Elitist Theory of Democracy,' *Apolitical Politics,* Charles A. McCoy and John Playford, eds (New York: Crowell, 1967), pp. 217–18.

10. Michael Mulkay, 'Some Aspects of Cultural Growth in the Natural Sciences,' *Social Research,* XXXVI (Spring, 1969), 22–52.

11. See, for example, Mary Roth Walsh, *Doctors Wanted. No Women Need Apply* (New Haven: Yale, 1977), Edward T. James, Janet Wilson James and Paul S. Boyer, *Notable American Women 1607–1950* (Cambridge, Mass.: Belknap Press, 1971), and H. J. Mozans, *Woman in Science* (Cambridge, Mass.: Massachusetts Institute of Technology, 1974).

12. See, for example, Ariel Dorfman and Armand Mattelart, *How to Read Donald Duck* (New York: International General, 1975) and Martin Carnoy, *Education as Cultural Imperialism* (New York: David McKay, 1974). One of the more interesting books for children which deals with some of these issues is Pal Rydlberg, *et al. The History Book* (Culver City, California: Peace Press, 1974).

13. Among the available bibliographies are *Women in U.S. History: An Annotated Bibliography* (Cambridge, Mass.: Common Women Collective, 1976) and Jim O'Brien, *et al. A Guide to Working Class History* (2nd edn: Somerville, Mass.: New England Free Press, n.d.).

14. The proposals for social action curriculum by Fred Newmann are interesting here. See his *Education for Citizen Action* (Berkeley: McCutchan, 1975). For a discussion of some of the problems with such proposals, see Michael W. Apple, 'Humanism and the Politics of Educational Argumentation,' *Humanistic Education: Visions and Realities,* Richard Weller, ed. (Berkeley: McCutchan, 1977), pp. 315–30.

15. David Easton and Jack Dennis, *Children in the Political System* (New York: McGraw-Hill, 1969), p. 162.

16. Ibid., pp. 271–6.

17. Dwayne Huebner, 'Politics and the Curriculum,' *Curriculum Crossroads,* A. Harry Passow, ed. (New York: Teachers College Press, 1962), p. 88.

3.3 PAULO FREIRE

Pedagogy of the Oppressed

Paulo Freire's philosophy of education was based on his belief in human liberation through the use of critical consciousness and dialogical methods of interaction between persons. He rejected traditional authoritarian "banking" conceptions of teaching, in which teachers "deposit" official knowledge in students' minds. He favored instead a "problem-posing" approach to teaching, in which teachers and students enter into a genuine dialogue devoted to developing their own visions of the world through the free exercise of their own voices. For Freire, education is "the practice of freedom." In the following selection, which is from *Pedagogy of the Oppressed* (Seabury Press, 1970), Freire critiques the "banking" method of teaching and promotes "problem-posing" approaches to the educational process.

Freire (1921–1997) was an educator of worldwide stature. In 1964, when *Pedagogy of the Oppressed* was first published in Brazil, the military government "invited" him to leave the nation. He first went to Chile and then to the United States, where he spent several years. The first English translation of *Pedagogy* appeared in 1970. Since that time it has become a modern classic. When a democratic government was elected in Brazil, Freire returned to his homeland. There he served as minister of education of the state of São Paulo, after which he moved back to the United States to work as a professor in the Harvard Graduate School of Education. He returned to teaching in Brazil, where he remained until his death.

Freire's many publications include *Letters to Cristina: Reflections on My Life and Work* (Routledge, 1996); *Letters to Guine-Bissau* (Seabury Press, 1978); *Cultural Action for Freedom* (Harvard Education Review Monograph No. 1, 1975 and 1983); *Education for Critical Consciousness* (Seabury Press, 1973); *Literacy: Reading the Word and the World*, coauthored with Donaldo Macedo (Bergin & Garvey, 1987); *Pedagogy of Hope: Reliving Pedagogy of the Oppressed* (Continuum, 1994); *A Pedagogy for Liberation: Dialogues on Transforming Education*, coauthored with Ira Shor (Bergin & Garvey, 1987); and *The Politics of Education: Culture, Power, and Liberation* (Bergin & Garvey, 1985).

Key Concept: education as the practice of freedom

A careful analysis of the teacher-student relationship at any level, inside or outside the school, reveals its fundamentally *narrative* character. This relationship involves a narrating Subject (the teacher) and patient, listening objects (the students). The contents, whether values or empirical dimensions of reality, tend in the process of being narrated to become lifeless and petrified. Education is suffering from narration sickness.

The teacher talks about reality as if it were motionless, static, compartmentalized, and predictable. Or else he expounds on a topic completely alien to the existential experience of the students. His task is to "fill" the students with the contents of his narration—contents which are detached from reality, disconnected from the totality that engendered them and could give them significance. Words are emptied of their concreteness and become a hollow, alienated, and alienating verbosity.

The outstanding characteristic of this narrative education, then, is the sonority of words, not their transforming power. "Four times four is sixteen; the capital of Pará is Belém." The student records, memorizes, and repeats these phrases without perceiving what four times four really means, or realizing the true significance of "capital" in the affirmation "the capital of Pará is Belém," that is, what Belém means for Pará and what Pará means for Brazil.

Narration (with the teacher as narrator) leads the students to memorize mechanically the narrated content. Worse yet, it turns them into "containers," into "receptacles" to be "filled" by the teacher. The more completely he fills the receptacles, the better a teacher he is. The more meekly the receptacles permit themselves to be filled, the better students they are.

Education thus becomes an act of depositing, in which the students are the depositories and the teacher is the depositor. Instead of communicating, the teacher issues communiqués and makes deposits which the students patiently receive, memorize, and repeat. This is the "banking" concept of education, in which the scope of action allowed to the students extends only as far as receiving, filing, and storing the deposits. They do, it is true, have the opportunity to become collectors or cataloguers of the things they store. But in the last analysis, it is men themselves who are filed away through the lack of creativity, transformation, and knowledge in this (at best) misguided system. For apart from inquiry, apart from the praxis, men cannot be truly human. Knowledge emerges only through invention and re-invention, through the restless, impatient, continuing, hopeful inquiry men pursue in the world, with the world, and with each other.

In the banking concept of education, knowledge is a gift bestowed by those who consider themselves knowledgeable upon those whom they consider to know nothing. Projecting an absolute ignorance onto others, a characteristic of the ideology of oppression, negates education and knowledge as processes of inquiry. The teacher presents himself to his students as their necessary opposite; by considering their ignorance absolute, he justifies his own existence. The students, alienated like the slave in the Hegelian dialectic, accept their ignorance as justifying the teacher's existence—but, unlike the slave, they never discover that they educate the teacher.

The *raison d'être* of libertarian education, on the other hand, lies in its drive towards reconciliation. Education must begin with the solution of the teacher-student contradiction, by reconciling the poles of the contradiction so that both are simultaneously teachers *and* students.

This solution is not (nor can it be) found in the banking concept. On the contrary, banking education maintains and even stimulates the contradiction through the following attitudes and practices, which mirror oppressive society as a whole:

1. the teacher teaches and the students are taught;
2. the teacher knows everything and the students know nothing;
3. the teacher thinks and the students are thought about;
4. the teacher talks and the students listen—meekly;
5. the teacher disciplines and the students are disciplined;
6. the teacher chooses and enforces his choice, and the students comply;
7. the teacher acts and the students have the illusion of acting through the action of the teacher;
8. the teacher chooses the program content, and the students (who were not consulted) adapt to it;
9. the teacher confuses the authority of knowledge with his own professional authority, which he sets in opposition to the freedom of the students;
10. the teacher is the Subject of the learning process, while the pupils are mere objects.

It is not surprising that the banking concept of education regards men as adaptable, manageable beings. The more students work at storing the deposits entrusted to them, the less they develop the critical consciousness which would result from their intervention in the world as transformers of that world. The more completely they accept the passive role imposed on them, the more they tend simply to adapt to the world as it is and to the fragmented view of reality deposited in them.

The capability of banking education to minimize or annul the students' creative power and to stimulate their credulity serves the interests of the oppressors, who care neither to have the world revealed nor to see it transformed. The oppressors use their "humanitarianism" to preserve a profitable situation. Thus they react almost instinctively against any experiment in education which stimulates the critical faculties and is not content with a partial view of reality but always seeks out the ties which link one point to another and one problem to another.

Indeed, the interests of the oppressors lie in "changing the consciousness of the oppressed, not the situation which oppresses them";[1] for the more the oppressed can be led to adapt to that situation, the more easily they can be dominated. To achieve this end, the oppressors use the banking concept of education in conjunction with a paternalistic social action apparatus, within which the oppressed receive the euphemistic title of "welfare recipients." They are treated as individual cases, as marginal men who deviate from the general configuration of a "good, organized, and just" society. The oppressed are regarded as the pathology of the healthy society, which must therefore adjust these "incompetent and lazy" folk to its own patterns by changing their mentality. These marginals need to be "integrated," "incorporated" into the healthy society that they have "forsaken."

The truth is, however, that the oppressed are not "marginals," are not men living "outside" society. They have always been "inside"—inside the structure which made them "beings for others." The solution is not to "integrate" them into the structure of oppression, but to transform that structure so that they can become "beings for themselves." Such transformation, of course, would undermine the oppressors' purposes; hence their utilization of the banking concept of education to avoid the threat of student *conscientização*.

The banking approach to adult education, for example, will never propose to students that they critically consider reality. It will deal instead with such vital questions as whether Roger gave green grass to the goat, and insist upon the importance of learning that, on the contrary, *Roger gave green grass to the rabbit*. The "humanism" of the banking approach masks the effort to turn men into automatons—the very negation of their ontological vocation to be more fully human.

Those who use the banking approach, knowingly or unknowingly (for there are innumerable well-intentioned bank-clerk teachers who do not realize that they are serving only to dehumanize), fail to perceive that the deposits themselves contain contradictions about reality. But, sooner or later, these contradictions may lead formerly passive students to turn against their domestication and the attempt to domesticate reality. They may discover through existential experience that their present way of life is irreconcilable with their vocation to become fully human. They may perceive through their relations with reality that reality is really a *process*, undergoing constant transformation. If men are searchers and their ontological vocation is humanization, sooner or later they may perceive the contradiction in which banking education seeks to maintain them, and then engage themselves in the struggle for their liberation.

But the humanist, revolutionary educator cannot wait for this possibility to materialize. From the outset, his efforts must coincide with those of the students to engage in critical thinking and the quest for mutual humanization. His efforts must be imbued with a profound trust in men and their creative power. To achieve this, he must be a partner of the students in his relations with them.

The banking concept does not admit to such partnership—and necessarily so. To resolve the teacher-student contradiction, to exchange the role of depositor, prescriber, domesticator, for the role of student among students would be to undermine the power of oppression and serve the cause of liberation.

Implicit in the banking concept is the assumption of a dichotomy between man and the world: man is merely *in* the world, not *with* the world or with others; man is spectator, not re-creator. In this view, man is not a conscious being *(corpo consciente)*; he is rather the possessor of *a* consciousness: an empty "mind" passively open to the reception of deposits of reality from the world outside. For example, my desk, my books, my coffee cup, all the objects before me—as bits of the world which surrounds me—would be "inside" me, exactly as I am inside my study right now. This view makes no distinction between being accessible to consciousness and entering consciousness. The distinction, however, is essential: the objects which surround me are simply accessible to my consciousness, not located within it. I am aware of them, but they are not inside me.

It follows logically from the banking notion of consciousness that the educator's role is to regulate the way the world "enters into" the students. His task is to organize a process which already occurs spontaneously, to "fill" the students by making deposits of information which he considers to constitute true knowledge.[2] And since men "receive" the world as passive entities, education should make them more passive still, and adapt them to the world. The educated man is the adapted man, because he is better "fit" for the world. Translated into practice, this concept is well suited to the purposes of the oppressors, whose tranquility rests on how well men fit the world the oppressors have created, and how little they question it.

The more completely the majority adapt to the purposes which the dominant minority prescribe for them (thereby depriving them of the right to their own purposes), the more easily the minority can continue to prescribe. The theory and practice of banking education serve this end quite efficiently. Verbalistic lessons, reading requirements,[3] the methods for evaluating "knowledge," the distance between the teacher and the taught, the criteria for promotion: everything in this ready-to-wear approach serves to obviate thinking.

The bank-clerk educator does not realize that there is no true security in his hypertrophied role, that one must seek to live *with* others in solidarity. One cannot impose oneself, nor even merely co-exist with one's students. Solidarity requires true communication, and the concept by which such an educator is guided fears and proscribes communication.

Yet only through communication can human life hold meaning. The teacher's thinking is authenticated only by the authenticity of the students' thinking. The teacher cannot think for his students, nor can he impose his thought on them. Authentic thinking, thinking that is concerned about *reality*, does not take place in ivory tower isolation, but only in communication. If it is true that thought has meaning only when generated by action upon the world, the subordination of students to teachers becomes impossible.

Because banking education begins with a false understanding of men as objects, it cannot promote the development of what Fromm calls "biophily," but instead produces its opposite: "necrophily."

> While life is characterized by growth in a structured, functional manner, the necrophilous person loves all that does not grow, all that is mechanical. The necrophilous person is driven by the desire to transform the organic into the inorganic, to approach life mechanically, as if all living persons were things.... Memory, rather than experience; having, rather than being, is what counts. The necrophilous person can relate to an object—a flower or a person—only if he possesses it; hence a threat to his possession is a threat to himself; if he loses possession he loses contact with the world.... He loves control, and in the act of controlling he kills life.[4]

Oppression—overwhelming control—is necrophilic; it is nourished by love of death, not life. The banking concept of education, which serves the interests of oppression, is also necrophilic. Based on a mechanistic, static, naturalistic, spatialized view of consciousness, it transforms students into receiving objects. It attempts to control thinking and action, leads men to adjust to the world, and inhibits their creative power.

When their efforts to act responsibly are frustrated, when they find themselves unable to use their faculties, men suffer. "This suffering due to impotence is rooted in the very fact that the human equilibrium has been disturbed."[5] But the inability to act which causes men's anguish also causes them to reject their impotence, by attempting

> ... to restore [their] capacity to act. But can [they], and how? One way is to submit to and identify with a person or group having power. By this symbolic participation in another person's life, [men have] the illusion of acting, when in reality [they] only submit to and become a part of those who act.[6]

Populist manifestations perhaps best exemplify this type of behavior by the oppressed, who, by identifying with charismatic leaders, come to feel that they themselves are active and effective. The rebellion they express as they emerge in the historical process is motivated by that desire to act effectively. The dominant elites consider the remedy to be more domination and repression, carried out in the name of freedom, order, and social peace (that is, the peace of the elites). Thus they can condemn—logically, from their point of view —"the violence of a strike by workers and [can] call upon the state in the same breath to use violence in putting down the strike."[7]

Education as the exercise of domination stimulates the credulity of students, with the ideological intent (often not perceived by educators) of indoctrinating them to adapt to the world of oppression. This accusation is not made in the naïve hope that the dominant elites will thereby simply abandon the practice. Its objective is to call the attention of true humanists to the fact that they cannot use banking educational methods in the pursuit of liberation, for they would only negate that very pursuit. Nor may a revolutionary society inherit these methods from an oppressor society. The revolutionary society which practices banking education is either misguided or mistrusting of men. In either event, it is threatened by the specter of reaction.

Unfortunately, those who espouse the cause of liberation are themselves surrounded and influenced by the climate which generates the banking concept, and often do not perceive its true significance or its dehumanizing power. Paradoxically, then, they utilize this same instrument of alienation in what they consider an effort to liberate. Indeed, some "revolutionaries" brand as "innocents," "dreamers," or even "reactionaries" those who would challenge this educational practice. But one does not liberate men by alienating them. Authentic liberation—the process of humanization—is not another deposit to be made in men. Liberation is a praxis: the action and reflection of men upon their world in order to transform it. Those truly committed to the cause of liberation can accept neither the mechanistic concept of consciousness as an empty vessel to be filled, nor the use of banking methods of domination (propaganda, slogans—deposits) in the name of liberation.

Those truly committed to liberation must reject the banking concept in its entirety, adopting instead a concept of men as conscious beings, and consciousness as consciousness intent upon the world. They must abandon the educational goal of deposit-making and replace it with the posing of the problems of men in their relations with the world. "Problem-posing" education, responding to the essence of consciousness—*intentionality*—rejects communiqués and em-bodies communication. It epitomizes the special characteristic of consciousness: being *conscious of,* not only as intent on objects but as turned in upon itself in a Jasperian "split"—consciousness as consciousness *of* consciousness.

Liberating education consists in acts of cognition, not transferrals of in-formation. It is a learning situation in which the cognizable object (far from being the end of the cognitive act) intermediates the cognitive actors—teacher on the one hand and students on the other. Accordingly, the practice of problem-posing education entails at the outset that the teacher-student contradiction be resolved. Dialogical relations—indispensable to the capacity of cognitive actors to cooperate in perceiving the same cognizable object—are otherwise impossible.

Indeed, problem-posing education, which breaks with the vertical pat-terns characteristic of banking education, can fulfill its function as the practice of freedom only if it can overcome the above contradiction. Through dialogue, the teacher-of-the-students and the students-of-the-teacher cease to exist and a new term emerges: teacher-student with students-teachers. The teacher is no longer merely the-one-who-teaches, but one who is himself taught in dialogue with the students, who in turn while being taught also teach. They become jointly responsible for a process in which all grow. In this process, arguments based on "authority" are no longer valid; in order to function, authority must be *on the side of* freedom, not *against* it. Here, no one teaches another, nor is any-one self-taught. Men teach each other, mediated by the world, by the cognizable objects which in banking education are "owned" by the teacher.

The banking concept (with its tendency to dichotomize everything) dis-tinguishes two stages in the action of the educator. During the first, he cognizes a cognizable object while he prepares his lessons in his study or his labora-tory; during the second, he expounds to his students about that object. The students are not called upon to know, but to memorize the contents narrated by the teacher. Nor do the students practice any act of cognition, since the ob-ject towards which that act should be directed is the property of the teacher rather than a medium evoking the critical reflection of both teacher and stu-dents. Hence in the name of the "preservation of culture and knowledge" we have a system which achieves neither true knowledge nor true culture.

The problem-posing method does not dichotomize the activity of the teacher-student: he is not "cognitive" at one point and "narrative" at another. He is always "cognitive," whether preparing a project or engaging in dialogue with the students. He does not regard cognizable objects as his private prop-erty, but as the object of reflection by himself and the students. In this way, the problem-posing educator constantly re-forms his reflections in the reflection of the students. The students—no longer docile listeners—are now critical co-investigators in dialogue with the teacher. The teacher presents the material to the students for their consideration, and re-considers his earlier considerations as the students express their own. The role of the problem-posing educator is to create, together with the students, the conditions under which knowledge at the level of the *doxa* is superseded by true knowledge, at the level of the *logos*.

Whereas banking education anesthetizes and inhibits creative power, problem-posing education involves a constant unveiling of reality. The former attempts to maintain the *submersion* of consciousness; the latter strives for the *emergence* of consciousness and *critical intervention* in reality.

Students, as they are increasingly posed with problems relating to themselves in the world and with the world, will feel increasingly challenged and obliged to respond to that challenge. Because they apprehend the challenge as interrelated to other problems within a total context, not as a theoretical question, the resulting comprehension tends to be increasingly critical and thus constantly less alienated. Their response to the challenge evokes new challenges, followed by new understandings; and gradually the students come to regard themselves as committed.

Education as the practice of freedom—as opposed to education as the practice of domination—denies that man is abstract, isolated, independent, and unattached to the world; it also denies that the world exists as a reality apart from men. Authentic reflection considers neither abstract man nor the world without men, but men in their relations with the world. In these relations consciousness and world are simultaneous: consciousness neither precedes the world nor follows it.

NOTES

1. Simone de Beauvoir, *La Pensée de Droite, Aujord'hui* (Paris); ST, *El Pensamiento político de la Derecha* (Buenos Aires, 1963), p. 34.

2. This concept corresponds to what Sartre calls the "digestive" or "nutritive" concept of education, in which knowledge is "fed" by the teacher to the students to "fill them out." See Jean-Paul Sartre, "Une idée fundamentale de la phénomenologie de Husserl: L'intentionalité," *Situations I* (Paris, 1947).

3. For example, some professors specify in their reading lists that a book should be read from pages 10 to 15—and do this to "help" their students!

4. Fromm, *op. cit.*, p. 41.

5. *Ibid.*, p. 31.

6. *Ibid.*

7. Reinhold Niebuhr, *Moral Man and Immoral Society* (New York, 1960), p. 130.

3.4 IVAN ILLICH

Deschooling Society

Ivan Illich believes that schools as we know them are a destructive force in the lives of the youth who are exposed to them. He feels that the hidden assumptions in school curricula encourage the young to accept indoctrination into the values of the hegemonic forces that are in control of society.

In the following selection, which is from *Deschooling Society* (Harper & Row, 1971), Illich portrays childhood as a social construct designed to encourage children to accept the authority of teachers and to allow those teachers to mold them to fit into socially acceptable roles. These roles, Illich argues, are predetermined by teachers, and they deny the young control over their own destinies. Illich critiques the Western cultural concept of childhood, saying that "childhood" is a burden to many of those few who are allowed it. He takes the position that if society were to abandon the concept of "childhood" and to permit the young to learn naturally in the world, rather than in schools under the direction of teachers, all children would be better off. Illich further argues that we have all learned most of what we know outside of the schools.

The following selection shows how Illich conceives of the phenomenology of schooling and the Western cultural conceptualization of childhood. Other publications that illustrate Illich's beliefs are *Celebration of Awareness: A Call for Institutional Revolution* (Doubleday, 1970); *H₂0 and the Waters of Forgetfulness: Reflections on the Historicity of "Stuff"* (Dallas Institute of Humanities and Culture, 1985); and *In the Mirror of the Past: Lectures and Addresses, 1978–1990* (Marion Boyars, 1992). Illich's lectures and addresses have also been widely circulated.

Key Concept: the phenomenology of school and childhood

WHY WE MUST DISESTABLISH SCHOOL

*T*he escalation of the schools is as destructive as the escalation of weapons but less visibly so. Everywhere in the world school costs have risen faster than enrollments and faster than the GNP [gross national product]; everywhere expenditures on school fall even further behind the expectations of parents, teachers, and pupils. Everywhere this situation discourages both the motivation and the financing for large-scale planning for nonschooled learning. The United States is proving to the world that no country can be rich enough to afford a school system that meets the demands this same system creates simply by existing, because a successful school system schools parents and pupils to the supreme value of a larger school system, the cost of which increases disproportionately as higher grades are in demand and become scarce.

Rather than calling equal schooling temporarily unfeasible, we must recognize that it is, in principle, economically absurd, and that to attempt it is intellectually emasculating, socially polarizing, and destructive of the credibility of the political system which promotes it. The ideology of obligatory schooling admits of no logical limits. The White House recently provided a good example. Dr. Hutschnecker, the "psychiatrist" who treated Mr. Nixon before he was qualified as a candidate, recommended to the President that all children between six and eight be professionally examined to ferret out those who have destructive tendencies, and that obligatory treatment be provided for them. If necessary, their re-education in special institutions should be required. This memorandum from his doctor the President sent for evaluation to HEW [Department of Health, Education, and Welfare]. Indeed, preventive concentration camps for predelinquents would be a logical improvement over the school system.

Equal educational opportunity is, indeed, both a desirable and a feasible goal, but to equate this with obligatory schooling is to confuse salvation with the Church. School has become the world religion of a modernized proletariat, and makes futile promises of salvation to the poor of the technological age. The nation-state has adopted it, drafting all citizens into a graded curriculum leading to sequential diplomas not unlike the initiation rituals and hieratic promotions of former times. The modern state has assumed the duty of enforcing the judgment of its educators through well-meant truant officers and job requirements, much as did the Spanish kings who enforced the judgments of their theologians through the conquistadors and the Inquisition.

Two centuries ago the United States led the world in a movement to disestablish the monopoly of a single church. Now we need the constitutional disestablishment of the monopoly of the school, and thereby of a system which legally combines prejudice with discrimination. The first article of a bill of rights for a modern, humanist society would correspond to the First Amendment to the U.S. Constitution: "The State shall make no law with respect to the establishment of education." There shall be no ritual obligatory for all.

To make this disestablishment effective, we need a law forbidding discrimination in hiring, voting, or admission to centers of learning based on previous attendance at some curriculum. This guarantee would not exclude performance tests of competence for a function or role, but would remove the present absurd discrimination in favor of the person who learns a given skill with the largest expenditure of public funds or—what is equally likely—has been able to obtain a diploma which has no relation to any useful skill or job. Only by protecting the citizen from being disqualified by anything in his career in school can a constitutional disestablishment of school become psychologically effective.

Neither learning nor justice is promoted by schooling because educators insist on packaging instruction with certification. Learning and the assignment of social roles are melted into schooling. Yet to learn means to acquire a new skill or insight, while promotion depends on an opinion which others have formed. Learning frequently is the result of instruction, but selection for a role or category in the job market increasingly depends on mere length of attendance.

Instruction is the choice of circumstances which facilitate learning. Roles are assigned by setting a curriculum of conditions which the candidate must meet if he is to make the grade. School links instruction—but not learning—to these roles. This is neither reasonable nor liberating. It is not reasonable because it does not link relevant qualities or competences to roles, but rather the process by which such qualities are supposed to be acquired. It is not liberating or educational because school reserves instruction to those whose every step in learning fits previously approved measures of social control.

Curriculum has always been used to assign social rank. At times it could be prenatal: karma ascribes you to a caste and lineage to the aristocracy. Curriculum could take the form of a ritual, of sequential sacred ordinations, or it could consist of a succession of feats in war or hunting, or further advancement could be made to depend on a series of previous princely favors. Universal schooling was meant to detach role assignment from personal life history: it was meant to give everybody an equal chance to any office. Even now many people wrongly believe that school ensures the dependence of public trust on relevant learning achievements. However, instead of equalizing chances, the school system has monopolized their distribution.

To detach competence from curriculum, inquiries into a man's learning history must be made taboo, like inquiries into his political affiliation, church attendance, lineage, sex habits, or racial background. Laws forbidding discrimination on the basis of prior schooling must be enacted. Laws, of course, cannot stop prejudice against the unschooled—nor are they meant to force anyone to intermarry with an autodidact—but they can discourage unjustified discrimination.

A second major illusion on which the school system rests is that most learning is the result of teaching. Teaching, it is true, may contribute to certain kinds of learning under certain circumstances. But most people acquire most of their knowledge outside school, and in school only insofar as school, in a few rich countries, has become their place of confinement during an increasing part of their lives....

PHENOMENOLOGY OF SCHOOL

Some words become so flexible that they cease to be useful. "School" and "teaching" are such terms. Like an amoeba they fit into almost any interstice of the language. ABM will teach the Russians, IBM will teach Negro children, and the army can become the school of a nation.

The search for alternatives in education must therefore start with an agreement on what it is we mean by "school." This might be done in several ways. We could begin by listing the latent functions performed by modern school systems, such as custodial care, selection, indoctrination, and learning. We could make a client analysis and verify which of these latent functions render a service or a disservice to teachers, employers, children, parents, or the professions. We could survey the history of Western culture and the information gathered by anthropology in order to find institutions which played a role like that now performed by schooling. We could, finally, recall the many normative statements which have been made since the time of Comenius, or even since Quintilian, and discover which of these the modern school system most closely approaches. But any of these approaches would oblige us to start with certain assumptions about a relationship between school and education. To develop a language in which we can speak about school without such constant recourse to education, I have chosen to begin with something that might be called a phenomenology of public school. For this purpose I shall define "school" as the age-specific, teacher-related process requiring full-time attendance at an obligatory curriculum.

Age. School groups people according to age. This grouping rests on three unquestioned premises. Children belong in school. Children learn in school. Children can be taught only in school. I think these unexamined premises deserve serious questioning.

We have grown accustomed to children. We have decided that they should go to school, do as they are told, and have neither income nor families of their own. We expect them to know their place and behave like children. We remember, whether nostalgically or bitterly, a time when we were children, too. We are expected to tolerate the childish behavior of children. Mankind, for us, is a species both afflicted and blessed with the task of caring for children. We forget, however, that our present concept of "childhood" developed only recently in Western Europe and more recently still in the Americas.[1]

Childhood as distinct from infancy, adolescence, or youth was unknown to most historical periods. Some Christian centuries did not even have an eye for its bodily proportions. Artists depicted the infant as a miniature adult seated on his mother's arm. Children appeared in Europe along with the pocket watch and the Christian moneylenders of the Renaissance. Before our century neither the poor nor the rich knew of children's dress, children's games, or the child's immunity from the law. Childhood belonged to the bourgeoisie. The worker's child, the peasant's child, and the nobleman's child all dressed the way their fathers dressed, played the way their fathers played, and were hanged by the neck as were their fathers. After the discovery of "childhood" by the bourgeoisie all this changed. Only some churches continued to respect for some time the dignity and maturity of the young. Until the Second Vatican Council, each child was instructed that a Christian reaches moral discernment and freedom at the age of seven, and from then on is capable of committing sins for which he may be punished by an eternity in Hell. Toward the middle of this century, middle-class parents began to try to spare their children the impact of this doctrine, and their thinking about children now prevails in the practice of the Church.

Until the last century, "children" of middle-class parents were made at home with the help of preceptors and private schools. Only with the advent of industrial society did the mass production of "childhood" become feasible and come within the reach of the masses. The school system is a modern phenomenon, as is the childhood it produces.

Since most people today live outside industrial cities, most people today do not experience childhood. In the Andes you till the soil once you have become "useful." Before that, you watch the sheep. If you are well nourished, you should be useful by eleven, and otherwise by twelve. Recently, I was talking to my night watchman, Marcos, about his eleven-year-old son who works in a barbershop. I noted in Spanish that his son was still a *"niño."* Marcos, surprised, answered with a guileless smile: "Don Ivan, I guess you're right." Realizing that until my remark the father had thought of Marcos primarily as his "son," I felt guilty for having drawn the curtain of childhood between two sensible persons. Of course if I were to tell the New York slum-dweller that his working son is still a "child," he would show no surprise. He knows quite well that his eleven-year-old son should be allowed childhood, and resents the fact that he is not. The son of Marcos has yet to be afflicted with the yearning for childhood; the New Yorker's son feels deprived.

Most people around the world, then, either do not want or cannot get modern childhood for their offspring. But it also seems that childhood is a burden to a good number of those few who are allowed it. Many of them are simply forced to go through it and are not at all happy playing the child's role. Growing up through childhood means being condemned to a process of inhuman conflict between self-awareness and the role imposed by a society going through its own school age. Neither Stephen Daedalus nor Alexander Portnoy enjoyed childhood, and neither I suspect, did many of us like to be treated as children.

If there were no age-specific and obligatory learning institution, "childhood" would go out of production. The youth of rich nations would be liberated from its destructiveness, and poor nations would cease attempting to rival the childishness of the rich. If society were to outgrow its age of childhood, it would have to become livable for the young. The present disjunction between an adult society which pretends to be humane and a school environment which mocks reality could no longer be maintained.

The disestablishment of schools could also end the present discrimination against infants, adults, and the old in favor of children throughout their adolescence and youth. The social decision to allocate educational resources preferably to those citizens who have outgrown the extraordinary learning capacity of their first four years and have not arrived at the height of their self-motivated learning will, in retrospect, probably appear as bizarre.

Institutional wisdom tells us that children need school. Institutional wisdom tells us that children learn in school. But this institutional wisdom is itself the product of schools because sound common sense tells us that only children can be taught in school. Only by segregating human beings in the category of childhood could we ever get them to submit to the authority of a schoolteacher.

Teachers and pupils.   By definition, children are pupils. The demand for the milieu of childhood creates an unlimited market for accredited teachers. School is an institution built on the axiom that learning is the result of teaching. And institutional wisdom continues to accept this axiom, despite overwhelming evidence to the contrary.

We have all learned most of what we know outside school. Pupils do most of their learning without, and often despite, their teachers. Most tragically, the majority of men are taught their lesson by schools, even though they never go *to* school.

Everyone learns how to live outside school. We learn to speak, to think, to love, to feel, to play, to curse, to politick, and to work without interference from a teacher. Even children who are under a teacher's care day and night are no exception to the rule. Orphans, idiots, and schoolteachers' sons learn most of what they learn outside the "educational" process planned for them. Teachers have made a poor showing in their attempts at increasing learning among the poor. Poor parents who want their children to go to school are less concerned about what they will learn than about the certificate and money they will earn. And middle-class parents commit their children to a teacher's care to keep them from learning what the poor learn on the streets. Increasingly educational research demonstrates that children learn most of what teachers pretend to teach them from peer groups, from comics, from chance observations, and above all from mere participation in the ritual of school. Teachers, more often than not, obstruct such learning of subject matters as goes on in school.

Half of the people in our world never set foot in school. They have no contact with teachers, and they are deprived of the privilege of becoming dropouts. Yet they learn quite effectively the message which school teaches: that they should have school, and more and more of it. School instructs them in their own inferiority through the tax collector who makes them pay for it, or through the demagogue who raises their expectations of it, or through their children once the latter are hooked on it. So the poor are robbed of their self-respect by subscribing to a creed that grants salvation only through the school. At least the Church gave them a chance to repent at the hour of death. School leaves them with the expectation (a counterfeit hope) that their grandchildren will make it. That expectation is of course still more learning which comes from school but not from teachers.

Pupils have never credited teachers for most of their learning. Bright and dull alike have always relied on rote, reading, and wit to pass their exams, motivated by the stick or by the carrot of a desired career.

Adults tend to romanticize their schooling. In retrospect, they attribute their learning to the teacher whose patience they learned to admire. But the same adults would worry about the mental health of a child who rushed home to tell them what he learned from his every teacher.

Schools create jobs for schoolteachers, no matter what their pupils learn from them.

Full-time attendance. Every month I see another list of proposals made by some U.S. industry to AID [Agency for International Development], suggesting the replacement of Latin-American "classroom practitioners" either by disciplined systems administrators or just by TV. In the United States teaching as a team enterprise of educational researchers, designers, and technicians is gaining acceptance. But, no matter whether the teacher is a schoolmarm or a team of men in white coats, and no matter whether they succeed in teaching the subject matter listed in the catalogue or whether they fail, the professional teacher creates a sacred milieu.

Uncertainty about the future of professional teaching puts the classroom into jeopardy. Were educational professionals to specialize in promoting learning, they would have to abandon a system which calls for between 750 and 1,000 gatherings a year. But of course teachers do a lot more. The institutional wisdom of schools tells parents, pupils, and educators that the teacher, if he is to teach, must exercise his authority in a sacred precinct. This is true even for teachers whose pupils spend most of their school time in a classroom without walls.

School, by its very nature, tends to make a total claim on the time and energies of its participants. This, in turn, makes the teacher into custodian, preacher, and therapist.

In each of these three roles the teacher bases his authority on a different claim. The *teacher-as-custodian* acts as a master of ceremonies, who guides his pupils through a drawn-out labyrinthine ritual. He arbitrates the observance of rules and administers the intricate rubrics of initiation to life. At his best, he sets the stage for the acquisition of some skill as schoolmasters always have. Without illusions of producing any profound learning, he drills his pupils in some basic routines.

The *teacher-as-moralist* substitutes for parents, God, or the state. He indoctrinates the pupil about what is right or wrong, not only in school but also in society at large. He stands *in loco parent is* for each one and thus ensures that all feel themselves children of the same state.

The *teacher-as-therapist* feels authorized to delve into the personal life of his pupil in order to help him grow as a person. When this function is exercised by a custodian and preacher, it usually means that he persuades the pupil to submit to a domestication of his vision of truth and his sense of what is right.

The claim that a liberal society can be founded on the modern school is paradoxical. The safeguards of individual freedom are all canceled in the dealings of a teacher with his pupil. When the schoolteacher fuses in his person the functions of judge, ideologue, and doctor, the fundamental style of society is perverted by the very process which should prepare for life. A teacher who combines these three powers contributes to the warping of the child much more than the laws which establish his legal or economic minority, or restrict his right to free assembly or abode.

Teachers are by no means the only professionals who offer therapy. Psychiatrists, guidance counselors, and job counselors, even lawyers, help their clients to decide, to develop their personalities, and to learn. Yet common sense tells the client that such professionals should abstain from imposing their opinion of what is right or wrong, or from forcing anyone to follow their advice. Schoolteachers and ministers are the only professionals who feel entitled to pry into the private affairs of their clients at the same time as they preach to a captive audience.

Children are protected by neither the First nor the Fifth Amendment when they stand before that secular priest, the teacher. The child must confront a man who wears an invisible triple crown, like the papal tiara, the symbol of triple authority combined in one person. For the child, the teacher pontificates as pastor, prophet, and priest—he is at once guide, teacher, and administrator of a sacred ritual. He combines the claims of medieval popes in a society constituted under the guarantee that these claims shall never be exercised together by one established and obligatory institution—church or state.

Defining children as full-time pupils permits the teacher to exercise a kind of power over their persons which is much less limited by constitutional and consuetudinal restrictions than the power wielded by the guardians of other social enclaves. Their chronological age disqualifies children from safeguards which are routine for adults in a modern asylum—madhouse, monastery, or jail.

Under the authoritative eye of the teacher, several orders of value collapse into one. The distinctions between morality, legality, and personal worth are blurred and eventually eliminated. Each transgression is made to be felt as a multiple offense. The offender is expected to feel that he has broken a rule, that he has behaved immorally, and that he has let himself down. A pupil who adroitly obtains assistance on an exam is told that he is an outlaw, morally corrupt, and personally worthless.

Classroom attendance removes children from the everyday world of Western culture and plunges them into an environment far more primitive, magical, and deadly serious. School could not create such an enclave within which the rules of ordinary reality are suspended, unless it physically incarcerated the young during many successive years on sacred territory. The attendance rule makes it possible for the schoolroom to serve as a magic womb, from which the child is delivered periodically at the schoolday's and school year's completion until he is finally expelled into adult life. Neither universal extended childhood nor the smothering atmosphere of the classroom could exist without schools. Yet schools, as compulsory channels for learning, could exist without either and be more repressive and destructive than anything we have come to know. To understand what it means to deschool society, and not just to reform the educational establishment, we must now focus on the hidden curriculum of schooling. We are not concerned here, directly, with the hidden curriculum of the ghetto streets which brands the poor or with the hidden curriculum of the drawing room which benefits the rich. We are rather concerned to call attention to the fact that the ceremonial or ritual of schooling itself constitutes such a hidden curriculum. Even the best of teachers cannot entirely protect his pupils from it. Inevitably, this hidden curriculum of schooling adds prejudice and guilt to the discrimination which a society practices against some of its members and compounds the privilege of others with a new title to condescend to the majority. Just as inevitably, this hidden curriculum serves as a ritual of initiation into a growth-oriented consumer society for rich and poor alike.

NOTES

1. For parallel histories of modern capitalism and modern childhood see Philippe Aries, *Centuries of Childhood*, Knopf, 1962.

PART TWO

Curriculum and Instruction

Chapter 4 Schooling 81

Chapter 5 Curriculum Theory and Practice 110

Chapter 6 Curriculum Development and the Language of Educational Debate 131

On the Internet . . .

Sites appropriate to Part Two

This site contains the position statement, key concepts, and practices of the American Montessori Society.

    http://www.amshq.org/key_concepts.html

The Center for Dewey Studies at Southern Illinois University at Carbondale was established in 1961 as the "Dewey Project." In the course of collecting and editing Dewey's works, the Center amassed a wealth of source materials for the study of philosopher-educator John Dewey. Links to information about these works can be found at this site.

    http://www.siu.edu/~deweyctr/index.html

In *Fairness and Core Knowledge,* sponsored by the Core Knowledge Foundation, E. D. Hirsch, Jr., argues for the adoption of a Core Knowledge Sequence in order to overcome educational injustice.

    http://www.trinity.edu/departments/
        education/core/articles/fair.htm

This site describes several major philosophical paradigms as they are applied to education.

    http://www.educ.drake.edu/romig/educ350/
        paradigms.html

CHAPTER 4 Schooling

4.1 MARIA MONTESSORI

Discipline

The following selection is taken from *The Montessori Method*, Maria Montessori's 1912 treatise on her theory of instruction. Specifically, it is from her chapter on "discipline" as the practice of liberty (freedom). In it, she describes how teachers can teach children to become self-disciplined persons. She discusses the concept of "active discipline," whereby teachers learn to observe student-initiated behaviors and to discern when to permit student-initiated action to proceed uninhibited. Montessori argues that teachers should interfere with antisocial or harmful student-initiated behaviors but that constructive student-initiated behavior should be encouraged. She provides examples of constructive student-initiated behaviors, defined as those that serve socially useful purposes in the classroom.

Montessori stresses that the child should not confuse "good" simply with "immobility," or "passivity," nor "evil" with "activity." The goal of school discipline should be the development of *self-disciplined*, free persons; this goal, Montessori argues, cannot be achieved simply by teaching children to be silent and obedient.

Montessori (1870–1952) earned her M.D. in 1896, making her the first woman in Italy to become a physician. She opened her first school, which she called a "Children's House," in 1905. By 1914 she was a world renowned figure in the field of education, and the "Montessori schools" that she developed featured kindergarten through eighth grade curricula. Her ideas had great influence in the development of the open primary and elementary schools in the United Kingdom in the 1930s and 1940s. Among her many important writings are *The Child in the Family*; *The Formation of Man*; *From Childhood to Adolescence*; *The Discovery of the Child*; *Dr. Montessori's Own Handbook*; *Education and Peace*; *Education for a New World*; and *To Educate the Human Potential*.

Key Concept: discipline through the use of liberty

*T*he pedagogical method of *observation* has for its base the *liberty* of the child; and *liberty is activity.*

Discipline must come through liberty. Here is a great principle which is difficult for followers of common-school methods to understand. How shall one obtain *discipline* in a class of free children? Certainly in our system, we have a concept of discipline very different from that commonly accepted. If discipline is founded upon liberty, the discipline itself must necessarily be *active.* We do not consider an individual disciplined only when he has been rendered as artificially silent as a mute and as immovable as a paralytic. He is an individual *annihilated,* not *disciplined.*

We call an individual disciplined when he is master of himself, and can, therefore, regulate his own conduct when it shall be necessary to follow some rule of life. Such a concept of *active discipline* is not easy either to comprehend or to apply. But certainly it contains a great *educational* principle, very different from the old-time absolute and undiscussed coercion to immobility.

A special technique is necessary to the teacher who is to lead the child along such a path of discipline, if she is to make it possible for him to continue in this way all his life, advancing indefinitely toward perfect self mastery. Since the child now learns to *move* rather than to *sit still,* he prepares himself not for the school, but for life; for he becomes able, through habit and through practice, to perform easily and correctly the simple acts of social or community life. The discipline to which the child habituates himself here is, in its character, not limited to the school environment but extends to society.

The liberty of the child should have as its *limit* the collective interest; as its *form,* what we universally consider good breeding. We must, therefore, check in the child whatever offends or annoys others, or whatever tends toward rough or ill-bred acts. But all the rest,—every manifestation having a useful scope,— whatever it be, and under whatever form it expresses itself, must not only be permitted, but must be *observed* by the teacher. Here lies the essential point; from her scientific preparation, the teacher must bring not only the capacity, but the desire, to observe natural phenomena. In our system, she must become a passive, much more than an active, influence, and her passivity shall he composed of anxious scientific curiosity, and of absolute *respect* for the phenomenon which she wishes to observe. The teacher must understand and *feel* her position of *observer:* the *activity* must lie in the *phenomenon.*

Such principles assuredly have a place in schools for little children who are exhibiting the first psychic manifestations of their lives. We cannot know the consequences of suffocating a *spontaneous action* at the time when the child is just beginning to be active: perhaps we suffocate *life itself.* Humanity shows itself in all its intellectual splendour during this tender age as the sun shows itself at the dawn, and the flower in the first unfolding of the petals; and we must *respect* religiously, reverently, these first indications of individuality. If any educational act is to he efficacious, it will be only that which tends to *help* toward the complete unfolding of this life. To be thus helpful it is necessary rigorously to avoid the *arrest* of *spontaneous movements and the imposition of arbitrary tasks.* It is of course understood, that here we do not speak of useless or dangerous acts, for these must be *suppressed, destroyed.*

Actual training and practice are necessary to fit for this method teachers who have not been prepared for scientific observation, and such training is especially necessary to those who have been accustomed to the old domineering methods of the common school. My experiences in training teachers for the work in my schools did much to convince me of the great distance between these methods and those. Even an intelligent teacher, who understands the principle, finds much difficulty in putting it into practice. She can not understand that her new task is apparently *passive,* like that of the astronomer who sits immovable before the telescope while the worlds whirl through space. This idea, that *life acts of itself,* and that in order to study it, to divine its secrets or to direct its activity, it is necessary to observe it and to understand it without intervening—this idea, I say, is very difficult for anyone to *assimilate* and to *put into practice.*

The teacher has too thoroughly learned to be the one free activity of the school; it has for too long been virtually her duty to suffocate the activity of her pupils. When in the first days in one of the "Children's Houses" she does not obtain order and silence, she looks about her embarrassed as if asking the public to excuse her, and calling upon those present to testify to her innocence. In vain do we repeat to her that the disorder of the first moment is necessary. And finally, when we oblige her to do nothing but *watch,* she asks if she had not better resign, since she is no longer a teacher.

But when she begins to find it her duty to discern which are the acts to hinder and which are those to observe, the teacher of the old school feels a great void within herself and begins to ask if she will not be inferior to her new task. In fact, she who is not prepared finds herself for a long time abashed and impotent; whereas the broader the teacher's scientific culture and practice in experimental psychology, the sooner will come for her the marvel of unfolding life, and her interest in it.

Notari, in his novel, "My Millionaire Uncle," which is a criticism of modern customs, gives with that quality of vividness which is peculiar to him, a most eloquent example of the old-time methods of discipline. The "uncle" when a child was guilty of such a number of disorderly acts that he practically upset the whole town, and in desperation he was confined in a school. Here "Fufu," as he was called, experiences his first wish to be kind, and feels the first moving of his soul when he is near to the pretty little Fufetta, and learns that she is hungry and has no luncheon.

"He glanced around, looked at Fufetta, rose, took his little lunch basket, and without saying a word placed it in her lap.

"Then he ran away from her, and, without knowing why he did so, hung his head and burst into tears.

"My uncle did not know how to explain to himself the reason for this sudden outburst.

"He had seen for the first time two kind eyes full of sad tears, and he had felt moved within himself, and at the same time a great shame had rushed over him; the shame of eating near to one who had nothing to eat.

"Not knowing how to express the impulse of his heart, nor what to say in asking her to accept the offer of his little basket, nor how to invent an excuse to justify his offering it to her, he remained the victim of this first deep movement of his little soul.

"Fufetta, all confused, ran to him quickly. With great gentleness she drew away the arm in which he had hidden his face.

" 'Do not cry, Fufu,' she said to him softly, almost as if pleading with him. She might have been speaking to her beloved rag doll, so motherly and intent was her little face, and so full of gentle authority, her manner.

"Then the little girl kissed him, and my uncle yielding to the influence which had filled his heart, put his arms around her neck, and, still silent and sobbing, kissed her in return. At last, sighing deeply, he wiped from his face and eyes the damp traces of his emotion, and smiled again.

"A strident voice called out from the other end of the courtyard:

" 'Here, here, you two down there—be quick with you; inside, both of you!'

"It was the teacher, the guardian. She crushed that first gentle stirring in the soul of a rebel with the same blind brutality that she would have used toward two children engaged in a fight.

"It was the time for all to go back into the school—and everybody had to obey the rule."

Thus I saw my teachers act in the first days of my practice school in the "Children's Houses." They almost involuntarily recalled the children to immobility without *observing* and *distinguishing* the nature of the movements they repressed. There was, for example, a little girl who gathered her companions about her and then, in the midst of them, began to talk and gesticulate. The teacher at once ran to her, took hold of her arms, and told her to be still; but I, observing the child, saw that she was playing at being teacher or mother to the others, and teaching them the morning prayer, the invocation to the saints, and the sign of the cross: she already showed herself as a *director.* Another child, who continually made disorganised and misdirected movements, and who was considered abnormal, one day, with an expression of intense attention, set about moving the tables. Instantly they were upon him to make him stand still because he made too much noise. Yet this was one of the *first manifestations,* in this child, of *movements* that were *coordinated* and *directed toward a useful end,* and it was therefore an action that should have been respected. In fact, after this the child began to be quiet and happy like the others whenever he had any small objects to move about and to arrange upon his desk.

It often happened that while the directress replaced in the boxes various materials that had been used, a child would draw near, picking up the objects, with the evident desire of imitating the teacher. The first impulse was to send the child back to her place with the remark, "Let it alone; go to your seat." Yet the child expressed by this act a desire to be useful; the time, with her, was ripe for a lesson in order.

One day, the children had gathered themselves, laughing and talking, into a circle about a basin of water containing some floating toys. We had in the school a little boy barely two and a half years old. He had been left outside the circle, alone, and it was easy to see that he was filled with intense curiosity. I watched him from a distance with great interest; he first drew near to the other children and tried to force his way among them, but he was not strong enough to do this, and he then stood looking about him. The expression of thought on his little face was intensely interesting. I wish that I had had a camera so that I might have photographed him. His eye lighted upon a little chair, and evidently he made up his mind to place it behind the group of children and then to climb up on it. He began to move toward the chair, his face illuminated with hope, but at that moment the teacher seized him brutally (or, perhaps, she would have said, gently) in her arms, and lifting him up above the heads of the other children showed him the basin of water, saying, "Come, poor little one, you shall see too!"

Undoubtedly the child, seeing the floating toys, did not experience the joy that he was about to feel through conquering the obstacle with his own force. The sight of those objects could be of no advantage to him, while his intelligent efforts would have developed his inner powers. The teacher *hindered* the child, in this case, from educating himself, without giving him any compensating good in return. The little fellow had been about to feel himself a conqueror, and he found himself held within two imprisoning arms, impotent. The expression of joy, anxiety, and hope, which had interested me so much faded from his face and left on it the stupid expression of the child who knows that others will act for him.

When the teachers were weary of my observations, they began to allow the children to do whatever they pleased. I saw children with their feet on the tables, or with their fingers in their noses, and no intervention was made to correct them. I saw others push their companions, and I saw dawn in the faces of these an expression of violence; and not the slightest attention on the part of the teacher. Then I had to intervene to show with what absolute rigour it is necessary to hinder, and little by little suppress, all those things which we must not do, so that the child may come to discern clearly between good and evil.

If discipline is to be lasting, its foundations must he laid in this way and these first days are the most difficult for the directress. The first idea that the child must acquire, in order to be actively disciplined, is that of the difference between *good* and *evil;* and the task of the educator lies in seeing that the child does not confound *good* with *immobility,* and *evil* with *activity,* as often happens in the case of the old-time discipline. And all this because our aim is to discipline *for activity, for work, for good;* not for *immobility,* not for *passivity,* not for *obedience.*

A room in which all the children move about usefully, intelligently, and voluntarily, without committing any rough or rude act, would seem to me a classroom very well disciplined indeed.

To seat the children in rows, as in the common schools, to assign to each little one a place, and to propose that they shall sit thus quietly observant of the order of the whole class as an assemblage—this can be attained later, as *the starting place* of *collective education.* For also, in life, it sometimes happens that we must all remain seated and quiet; when, for example, we attend a concert or a lecture. And we know that even to us, as grown people, this costs no little sacrifice.

If we can, when we have established individual discipline, arrange the children, sending each one to *his own place, in order,* trying to make them understand the ideal that thus placed they look well, and that it is a *good thing* to be thus placed in order, that it is a *good and pleasing arrangement in the room,* this ordered and tranquil adjustment of theirs—then their remaining in their places, *quiet* and *silent,* is the result of a species of *lesson,* not an *imposition.* To make them understand the idea, without calling their attention too forcibly to the practice, to have them *assimilate a principle of collective order*—that is the important thing.

If, after they have understood this idea, they rise, speak, change to another place, they no longer do this without knowing and without thinking, but they do it because they *wish* to rise, to speak, etc.; that is, from that *state of repose and order,* well understood, they depart in order to undertake *some voluntary action;* and knowing that there are actions which are prohibited, this will give them a new impulse to remember to discriminate between good and evil.

The movements of the children from the state of order become always more co-ordinated and perfect with the passing of the days; in fact, they learn to reflect upon their own acts. Now (with the idea of order understood by the children) the observation of the way in which the children pass from the first disordered movements to those which are spontaneous and ordered—this is the book of the teacher; this is the book which must inspire her actions; it is the only one in which she must read and study if she is to become a real educator.

For the child with such exercises makes, to a certain extent, a selection of his own *tendencies,* which were at first confused in the unconscious disorder of his movements. It is remarkable how clearly *individual differences* show themselves, if we proceed in this way; the child, conscious and free, *reveals himself.*

There are those who remain quietly in their seats, apathetic, or drowsy; others who leave their places to quarrel, to fight, or to overturn the various blocks and toys, and then there are those others who set out to fulfill a definite and determined act—moving a chair to some particular spot and sitting down in it, moving one of the unused tables and arranging upon it the game they wish to play.

Our idea of liberty for the child cannot be the simple concept of liberty we use in the observation of plants, insects, etc.

The child, because of the peculiar characteristics of held lessness with which he is born, and because of his qualities as a social individual is circumscribed by *bonds* which *limit* his activity.

An educational method that shall have *liberty* as its basis must intervene to help the child to a conquest of these various obstacles. In other words, his training must be such as shall help him to diminish, in a rational manner, the *social bonds, which limit* his activity.

Little by little, as the child grows in such an atmosphere, his spontaneous manifestations will become more *clear, with the clearness of truth,* revealing his nature. For all these reasons, the first form of educational intervention must tend to lead the child toward independence.

No one can be free unless he is independent: therefore, the first, active manifestations of the child's individual liberty must be so guided that through this activity he may arrive at independence. Little children, from the moment in which they are weaned, are making their ways toward independence.

What is a weaned child? In reality it is a child that has become independent of the mother's breast. Instead of this one source of nourishment he will find various kinds of food; for him the means of existence are multiplied, and he can to some extent make a selection of his food, whereas he was at first limited absolutely to one form of nourishment.

Nevertheless, he is still dependent, since he is not yet able to walk, and cannot wash and dress himself, and since he is not yet able to *ask* for things in a language which is clear and easily understood. He is still in this period to a great extent the *slave* of everyone. By the age of three, however, the child should have been able to render himself to a great extent *independent* and free.

That we have not yet thoroughly assimilated the highest concept of the term *independence,* is due to the fact that the social form in which we live is still *servile.* In an age of civilisation where servants exist, the concept of that *form of life* which is *independence* cannot take root or develop freely. Even so in the time of slavery, the concept of liberty was distorted and darkened.

Our servants are not our dependents, rather it is we who are dependent upon them.

It is not possible to accept universally as a part of our social structure such a deep human error without feeling the general effects of it in the form of moral inferiority. We often believe ourselves to be independent simply because no one commands us, and because we command others; but the nobleman who needs to call a servant to his aid is really a dependent through his own inferiority. The paralytic who cannot take off his boots because of a pathological fact, and the prince who dare not take them off because of a social fact, are in reality reduced to the same condition.

Any nation that accepts the idea of servitude and believes that it is an advantage for man to be served by man, admits servility as an instinct, and indeed we all too easily lend ourselves to *obsequious service,* giving to it such complimentary names as *courtesy, politeness, charity.*

In reality, *he who is served is limited* in his independence. This concept will be the foundation of the dignity of the man of the future; "I do not wish to be served, *because* I am not an impotent." And this idea must be gained before men can feel themselves to be really free.

Any pedagogical action, if it is to be efficacious in the training of little children, must tend to *help* the children to advance upon this road of independence. We must help them to learn to walk without assistance, to run, to go up and down stairs, to lift up fallen objects, to dress and undress themselves, to bathe themselves, to speak distinctly, and to express their own needs clearly. We must give such help as shall make it possible for children to achieve the satisfaction of their own individual aims and desires. All this is a part of education for independence.

We habitually *serve* children; and this is not only an act of servility toward them, but it is dangerous, since it tends to suffocate their useful, spontaneous activity. We are inclined to believe that children are like puppets, and we wash them and feed them as if they were dolls. We do not stop to think that the child *who does not do, does not know how to do.* He must, nevertheless, do these things, and nature has furnished him with the physical means for carrying on these various activities, and with the intellectual means for learning how to do them. And our duty toward him is, in every case, that of *helping him* to make a conquest of such useful acts as nature intended he should perform for himself. The mother who feeds her child without making the least effort to teach him to hold the spoon for himself and to try to find his mouth with it, and who does not at least eat herself, inviting the child to look and see how she does it, is not a good mother. She offends the fundamental human dignity of her son,—she treats him as if he were a doll, when he is, instead, a man confided by nature to her care.

Who does not know that to *teach* a child to feed himself, to wash and dress himself, is a much more tedious and difficult work, calling for infinitely greater patience, than feeding, washing and dressing the child one's self? But the former is the work of an educator, the latter is the easy and inferior work of a servant. Not only is it easier for the mother, but it is very dangerous for the child, since it closes the way and puts obstacles in the path of the life which is developing.

The ultimate consequences of such an attitude on the part of the parent may be very serious indeed. The grand gentleman who has too many servants not only grows constantly more and more dependent upon them, until he is, finally, actually their slave, but his muscles grow weak through inactivity and finally lose their natural capacity for action. The mind of one who does not work for that which he needs, but commands it from others, grows heavy and sluggish. If such a man should some day awaken to the fact of his inferior position and should wish to regain once more his own independence, he would find that be had no longer the force to do so. These dangers should be presented to the parents of the privileged social classes, if their children are to use independently and for right the special power which is theirs. Needless help is an actual hindrance to the development of natural forces.

Oriental women wear trousers, it is true, and European women, petticoats; but the former, even more than the latter, are taught as a part of their education the art of *not moving.* Such an attitude toward woman leads to the fact that man works not only for himself, but for woman. And the woman wastes her natural strength and activity and languishes in slavery. She is not only maintained and served, she is, besides, diminished, belittled, in that individuality which is hers by right of her existence as a human being. As an individual member of society, she is a cypher. She is rendered deficient in all those powers and resources which tend to the preservation of life. Let me illustrate this:

A carriage containing a father, mother, and child, is going along a country road. An armed brigand stops the carriage with the well-known phrase, "Your money or your life." Placed in this situation, the three persons in the carriage act in very different ways. The man, who is a trained marksman; and who is armed with a revolver, promptly draws, and confronts the assassin. The boy, armed only with the freedom and lightness of his own legs, cries out and be-takes himself to flight. The woman, who is not armed in any way whatever, neither artificially nor naturally (since her limbs, not trained for activity, are hampered by her skirts), gives a frightened gasp, and sinks down unconscious.

These three diverse reactions are in close relation to the state of liberty and independence of each of the three individuals. The swooning woman is she whose cloak is carried for her by attentive cavaliers, who are quick to pick up any fallen object that she may be spared all exertion.

The peril of servilism and dependence lies not only in that "useless consuming of life," which leads to helplessness, but in the development of individual traits which indicate all too plainly a regrettable perversion and degeneration of the normal man. I refer to the domineering and tyrannical be-haviour with examples of which we are all only too familiar. The domineering habit develops side by side with helplessness. It is the outward sign of the state of feeling of him who conquers through the work of others. Thus it often happens that the master is a tyrant toward his servant. It is the spirit of the task-master toward the slave.

Let us picture to ourselves a clever and proficient workman, capable, not only of producing much and perfect work, but of giving advice in his workshop, because of his ability to control and direct the general activity of the environment in which he works. The man who is thus master of his environment will be able to smile before the anger of others, showing that great mastery of himself which comes from consciousness of his ability to do things. We should not, however, be in the least surprised to know that in his home this capable workman scolded his wife if the soup was not to his taste, or not ready at the appointed time. In his home, he is no longer the capable workman; the skilled workman here is the wife, who serves him and prepares his food for him. He is a serene and pleasant man where he is powerful through being efficient, but is domineering where he is served. Perhaps if he should learn how to prepare his soup he might become a perfect man! The man who, through his own efforts, is able to perform all the actions necessary for his comfort and development in life, conquers himself, and in doing so multiplies his abilities and perfects himself as an individual.

We must make of the future generation, *powerful men,* and by that we mean men who are independent and free.

The Dewey School

Katherine Camp Mayhew and Anna Camp Edwards were teachers in the Laboratory School of the University of Chicago, which was founded by John Dewey in 1896. This school was an educational laboratory for exploring the ideas on curriculum and instruction being developed by Dewey. The school, which later became the School of Education, was created to involve parents, teachers, and professors in dialogue regarding the 10 ideas about experience-based pedagogy being developed by Dewey and other progressive educators. Mayhew and Edwards published a now-classic book on the early years of this experimental school entitled *The Dewey School: The Laboratory School of the University of Chicago, 1896–1903* (D. Appleton-Century, 1936). The selection that follows is from that book.

The students of the Dewey school were broken into groups by relative age. Each group was designated by a Roman numeral. To give the reader a flavor of how the school was conducted, this selection includes the authors' descriptions of the experiments in specialized activities by "Group XI" (ages 14 to 15) for the 1901–1902 school year. Also included are brief comments by Mayhew and Edwards regarding the school's philosophy of student growth.

Key Concept: the Dewey school

EXPERIMENTS IN SPECIALIZED ACTIVITIES

Group XI (Age Fourteen to Fifteen)

In a developing experiment such as that of the school, the work of the oldest children is of necessity highly exploratory and tentative in character. Because of the school's early demise also, many of the courses for this age were repeated but once, or at the most twice. An account of them is, therefore, only suggestive of a way in which the interests and activities of the elementary stage may be guided into the deviating paths of the more specialized interests and subject-matter of the secondary period.

Careful study of the school's brief and very condensed records during the year 1901–1902 seems to indicate that in this year the two older groups were united into one. This was true for at least certain of their studies. The oldest

*Katherine Camp
Mayhew and
Anna Camp
Edwards*

members of this united group (who normally would have been classified as Group XII) were given special tutoring and review courses in preparation for their college board examinations, which were complicating the program. Had the group consisted solely of those who had followed the consecutively developing program of the school, and had it not been hampered by the demands of college entrance examinations, the various courses for the oldest children doubtless would have followed a far different and more logical plan, hints of which appear in the records. Roman history would have been studied from the point of view of the political state; the history of industry and of social groupings would have been developed; and more of the specialized sciences gradually would have found their places in the curriculum. As it was, the theoretical plan for the oldest children was greatly altered by circumstances. There was also lack of space and of proper laboratories and equipment for older children. Many of these difficulties were swept away in the following year when the Laboratory School, for one year, became a part of the School of Education, and moved into its beautiful new building. Records of the work of that year (1902–1903), however, were not available; hence the history of the school ends with the records of Group XI.

The Work of the Fall Quarter

For two years the course in general science for these children had been separated into its physiographical and biological aspects. The year before the children had continued the study of the various forms of energy with special emphasis on light. This course had included a fundamental consideration of various theories of energy and had been in the nature of an introduction to the technical study of physics, which would soon enter the program of those preparing for college entrance examinations. The science course planned for Group XI was a continued and more detailed consideration of their earlier study of existing types of animal life. This was constantly related to the evolutionary processes touched upon in the geological study of North America the preceding year. It was characterized by more laboratory work and outdoor excursions than usually mark a study of biology in the secondary period. The aim was to preserve the spirit of individual investigation and rediscovery that had characterized the children's scientific work from the beginning.

The study of mathematics also became more highly specialized. The work in algebra included involution, evolution, the theory of exponents, and operations involving radical quantities. In geometry, each member of the group worked out, for the most part independently, from twenty to thirty propositions and exercises and wrote up his demonstrations with a varying degree of care. In addition to that of clarifying the children's fundamental mathematical ideas, three ulterior purposes were kept in view by the teacher of this course: to train each individual into the highest degree of independence and perseverance in attacking new and difficult work, to aid him in developing a clear concept of what constitutes a geometrical demonstration, to attain clear, definite, and concise expression.

In the second quarter the pupils used Will's *Essentials of Geometry* as the basis of their work and were able to work more rapidly than when they had had to make constructions as well as work out demonstrations from dictated exercises. The propositions of Book I and many other related exercises were covered —in all about one hundred. In order to have time to finish the desired work in algebra, geometry was discontinued in May without reviewing the work done. The remainder of the quarter was spent in the study of radical equations, quadratic equations, the theory of quadratics, and problems involving quadratics. Although all the work usually prescribed for college entrance was taken up, only a few of the group completed the course in a satisfactory way. Some of them were hampered by lack of a ready command of fundamental principles and processes. Others did not put sufficient time on study to acquire familiarity with and ready application of the principles. The work of three was highly satisfactory, but even these needed a month of review before taking college examinations. It was felt that other members of the group would require at least another quarter's work on the important and more technical parts of the subject.

The work in history was also more specialized than in previous years. Six years' study of social living the world over, as well as that of their own present, had more or less adequately prepared these children to appreciate a study of certain thoroughly differentiated and, so to speak, peculiar types of social life. It was hoped that on the basis of their rather thorough knowledge of both the principles and facts of social life they would be able to discover for themselves the special significance of each civilization and the particular contribution it had made to the world's history. The plan, therefore, was to change from the psychological approach to a study of history to the chronological, to begin with the ancient world around the Mediterranean and come down again through the European story to the peculiar and differentiating factors of American history. The plan, however, was tried for two years only, and the records of the work of the last year are too meagre for inferences of any value to be drawn as to its ultimate success. In history, much time was also given to making up the lacks in the consecutive study of history required by college entrance examinations.

The shop-work of this group for the quarter was not up to the standard of that of Groups VIII or IX. The pupils chose their own work, and the results were unsatisfactory. Some showed a lack of ambition to undertake any worthy object; some were ambitious beyond their skill; and some lacked decision and perseverance. When careful work was required, most of the group worked very slowly. The boys took some time to complete the tool drawers in their benches, did some repair work about the school and finished a tripod for a camera and a bread board. The girls completed tool boxes, a mail box, two or three book racks, a window seat, an oak table, an oak music rack, and other smaller articles. The whole-hearted effort and genuine interest of other years seems to have been lacking. The cooking as a course had been discontinued with Group IX, but on occasions when distinguished guests were present at luncheon, the older groups were called in to plan, prepare, and serve the meal.

The work in languages, French, Latin, and English, took on a specialized character. In Latin, before beginning Caesar's Commentaries, the class read his biography from *Viri Romae*. In translation, emphasis was laid on syntax. In composition, the aim was to help the children to gain a free use of Latin idioms in their translation of English into Latin and in their condensed historical reports. Sight reading was also part of the program, and in connection with work on the Gallic wars a detailed study of the life of Caesar's times was made, of its outstanding men and the social, intellectual, and political events of the period. In this year the children also started their first formal study of the English language, and English was chosen as the subject for special emphasis during the year. Some intensive work was done on Latin derivatives. The points emphasized were: (1) consonant and vowel changes; (2) suffixes and prefixes, their value and changes; (3) growth and change in the meaning of derivatives. Coöperation with the French teacher was necessary as the Latin element in the English language, while partly derived directly from Latin, has, in the main, come through French, and has been largely modified in the process.

*Katherine Camp
Mayhew and
Anna Camp
Edwards*

The first piece of work in composition was a theme relating to summer experience. The children's style was clear and fluent, but inclined to be loose and inaccurate in sentence structure. Careful criticism brought out some difficult grammatical points which were analyzed and discussed; considerable logical power was evidenced in attacking these grammatical problems. After this preliminary work, the reading of one of Shakespeare's plays was undertaken. As these children had not the habit of reading aloud, they were very awkward. They had never read a play, with the exception of two pupils. They knew nothing of Shakespeare, nor of dramatic history, so a brief sketch of Shakespeare's life and the prominent social features of his time was made from books which the children read themselves. They had no way of expressing their ideas of meter and in the beginning found it difficult to tell when they omitted a syllable or inserted one which did not belong in the phrase. As their attention had to be continually interrupted to discover errors in reading, the work went very slowly at first. They had had Roman History so that they understood the story of the play. They committed to memory some couplets and short passages, and as soon as the study of the first act was completed, they prepared an abstract. By this time they had enough command of method to understand the character of work expected of them, and their interest in the story and the dramatic setting was thoroughly aroused. The play was completed by Christmas time; abstracts of each act were written; and an outline of the entire play given by every pupil in the class. In a general way they understood the difference between the Shakespearean drama and preceding English drama. They were familiar with the versification so far as its use went, although no technical terms were given to them. The class showed particular interest in the character study. Two members carried on a two-day debate over the comparative virtues of Brutus and Cassius. Each member of the class had weighed all the main characters and could give an opinion on their virtues or vices and the relative importance of the part each had in the drama.

This study cleared the way for a return to a study of the village life and history of Shakespeare's time. Notes were made of the many incidental allusions to the commercial changes which were taking place in England. To explain these allusions a study of the Tudor family's position and importance in history was made in the winter quarter. The religious attitude of France, Spain, Italy, and the Netherlands was also discussed. Since the pupils had no idea of the reasons why this period was called the Renaissance of Learning, biographies of the great discoverers in science were read. The discovery of the New World and its commercial importance they already understood. They studied the lives of Copernicus, of Sir Thomas More, Martin Luther, the inventors of printing, and the story of the rise of Protestantism and the settlement of Ireland. Working back in history from Shakespeare and Queen Elizabeth to the Wars of the Roses, they studied Shakespeare's *King Richard III,* following the same method used in *Julius Caesar.* About five or six weeks were spent on the play. The class was much shocked by the evil portrayed, and interest was somewhat depressed by the shock to their feelings. The outlines and abstracts of the acts were prepared, and a very good idea of the historical setting was gained. The class was somewhat critical of the play and inclined to compare it with *Julius Caesar,* which they considered much superior. However, in the end they were all impressed by the intellect of King Richard, as well as horrified by his wickedness.

The Work of the Spring Quarter

In the spring quarter work followed quite different lines. It consisted of a critical analysis of the class papers prepared in science. The subjects of these papers were volcanoes, glaciers, and other physiographical features. The first task was to prepare an outline of what they themselves were to write. They had no idea how to attack this and in the first attempt were quite as likely to put descriptions into their outlines as to separate the headings or main topics. However, as the subject-matter had been given them in logical order in the science class, they soon grasped the idea that the order of composition was simply the logic of thought or subject-matter, and rapidly gained power to prepare clear and accurate outlines. The only details taken up were those of grammar and sentence structure. The differentiation between English and Latin caused them some difficulty. In the former, they had to learn to depend upon their own analysis to determine the relation of a word to the sentence. They were inclined at first to define such terms as subject and object in too restricted a way. They came to see that where no endings existed to place the word, the difficulty of defining its use was increased. The main points in sentence analysis, they soon grasped. Certain forms of diagramming sentences were given, but these were not used for more than two days, although the class showed an inclination to come back to them. As time went on, they improved greatly in definiteness of statement and in ability to criticize their own forms of expression. Considerable time was spent throughout the entire year in studying the derivations of words and the historical development of their meanings. At the beginning of the year the whole class was satisfied with a very loose explanation of the meaning of a word, but after the year's study not one was satisfied until he had looked it up in the Century Dictionary. They often followed a word to its roots in other languages.

Group XI also carried on the printing of a daily newspaper for a short time, as did other groups. This did much to interest the children in language expression. On account of the pressure of time, inconvenient quarters, and type of press, the work was more limited than it might have been under more flexible conditions. At one time the press was of great service in printing the reading lessons for the younger children. Developments in later progressive schools have shown that carried out in the same way in which other occupations in the school were pursued, printing might have been an absorbing interest and of great educational value.

Katherine Camp
Mayhew and
Anna Camp
Edwards

The group was active in school clubs and in the club-house project. The Educational Club was under the special guidance of these children. It started out with fine spirit the last year of the school. The constitution of the club allowed any member of the school to become a member, and several new names were voted on. A committee was appointed to attend to the finances of the club-house and to confer with an adviser to consider the best method of raising the money for it. A new president, secretary, and treasurer were elected. The club then voted to take charge of the Friday afternoon exercises of the school. A committee of three members was appointed for this purpose. The children voted to have a general adviser, and a teacher was appointed. At a special meeting the Monday before Thanksgiving, the club decided to raise the dues of club members to twenty-five cents a month until the house was paid for. They also formed an athletic department, and the president appointed a committee of three to decide definitely on the work of this department.

Development of Expression Through the Weekly Assembly

The weekly general assembly of the older children on Friday afternoon of each week was always a social occasion and was usually directed by the older groups. In the beginning, one of the girls read a story of her own composition. The children were then asked to bring in suggestions for programs. One offered to have a friend come and play the piano. A girl offered the play that she had been writing, volunteering to select the actors and actresses and drill them in it. They all voted to ask Professor Judson of the University to come to talk about the trouble in China, requesting that they be allowed to ask all the questions they wished. Extracts from the records of some of these assemblies follow:

At the general exercises held on the Wednesday afternoon before Thanksgiving, the children sang their songs of last year. Professor MacClintock read a Thanksgiving story—Whittier's *The Pumpkin*. On another occasion, papers written by the children of the various groups on their class work were read. One read a long account of the conquest of Peru, another, an account of a series of experiments carried on in science during the fall.

One week Mr. F— gave a very informal talk to the children about his experiences in Cuba during the late war. The children were so much interested that they stayed half an hour afterwards asking questions. In February Mr. Jenkin Lloyd Jones was invited to talk on the subject of Lincoln. He accepted the invitation and entertained them for half an hour with stories illustrating Lincoln's characteristics.

At the next meeting the children celebrated Washington's birthday, Group IX prepared the program, in which each child had a part. One played the boyhood of Washington; another, his school-days; another, his part in the French and Indian War; Washington in the Revolution; Washington as president; and Washington at home. One girl said that she knew several stories of Washington which did not come under any of these heads, so she wrote and read a paper on "Incidents in the life of Washington." On this occasion they worked together as a class better than ever before. Another afternoon Miss Harmer talked to the children on the Horace Mann School, and they asked many questions and seemed interested in the subject. At the next assembly Dr. Coulter gave a description of his trip to the Yellowstone Park in 1870 when he went out with an expedition appointed by the government to explore the Wyoming geysers. On one occasion when a speaker failed to come, the children had an old-fashioned spelling contest, Groups IX and X doing themselves credit. On another, to which friends were invited, the program consisted of a German play, the composition of which had formed the basis of Group VIII-*b's* work for the winter quarter; in addition there were songs and English and French recitations.

In the later years of the school the debating society became very active and frequently took charge of the assembly program. It was noticeable that a child speaking to children always got rapt attention, and judgment of points in a debate grew to be very discerning. All these weekly assemblies were productive of good results, but a great handicap was the lack of an auditorium and any stage facilities.

The boys and girls of Group XI were divided for their music periods. The latter sang well and with much enthusiasm. Sight singing was emphasized, and they learned Schumann's "The Wanderer," Schubert's "Haiden Roslein" (in German) by note and spent a large portion of their time in writing a long two-part song which they notated on the board and copied. The boys of the group, having completed the work on key and time signatures, were told that unless they wished to sing, there was nothing further to do, for them, in music. They responded to this by suggesting that they write a song and chose as a topic "La Journée" such as they had seen described in their recent study of *Ivanhoe* in a literature course. The words finished, they were at a loss for the music, and finally decided that the teacher had better write it. Accordingly, she put a phrase of music on the board which they proceeded to change by telling on what line or space each note should be placed. They then listened to and criticized the result. In this manner the song was completed. The three older groups were allowed to learn it. They were then to invite the composers to chorus practice and sing it for them. The latter, however, were not pleased with the result, saying the voices were too high to do justice to the song, and finally decided to learn to sing it themselves. This they did and, finding they could, continued to sing for the rest of the quarter.

The work in the art studio centered around the furnishing and decorating of the now completed club-house. All the groups of the school had been drawn into interested participation in the final touches on the cherished project, but the older groups designed and made most of the furniture, hangings, and rugs. At various times the center of activity shifted from the studio to the science laboratory for experimentation on vegetable dyes (aniline dyes were viewed with scorn) or for the right mixture of stain for the woodwork; again the carpentry shop was sought out for some necessary construction of wood or metal; or it was back to the textile studio for sewing and embroidery of the curtains, or weaving the rugs already planned and designed. Through all these activities ran the artistic motive—a genuine longing that the house and all that was to be put therein should be beautiful and appropriate. Interest and effort harnessed as a team, driven by genuine desire that sprang from genuine need, accomplished results of real quality. Although skilled guidance was at hand and irremediable errors were not permitted, the children had great freedom in directing their project. Naturally many mistakes were made, some of which took much time and hard labor to correct, but which taught much otherwise never learned. The groups primarily responsible for the project had organized themselves into various executive committees. The committee on house decoration decided in favor of a dark stain (then in vogue) for the woodwork of the house and, in spite of the advice of those guiding the work, carried their idea through. They were much criticized by the rest for the gloomy effect of their choice, a criticism some of them recall to this day.

Summary

The little house when finished represented the best thought and genuine interest as well as labor of many children, and it grew out of genuine need. Its construction and decoration had been guided by skilled persons, interested in helping the children to conceive and achieve their ideals, and in the process to learn to judge and critically evaluate their own results. With these older children, as with all the groups in the school, the motives for art expressions sprang out of other activities and thus held vital relations for the children. The ideal of the school was that skill in the technique of artistic expression should keep pace with the children's intellectual concepts of the way they wished to refine, adorn, or represent in line, color, or clay the thing they were making. This was an ideal difficult to attain and more often than not failed of achievement. That it was achieved, in a measure, in art, in music, and to a still more limited degree in drama was a real achievement for those in charge. These were pioneer days, and previous attempts to cultivate artistic quality of expression from the kindergarten to the studio were quite unknown. Since these early days great progress has been made in the teaching of the musical and those representative activities usually called the fine arts. There is great value in this type of activity for securing freedom of expression and joyous creative effort. For the child this is what might be called consummatory experience.

In justice it should be said that at all times the experiment was much hampered by its limited quarters and equipment. Because of the lack of library and laboratory facilities especially, many of the things done with the three older groups were second choices as to subject-matter. The very nature of the school also made it necessary for the children to concentrate under difficult conditions of noise and interruption. This was not conducive to the development of the habit of consecutive study necessary to the best expression of individual thought in language or in any other medium. Lack of a library, lack of quiet, lack of beauty, lack of adequate space for club meetings, all made it impossible to carry out many individual and group plans. As was stated at the time, "It was never practically possible to act adequately upon the best ideas obtained, because of administrative difficulties, due to lack of funds, difficulties centering in the lack of a proper building and appliances and in inability to pay the amounts necessary to secure the complete time of teachers in some important lines. Indeed, with the growth of the school in numbers and in the age and maturity of the pupils, it was always a grave question how long it was fair to the experiment to carry it on without more adequate facilities."

Although the school had a number of children who were finishing the third stage of growth of the elementary period, it was not in existence long enough so that many typical inferences as to results for this period could be safely drawn. There did seem reason to hope, however, that with the consciousness of difficulties, needs, and resources gained in the experience of five years, children can be brought to and through this period not only without sacrifice of thoroughness, mental discipline, and command of the technical tools of learning, but also with a positive enlargement of life, and a wider, freer, and more open outlook upon it.

At least it can be said that at fourteen these children had the background of an unusually wide first-hand experience upon which to base their more technical study, not only of artistic forms and appreciations, but of all forms of knowledge, whether scientific or practical, that had come within the range of their activities. Where these experiences had taken root in the good soil of native aptitudes, tendrils of intellectual and spiritual appreciations of beauty of color, line, and form, of harmony and rhythm, of ethical, social, and moral values and responsibilities were reaching out, searching for the light of broader opportunities. They represented permanently rooted motives and vocational interests which, given a chance, would grow into continuing purposes and well-planned social action. This was by no means true of all the children who had come through the processes of the school. It possibly was true only of a very few, but it is not too much to hold that what was accomplished gave those who had eyes to see and ears to hear faith to believe that here lay the way of an education that was also the way of developing life.

PRINCIPLES OF GROWTH GUIDING SELECTION OF ACTIVITIES

In the school, education was recognized as a maturing process, in which the young child grows in body and mind and in ability to handle himself in his physical environment and in his social relationships. The conditions for healthy bodily growth had long been recognized, but the idea that power to think depends upon the healthy growth and proper functioning of the mechanism of thought and its expression was, at that time, quite new. The bearing upon education of psychological science as a study of this mechanism, and of the conditions that minister to and promote its normal development in mental power and intelligent action was still for the most part unrecognized.

Two psychological assumptions of the school's hypothesis, basic to its theory and controlling its practices, were radically different from those that underlay the prevalent educational theory and practice. The first of these recognized a psychological and biological distinction between the child and the adult, as a result of which it is neither physiologically nor mentally possible to describe children as "little men and women." The adult is a person with a calling and position in life. These place upon him specific responsibilities which he must meet. They call into play formed habits. The child's primary calling is growth. He is forming habits as well as using those already formed. He is, therefore, absorbed in making contacts with persons and things and in getting that range of acquaintance with the physical and ideal factors of life which should be the background and afford the material for the specialized activities of later life. Recognition of this difference, therefore, conditioned the selection and arrangement of all school materials and methods in order to facilitate full normal growth. It also required faith in the results of growth to provide the power and ability for later specialization.

The second assumption was that the conditions which make for mental and moral progress are the same for the child as for the adult. For one, as for the other, power and control are obtained through realizing personal ends and problems, through personal choosing of suitable ways and means, and through adapting, applying and thereby testing what is selected in experimental and socially acceptable action.

The Child-Centered School: An Appraisal of the New Education

Harold Rugg and Ann Shumaker published *The Child-Centered School: An Appraisal of the New Education* (World Book) in 1928. This important book described and synthesized the basic underlying principles of the rapidly growing progressive, child-centered school movement in America. Rugg (1886–1960) went on to publish 57 more books on education. Through his works, he interpreted the socially conscious ideas on education that developed in the first six decades of the twentieth century. Shumaker (1899–1936) was a teacher at the Lincoln School, the experimental elementary school at Teachers College, Columbia University, where she did her graduate studies. Her enthusiasm for the ideas of John Dewey and William Heard Kilpatrick shines through in the following excerpt from *The Child-Centered School*. Shumaker is considered by many to be America's first published woman philosopher of education.

In the first part of Rugg and Shumaker's book, the authors explore how the early writings of Dewey and Kilpatrick on child-centered ideas about teaching have influenced education, and they note several of the experimental schools that developed in the United States in the first 25 years of the twentieth century. In the excerpt that follows, the authors describe the "new articles of faith"—the bases of the child-centered school—in what they consider to be the revolution in educational thought.

Key Concept: child-centered schooling

It was John Dewey,... Professor of Philosophy and Head of the Department of Education at the University of Chicago from 1894 to 1904, who ignited the first flame of the current educational revolution. Dewey, curious combination of the arid New England Puritanism and Middle West democratic practicality, first phrased the educational philosophy of the developing American culture. Thoroughgoing Darwinian and firm believer in democracy, he, more than all others, rationalized the rapidly evolving industrial civilization. He was third in the line of the pragmatic succession. Two other original thinkers preceded him in phrasing the hypotheses of the new Americanism: Charles Sanders Peirce, engineer, statistician, professor of logic, inventor of pragmaticism; and William James, organizer of the first psychological laboratory in America, true experimental scientist, phraser of the philosophy of radical empiricism, for whom "there was no conclusion."

It is to Dewey's everlasting credit that his mind was able to stay above the maelstrom of economic exploitation, rapid urbanization, mass education, and to frame critical hypotheses for the intellectual base of the new national school system.

It was in 1896 that John and Alice Dewey, in company with colleagues and neighbors, started their little laboratory school. A thoroughly radical institution it was, with neither school subjects nor conventional furniture, the first important overt expression of the growing protest against the formal school. Of course, in this, their first escape from the conventional order, they swung far with the experimental pendulum. Many thought that their experiment exemplified only scholastic chaos. For several years it grew slowly, a true innovation, throwing overboard most of the established principles of order. Leading "educators" of the country visiting it went away determined not to practice that form of educational anarchy in their own institutions.

Nevertheless, it was in these formative years and through the trial and error of radical experimentation that John Dewey succeeded in phrasing the new doctrines of educational reconstruction. Under the impetus of round-table staff meetings, lectures to the parents and teachers of the laboratory school, there emerged the essays, "School and Society" and "The Child and the Curriculum." Papers were contributed to the proceedings of the Herbart Society and of the National Education Association on the practical reconstruction of the elementary and secondary schools. Dewey displayed a catholicity of interests. Hence his "Interest as Related to Will,"[1] and also "Ethical Principles Underlying Education,"[2] the essay in which he developed the basic theses of his orienting theory.

In striving to cut through the crust of the disciplinary conception he seized upon the doctrine of growth and activity. This leader of the first real protest school of our times was guided, therefore, by children's "full spontaneous interests and intentions." Hence, school subjects—reading, writing, arithmetic— were to develop out of children's "life activities," out of methods of living and learning, not out of the memorization of "distinct studies."

According to Dewey's theory, therefore, the life of the school was to be active, not passive; the children were to work, not merely to listen. The curriculum was to be organized around four chief impulses: the social instinct of the children, the instinct of making—the constructive impulse, the expressive instinct —the art instinct, and the impulse toward inquiry or finding out things.[3]

The preparatory work was going on, however, and then appeared William H. Kilpatrick and his monograph, *The Project Method*.

Professor Kilpatrick,[4] strategically located in the first and most influential of the new teachers' colleges, has succeeded not only in making the philosophy of the child-centered school intelligible to thousands of teachers in service, but also in inciting widespread experimentation with the new point of view. In 1910 the movement needed analysis and concrete illustration. Vigorous preachment was required in order to provide the impulse for the next step—widespread experimentation.

NEW ARTICLES OF FAITH

The pageant historical of the new schools has passed in review, a procession of novel educational tableaux. The parade convinces the spectator that at last rebellious preachment is producing action in the school.

The new school is different—different in practice, different in theory. Dynamic articles of faith have been precipitated from the reaction of the new culture of industrialism on the Puritan scene.

Semi-phrased; relatively unformulated; beyond such catch slogans as freedom, initiative, activity, interest, self-expression, was the theoretical basis of most of the radical innovations. For years little advance was made in theory. Until 1920 Dewey's philosophic writings, supplemented by Kilpatrick's pamphlets, constituted the bulk of frontier thinking. Then suddenly emerged an accumulating wealth of description—yearbooks, records, bulletins, reprinted addresses, what not. And in 1919 the need of the rebels for mutual support, for discussion, for comparison of practices produced the Progressive Education Association[5] and in 1924, its magazine, *Progressive Education*. In Europe the corresponding New Education Fellowship and its tri-language magazine[6] perform a similar service.

The meetings of the American as well as the European organization have brought out encouraging reiterations and confirmations of faith, and thrilling exhibits of the productivity of the creative environment. Slowly this fellowship has helped to focus and clarify the vocabulary (and correspondingly the thinking) of the new educationists. Haltingly the new philosophy is being evolved; bit by bit a mosaic of theory is being constructed, mostly of excerpts culled from the educational writings of Dewey and his followers. Gradually basic articles of faith are emerging, to which all these new schools subscribe. For back of the varying, overt manifestations of the new spirit stand a few fundamental beliefs, a few distinctly new conceptions of growth, experience, the course of learning and of education.

Freedom vs. Control

And the first of these articles of faith is freedom. "Free the legs, the arms, the larynx of a child," say these advocates of the new education, "and you have taken the first step towards freeing his mind and spirit."

Hence the revolution in school furniture, schedules of work, all the paraphernalia of administration. Fixed seats nailed to the floor, lock-step precision, rigidity, conformity, are disappearing. In their places are coming the informal, intimate atmosphere—the air of happy, cheerful living. Light, movable tables and chairs that may be shoved aside at any time to make room for work or play; children moving freely about, talking with one another, leaving the room to go to other parts of the building relatively at their own discretion. The fixed, elaborate machinery of mass education is being abandoned: large classes; emphasis upon grades; housing in stereotyped, barrack-like buildings; adherence to strict time schedules; the oppressive silence of restraint; the labored compulsion—all the stringent coercion of the old order is passing.

The new freedom reveals itself, therefore, in an easier, more natural group life. At great expense to itself it maintains mere corporal's guards of classes—ten, twelve, fifteen, rarely over twenty pupils—in sharp contrast to the huge regiments of the formal, graded school. Thus the formal question-and-answer recitation is giving way to the free interchange of thought in group conferences and progress through individual work.

Freedom to develop naturally, to be spontaneous, unaffected, and unselfconscious, is, therefore, the first article of faith.

Child Initiative vs. Teacher Initiative

What is this new freedom based upon? Nothing less than the reorientation of the entire school around the child. These schools are child-centered institutions in contrast to the teacher-centered and principal-centered schools of the conventional order. They believe that the ability to govern one's self grows only through the practice of self-government. They have learned wisely the lesson of democracy in the western world; namely, that no people, however potentially able, will learn how to carry on its collective affairs except under freedom to practice self-government. Wherever adult societies have imposed democratic forms of government on a people uneducated in democracy, chaos has resulted. Throughout a century of national history in America our schools have adopted the form and the catch slogans of democracy, but never its true technique.

In this respect, however, another day has come in the new schools. These schools believe that boys and girls should share in their own government, in the planning of the program, in the administering of the curriculum, in conducting the life of the school. In the elementary division of some of these schools, during an informal morning discussion period, children, with the teacher as a wise but inconspicuous adult member of the group, consider together what they are to undertake during the day. The routine needs of the school, as well as the lesson assignments, the planning of excursions and exhibits, and the criticism of reports are taken over by the pupils. This is, indeed, a revolution in educational procedure and stands in sharp contrast to the conventional mode of conducting a school.

The difference in amount of work done by teachers and pupils respectively under these two plans of work—the pupil-initiating plan *vs.* the teacher-initiating plan—is conspicuous. In the formal school of today the teacher still does the thinking, planning, and initiating. Pupils are passive, quiescent, generally uninterested if not actively antagonistic. Learning is at a low ebb, if not at a standstill. In the child-centered school, however, pupils are alive, active, working hard, inventing, organizing, contributing original ideas, assembling materials, carrying out enterprises. As individuals and as social groups pupils grow, and they grow in the capacity to govern themselves, to organize machinery for handling their collective affairs, as well as in individual capacity for creative self-expression. So it is that the true theory of democracy is being put into practice in these new schools.

This centering of responsibility and initiative in the pupil brings into the forefront the child's own needs. His immediate interests are to furnish the starting point of education, according to the new schools. But, even of the most rebellious reformers, few advocate that the entire work of the school be based solely upon these naïve and spontaneous interests of children. However, the last twenty-five years of experimentation have undoubtedly contributed no more revolutionary articles of faith than that involved in this reorientation of the school about the child.

The Active School

Freedom, pupil initiative—therefore, the active school.

Naturally, from the free atmosphere in which pupil initiative plays the chief role it is but a next step to pupil activity. In these free, child-centered schools, therefore, pupils are active—physically active, mentally active, artistically active. There is a large amount of actual physical exertion, of overt bodily movement, of a wide variety of sensory contacts, of the type of energy-release which is ordinarily designated as play. Hence the terms, "activity schools," "play schools," and so on.

Education is to be based on child experience—experience not only in the physical sense but in the intellectual and emotional sense too. Thus do these child-centered schools want experience to be real. They depend as little as possible upon described experience. The wiser among their leaders know, of course, that in the adult world much real experience is abstract, described, vicarious, verbal. Therefore the child who is growing toward adulthood will appropriate to his uses an increasingly larger amount of described experience. In the higher reaches of the school, indeed, many described experiences must be made the very center of educational development. However, as far as possible, and predominantly in the lower years of the child-centered schools, real life is reproduced in physical miniature. Excursions are made into the neighborhood, the community. The scholastic environment is extended outward to include *realia* of a variegated sort, and within the school itself plants, animals, tools, materials, machines, are provided to stimulate activity and to give rise to interests which will require activity in their development. Much free play is permitted for the experiences in self-direction it affords.

Now the most deep-seated tendency in human life is movement, impulse, activity. The new schools, therefore, are experimenting vigorously with this fundamental psychological law—that the basis of all learning is reaction. That they are making a contribution is unquestioned.

In the formal schools the conditions of true growth were exactly reversed. One found outward quiet, orderliness, apparent concentration, little physical movement. Actually, however, this condition was one of restlessness, of much inner activity—a continual mutiny against the aims of the school. The iron rule of the school succeeded only in inhibiting the outward symptoms of inattention. There was fidgeting, uneducative scattering of interest and attention, and little conscious reflection on the matters in hand.

*Harold Rugg
and Ann
Shumaker*

The new schools, with freedom of activity and movement, with apparent lack of concentration, produce nevertheless a much more truly educative absorption. The newer education regards the active child as the truly growing child. Not activity for activity's sake—energy exploding in random movements—but activity which is a growing toward something more mature, a changing for the better. The true criterion of educative activity is prolonged attention and concentrated effort. Such then is the activity which the new education writes into its articles of faith.

Child Interest as the Basis of the New Educational Program

Freedom, not restraint.

Pupil initiative, not teacher initiative.

The active, not the passive, school.

There is a fourth new article of faith—child interest as the orienting center of the school program.

In the formal schools, even in those of today, the program of the child's education is organized about school subjects. Not so in the new schools. We find a new educational vocabulary exponential of a unique educative program. Compare the schedules of the new and the old schools. What a difference! The logically arranged subjects of the past—reading, writing, arithmetic, spelling, geography, history—are replaced by projects, units of work, creative work periods, industrial arts, creative music, story hour, informal group conferences, and other vastly intriguing enterprises.

This curriculum does not look well on paper. It is a chaos of irregular time allotments. School principals might have a difficult time trying to fit the orderly movement of a large school into it. But it does give promise of active learning.

The new school is setting up a program of work which has a personal connection with the immediate life of the child. It starts from his needs and interests. The units of the new program approximate as nearly as possible what to the children are real-life situations. Hence the new school organizes its program around the centers of interest rather than around academic subjects. Wherever school subjects, however, coincide with life needs, then the new centers of interest coincide with the old school subjects; for example, the subjects of reading and creative music, the story hour. But because the formal school subjects were the product of academic research interests, most of them do not coincide with life interests, either of children or of adults. Hence in the new educational order they must go. This new plan of organizing the curriculum around units of pupil activity gives greater promise of wide-spreading, educational achievement for the pupil than does the dry, intellectualized, logical arrangement of subjects-to-be-learned of the old school. It is vitalized by interesting and purposeful activity that has an intimate connection with the child's personal life.

That the new schools are evolving an educational program in which school subjects are rejected in favor of broader and more integrative centers of work is illustrated also in the tendency to organize materials in a few broad departments of knowledge. The old school organized knowledge into many minute, disparate, academic departments. In the upper grades of some of the new schools the initiating center of organization is the interest of the child in some contemporary institution or problem. In the lower grades the focus is the immediate school scene. In the higher grades the emphasis shifts to adult society; in the foreground always stand the fundamental movements or trends, the crucial institutions or problems of contemporary life.

All this does not mean that the new school entirely avoids school subjects, but the subjects in these schools differ materially from those of the formal school. The new-school subjects represent new departmentalizations of knowledge which include a broad view of race experience rather than mere devitalized definitions and long lists of factual enumerations. They are concerned at bottom with big concepts, themes, movements, that explain broad, fundamental phases of human life.

The old school spent its time and energy in drilling pupils into a state of passable efficiency in minimal essentials. The new school treats these minimal essentials, which are largely skills, as by-products of the educative situation. Usually it has succeeded in teaching them much more adequately than the old school, and in less time.

Creative Self-Expression

"I would have a child say not, 'I know,' but, 'I have experienced.'"

Education as conformity *vs.* education as creative self-expression, adaptation and adjustment *vs.* creative experience—these are some of the phrases which are recurring with accumulating momentum in the discussions of the new education.

We find as sharp a contrast in theory between the old and the new at this point in our analysis as in our consideration of other aspects. The spirit of the old school was centered about social adjustment, adaptation to the existing order. The aim of conventional education was social efficiency. Growth was seen as increasing power to conform, to acquiesce to a schooled discipline; maturity was viewed from the standpoint of successful compliance with social demands.

In the new school, however, it is the creative spirit from within that is encouraged, rather than conformity to a pattern imposed from without. The success of the new school has been startling in eliciting self-expression in all of the arts, in discovering a marvelously creative youth. The child as artist, poet, composer, is coming into his own.

This success is due not so much to the changed viewpoint concerning the place of art in education as to the whole new theory of self-expression, the emphasis on the place of creative originality in life. Art in the new school is permitted; in the old it was imposed. The new school assumes that every child is endowed with the capacity to express himself, and that this innate capacity is immensely worth cultivating. The pupil is placed in an atmosphere conducive to self-expression in every aspect. Some will create with words, others with light. Some will express themselves through the body in the dance; others will model, carve, shape their ideas in plastic materials. Still others will find expression through oral language, and some through an integrated physical, emotional, and dramatic gesture. But whatever the route, the medium, the materials—each one has some capacity for expression.

The artist in Everyman's child is being discovered, not only in the unusual, the gifted, the genius; the lid of restraint is being lifted from the child of the common man in order that he may come to his own best self-fulfillment. The new schools are providing "drawing-out" environments in sharp contrast to the "pouring-in" environments of the old.

Art in the new schools is naïve, neo-primitive. The child is permitted to set his own standards as he works. The "masters" are not set out to be worshiped respectfully—they are admired in the frank and critical spirit of intimate companionship. Appreciation of the finished works of genius is best built up, say the new schools, by first encouraging the creative products of the child's own pen, voice, brush. The emphasis is not upon finished work, skill, and technical perfection, but upon the release of the child's creative capacities, upon growth in his power to express his own unique ideas naturally and freely, whatever the medium.

Personality and Social Adjustment

The leaders of our schools are confronted by no more important and overwhelming problem than that of providing an environment by which each child can learn to live with others and yet retain his personal identity. To live with others, learn how to adjust himself to them, and yet grow in the confident knowledge that he, like each of them, is a unique individuality, a rare personality; to live with others and yet grow in the assurance that he too is superior, that he, and he alone, is distinctive in some trait or traits and that he has something unique to contribute to the groups in which he lives. How are the new and the old schools trying to solve this problem?

The old school, with its mass-education machinery, seemed to treat children in social groups, to develop social attitudes, but in reality it sacrificed the individual to mythical group needs. Social contacts during school hours were dominated by an arbitrary authority—the teacher—and had to conform to a rigid formality in order that discipline might be maintained. The old school, therefore, left the child entirely unaided in coping with social situations. Under mass education—hyper-intellectual, hyper-individualistic—with pupils isolated in seats, no opportunity was offered to practice cooperative living except in the undirected out-of-school contacts. The child was not assisted in learning to work effectively with a group at a common interest. A false notion of individuality was erected; namely, that superiority could be asserted only through personal competition. The old school over-emphasized competition because it was a convenient, effective, and inexpensive device for attaining greater effort from pupils. However, it was often used at the cost of successful social living.

The new school, on the other hand, encourages the child to be a distinct personality, an individualist, to believe in his ability—but of course not to an unjustifiable degree. It sets up situations which provide constant practice in cooperative living. It encourages activities in which he can make a personal contribution to group enterprises; in which he has social experiences, graded to fit his level of social development; in which he feels himself an accepted and respected member of a society of which he himself approves.

The new school bridges the gap, therefore, between the development of individuality on the one hand and successful social participation on the other by insisting that the true development of the individual and the fulfillment of personality are best attained as one expresses himself most successfully and adequately *with* others and *toward* others.

How does the new school propose to secure this cooperative endeavor?

It does so by means of a wide variety of group activities. Dramatics which require concerted effort toward a common goal; assemblies through which frequent interchange of mutually interesting ideas takes place; student committees and clubs managing student affairs; miniature social organizations and group games—these are some of the social situations which the new school deliberately encourages. The group dance also is coming into its own as a vehicle for more than rhythmic physical development. Indeed, rhythmics gives promise of usurping the place in the lower school that has formerly been given to competitive athletics. Active experience in grace and physical poise, as an agency for the education of personality of each and every individual, is the aim, rather than development of a few stellar performers with the mass remaining mere passive, untransformed observers.

The new school has no extracurricular activities. These group activities are a regular and important part of school life—they are not a side issue indulged in at the end of the day or week as unrelated recreation or relief from the real business of the school.

Again, where the old school maintained a noisy silence as the ideal schoolroom atmosphere, the new removes the ban from speech, encourages communication as a vehicle for social understanding and personal development. Indeed the new school has gone so far in this respect as to be accused at times of being garrulous. However, it is well known that practice in the free use of language, with guidance, helps to develop qualities desirable for successful social living. Fluent, natural speech is the basis for effective self-expression and mutual understanding.

In ways like these the new school is evolving its informal real-life organization, encouraging common aims and purposes, the interpenetration of minds, producing in the school a life of happy intimacy—creating a "wholesome medium for the most complete living."[7]

1. First Yearbook of the Herbart Society for the Scientific Study of Teaching. University of Chicago Press; 1894.

2. Third Yearbook of the National Herbart Society. University of Chicago Press; 1897.

3. Dewey, John. *School and Society*, page 11. University of Chicago Press; 1899.

4. William Heard Kilpatrick (1871–), teacher and principal of public schools of Georgia until 1907; Professor of Mathematics, 1897–1906, Acting President 1903–1905 at Mercer University; Lecturer in Education, 1909–1911, Assistant Professor, 1911–1915, Associate Professor, 1915–1918, Professor Philosophy of Education, from 1918, at Teachers College, Columbia University. Author: *The Dutch Schools of New Netherland and Colonial New York*, 1912; *The Montessori System Examined*, 1914; *Froebel's Kindergarten Principles Critically Examined*, 1916; *Source Book in the Philosophy of Education*, 1923; *Foundations of Method*, 1925; *Education for a Changing Civilization*, 1926; and numerous articles on educational topics.

5. Headquarters, 10 Jackson Place, Washington, D.C.

6. The *New Era*, edited by Beatrice Ensor. 11, Tavistock Square, London, W.C. 1. *Das Werdende Zeitalter*, edited by Dr. Elizabeth Rotten. Kohlgraben, bei Vacha (Rhön), Berlin. *Pour L'ère Nouvelle*, edited by Dr. Adolph Ferrière. Chemin Psechier 10, Geneva. There are also Bulgarian, Hungarian, Italian, Spanish, and other editions. The various editions are not translations of each other, each editor being free to fill the special needs of his own readers.

7. Tippett, James S., and Others. *Curriculum Making in an Elementary School*, page 8. Ginn & Co., Boston; 1927.

*Harold Rugg
and Ann
Shumaker*

CHAPTER 5 Curriculum Theory and Practice

5.1 HILDA TABA

Current Conceptions of the Function of the School

Hilda Taba (1902–1967) was a major influence on curriculum theory and practice during her career in teacher education. Strongly grounded in educational theory and philosophy, Taba committed herself to working in schools and observing relations among students and teachers. She conducted pioneering longitudinal research studies on human relations in school settings, and she wrote books and guides on improving intergroup understanding in schools. Her work laid a solid foundation in curriculum theory and development for what would later be called multicultural education.

The selection that follows is from Taba's *Curriculum Development: Theory and Practice* (Harcourt, Brace & World, 1962), which was heavily cited by the United States Commission on Civil Rights in its 1975 report *A Better Chance to Learn.* Taba believed that it is important to understand the social context of education and the cultural forces that impact those who create school curricula. Here she provides a synthesis of the leading theories of her time on the roles that schools play in human cultures.

Key Concept: schools and society

*S*ociety's concept of the function of the public school determines to a great extent what kind of curriculum schools will have. Yet, in a complex culture with a pluralistic value system, it is difficult to establish a single central function for any agency. In a democratic society these formulations are further complicated by the fact that different layers of society participate in the process of determining what education in general and public schools specifically should be and do. It is, therefore, more difficult to determine the central function of schools in a democracy than in a totalitarian society where a small power group decides both what society should be and what role schools shall play in it.

Our society today has by no means agreed about what the central function of the school should be. One could even say that "the great debate about schools and their function" is in effect a debate about many of the issues our society faces: the balance between freedom and control and between change and tradition, whether the elite should be of power or of intellect, who should participate in shaping the public policy, and many others. It is generally agreed that the main outlines of the "crisis in education" are shaped and complicated by the convergence of two phenomena: the transformative effects of science and technology on society and the emergence of Communist totalitarianism as an expanding imperialist power. In the light of this setting the examination of the functions of the public school is highly pertinent, but extremely difficult, because the issues tend to be confused and the viewpoints somewhat less than objective.

Whatever the specific viewpoints regarding the functions of the public schools, there seems to be little disagreement about the importance of the role of education. American society has always expected a great deal of education and, in Walter Lippmann's phrase, has expressed great faith in it as the "life-giving principle of national power." Historically the American people have assumed that education has the power to reduce poverty and distress, to prevent child delinquency and crime, and to promote the well-being of the individual, the intelligent use of suffrage, and the welfare and stability of the state. Indeed, even today education, if not the public school, is considered an antidote against evils in the minds of men and an ally in achieving all good causes. The very attacks on the schools express the faith of the American public that the schools matter because of their influence not only on individuals, but on society as well. Some critics, for example, seem to reason that the strength of our current enemies is the *result* of *their* education and, correspondingly, that the weakness in our position is the *fault* of *our* education.

These high expectations and the naive faith in the power of education are at once a curse and a blessing. No doubt they have given American education a certain vigor by insisting that it respond to social ideologies and needs. They have also made it more subject to passing hysterias and changing moods of the public than may have been good for a healthy development. Anyone tracing the various "trends" in curriculum development in the United States will note a zigzag movement in which one "trend" swallows and annihilates the preceding one with an almost unbelievable discontinuity in theoretical thought. When education is overly sensitive to public opinion, changes are bound to be made thoughtlessly. Continuity in capitalizing on past achievements is jeopardized in the heat of hastily formulated reforms and changes. It is no wonder, then, that in periods of crisis the question of the central function of schools in society becomes a subject of heated controversy, with the nature of the relationships of education to society at the very core of that controversy. It is no wonder also that there are many variations in the conceptions of what the essential function of the public school is.

There is relatively little disagreement also about the idea that schools function on behalf of the culture in which they exist. The school is created by a society for the purpose of reproducing in the learner the knowledge, attitudes, values, and techniques that have cultural relevancy or currency. There is generally also no quarrel with the idea that of the many educative agencies of society, the school is the one which specializes in inducting youth into the culture and is thus responsible for the continuity of that culture.

However, opinion is divided about the precise nature of this function. The differences range from conceptions which assume a strong cultural determination of everything schools do and should do to postulations about ideals of individual development which are quite independent of cultural norms. This division of opinion extends also to views on the extent to which the program of the school is or should be subject to the values and norms of the culture, and in what measure the materials it uses and the ideologies that control its shaping should be drawn from the life of the culture. While in all concepts it is accepted that schools must transmit culture, there are sharp differences about what should be transmitted and the manner in which it is to be done. Some conceptions emphasize education as an agent of change, while others stress its preserving functions.

Sometimes, especially in theoretical discussions, these divisions of views appear as rather stark and even unrealistic alternatives. Speaking of the function of general education, Conant states one such alternative neatly:

> Roughly speaking, the basic argument about general education turns on the degree to which the literary and philosophical traditions of the western world, as interpreted by scholars and connoisseurs before World War I, should be the basis of the education of *all* American youth. The watershed between two fundamentally opposed positions can be located by raising the question: For what purpose do we have a system of public education? If the answer is to develop effective citizens of a free democratic country, then we seem to be facing in one direction. If the answer is to develop the student's rational powers and immerse him in the stream of our cultural heritage, then we appear to be facing in the opposite direction. By and large, the first position represents the modern approach to education; the latter the more conventional view. Those who look down one valley regard conventional "book learning" as only one element in the landscape; those who look down the other believe that developing the "life of the mind" is the primary aim of civilization and this can be accomplished only by steeping youth in our literary and philosophical heritage.

All the same, the overlappings in these conceptions are too great to make possible a refined classification of concepts of the function of education. . . .

EDUCATION AS PRESERVER AND TRANSMITTER
OF THE CULTURAL HERITAGE

One group of theorists stresses the preserving function of education: the preserving of the cultural heritage, especially that of the Western culture. This group argues that since all cultural traditions have roots, cultural continuity is possible only if education preserves this heritage by passing on the truths worked out in the past to the new generation, thus developing a common cultural background and loyalties. The specific ideas regarding what this heritage consists of are not always clear. In the main the transmission of the accumulated wisdom of the race and of basic truths and values is emphasized.

The Harvard Report on General Education is one example of an emphasis on the importance of preserving tradition and maintaining roots from the past. This report argues that education can develop a unifying purpose and idea only as it develops this sense of heritage, which in turn requires a common ground in training and outlook. This heritage is basic to education because it uses the past to clarify or even to determine what is important in the present. The report points out that it is the function of education to pass on the *inherited* (italics mine) view of man and society, and that its main task is to perpetuate such ideas as the dignity of man and common beliefs in what is good. "Classical antiquity handed on a working system of truths which relied on both reason and experience and was designed to provide a norm for civilized life." It is the business of education to instill a commitment to these truths.

This assertion of the necessity for imparting the common heritage is, however, modified by a certain recognition of the role of new experience and change. The report attempts to reconcile the necessity for common belief with the equally obvious necessity for new and independent insight by pointing out that a certain tough-mindedness in reaching conclusions by scientific methods of thought, a curiosity, and a readiness for change are also necessary; that education cannot be wholly devoted to the commitment to tradition or to the view that means are valuable apart from ideals; that it upholds at the same time the tradition and the experiment, the ideal and the means, and, like our culture itself, change within the commitment. While the report makes a bow to experiment and change, it seems to say that the basic ideals of what constitutes a good man in our society come from tradition. In other words, since the modern society is only an extension of the traditional one, changes will come from applying the ancient truths to the modern scene. Because the common heritage is a way of building unity in culture, and since the classical tradition has handed down a norm for civilized life, the task of education is to "shape the student" to "receive" this ideal.

This preserving or conserving function of education is still more strongly accentuated by a group of theorists philosophically classified as rational humanists and classicists. Their conception of the function of education is intimately bound up with and derived from their conception of human nature, which has as its major premise that the essence of human nature is its rational character. Rationality is a common characteristic of all men, apart and independent of the culture in which they exist. The world can be understood by the exercise of this faculty of rationality. Therefore, the chief function of education is to develop this rationality, and the understanding of the eternal truths revealed by these rational faculties. "Education, if it is rightly understood, is the cultivation of the intellect. Only this is what belongs to man as man, and his individuality is only his caprice, self-will, and unique propensities."

Being preoccupied with the essence of things, this viewpoint also insists that learning should be concerned with *essentials*, that is, the first principles articulated in the great books and the classical tradition. Since rationality is essential, the subjects of greatest rational content should also have priority in the curriculum. These subjects are the liberal arts and, among the liberal arts, the humanities.

This viewpoint does not deny that societies differ, that education must train citizens for its own society, or that problems of societies vary. However, it insists that these differences are ephemeral and idiosyncratic and that these problems must be understood and interpreted in the light of the universal eternal truths embodied in the classical literature of great books. Such truths are our main cultural heritage, which education must transmit. They constitute the liberalizing education. Further, liberalizing education is the same everywhere, because "truth" is the same everywhere. Thus is set the case not only for the preserving function of education, but also for the requirements for "essentials" and for the uniformity of curriculum.

A rejection of technical subjects and of vocational education of any sort as a narrowing influence is the logical consequence of this viewpoint. That type of "education" is considered to be not education, but training. It is an uncalled-for "encroachment" on the essential task of liberal education.

While this view of the function of education was originally put forth in reference to college education, recently the same orientation has been applied to criticism of and proposals for the public-school curriculum by a group organized around the concept of basic education. This group insists also that the transmission of cultural heritage is the chief function of public schools. This heritage is defined by stress on three points, each of which has consequences on what may be proposed for the curriculum.

First, a strong case is made for intellectual development as the distinctive function of public schools. As defined by Bestor this intellectual development must stress the understanding of principles and the ability to handle and to apply complex ideas, to make use of a wide range of accurate knowledge, and to command the means of effective communication. No one would quarrel with this definition. But there is reason to quarrel with another assumption Bestor makes—namely, that because education has been extended to classes and groups which have hitherto been deprived of it, any "weakness" in intellectual training creates a void into which steps anti-intellectualism. In order to prevent this from happening, the case for this intellectual purpose of the school must be made so clear that the anti-intellectual masses cannot distort it.

Second, this type of intellectual training is possible only by centering the educational effort on basic skills and disciplines: reading, writing, and arithmetic on the lower level, and logic, history, philosophy, mathematics, science, art, and philosophy on the higher levels. These lead the hierarchy of subjects, or the "basics" of education. The assumption that there is a hierarchy of subjects according to "their power to enhance intellectual development" and that the traditional liberal arts subjects are at the top of that hierarchy runs through most of the writings of the basic educators.

This belief that certain subjects are superior to others as means for intellectual training is made perfectly clear by Clifton Fadiman, who argues that since the cultural tradition includes many more things than can be handled in schools "without running into chaos," men in the past have imposed on cultural tradition a form and a hierarchy which is constituted into the disciplines of liberal arts, as encompassed in a New York City public school he attended. . . .

The third characteristic of "basic education" is a complete rejection of certain current functions of the schools, among them education for democratic citizenship, for moral values, and for ability to deal with social problems, and the concern for the "whole child" or any form of "life adjustment," including education for vocations. These functions put basic educators in an especially aggressive and combative mood. According to Bestor, modern education suffers from an enormous extension of functions which schools have no business in assuming: In this extension there is peril to basic education and to the development of intelligence. This extension also unnecessarily pre-empts the functions of other agencies. Thus, job training is the problem of industry. Training in cultural traits, mores, and the ethical systems belongs to the family and the church. Neither should the school be concerned about "social conditioning," partly because it works against tremendous odds and therefore is ineffectual, partly because the socialization of the individual is the very means of squelching the creativity and independence of the intellect. A thoughtless transfer of functions from one agency to another only creates problems; this transfer should be resisted, even though pressures exist for it.

In other words, basic education is a case against any goals for schools beyond those for intellectual development, for a return to the pure form of disciplines as defined by classical tradition, and for limiting general education to those who show a certain level of intellectual promise.

There are, of course, many criticisms of and questions about this definition of the function of the public school. One criticism pertains to the validity of the assumption that, since men are rational and truth is everywhere the same, education everywhere must be uniformly addressed to these truths and to the exclusive task of developing the rational powers. The recent explosion of knowledge seems to have disestablished many truths that were considered perennial. Rational powers seems to be interlocked with cultural conditions and personal factors in a way that forces reinterpretation of ancient truths. "Ancient truths" are not always applicable to the realities and the needs of modern society except in a sense so general as to be unachievable short of a lifetime of study. Further, modern social analysis seems to indicate a greater break with tradition than any of the basic educators are willing to admit, and therefore the transmission of outdated wisdom might even be dangerous. It seems more likely that society today needs to create its own image of the true, the beautiful, and the just.

It is questionable also whether intellectual development can take place effectively in such a grand isolation from the cultural milieu as the advocates of this viewpoint seem to assume. This assumption contradicts the tenor of many studies which point to the relationship between the development of an individual and his cultural milieu. Further, while there is a general agreement about the central importance of intellectual development, the weight of recent knowledge about learning points to the fact that intellectuality cannot be neatly separated from other aspects of personality development without the danger of cultivating an academic intellectuality instead of a functioning intelligence.

Finally, the argument for the purified liberal arts disciplines as a sole way to wisdom is strongly contradicted by the very developments in these disciplines. Often so-called practical application of what is known becomes the very mainspring of theory, or "pure" thought.

EDUCATION AS AN INSTRUMENT FOR TRANSFORMING CULTURE

An opposing view is held by many educators and social analysts who maintain, in effect, that education can and does play a creative role in modifying and even reshaping the culture in which it functions, that education and public policy are intimately related, and that progress in one is limited without progress in the other. They maintain that education must deal with the needs of current culture and even help to shape the future.

The idea that education has a constructive role to play in shaping the society has deep roots in American tradition. It is implicitly expressed in the general public faith in the power of education to deal with problems of culture. It is also articulated in much of educational writing over a long period of time. Horace Mann underscored the integral relationship between popular education and social problems, such as freedom and the republican government. This theme resounds through his twelve reports: "A nation cannot long remain ignorant and free. No political structure, however artfully devised, can inherently guarantee the rights and liberties of citizens, for freedom can be secure only as knowledge is widely distributed among the populace." Facing the social reality of the times, the public discord of a nation not yet unified, and "Fearing the destructive possibilities of religious, political and class discord," he sought a common value system which might undergird American republicanism and within which a healthy diversity might thrive. His quest was for *public philosophy,* a sense of community which might be shared by Americans of every variety and persuasion. His effort was to use education to fashion a new American character out of a maze of conflicting cultural traditions. And his tool was the *Common School.* The common school for him was the instrument for his limitless faith in the perfectibility of human life and institutions. In this sense, then, Horace Mann regarded education as an arm of public policy and an instrument for dealing with the problems facing the nation at that time.

A flowering of the idea that education is a social process, the primary and most effective instrument of social reconstruction, came with the work and writings of Dewey and his followers. The main thesis of this group was that the school is not merely a residual institution to maintain things as they are: education has a creative function to play in the shaping of individuals and through them in the shaping of the culture. Dewey consistently saw the function of the school in both psychological and social terms. As early as 1897 he wrote:

> I believe that: all education proceeds by the participation of the individuals in the social consciousness of the race. This process... is continually shaping the individual's powers, saturating his consciousness, forming his habits, training his ideas, and arousing his feelings and emotions.... The most formal and technical education in the world cannot safely depart from this general process.... This educational process has two sides—one psychological, and one sociological and... neither can be subordinated to the other, or neglected, without evil consequences... knowledge of social conditions of the present state of civilization is necessary in order to properly interpret the child's powers... and that the school is primarily a social institution.

In subsequent development one fork of this dual orientation of Dewey on the function of education matured into an elaboration of the social responsibilities of the school, while the other centered more emphatically on individual development.

Dewey's concept of democracy was that of an intentionally progressive society, committed to change, organized as intelligently and as scientifically as possible. The role of education in such a society is to inculcate the habits that would make it possible for individuals to control their surroundings rather than merely to submit to them. A progressive society would "endeavor to shape the experience of the young so that instead of reproducing current habits, better habits shall be formed, and thus the future adult society be an improvement on their own.... We are doubtless far from realizing the potential efficacy of education as a constructive agency of improving society, from realizing that it represents not only a development of children and youth but also of the future society of which they will be the constituents."

This viewpoint dictated priorities for curriculum. Dewey was concerned that essentials be placed first and refinements second, but he defined as essentials the things which are most fundamental socially, which have to do with experience shared by the widest groups. He was also deeply critical of the dualism between culture and vocation and concerned with the effects on democracy of a scheme of education in which there is a narrow utilitarian education for one class of people and a broad liberal education for another. In addition to insisting on the cultivation of the "method of intelligence" and of scientific inquiry as the first tasks of the curriculum, he also stressed the necessity of introducing vocational subjects not merely to build utilitarian skills but as "points of departure" for increasingly intellectualized ventures into the life and meaning of industrial society.

The subsequent elaborations of the social function of the school took on several different shadings, which ranged from emphasis on changing society by changing individuals to stress on planned reconstruction of the social system.

Some of the elaborations stress primarily the responsibility of the school to meet current social needs. The deeper interpretation of this responsibility involves shaping the school program according to a long-term perspective on the realities of the changing society, and an adequate study of a whole range of social needs. A shallower interpretation makes demands on the school on behalf of immediate difficulties and problems. The current insistence on redoubled study of mathematics and physical science, growing in part out of the "somewhat adolescent feeling of national humiliation" at Soviet advances in missile technology and in part out of temporary anxieties regarding manpower needs in these fields, illustrates the shallow perspective.

Others see the social function of education as one of promoting a critical orientation toward the current scene. This interpretation has led to an emphasis on problem solving in the social sciences and to the introduction of problem courses. An emphasis on an understanding of the social forces that generate cultural lag and dislocation is part of this orientation. Some educators interpret the social function of education chiefly as an instrument for social change, either through gradual reform by reshaping the outlook of the oncoming generation or through planned effort at reconstruction.

But whatever the variations in concepts of the social functions of education, certain fundamental ideas tend to run through all. One is the understanding that education must, and usually does, work in the cultural setting of a given society, at a given time, in a given place, shaping the individual in some measure to participate in that society. All decisions about education, including those about curriculum, are made within the context of a society. The values and forces of that society determine not only what manner of man exists but also to some extent what manner of man is needed. The decision-makers themselves are immersed in the culture and therefore subject to the culturally conditioned conceptions of how education is to serve that society. As Childs puts it, the schools are doubly social in nature. They are the arm instituted by society for the education of the young. But the very materials which constitute the program of the school are also drawn from the life of that society.

This concept means that not only is intellectual training to be directed to understanding the forces of the culture and to mastering the intellectual tools necessary for that understanding, but also that there is a fundamental responsibility for training in the culture's essential values and loyalties. In this view, then, social cohesion depends not so much on transmission of the common knowledge as the sharing of common values and concerns.

A second important element in these concepts is the profound appreciation of the fact of change in modern culture and of the meaning of social change. If the society and the culture are changing, then it is the task of schools to play a constructive role in that change. Education must adjust its aims and program to changing conditions, and, if possible, foreshadow them, especially under the conditions of rapid change introduced by modern technology. Without a continual reorientation to changing conditions, education becomes unreal and in a sense useless because it does not prepare youth for life's problems and responsibilities. To meet changing conditions means, of course, that both the aims of education and the programs devised to implement these aims, including the orientation brought to bear on materials used, must be changed also. It is of central importance to use critical intelligence (not intellectuality as described in the preceding section) and scientific attitudes in understanding and solving human and social problems. These qualities of mind can be cultivated to the extent that the "subject matter" of education is significant to the ongoing experience and concerns of the culture, and that experience is used as the key for giving meaning to knowledge and for translating subject matter into behavior and action.

The third important element of this concept is the idea that education is a moral undertaking. It begins and ends with value decisions. Educational decisions, whether regarding aims or curricular selections, always involve value judgments. For this reason education always will involve an element of prescription. Although scientific inquiry will determine what is, it will not prescribe what should be. Education is a moral enterprise also in that it selects which parts of the culture, what wisdom, which values, what ideals to transmit. No school in any society can be completely neutral; the difference lies in whether the basis for selection is made clear and whether the selection is made with some degree of rational method and scientific inquiry.

The concept of education as a reconstruction of society goes further than any of the above. The proponents of this view speak of education as management and control of social change and as social engineering, and of educators as statesmen. The idea that education should not only foster changes in society but should change the very social order was first expressed by Counts. It was later reiterated in *The Educational Frontier,* the thesis of which was that the task of education is "to prepare individuals to take part intelligently in the management of conditions under which they live, to bring them to an understanding of the forces which are moving, to equip them with the intellectual tools by which they can themselves enter into the direction of these forces." To implement such an education it would be necessary to launch a massive adult program that would build political and educational support for a radically different school curriculum, to develop a public which is education conscious and wise in the realities of industrial civilization, to reorient professional education, and to alert teachers to the pressing social issues of the day.

More recently a group of educators who call themselves the "reconstructionists" have argued in a similar vein and with the same sense of urgency about the social mission of education. In analyzing the orientation needed for developing a curriculum theory, B. Othanel Smith concludes by observing: "It is clear that the time for building a comprehensive social perspective is here. We are now living in a time when we can no longer depend upon custom and unconscious control to regulate our social existence. There is no longer any substitute for human management of the vast social machine. As a people we have much knowledge of and techniques for social engineering. The question is: can we learn to use it rapidly enough to control the social machine before it either enslaves us or destroys us?"

The main theses of the reconstructionist position are somewhat as follows: the transformation of society by technological and scientific revolution is so radical as to require a new moral and intellectual consensus capable of molding and directing this transformation. It is the task of educators to analyze the social trends, to discern the problems society is facing, to speculate on the consequences of the current social dynamics, and to project the values and the goals which need to be sought to maintain a democratic way of life. Because social changes today are rapid and radical, and because there are blind consequences to the technological revolution which seem to endanger the democratic way of life, tradition is a poor guide. A continuous critical reexamination of the meaning of the democratic way of life under the altered social conditions is needed. Critical examination and reconstruction of the cultural heritage—or social ideas, beliefs, and institutions—in the light of current problems and conditions, rather than inculcation of traditional ideas, must constitute the core of the educational program of today. In addition, educators must be statesmen, and in cooperation with other agencies must study and discuss the implication of the new "intellectual and moral order" for the "institutional structure of society."

In this scheme a rather exalted role is allotted to education and the schools. Educators must take close account of social forces, of the social institutions, and of their educative effects. They must translate this knowledge of culture and society into "educational policy," that is, a curriculum which will aid students in understanding these forces and in developing the techniques and attitudes necessary for participation in democratic reconstruction. The total educative impact of the school must encompass and coordinate changes in beliefs, personality structures, and social arrangements. Educators must carry the rest of the community to an agreement with their proposals. Curriculum planning needs to focus on building "social goals" and a "common social orientation." Individual goals and diverse group goals must be integrated into a system of social ends. Curriculum development in this sense becomes a way of making public policy.

The capacity of education in general and of public schools in particular to assume a leading role in changing the society and particularly the social structure has been seriously questioned. To sociologists concerned with the relationship of school and society it seems altogether unrealistic for schools to be animated by goals which differ radically from those of the culture in which they work. They point out that usually the aims of education are conservative —that is, they are consonant with the conceptions of the ideal adult which society wishes to produce—and educational institutions can pursue only those aims that society considers desirable. Historically, the aims of education have shifted, but these shifts have followed, not preceded, the changes in society's ideals of a desirable adult. It is therefore somewhat utopian to think of education as a means for a radical reconstruction of society, such as a new social order.

Other critics suggest, in addition, that it is easy to exaggerate both the actual and the potential ability of any formal institution, including the schools, to contribute to consensus in society, whether the means to achieve this consensus be the formation of basic personality or inculcation of a common set of values. This is especially so in industrial societies with their mass patterns of educational service, in which instruction looms larger than education, and in school settings in which it is impossible except under extreme conditions either to isolate or to exclude from its personnel those groups who do not share the dominant goals of the institution. It is possible, of course, that the sociologists and other critics may because of their own limited insight into the dynamics of the educational process underestimate what schools can do. The conditions under which creative educational aims can be conceived and implemented might well form the subject of further serious study and research.

5.2 THEODORE R. SIZER

Horace's Hope: What Works for the American High School

In the selection that follows, Theodore R. Sizer discusses the possibilities for the future of the American public schools. He uses as the vehicle for his discussion the character of Horace Smith, a fictional high school teacher who Sizer first portrayed in *Horace's Compromise: The Dilemma of the American High School* in 1992. In *Horace's Hope: What Works for the American High School* (Houghton Mifflin, 1996), from which the following selection has been taken, Sizer outlines the current debate on school reform and the renewed dialogue on how to improve the public schools.

In his discussion, Sizer notes the obstacles to change in the field of public education. He argues that public schools should be funded primarily at the state level rather than at the local level in order to better equalize the funding of schooling for all students. He further supports "choice" in terms of tax funds for schooling following students into either public or private schools and contends that such a policy is consistent with current public sentiment. Sizer believes that the current dialogue under way regarding how to create alternative visions of academic excellence in schools will lead to great variety in the modes of schooling as well as to higher levels of student achievement. Sizer concludes that Horace Smith has grounds to be hopeful regarding the future of public education.

Sizer served as dean of the Harvard Graduate School of Education for several years. He is a professor at Brown University and one of the founders of the Coalition for Essential Schools, an effort to help schools develop better educational programs based on nine common principles of education. Some of his other books include *Places for Learning, Places for Joy* (Harvard University Press, 1973) and *Horace's School: Redesigning the American High School* (Houghton Mifflin, 1993).

Key Concept: the future of American public education

*H*orace Smith, to the surprise of many of his colleagues, is hopeful about the future of American public education. Horace has hope not because he believes that there will be a return to some purported good old days or that the status quo is fine, bedeviled only by a temporary public relations problem. Quite the contrary. And that is what his colleagues who cannot fathom his optimism do not understand.

I have learned to share Horace's hope, ... however I absorb the sour messages abroad about schools and schooling, about incompetent teachers, rigid bureaucracies, embarrassing test scores, lazy and indulgent students, and high budgets.

Paradoxically, perhaps, all the public controversy itself provides a cause for hope. It is not that all the criticisms are well taken and all those at work in public education deserve the raking-over they are getting. It is, rather, that the invective, whether accurate or far off the mark, has legitimized a searching rethinking of what schooling is all about. What used to be unsayable now is being said—and listened to. No idea is peremptorily dismissed. The taxing ambiguities have brought a freshening of ideas.

For many, this is a frightening moment. It is also a highly promising one. Out of such turbulence can come better schools—or worse, Horace knows, if we blow the opportunity the times are providing us. To my eye, however, some of the trends are very much in the right direction.

Horace Smith is part of a grass-roots movement for reform, one given increasing running room by those very public authorities who are now so assaulted with criticism. It is not without hassle: the lurches of state legislatures, state departments of education, and school boards are a nuisance and often a barrier to the changes Horace wishes to make. Inappropriate regulations, poorly designed but influential assessment systems, and tighter and more paranoid collective bargaining agreements get in the way.

Nonetheless, school-level reform now has visible momentum. This momentum and the increasing public attention that it is receiving are important. As the reform quickens, Horace Smith can take its imperatives as much into account as he takes the dictates from above. Pressure to try new ways to do better has its own authority and public approval and is every bit as powerful as the pressure that says, "Do what you are told and toe the line." Horace is getting into the habit of saying that he won't do as he is told if he is told to do something mindless or ill-advised.

Today there is something for Horace to join, something to make cause with, something that is not wholly a creation of government and the corrosive politics that currently infests so much of it, something that speaks directly to the compromises that so dismay him. It is something more than mere talk, something with an edge, something to do. This something may be an identifiable enterprise, such as the Coalition of Essential Schools, or Dr. James Comer's School Development Project, or E. D. Hirsch's Core Knowledge Foundation, or the Accelerated Schools Project, led by Henry Levin, or Harvard Project Zero. Or, more likely, it may be an informal but sustained gathering of earnest friends or a fresh attitude found in a faculty room or at the meetings of a regional professional group. It gives hope, and the energy to tackle persistent compromises that hope inspires. As a veteran teacher told his younger colleagues at a meeting which I recently attended, "I don't have to apologize anymore." Here and there, more and more, the compromises are being addressed from the grass roots, often in spite of the higher-ups.

Horace knows that the stereotype of the teacher is a crabbed one, and that many in his profession, which is devoted to the task of helping young people learn to use their minds well, have little idea what serious intellectual work in fact involves. They have rarely experienced it themselves, having been through an educational system, including college, that rewarded them for merely showing up and passing through, rather than for presenting serious, rigorous academic work. As a result, coming up with demanding intellectual work for the adolescents they teach is difficult, often poignant labor. It starts with the teachers themselves.

Many critics thus protest. Give authority to these school-level people, with all their well-documented limitations? They will botch it. This, however, is a self-fulfilling prophecy. Tell people of any age that they are not to be trusted, and they will soon believe it and act accordingly. Give a job authority and accountability and able people will flock to it. They will especially gravitate to teaching, with its inherent excitement, variety, and legitimate sense of service—a phenomenon long seen in some private schools and prestigious public magnet schools (not all of which serve only well-scrubbed, academically inclined students) and increasingly seen today.

Horace also appreciates what so many far from the neighborhoods and their schools fail to see: the stubborn quality of decency in so many citizens. There are, as always, the complainers and the people who walk away from their responsibilities for their children. However, too much can be made of them: they are good newspaper copy. Many more people rally around in most communities, especially in an emergency.

Take heart from the school's neighbors? Some will think Horace is blind. The people care? Yes, Horace tells me, the parents and many parents by association (most of us older citizens) do give a damn, and if we see a way to help our public schools, we join in. True, if we are patronized or told that we can briefly "advise" and then "come aboard" when we have had little role in shaping a plan, we tune out. I have experienced happy engagement recently with parents and community members starting a regional public charter school. Meetings of its board of trustees, as provided by the state's legislation for all public schools, are open to all, but the engagement at this school is special. Parents—on the board and in the audience—raise issues, shape the agenda, insistently demand to be consulted, heard, involved, put to work, respected. All feel the power that comes with having chosen this school.

A recent meeting dealt with the "tone of decency" (as the agenda put it) of the school, and it eventually spilled into the collective "tone of decency" of the school's larger community, including what happens at home. (Were rap CDs that are contemptuous of and vicious toward women tolerated at home at the same time that they were banned from school? If so, what does this teach?) This kind of involvement, while it leads to long meetings, will surely serve the children well. Of course, it is possible only in human-scale communities, ones that have real authority over their work. Roaring debates at meetings of school boards representing large constituencies are usually led by factions and special-interest groups. The voice of a parent of a particular youngster with a particular problem is rarely heard, and the energy and commitment of that parent is thus rarely energized.

If people of any age are treated with the dignity they deserve, they respond, in community after community. We see it daily. Often it takes a crisis—a flood on the Mississippi or a bombing on Wall Street or in Oklahoma City—to highlight it. It is patently there. It is a cause for hope.

Doomsayers say that democracy is dying. The number of registered voters who cast ballots drops. The pundits suggest to us, persuasively, that Americans are disgusted with their politicians, that they distrust the system and the government that is its agent. However, being disgusted with the status quo does not mean that we are giving up on democracy. Paradoxically, the opposite is true. So many are unhappy precisely because we believe in the system. We know it can work, and we believe that the alternatives are much worse than the system of government we now have, warts and all.

We complain when we see organized forces outside the democratic system seizing excessive influence. We are sick of being manipulated and lied to ("I merely misspoke . . . "), of being the subjects not of respectful persuasion but of an advertising campaign, of being targets of the same sort of sell that gets us to buy a deodorant or cigarettes. We believe that the American way is better than that and that blatant influence-peddling corrupts what we admire.

People do not want to be patronized and manipulated by their government. They want government to work. They want to admire their government. Is this naive, sentimental patriotism? Not entirely, and there is nothing necessarily wrong with patriotism. We should note the extraordinary surge of interest in local action that followed President Clinton's announcement of Ambassador Walter Annenberg's $500 million personal challenge to the nation for school reform. Annenberg's simple idea—that democracy is at risk of destruction through neglect and violence and that local public schools are the necessary and principal bulwark to resist this decay—struck a powerful chord. Sentimental? Perhaps. Purposeful? Certainly. Realistic? It has to be. What is the alternative, save more decay? People have stepped forward.

There is a host of examples. For instance, I have seen an explosion of energy in parents and local citizens in support of a new district high school in which they will have a respected role and which is designed with their particular children, rather than some stereotype of a child of a certain age (hatched in a remote office building), in mind. A sense of community responsibility is latent in many American neighborhoods, I have found, even those that are racked by poverty and crime or awash in the entitlements of affluence. Too many Americans know that their worlds can be better, that with encouragement those worlds are theirs and they can take charge of them. Give people a cause worth following and the dignity of a necessary role for everyone of every age and they will respond—not quickly or easily, perhaps, but if patiently gathered, they will respond.

I am invited to graduations at Essential schools. Several in communities serving low-income families stick especially in my mind. Most of the young people at these schools have stayed the course, have not dropped out, and have publicly presented their final Exhibitions. Many who never dreamed of going to college are going to college.

Their families know this, and the atmosphere at these gatherings is electric. At one school, student after student gave brief remarks, one coming up after another, spontaneously. Their sustained theme was a poignant and powerful one: "We did what America did not believe we could do." The momentum of this message at this particular gathering—a sad message in its way, as it reminded those assembled that these adolescents knew they were perceived to be people of limited merit—gained force as the long ceremony, some of it colorfully out of control, seemed to burst forth in radiant optimism and determination. Such young people are the fuel of hope. Their schools have made a difference for them, a life-altering difference. Horace has good reason to be hopeful.

The likely shape of a different and useful system of American schools—one created in large part anew—is dimly visible. Key details are still murky and still very much in play, but some outlines are there. The best of these follow.

There will be choice. Every family (not just rich families) will have the ability —indeed, the obligation—to choose among schools for their children. The state will assure that parents do in fact have meaningful choices among schools.

The substance, standard, and culture of each school will be shaped significantly by the families who choose it and the staff who elect to work at it rather than primarily by the deliberations of those families' and the larger communities' elected representatives. Schools will thus differ from one another, often significantly.

Finance will completely or largely be a state (rather than a local) responsibility, and the money will follow the child directly, the full per-pupil allotment going to his or her school. The drift toward state rather than local funding has been under way since the early 1970s. It will continue.

To be a truly public school, worthy of state funding, each school, wherever it is located, will admit every applicant from that state; if there are more applicants than places at the school, it will admit students by lottery. No public policy can more dramatically create the truly common school than this. Civil rights should not and do not need to be weakened by a system of parental choice.

Given general state funding, accountability by and for the schools will be due both to those who chose them—the families, who come first—and to the state. Given the rights of the former, each school should be accountable for the way in which it presents itself and the standard of its work. The state will regularly inspect that school on the basis of the school's own assessment design, objecting only in the most severe cases. The state's essential obligation will be to insist on frequent and public displays by each school of its progress, defined largely by the observable work of its students, which will help provide parents with an accurate picture of the schools. Wise schools will engage outside authorities of their choice to assist in their assessment and public display as they do today with both profit-making and nonprofit agencies, from test publishers to the College Board.

Gradually a spectrum between traditional schooling and formal home schooling will evolve, with what takes place in any one schoolhouse deliberately orchestrated with serious learning activity at home, usually at a computer or book, at a workplace, in an orchestra, as part of a team, as a member of a small neighborhood seminar that is an extension of a larger regional school. "Homework" will change its meaning. Rather than being only studies supplementary to classroom work, it will become activity that is largely independent of the daily, formal school routine, especially for older students. The standard to which the students are held will be met by work at and beyond the formal schoolhouse. The expectation will be that each adolescent will prepare for that standard beyond the immediate shepherding of his teacher in school.

As this configuration of deliberate education emerges, technology—and particularly software—will adapt. Programs will be designed not only to reinforce classroom activity or to entertain in some educational way. They will be freestanding ventures, designed to be used in a variety of ways and organized to prepare a student for an ultimate Exhibition.

In this way students will go to multiple schools, places that in planned combination provide for formal education. For most contemporary adolescents, this will at first appear to call for just a modest change in behavior, as their learning is now influenced powerfully by multiple sources of information. What will be starkly new for them, however, is finding that these sources can and must be taken seriously. Educators, parents, and the media and publishing industries will have to create incentives for students to use all of these sources resolutely —no mean feat. But it will happen, because that is the way the culture increasingly educates itself and because configurations make as much financial as educational sense. Better yet is the fact that these "beyond the schoolhouse" opportunities can at one leap transcend the boundaries of geography and thus of class, ethnicity, and race.

As a practical matter, *systems of schools will emerge,* each representing a particular educational style or opportunity and each governing itself within state authority. For example, one set of schools might emphasize a particular teaching approach, such as that arising from the work of Maria Montessori or from E. D. Hirsch's Core Knowledge Foundation or from the Coalition of Essential Schools. Another might involve a substantial system of computer-driven connected instruction. Others might emphasize, for adolescents, substantial time and formal learning in a workplace other than a traditional school building. The momentum of tradition and expected practice will, at least for a generation, hold these approaches to substantial common ground, as they do today. The temptation of central authorities to micro-manage them, however, will have to be stoutly resisted. These systems of schools would overlap. The options available to families would appear much like those now represented by higher education.

Choice. Variety. Truly open schools. Equitable finance. Power deliberately tilted toward the families of the children served and the professionals who teach them. The deliberate use of various orchestrated configurations of learning, not just the schoolhouse. All of these issues are more or less on the political table today. Over the past decade, interest in them has picked up substantial momentum.

These ideas are consistent with the drift of contemporary public sentiment as expressed in policy or implicitly, by what is happening in practice. They reflect the prevalent view that centralized government is an inept and inappropriate tool to set and shape the substance and standards of school policy and practice. They reflect the view that disproportional authority for these purposes should be given to the families affected and the professionals to whom those families entrust their children. Centralized government is needed as a financier (that is, the dispenser of the people's money), as a documenter, persuader, supporter, advocate for neglected children, truth-teller, but not, except at the extremes, a director.

These ideas reflect the belief that a market—involving competition and real choice among schools—is a better, if not complete or perfect, regulator of schooling than the traditional educational and political authorities and their expert allies in the teaching profession.

They reflect a prominent view loudly expressed today in the context of the debate over national health care: I wish to choose my own doctor rather than be assigned one by the state. In like manner, I wish to pick my children's school rather than have the state do the choosing.

These ideas address reality, however painful or inconvenient that reality is. They are attuned to the extraordinary variety of communities and interests in this country, a variety that is ill served by centralized control, which usually demands standardization. What works well for a small town in northeastern Arizona might be inappropriate for a precinct in Pittsburgh. These ideas recognize and dignify our diversity.

They provide an end run around the *Milliken* decision of the United States Supreme Court, which ruled that the suburbs (usually wealthy and white) have no constitutional responsibility to join in racial integration with the school systems in the central cities (usually poor and disproportionately nonwhite). If the money follows the child and if that child's family can enter him or her in its school of choice, *wherever that may be*—a school that must admit all applicants, using a lottery system if necessary, in order to receive public funding—the opportunity for more class and racial integration, where it is desired, can proceed. Currently it cannot proceed at all, at least for the poor, even if some families —poor and rich—wish that it could. Geographical boundaries, mostly reflecting the demographic and political priorities of the past, dictate current school policy. These boundaries will be pierced.

These ideas address the fact that there are deep and understandable disagreements not only among citizens but among experts on just what an excellent education might be and how we would know it when we saw it. In the emerging public school system, no one point of view dominates; the market of ideas allows both variety and contention among serious positions. This will be untidy, and those who believe that there is a virtue in cultural orderliness will no doubt be unhappy. Unfortunately, our world is untidy, free minds are untidy, and to be genuine and useful, our institutions must reflect that rather than present a spurious uniformity.

They address the compromises that so trouble Horace Smith, by providing channels and incentives for the creation of new schools or the redesign of existing schools that follow more sensible regimens than those now widely in use and largely cemented in place by regulatory practice. This encourages Horace, keeps him at his work, and attracts imaginative and talented people into the school business.

These ideas carry with them important side effects. They imply that school leaders must become more entrepreneurial than exclusively managerial, becoming leaders of schools that have a distinct character rather than agents of someone else's idea of what a school ought to be.

They put an extraordinary responsibility on the profession and the academic community at large to seek out and place before the public evidence of what is working in schools, by a variety of definitions, and what is not, and to define what kinds of investment different goals require, thus pushing into visibility the weaknesses and strengths of the diverse schools that citizens are choosing among. The watchdogs have to be the people themselves, not central governments (except at the extremes, such as when a school gives evidence of appalling neglect or has doctored evidence about its graduates' performance).

These ideas will challenge, directly or by circumvention, the elaborate thickets of educational regulation, certification, and accreditation, which more often than not reflect the vagaries of past academic politics and distrust of local authorities rather than considered and proven practices. They depend on persuasion rather than coercive control.

These systems will be messy, both in their diversity and in the confrontations that will result from their competition. Many will find this aggravating, undercutting the (spurious) spirit of togetherness expressed by main-line education groups.

But these ideas force a test of the proposition that healthy democracy depends on an ultimate trust in and of the people, no matter how small the unit in which the people are gathered for a particular purpose is. Either we trust the people or we don't.

These ideas challenge the notion that the primary purpose of the public schools is to teach a common culture, an American way, American ideals. Diversity is centrifugal, some will argue; the common school is the only way to give coherence to what it is to be an American. However, the reality is that we have in the media the most powerful common carrier of mass culture in history. It is so powerful that its existence changes the necessary role for schools from creators of the culture to respectful critics of that culture.

In this regard, the federal government has new and heavy responsibilities. The mass media must be seen as a fundamental piece of public education, a full participant with the schools. Federal responsibility might play out in a number of ways. The financing of useful programming and the maintenance of independent channels devoted to educational purposes is a clear governmental responsibility. Free access by all citizens to the artistic and intellectual treasures of the society must become an absolute right, like free public education itself. The electronic library is the lineal descendant of the public library and is crucial for the support of an intelligent people. Its costs should be wholly met by a tax on those making commercial use of the common good represented by the broadcast channels. There is growing public sentiment for these ideas, only just now powerful enough to affect federal policy.

The outlines of a new kind of public education, then, are visible. One danger is that government will adopt the easy parts and ignore the difficult ones, such as providing fair compensatory funding or access to technology for each poor or handicapped child, or providing access to any publicly financed school in the state, not only those within a historically established district. Another is that the leap from dependence on a rule-driven hierarchical system to trust of families is more than the political system can tolerate and the temptation on the part of the state to keep control will be too strong. Loosening control is always more difficult than tightening it. A third is the danger that removing education from the administrative status it now enjoys within government, weak though that is, will lessen leaders' interest in keeping an eye on the educational needs of its citizens.

All these concerns are real ones. Are they greater than those implicit in going along with the present system? We must always measure the risks of the new against those of the old. The reality is that the currents toward a new sort of American educational system are already flowing. There can be no turning back. The trick will be to understand those new currents and to ride, and thus direct, the best of them.

The traditional American system of schools was in large measure designed exactly a century ago. It has served us well, but times and conditions change. America in 1995 is not the America of 1895. Not surprisingly, a new system of schools is emerging, one that is more complex and potentially more powerful than the one we inherited. If wisely and resolutely shaped, such a system can serve the people and democracy well. Such is a source of Horace's hope. . . .

Public education is an idea not a structure. The idea is that every citizen must have access to the culture and to the means of enriching that culture. It arises from the belief that we are all equal as citizens, and that we all thereby have rights and obligations to serve the community as well as ourselves. To meet those obligations, we must use our informed intelligence. Schools for all assure the intelligence of the people, the necessary equipment of a healthy democracy. A wise democracy invests in that equipment.

Public education, then is not at all or necessarily the same thing as our current system of schools. Other means to give the people access and intelligence— new configurations of educating institutions—may be better, more appropriate to our time, more respectful of current exigencies. If we are wise, we will consider them, however much they may challenge the conventional ways of doing things.

To the extent that we embrace that challenge and the fundamental American philosophy behind it—that a free and powerful education is the absolute right of every citizen and that this education must be first and foremost seen as the mainspring of a democratic community—we can be hopeful.

For Horace Smith, the hope is also more personal, arise from the particular adolescents all around him—their color and brashness, their gawkiness, their risk-taking, their naiveté about the world, which sucks so many of them into optimism, however unrealistic. The high theater of the school hallway never ceases to amuse him, and the diversions of the kids' little passions tickle his love of fiction, creating tiny comic stories in his head. The dance of youth is timeless and beautiful in its awkwardness.

Most of the young people are resilient in the face of either the lures of affluence or the savagery of neglect. Horace worries more about them than they do about themselves, and he is ashamed when it dawns on his students how little American culture actually values them. Most of the kids, however, sweep this away, not so much with anger as with tacit rejection. *To hell with you, old-timer. We'll go it on our own, and we'll make it.*

Horace knows that some will and many won't. But the energy is there, fueled as much by inexperience as by grit. With all its unreality, it yet insistently radiates the strength and inventiveness of humankind. In dark days, such light brings hope.

CHAPTER 6 Curriculum Development and the Language of Educational Debate

6.1 PETER McLAREN

Multiculturalism and the Postmodern Critique

Peter McLaren is an associate professor of administration, curriculum, and teaching studies. He earned his Ph.D. in curriculum and educational theory in 1983 from the Ontario Institute for Studies in Education at the University of Toronto, Canada. His current research interests include postcolonial and postmodern theories as applied to curriculum development and instruction. He has published many books, including *Critical Pedagogy and Predatory Culture: Oppositional Politics in the Postmodern Era* (Routledge, 1995) and *Schooling as a Ritual Performance: Towards a Political Economy of Educational Symbols and Gestures,* 2d ed. (Routledge, 1993).

The selection that follows is from "Multiculturalism and the Postmodern Critique: Toward a Pedagogy of Resistance and Transformation," in Henry A. Giroux and Peter McLaren, eds., *Between Borders: Pedagogy and the Politics of Cultural Studies.* In it, McLaren offers insight into the state

132

*Chapter 6
Curriculum
Development
and the
Language of
Educational
Debate*

of injustice in present-day society and discusses how the struggle for social justice can be engaged by educators and other cultural workers. McLaren positions the discussion of "multiculturalism" in the competing social and ideological contexts of our time. He argues that a "resistance" postmodernist method of social critique can help teachers and students to clarify issues relating to "difference" and "diversity" and the importance of accepting cultural and personal differences and diversity.

McLaren argues that social and personal justice needs to be continually created—that the quest for justice in society is a constant struggle. Educators and other cultural workers can help the young to position themselves in this struggle by learning to define and locate their own voices in their own localities in critiquing local and national social practices and policies. He points out that in applying resistance postmodernist methods of social critique, individuals need to always rethink the relationship between identity and difference. A resistance postmodernist educational critique, McLaren maintains, must *not* see cultural differences as merely "other than white"; the concept of white ethnicity must itself be critiqued as part of creating accurate awareness of its hegemonic (dominating) impact.

Key Concept: multiculturalism and postmodernism

For the proletariat does not need all the thousands of little words by which the bourgeoisie masks class struggles in its own pedagogy. The "unprejudiced," "understanding," "empathetic" bourgeoisie practices, the "child-loving" teachers—these we can do without.

—Walter Benjamin, "Program for a Proletarian Children's Theater"

SOCIAL JUSTICE UNDER SIEGE

We inhabit skeptical times, historical moments spawned in a temper of distrust, disillusionment, and despair. Social relations of discomfort and diffidence have always preexisted us but the current historical juncture is particularly invidious in this regard, marked as it is by a rapture of greed, untempered and hypereroticized consumer will, racing currents of narcissism, severe economic and racial injustices, and heightened social paranoia. The objective conditions of Western capitalism now appear so completely incompatible with the realization of freedom and liberation that it is no understatement to consider them mutually antagonistic enterprises. Situated beyond the reach of ethically convincing forms of accountability, capitalism has dissolved the meaning of democracy and freedom into glossy aphorisms one finds in election campaign sound bytes or at bargain basement sales in suburban shopping malls. The American public has been proffered a vision of democracy that is a mixture of Sunday barbecue banality, American Gladiator jocksniffery, AMWAY enterprise consciousness, and the ominous rhetoric of "New World Order" jingoism.

The heroic cult of modernism which has naturalized the power and privilege of "dead white men" and accorded the pathology of domination the status of cultural reason has all but enshrined a history of decay, defeat, and moral panic. As illustrated so vividly in Oliver Stone's television mini-series, *Wild Palms*, greed, avarice, and cynicism have insinuated themselves into virtually every aspect of cultural life, and have become rationalized and aestheticized as necessary resources that must be fed into a vast technological machine known as Western civilization. It is history that has installed Willie Horton into our structural unconscious and helped make possible and desirable the legal torture and dehumanization of Rodney King and peoples of color in general. That the fortified, postmodern *noir* metropolises of this fin-de-siècle era have grown more Latinophobic, homophobic, xenophobic, sexist, racist, and bureaucratically cruel is not reflective of the self-understanding of the public at large but of the way that the public has been constructed through a politics of representation linked to the repressive moralism of the current conservative political regime and current counterattacks on cultural democracy from the Right. We should not forget, as well, the spectatorial detachment of those postmodern free-floating intellectuals who, despite their claim to be part of a collective deconstructive project, often fail to mobilize intellectual work in the interest of a liberatory praxis.

The present moral apocalypse, perhaps most vividly represented by the maelstrom of anger and violence under the smoke-filled skies of Los Angeles—what Mike Davis calls the "L.A. Intifada" (Katz and Smith, 1992)—has not been brought on simply by the existence of midnight hustlers, the drug trade, skewered ambition, or gang members taking advantage of public outrage over the justice system but by shifting economic, political, and cultural relations that have worsened over the last two decades. We have been standing at the crossroads of a disintegrating culture for the last two decades where we have witnessed a steady increase in the disproportionate level of material wealth, economic dislocation, and intergenerational poverty suffered by African-Americans, Latinos, and other minorities. Such conditions have been brought about by the frenetic and, at times, savage immorality of the Reagan and Bush administrations, as evidenced in their direct attacks on the underclass, the disintegration of social programs, and the general retreat from civil rights that occurred during their tenure in office.

Other characteristics of this current juncture include: changes in the structure of the U.S. economy; the declining inner-city job market; growing national "unemployment rates; a drastic decline in the number of unskilled positions in traditional blue-collar industries in urban areas; the increasing numbers of youth competing for fewer and fewer entry-level unskilled jobs; the automation of clerical labor; the movement of the African-American middle class out of the once multiclass ghetto; the shifting of service-sector employment to the suburbs" (Kasinitz 1988); the destructive competition among nations that results from a free-trade policy fueled by the retrograde notion that other nations can achieve economic growth by unbalanced sales to the U.S. market; increased global competition provoking capitalist manufacturing firms to reduce costs by exploiting immigrant workers in U.S. cities or "out-sourcing" to Third World countries; and a post-Fordist demonopolization of economic structures and the

134

*Chapter 6
Curriculum
Development
and the
Language of
Educational
Debate*

deregulation and globalization of markets, trade, and labor as well as deregulated local markets "that [make] local capital vulnerable to the strategies of corporate raiders" (Featherstone 1990, 7).

In addition, we are faced with an increasing assault on human intelligence by the architects of mass culture, an increasing dependency on social cues manufactured by the mass media to construct meaning and build consensus on moral issues, and the strengthening of what Piccone (1988, 9) has called the "unholy symbiosis of abstract individualism and managerial bureaucracies." The white-controlled media (often backed by victim-blaming white social scientists) have ignored the economic and social conditions responsible for bringing about in African-American communities what Cornel West has called a *"walking nihilism* of pervasive drug addiction, pervasive alcoholism, pervasive homicide, and an exponential rise in suicide" (cited in Stephanson 1988, 276).

Furthermore, the white media have generated the racially pornographic term "wilding" to account for recent acts of violence in urban centers by groups of young African-Americans (Cooper 1989). Apparently the term "wilding," first reported by New York City newspapers in relation to the Central Park rapists, was relevant only to the violence of black male youth, since it was conspicuously absent in press reports of the attack of white male youths on Yusef Hawkins in Bensonhurst (Wallace 1991). Thus, the postmodern image which many white people now entertain in relation to the African-American underclass is one constructed upon violence and grotesquery—a population spawning mutant Willie Horton–type youths who, in the throes of bloodlust, roam the perimeter of the urban landscape high on angel dust, randomly hunting whites with steep pipes.... Latino youth fare no better in the public eye.

THE DILEMMA OF POSTMODERN CRITIQUE AND THE DEBATE OVER MULTICULTURALISM

I have foregrounded the social and cultural situatedness of oppression as a background for my discussion of multiculturalism since I share Michele Wallace's conviction that the debates over multiculturalism cannot afford to have their connection to wider material relations occulted by a focus on theoretical issues divorced from the lived experiences of oppressed groups. She is worth quoting on this issue:

> Many individual events on the current cultural landscape conspire to make me obsessed with contemporary debates over "multiculturalism" in both the art world and the culture at large, but my concern in grounded first and foremost in my observation of the impact of present material conditions on an increasing sector of the population. These material conditions, which include widespread homelessness, joblessness, illiteracy, crime, disease (including AIDS), hunger, poverty, drug addiction, alcoholism as well as the various habits of ill health, and the destruction of the environment are (let's face it) the myriad social effects of late multinational capitalism. (1991, 6)

A focus on the material and global relations of oppression can help us to avoid reducing the "problem" of multiculturalism to simply one of attitudes and temperament or, in the case of the academy, to a case of textual disagreement and discourse wars. It also helps to emphasize the fact that in the United States the concoction called "multiculturalism," which has resulted from a forensic search for equality and the political ladling of the long-brewing "melting pot," has produced an aversion to rather than a respect for difference. Regrettably, multiculturalism has been too often transformed into a code word in contemporary political jargon that has been fulsomely invoked in order to divert attention from the imperial legacy of racism and social injustice in this country and the ways in which new racist formations are being produced in spaces culturally dedifferentiated and demonized by neoconservative platforms that anathematize difference through attacks on the concept of heterogeneous public cultures (see Ravitch 1990, 1991; Kimball 1991; Browder 1992).

In the sections that follow, I want to discuss recent articulations of the postmodern critique in order to examine the limitations of current conservative and liberal formulations of multiculturalism. In doing so, I would like to pose an alternative analysis. I shall argue that, despite its limitations for constructing an emancipatory politics, postmodern criticism can offer educators and cultural workers a means of problematizing the issue of difference and diversity in ways that can deepen and extend existing debates over multiculturalism, pedagogy, and social transformation. Certain new strands of postmodern critique that fall under the rubric of "political" and "critical" postmodernism deserve serious attention in this regard.

More specifically, I shall redraw the discussion of multiculturalism from the perspective of new strands of postmodern critique that emphasize the construction of "a politics of difference." I will conclude by urging critical educators to reclaim the importance of relational or global critique—in particular the concept of "totality"—in their efforts to bring history and materiality back into theoretical and pedagogical discourses. . . .

MULTICULTURALISM AND THE POSTMODERN CRITIQUE

In this section I want to bring a critical or resistance postmodernist perspective to bear on the issue of multiculturalism. For me, the key issue for critical educators is to develop a multicultural curriculum and pedagogy that attends to the specificity (in terms of race, class, gender, sexual orientation, etc.) of difference (which is in keeping with ludic postmodernism) yet at the same time addresses the commonality of diverse Others under the law with respect to guiding referents of freedom and liberation (which is in keeping with resistance postmodernism).

Viewed from the perspective of resistance postmodernism, the liberal and conservative attacks on multiculturalism as separatist and ethnocentric

136

*Chapter 6
Curriculum
Development
and the
Language of
Educational
Debate*

carry with them the erroneous assumption that North American society fundamentally constitutes social relations of uninterrupted accord. This view furthermore underscores the idea that North American society is largely a forum of consensus with different minority viewpoints simply accretively added on. This constitute a politics of pluralism which largely ignores the workings of power and privilege. More specifically, it "involves a very insidious exclusion as far as any structural politics of change is concerned: it excludes and occludes global or structural relations of power as 'ideological' and 'totalizing'" (Ebert forthcoming). In addition, it presupposes harmony and agreement —an undisturbed space in which differences can coexist. Yet such a presupposition is dangerously problematic. Chandra Mohanty (1989/90) notes that the difference cannot be formulated as negotiation among culturally diverse groups against a backdrop of presumed cultural homogeneity. Difference is the recognition that knowledges are forged in histories that are riven with differentially constituted relations of power; that is, knowledges, subjectivities, and social practices are forged within "asymmetrical and incommensurate cultural spheres" (1989/90, 181).

Too often liberal and conservative positions on diversity constitute an attempt to view culture as a soothing balm—the aftermath of historical disagreement—some mythical present where the irrationalities of historical conflict have been smoothed out. This is not only a disingenuous view of culture, it is profoundly dishonest. The liberal and conservative positions on culture also assume that justice already exists and needs only to be evenly apportioned. However, both teachers and students need to realize that justice does not already exist simply because laws exist. Justice needs to be continually created, constantly struggled for. The question that I want to pose to teachers is this: Do teachers and cultural workers have access to a language that allows them to sufficiently critique and transform existing social and cultural practices that are defended by liberals and conservatives as democratic? ...

CRITICAL PEDAGOGY: TEACHING FOR A HYBRID CITIZENRY AND MULTICULTURAL SOLIDARITY

"There's room for all at the rendez-vous of victory"

—Cesaire

Resistance postmodernism has figured prominently in the development of new forms of pedagogical praxis concerned with rethinking educational politics in a multicultural society (Giroux 1992; McLaren and Leonard, forthcoming; McLaren forthcoming; Aronwitz and Giroux 1991). Of particular significance is Giroux's concept of a "border pedagogy" which enables educators to affirm and legitimate local meanings and constellations of meanings that grow out of particular discursive communities but at the same time interrogate the interests, ideologies, and social practices that such knowledges serve when viewed from the perspective of more global economies of power and privilege.

A pedagogy informed significantly by resistance postmodernism suggests that teachers and cultural workers need to take up the issue of "difference" in ways that don't replay the monocultural essentialism of the "centrisms"—Anglocentrism, Eurocentrism, phallocentrism, androcentrism, and the like. They need to create a politics of alliance building, of dreaming together, of solidarity that moves beyond the condescensions of, say, "race awareness week," which actually serves to keep forms of institutionalized racism intact. A solidarity has to be struggled for that is not centered around market imperatives but develops out of the imperatives of freedom, liberation, democracy, and critical citizenship.

The notion of the citizen has been pluralized and hybridized, as Kobena Mercer notes, by the presence of a diversity of social subjects. Mercer is instructive in pointing out that "solidarity does not mean that everyone thinks the same way, it begins when people have the confidence to disagree over issues because they 'care' about constructing a common ground" (1990, 68). Solidarity is not impermeably solid but depends to a certain degree on antagonism and uncertainty. Timothy Maliqualim Simone calls this type of multiracial solidarity "geared to maximizing points of interaction rather than harmonizing, balancing, or equilibrating the distribution of bodies, resources, and territories" (1989, 191).

While guarding against the privileging of a false universalism, a false unity that denies the internal rifts of bodily desire, both teachers and students need to open themselves to the possibility of Otherness so that the particularity of individual being can become visible in relation to larger relations of power and privilege. Students especially need to be provided with opportunities to devise different assemblages of the self by dismantling and interrogating the different kinds of discursive segmentarity that inform their subjectivities, subverting those stratified and hierarchized forms of subjectivity that code the will, and developing nomadic forms of individual and collective agency that open up new assemblages of desire and modes of being-in-the-world (Grossberg 1988).

Educators must examine the development of pedagogical discourses and practices that demonize Others who are different (through transforming them into absence or deviance). A resistance postmodernism that takes multiculturalism seriously calls attention to the dominant meaning systems readily available to students—most of which are ideologically stitched into the fabric of Western imperialism and patriarchy. It challenges meaning systems that impose attributes on the Other under the direction of sovereign signifiers and tropes. And this means not directing all our efforts at understanding ethnicity as "other than white," but interrogating the culture of whiteness itself. This is crucial because unless we do this—unless we give white students a sense of their own identity as an emergent ethnicity—we naturalize whiteness as a cultural marker against which Otherness is defined. Coco Fusco warns that "to ignore white ethnicity is to redouble its hegemony by naturalizing it. Without specifically addressing white ethnicity there can be no critical evaluation of the construction of the other" (cited in Wallace 1991, 7). White groups need

138

*Chapter 6
Curriculum
Development
and the
Language of
Educational
Debate*

to examine their ethnic histories so that they are less likely to judge their own cultural norms as neutral and universal. "Whiteness" does not exist outside of culture but constitutes the prevailing social texts in which social norms are made and remade. As part of a politics of signification that passes unobserved into the rhythms of daily life, and a "politically constructed category parasitic on 'Blackness' " (West 1990, 29), "whiteness" has become the invisible norm for how the dominant culture measures its own civility.

With this in mind, a critical pedagogy that embraces a resistance postmodernism needs to construct a politics of refusal that can provide both the conditions for interrogating the institutionalization of formal equality based on the prized imperatives of a white, Anglo male world and for creating spaces to facilitate an investigation of the way in which dominant institutions must be transformed so that they no longer serve simply as conduits for a motivated indifference to victimization for a Euroimperial aesthetics, for depredations of economic and cultural dependency, and for the production of asymmetrical relations of power and privilege. . . .

INTENSIFYING THE OBVIOUS AND ACCELERATING THE MUNDANE

A pedagogy that takes resistance postmodernism seriously does not make the nativist assumption that knowledge is preontologically available and that various disciplinary schools of thought may be employed in order to tease our different readings of the same "commonsense" reality in a context of impartiality. Rather, the discourses that inform the educator's problematics are understood as constitutive of the very reality that he or she is attempting to understand. Consequently, the classroom is the site of the teacher's own embodiment in theory/discourse, ethical disposition as moral and political agent, and situatedness as a cultural worker within a larger narrative identity. In recognizing the important role played by "place" in any critical pedagogy, it should be clear that we are talking not about the physical milieu where knowledge is made visible within preordained and circumscribed limits but rather the textual space that one occupies and the effective space one creates as a teacher. In other words, the discursive practice of "doing pedagogy" does not simply treat knowledge outside of the way that it is taken up by both teachers and students *as a form of dialogue.* I am referring here to the multi-voicedness of democratic discourse not in the sense of unrestrained intersubjective exchange but rather as challenging "the logic of dialogue as equal linguistic exchange." Such a challenge involves interrogating the ideological interests of the speaker, the social overdeterminations of utterances, and the social context in which utterances are both historically produced and culturally understood (Hitchcock, 1993, 7). Knowledge can never be treated as a cultural artifact or possession that serves as a pristine, prefigurative source of cultural authenticity inviting unbiased analysis.

The project of critical pedagogy means bringing the laws of cultural representation face to face with their founding assumptions, contradictions, and paradoxes. It also means encouraging teachers to participate in the affective as well as intellectual cultures of the oppressed, and to challenge in the spirit of Ernst Bloch's "militant optimism" ethical and political quietism in the face of operating homilies such as "progress is inevitable" or what might seem like historical inevitability—a perspective that leads to the cult of the mausoleum. Educators can no longer project onto the student-as-Other that part of themselves that out of fear and loathing they rejected or subtracted from their identities in their attempt to become unified subjects—that "split-off" part of themselves which prevents them from becoming whole, that disfiguring surplus that they have cast out in order to become white or live in the thrall of racelessness, that metaphysical double that guarantees their own self-regarding autonomy. From this point of view, liberation is never an encapsulated fulfillment of some prefigured end constructed in the temple of memory but a lived tension between the duration of history and the discourse of possibility. It resides in an approach to the *"Aufhebung"*—our passing *into* the "not-yet," and seeking the immanent utopia in the crisis of meaning and the social relations that inform it. It is found, too, in the proleptic consciousness of liminality—the liberating intention of the reflective will caught in the "subjunctive" moment of the "ought" and disabused of metaphysical illusion. It is formed out of an ethical intent commensurate with the love that Paulo Freire and Che Guevara both argue constitutes the ground from which all revolutionary action should take place....

Educators need to do more than to help students redescribe or represent themselves in new ways—although the way we seek to imagine ourselves is an important step in the struggle for liberation. As Sander L. Gilman has pointed out in his study of stereotypes of sexuality, race, and madness, "we view our own images, our own mirages, our own stereotypes as embodying qualities that exist in the world. And we act upon them" (1985, 242). More specifically, a pedagogy must be made available to teachers that will enable them along with their students to outface the barrenness of postmodern culture by employing a discourse and set of social practices that will not be content with infusing their pedagogies with the postmodern élan of the ludic metropolitan intellectual, with resurrecting a nostalgic past which can never be reclaimed, or with redescribing the present by simply textualizing it, leaving in place its malignant hierarchies of power and privilege, its defining pathologies. For these latter acts only stipulate the lineage of and give sustenance to those social relations responsible for the very injustice critical educators are trying to struggle against. Educators need to stare boldly and unflinchingly into the historical present and assume a narrative space where conditions may be created where students can tell their own stories, listen closely to the stories of others, and dream the dream of liberation. Identity formation must be understood in terms of how subjectivity is contextually enacted within the tendential forces of history (Grossberg, 1992). The exploration of identity should consist of mapping one's subject position in the field of multiple relationships and should be preceded by a critique of hegemony (San Juan, Jr. 1992, 128). This suggests that educators and students need to uncouple themselves from the "disciplined mobilizations" that regulate their social lives and rearticulate the sites of their affective investments in order to create new strategies and alliances of struggle.

140

*Chapter 6
Curriculum
Development
and the
Language of
Educational
Debate*

A critical pedagogy also demands political and cultural tactics that can fight multiple forms of oppression yet achieve a cohesiveness with divergent social groups working toward liberatory goals. To this end, Chela Sandoval (1991) suggests that cultural workers develop "tactical subjectivities" which she describes as forms of oppositional and differential consciousness and counter-hegemonic praxis (which she discusses in the context of feminism). Tactical subjectivity enables teachers as social agents to recenter their multiple subjectivities with respect to the kind of oppression that is being confronted and "permits the practitioner to choose tactical positions, that is, to self-consciously break and reform ties to ideology, activities which are imperative for the psychological and political practices that permit the achievement of coalition across differences" (Sandoval 1991, 15).

REFERENCES

Aronowitz, Stanley, and Giroux, Henry (1991). *Postmodern Education.* Minneapolis, Minn.: University of Minnesota Press.

Browder, Leslie H. (1992). "Which America 2000 Will Be Taught in Your Class, Teacher?" *International Journal of Educational Reform 1,* no. 2:111–33.

Cooper, B. M. (1989). "Cruel and the Gang: Exposing the Schomburg Posse." *Village Voice* 34, no. 19:27–36.

Ebert, Teresa (forthcoming). "Writing in the Political Resistance (Post) Modernism."

Featherstone, Mike (1990). "Global Culture: An Introduction." *Theory, Culture, and Society* nos. 2–3:1–14.

Gilman, Sander L. (1985). *Difference and Pathology.* Ithaca, New York: Cornell University Press.

Giroux, Henry (1992). *Border Crossings.* London and New York: Routledge.

Grossberg, Larry (1988). *It's a Sin.* University of Sydney, Australia: Power Publications.

Grossberg, Larry (1992). *We Gotta Get Out of This Place.* New York and London: Routledge.

Hitchcock, Peter (1993). *Dialogics of the Oppressed.* Minneapolis and London: University of Minnesota Press.

Kasinitz, P. (1988). "Facing Up to the Underclass." *Telos* 76:170–80.

Katz, Cindi and Smith, Neil (1992). "L.A. Intifada: Interview with Mike Davis." *Social Text.* 33:19–33.

Kimball, Roger (1991). "Tenured Radicals: A Postscript." *The New Criterion 9,* no. 5:4–13.

McLaren, Peter (ed.) (forthcoming). *Postmodernism, Postcolonialism and Pedagogy.* Albert Park, Australia: James Nicholas Publishers.

McLaren, Peter, and Leonard, Peter (1993). *Paulo Freire: A Critical Encounter.* London and New York: Routledge.

Mercer, Kobena (1990). "Welcome to the Jungle: Identity and Diversity in Postmodern Politics." In Jonathan Rutherford (ed.), *Identity: Community, Culture, Difference.* London: Lawrence and Wishart. 43–71.

Mohanty, Chandra (1989/90). "On Race and Voice: Challenges for Liberal Education in the 1990s." *Cultural Critique* 19:179–208.

Piccone, Paul (1988). "Roundtable on Communitarianism." *Telos* no. 76:2–32.

Ravitch, Diane (1990). "Multiculturalism: E Pluribus Plures." *The American Scholar 59,* no. 3:337–54.

Ravitch, Diane (1991). "A Culture in Common." *Educational Leadership* (December): 8–16.

Sandoval, Chela (1991). "U.S. Third World Feminism: The Theory and Method of Oppositional Consciousness in the Postmodern World." *Genders* no. 10:1–24.

San Juan, Jr., E. (1992). *Racial Formations/Critical Formations.* New Jersey and London: Humanities Press.

Simone, Timothy Maliqualim (1989). *About Face: Race in Postmodern America.* Brooklyn, NY: Autonomedia.

Stephanson, Anders (1988). "Interview with Cornel West." In Andrew Ross (ed), *Universal Abandon? The Politics of Postmodernism.* Minneapolis: University of Minnesota Press. 269–86.

Wallace, Michele (1991). "Multiculturalism and Oppositionality." *Afterimage* (October): 6–9.

West, Cornel (1990). "The New Cultural Politics of Difference." In Russell Ferguson, Martha Gever, Trinh T. Minh-ha, and Cornel West (eds.), *Out There: Marginalization and Contemporary Cultures.* Cambridge, Mass.: MIT Press and the New Museum of Contemporary Art, New York. 19–36.

The Common School and the Common Good

E. D. Hirsch, Jr. (b. 1928) is the Linden Kent Memorial Professor of English at the University of Virginia in Charlottesville, Virginia, and president of the Core Knowledge Foundation. He is the author of *Cultural Literacy: What Every American Needs to Know* (Houghton Mifflin, 1987); coauthor, with Joseph F. Kett and James Trefil, of *The Dictionary of Cultural Literacy* (Houghton Mifflin, 1988); and coeditor, with William G. Rowland, Jr., and Michael Stanford, of *First Dictionary of Cultural Literacy* (Houghton Mifflin, 1989).

The following selection is from *The Schools We Need and Why We Don't Have Them* (Doubleday, 1996). In it, Hirsch argues for grade-by-grade standards for American schools. He summarizes his beliefs as to why the quality of cultural literacy in the United States is unacceptable. Hirsch supports the concept of basic national curriculum content standards partly because of the high mobility of American children in attending different schools. That is, because many children move from school to school, the principle of isolated localism in curriculum development cannot be followed. We cannot allow, Hirsch argues, each local school district to develop a curriculum without regard to the school curricula in other districts. There must be a common core of basic knowledge that is to be taught in all American schools. Hirsch concludes that it is the duty of educators to create a common basic core of knowledge, which he refers to as a "domain of public communicability" and a "shared public culture."

Key Concept: a common core curriculum

*E*very nation that manages to achieve universal readiness in the early grades for all its children—a few examples are France, Hungary, Norway, Japan, Korea, Sweden, and Denmark—does so by following grade-by-grade standards. In large, diverse nations as well as small, homogeneous ones, a common core curriculum appears to be the only practical means for achieving universal readiness at each grade level. Universal readiness, in turn, is the only means for achieving universal competence and for combining excellence with fairness. In contrast, no nation that *dispenses* with grade-by-grade standards has managed to achieve universal readiness, excellence, and fairness. The Netherlands, for example, is a non-core-curriculum nation that has managed to attain a high average level of excellence because of very high achievement among the top half of its students, but it has failed to achieve universal competence and fairness. Indeed, the Netherlands, the only non-core-curriculum nation of Northern Europe, exhibits the lowest degree of educational fairness in that region, with some 16 percent of its schools falling below minimum competency, as contrasted with about 2.5 percent among its core-curriculum neighbors. (The United States figure is 30 percent of schools below minimum competency.)

An informative exception to this correlation is found in Switzerland, which lacks a national core curriculum but achieves the best combination of excellence and fairness in the world, having the highest average level of achievement coupled with the smallest standard deviation. But on closer inspection, we find that in fact Switzerland has one of the most detailed and demanding core curriculums in the world, with each canton specifying in detail the minimum knowledge and skill that each child shall achieve in each grade, and an accountability system that ensures the attainment of those universal standards. There is some commonality in standards among the cantons, but equally important, Swiss children rarely move from one canton to another in the course of their schooling. Each child therefore receives a highly coherent, carefully monitored sequence of early learnings such as children receive in countries that have grade-by-grade standards nationwide.

To the reader who may feel that these international data have little relevance to the United States, with its anticentralized educational traditions and its diversity, the Swiss example, in which each state fixes its own core curriculum, may appear to have the greatest affinity which our own tradition of state and local control. That would be the case, however, only if our children did not move so frequently from one school to another, and stayed put as the Swiss do. In the 1930s, William Bagley summarized the problem of American nomadism (which has grown more acute since he wrote):

> The notion that each community must have a curriculum all its own is not only silly, but tragic. It neglects two important needs. The first, as we have already seen, is the need of a democracy for many common elements in the culture of all the people, to the end that the people may discuss collective problems in terms that will convey common meanings. The second need is extremely practical. It is the need of recognizing the fact that American people simply will not "stay put." They are the most mobile people in the world.... Under these conditions, failure to have a goodly measure of unformity in school subjects and grade placement is a gross injustice to at least ten million school children at the present time.

The injustice that Bagley identified has intensified for many reasons, and it now extends to many more than ten million children. The average inner-city mobility rates (the percentage of children in a school who transfer in or out during the school year) lie routinely between 45 and 80 percent. Some inner-city schools have mobility rates of over 100 percent. A recent analysis from the United States General Accounting Office reported that one sixth of all third graders attend at least three schools between first and third grade. Given the

144

*Chapter 6
Curriculum
Development
and the
Language of
Educational
Debate*

curricular incoherence of schooling even for those who stay at the same school, the fragmentation and incoherence of the education provided to frequently moving students are heartbreaking.

In sum, the high mobility of our children, especially of those who can least afford educational disruption, makes common learnings *more* needed in the United States than in most other nations. The argument that we are different from others and require different educational arrangements points to more, not less, commonality in our educational standards. It is certainly true that we cannot reasonably be compared to Switzerland, but our children's high mobility rates are all the more reason why we cannot reasonably follow the Swiss principle of isolated localism. Our diversity, size, and nomadism are arguments in favor of, not against, common, grade-by-grade standards. Until very recently, of course, the idea of common standards in the United States has been unthinkable among American educational experts. Localism remains a quasi-sacred principle, despite the fact that few localities actually impose explicit content standards. But many people are coming to feel that, considering the glaring knowledge gaps and boring repetitions that children experience even when they stay in the same school, continuing our educational incoherence, nonaccountability, and inequity would be even more unthinkable.

Bagley's other point, that common learnings are necessary to a functioning democracy, is an educational principle that has been accepted in most democracies of the world, including our own in its earlier years. The institution of the common school, proposed by Jefferson and fostered by Horace Mann, had the goal of giving all children the shared intellectual and social capital that would enable them to participate as autonomous citizens in the economy and policy of the nation. When Jefferson said that if he had to choose between newspapers and government, he would choose newspapers, he went on to say that his remark was premised on each citizen's being able to read and understand the newspapers. It was a prescient addendum. A citizenry cannot read and understand newspapers, much less participate effectively in a modern economy, without sharing the common intellectual capital that makes understanding and communication possible. In a large, diverse nation, the common school is the only institution available for creating a school-based culture that, like a common language, enables everyone to communicate in the public sphere.

The principle that children should enter a new grade already sharing the background knowledge required to understand the teacher and each other is at bottom the principle that enables the functioning of an entire community or nation. People cannot effectively meet in the classroom or in the marketplace unless they can communicate with and learn from each another. It is the duty of a nation's educational system to create this domain of public communicability. It cannot do so without the common school, and the common school cannot be truly such without providing each child the shared intellectual capital that will be needed in each early grade, and needed ultimately in society after graduation. A shared public culture that enables public communicability is essential to an effective community at every age and stage of life, and most emphatically in the early grades, when deficits can be made up. Once out of school, a citizen must continue to share in the common intellectual capital of the nation in order to communicate and learn.

The need to develop and nurture this cultural commons was implicitly understood by the founders, and is consistent with their motivation for having a First Amendment clause that forbids the establishment of a state religion. Divisiveness was to be excluded from the cultural commons. Guided by the principle of public toleration enunciated by John Locke and others after the bloody seventeenth-century wars of religion, the founders desired that the laws and customs of the public sphere should favor no single sect but should promote the general welfare. Customs devisive and dangerous to the internal peace of the nation, chiefly sectarian religions, were to be relegated to the private sphere, enabling all to meet in the public sphere as fellow citizens and equals. The deliberately artificial wall of separation helped create and nurture a public domain of toleration and civility, while leaving everyone as free as possible in their private lives. It was a brilliant Enlightenment political innovation for encouraging internal peace and solidarity in a large nation, and it led to the development of a uniquely American public culture. The development of this cosmopolitan culture was thus no accident. It had been openly discussed in the later Enlightenment, notably in the writings of Immanuel Kant. In the minds of Jefferson, Mann, and other democratic theorists in France and elsewhere, the common school was to be not just the instrument of knowledge, literacy, and equality of opportunity but also the agent of a cosmopolitan culture that would promote universal respect and civility.

In our own day, the chief danger to this ecumenical, cosmopolitan public culture is not a religious but an ethnic sectarianism. The two kinds of sect, religious and ethnic, are highly similar in their divisiveness and their danger to the shared public sphere. Had the idea of ethnic strife been as present in the minds of the Founding Fathers as the idea of religious strife, our founding laws might have included a clause forbidding the establishment of a narrow ethnic culture. Just as the invocations of the Divinity in our public ceremonies are deliberately nonsectarian, hybrid affairs, engaged in by rabbis as well as priests, so our public culture is a hybrid construct that contains heterogeneous elements from various ethnic groups. Recently, Orlando Patterson has spoken of "cross-pollinating our multi-ethnic communities" in order to "promote that precious overarching national culture—the envy of the world—which I call ecumenical America." But Patterson sees a serious danger to that overarching culture in

> balkanizing America both intellectually and culturally. One has only to walk for a few minutes on any large campus (the unfortunate coalescence of the left separatists and the right republican anti-communitarian individualists/separatists!) to witness the pervasiveness of ethnic separatism, marked by periodic outbursts of other chauvinisms and hostilities.

Patterson urges instead a return to the cosmopolitan ideal of the commons:

> Universities and businesses should return to the principle of integration, to the notion that diversity is not something to be celebrated and promoted in its own right, but an opportunity for mutual understanding and the furtherance of an ecumenical national culture.

146

*Chapter 6
Curriculum
Development
and the
Language of
Educational
Debate*

Patterson and others, notably Arthur Schlesinger, Jr., have been urging that the principle of multiculturalism should be guided into this ecumenical, cosmopolitan direction for the good of the nation rather than fostering its all-too-prevalent tendency toward angry separatism and mutual hostility. [I] strongly [support] that view. Whether multiculturalism should be given a Romantic, separatist form (in the tradition of Fichte) or an Enlightenment, cosmopolitan form (in the tradition of Kant) has an obvious bearing on the educational question of common learnings in the early grades. In my view, the Romantic version of ethnicity is as deleterious to public education as the Romantic conception of pedagogy. The common learnings taught in school should promote a cosmopolitan, ecumenical, hybrid public culture in which all meet on an equal footing—a culture that is as deliberately artificial and nonsectarian as our public invocations of the Divinity. This school-based culture belongs to everyone and to no one. Its function is analogous to that of the hybrid lingua francas of the medieval marketplace, which were the antecedents of the major national languages—themselves hybrid, artificially constructed affairs, mostly codified by committees.

In the United States, the process of reaching agreement about a sequence of common learnings in the early grades is likely to be lengthy, conflict-ridden, and, at the start, unofficial. A highly specific common core of content is still repellent to many Americans. Gradually, however, general agreement on such a core might be developed if the public and the educational community became fully persuaded that some degree of grade-by-grade commonality is necessary to educational excellence and equity. (A 50 percent common core has proved to be acceptable to parents in Core Knowledge schools.) The public will be all the more likely to reach this conclusion when it becomes more fully aware that educational formalism has turned the jealously guarded principle of local curriculum control into a myth. As far as specific content is concerned, the local curriculum, with few exceptions, does not exist. One cannot reasonably endorse something that does not exist, though one can demand that it come into existence. If the public simply insisted upon a true common core of learnings at the local level, that would mark a huge advance in our educational arrangements, and might in time lead to still broader commonalities.

Because this [writing] has been focused mainly on kindergarten through grade eight—decisive grades for determining the excellence and equity of schooling—I have paid scant attention to high school. That is a conscious omission. If the principles of early education advanced here were to be followed, American high schools would change perforce for the better. Their incoming students would have already received the foundational knowledge and skill needed for good citizenship. (In earlier eras, many exemplary citizens-to-be were compelled to leave school by the end of grade eight.) Students would not need to be shepherded into so many elementary courses; they could follow more varied and intensive strands of academic or vocational study according to their interests and abilities. As a consequence, the American high school would become a more interesting and effective place for all types of students.

Beyond urging agreement at the local level, I have not made many suggestions regarding the large-scale policies needed to create more demanding elementary schools. I haven't answered questions like What shall we do tomorrow? and Who shall be in charge? The possible administrative means for accomplishing the task are many, but there can be no substitute for the main elements of the task itself. Schools need to have a coherent, cumulative core curriculum which instills consensus values such as civic duty, honesty, diligence, perseverance, respect, kindness, and independent-mindedness; which gives students step-by-step mastery of *procedural knowledge* in language arts and mathematics; which gives them step-by-step mastery of *content knowledge* in civics, science, the arts, and the humanities; and which holds students, teachers, schools, and parents accountable for acceptable progress in achieving these specific year-by-year goals. Every school, in short, should have [certain] basic characteristics . . . :

> All teachers at our school have not only pedagogical training but also a detailed knowledge of the subject matter that they teach. We instill in all children an ethic of toleration, civility, orderliness, responsibility, and hard work. Our staff has agreed on a definite core of knowledge and skill that all children will attain *in each grade*. We make sure that every child learns this core, and gains the specific knowledge and skill needed to prosper at the next grade level, thus enabling knowledge to build upon knowledge. Our teachers continually confer with their colleagues about effective ways of stimulating children to learn and integrate this specific knowledge and skill. The specificity of our goals enables us to monitor children, and give focused attention where necessary. To this end, we provide parents with a detailed outline of the *specific* knowledge and skill goals for each grade, and we stay in constant touch with them regarding the child's progress. Through this knowledge-based approach, we make sure that *all* normal children perform at grade level, while, in addition, the most talented children are challenged to excel. Attaining this specific and well-integrated knowledge and skill gives our students pleasure in learning as well as self respect, and it ensures that they will enter the next grade ready and eager to learn more.

Since this emphasis on content and coherence requires a restructuring of ideas, and because ideas are slow to change, my colleagues and I have been pursuing a school-by-school grassroots effort in which the leadership of one group of parents or teachers, or of a single principal or superintendent, can revolutionize the ideas and practices of an individual school. That school's success then sometimes encourages other schools to rethink their assumptions. This school-by-school effort is slow, but it is at least an avenue that can be taken now, without delay—the kind of initiative greatly facilitated by large-scale policies that consciously liberate individual initiative, policies such as "parental choice" and "charter schools," which give parents and teachers the power to change their own individual schools, so long as their students are trained to high standards of skill and knowledge.

It has taken nearly seventy years for Romantic progressivism to exercise virtually totalitarian intellectual dominion over not just schools of education but a large percentage of policymakers and the general public as well. Nothing truly effective in the way of large-scale policy change—through federal, state, or local mechanisms—can be accomplished, no new power relationships can be forged, until there is a change of mind by the general public—among whom I

148

*Chapter 6
Curriculum
Development
and the
Language of
Educational
Debate*

include two and a half million teachers. Once that occurs, many different public policies could be successful.

The strongest resistance to commonality in schooling may come from a widespread fear of uniformity—the last bastion of misguided Romanticism. It is said that common elements in the curriculum would destroy our American essence, which is diversity. There is no evidence whatever that this fear of uniformity, which is widespread and often expressed, has any real-world foundation, or that a moiety of commonality in the school curriculum will turn everyone into interchangeable automatons. To the extent that this antisameness sentiment has any concrete implication for the curriculum, it would seem to be the current laissez-faire idea that if all schools and teachers do their own thing, then the invisible hand of nature will cause our children to be educated effectively, and thus ensure their individuality and diversity. The foundation for this curricular confidence (which has in fact resulted in huge knowledge gaps, boring repetitions, and glaring inequalities) would seem to be a Romantic faith in the watchful beneficence of nature, which "never did betray the heart that loved her." It is an expression of the same optimistic naturalism which supposes that the pace and quality of each child's scholarly attainments are determined naturally, and will follow an innate course of development which should not be interfered with by external impositions of drills and hard work.

Improving the effectiveness and fairness of education through enhancing both its content and its commonality has a more than educational significance. The improvement would, as everyone knows, diminish the economic inequities within the nation. Nothing could be more important to our national well-being than overcoming those inequities, which have grown ever greater in recent decades. But something equally significant is at stake. Many observers have deplored the decline in civility in our public life, and with it the decline in our sense of community. The interethnic hostilities that have intensified among us recently, the development of an us-versus-them mentality in political life, the astonishing indifference to the condition of our children—all bespeak a decline in the communitarian spirit, which used to be a hallmark of what Patterson calls our "ecumenical national culture." Bringing our children closer to universal competence is important. But an equally important contribution of the truly common school would be the strengthening of universal communicability and a sense of community within the public sphere. In the long run, that could be the common school's most important contribution to preserving the fragile fabric of our democracy.

PART THREE

Schools in a Multicultural Society

Chapter 7 The Struggle for Freedom in Education 151

Chapter 8 The Critical Perspective on the Struggle for Freedom in Education 193

Chapter 9 Women and Education 212

On the Internet . . .

Sites appropriate to Part Three

This is the home page of the American Association of University Women, a national organization that promotes education and equity for all women and girls.

```
http://www.aauw.org/
```

The W. E. B. Du Bois Virtual University is a series of pages detailing various aspects of Du Bois studies. It has been created to serve as a clearinghouse for information on Du Bois and to spur intelligent scholarship and discussion of his life, legacy, and works.

```
http://members.tripod.com/~DuBois/
    index.htm
```

This site offers a brief description of the role that the Tuskegee Institute played in dividing black intellectual leaders Booker T. Washington and W. E. B. Du Bois.

```
http://www.york.cuny.edu/~gibson/
    Tuskegee.html
```

CHAPTER 7 The Struggle for Freedom in Education

7.1 DIANE RAVITCH

Postwar Initiatives

In the selection that follows, which is from *The Troubled Crusade: American Education, 1945–1980* (Basic Books, 1983), Diane Ravitch discusses the civil rights and race relations situation in America late in World War II and in the years immediately following the war. She documents the vast inequalities of educational opportunities between white and African American students in 1945 and the terrible effects of racial segregation in the schools. She further documents the tragic impact of racism on the field of education and the hostile state of race relations in the United States in the mid and late 1940s.

Ravitch describes the work and the resulting report of the President's Committee on Civil Rights appointed by President Harry S. Truman on December 5, 1945, as well as Truman's charge to this committee. She discusses the choices and options that were open to the committee and the political context in which its deliberations occurred. She notes that President Truman bravely supported the struggle for civil rights. This selection sets the thematic stage for the other selections in this chapter regarding the struggle for freedom and equality in education in America.

Ravitch is a senior research scholar at New York University in New York City and a fellow of the Brookings Institution, a private, nonprofit organization devoted to research, education, and publication in economics,

151

government, foreign policy, and the social sciences. She also served as assistant secretary of education during the Bush administration. In addition to *The Troubled Crusade,* she is the author of *National Standards in American Education: A Citizen's Guide* (Brookings Institution, 1995) and coeditor, with Joseph Viteritti, of *New Schools for a New Century: The Redesign of Urban Education* (Yale University Press, 1997).

Key Concept: racism in America and segregation of schools on the basis of race

*I*n early 1945, with the war in Europe coming to an end, the Senate Committee on Education and Labor opened hearings on a proposal for federal aid to education. The most insistent claimants for federal help were poor districts, which had a difficult time adequately financing their public schools from local property taxes. In addition to the usual statements of support and opposition from interest groups, several teachers told the senators about conditions in their schools. Miss Wilma Upchurch, a teacher from rural Nebraska, stated that her school had 487 pupils and twelve teachers, only seven of whom had college degrees. Because of low salaries, teacher turnover had been 50 percent the year before, and one out of every five teachers in the state had a temporary emergency teaching certificate, usually because of lack of qualifications. Her district, a poor one, taxed itself to the limit and yet was able to spend only forty to forty-seven dollars per pupil annually. "I am sure I could get a job in another state, or maybe I could work at the bomber plant," Miss Upchurch testified, "but I would rather stay in the teaching profession. Somebody has got to teach those children, and I would like to do it."

Mrs. Florence Christmas, a black teacher from Copiah County, Mississippi, described her school of 190 children and three teachers. As principal, she taught all subjects in four grades (fifth through eighth) and received $60 per month for six months. The other two teachers were paid, respectively, $292 and $288 for the six-month term. Mrs. Christmas said:

> Our school is called Antioch and is located on the same ground as the Antioch Baptist Church. Some of our people in the community are small truck farmers. They have a great love for education. They built their own schoolhouse. It has grown from one room to a three-teacher type school. The money for the building was raised by the teachers, children, and patrons. We gave programs, entertainments, secured pledges from the parents and friends, and gave money from our salaries to help with the building. We have been able to put on one coat of paint, inside and out.

Parents and teachers were still trying to raise $12.57, Mrs. Christmas said, to "finish paying for the paint," and their next project was to get enough benches "so that all the children may have seats, especially those in the primary room."

Of six thousand Negro teachers in Mississippi, said Mrs. Christmas, five thousand received less than $600 per year. During the months when school was not in session, she held a factory job, making containers for vegetables, where she earned almost as much in a week as in a month of teaching. When he heard this, Senator William Fulbright of Arkansas asked her, "Why do you do teaching?"

Mrs. Christmas responded, "Teaching is my profession. I would rather teach."

It was matter-of-factly noted in the record that in Copiah County, where Mrs. Christmas taught, the average salary for white teachers was $889.53, compared to an annual average for black teachers of $332.58; the length of the school term was eight months for whites and six months for blacks; of 91 white teachers in the county, 44 had no college degree, while of 126 black teachers, 122 had no college degree. The daily attendance rate for white children was 48 percent; for black children, it was 60 percent. At the Antioch school, the black parents dug down into their pockets to keep the school open for a seventh month.

Educational conditions throughout the South, particularly in rural areas, were equally depressed. Dr. E. B. Norton, the chief state school officer of Alabama, noted that "the only difference between our state and some of the others is that our emergency is not temporary, ours seems to be a permanent emergency." Some eleven thousand of Alabama's twenty thousand teachers had left their jobs in the three years after Pearl Harbor; many of their replacements had no college training. Low pay was one reason: the annual salary for white teachers was $976, and for black teachers only $600. Furthermore, more than half the school buildings in the state were heated with open stoves, and more than half lacked electricity. . . .

Although racism was deeply embedded in American life and law, the experience of the war heightened the contradiction between the reality of racism and the ideals of American democracy. The painfulness of the contrast was presented most acutely to blacks, particularly the one million blacks who served in the armed forces. They had encountered racism in their daily lives before the war, but as members of the armed services, they found themselves in the odd position of being discriminated against by the American government, a government that daily proclaimed that the goal of the war was to defend the principles of democracy and to defeat malignant exponents of racial superiority. Northern blacks stationed in the South were subjected to the humiliating laws and practices of the segregated states; southern blacks who traveled North realized that the rigid racial separatism of their home communities was not immutable; and those who were sent overseas encountered cultures where racial prejudice was unknown. Among many who served in the military or who had, for the first time, a good job in a war industry, the war years were the beginning of a new consciousness, a new willingness to insist that the society make real the promises of its democratic creed.

The war and the democratic rhetoric it inspired contributed to delegitimating prejudice. Recognizing that the United States could not fight racism abroad while practicing it at home, a growing number of whites began to criticize openly the nation's racial caste system. Wendell L. Willkie, the unsuccessful Republican presidential candidate in 1940, wrote in 1944 that the war "has made us conscious of the contradiction between our treatment of our Negro minority and the ideals for which we are fighting." The perpetuation of racism, he declared, would harm America's standing in the world, for so long as "we continue to practice an ugly discrimination at home against our minorities... we cannot expect small nations and men of other races and colors to credit the good faith of our professed purposes." *Fortune* magazine sharply criticized both employers and labor unions for their continuing exclusion of blacks from employment. Racial discrimination, wrote the editors in 1942, impaired the war effort, damaged America's relations with other nations, and corroded the national conscience. "No serious review of the nation's status could ever overlook the contradiction between America's dream and the Negro reality," they stated. "In the consciousness of all peoples in the world this war is being fought for and against the idea of racial superiority. America's Constitution, like Christianity, is based on the principle that every man is born with the inalienable right to equality of opportunity. Whether or not this assumption is 'realistic'—we must either stick to it or change sides." The erosion of prejudice was also advanced by social scientists, whose research on the irrationality of group prejudice undermined the ideology of white supremacy. Of particular importance as a powerful indictment of racism was Gunnar Myrdal's *An American Dilemma*, published in 1944, which surveyed racial relations and summarized the findings of modern social science.

Nonetheless, the outlook for political change on racial matters was not promising at the end of the war. Reactionaries and racists held key seats in Congress, and the Democratic party—which had won the allegiance of blacks during the Depression—was dependent on the electoral votes of the "solid South." Even President Roosevelt, beloved as a friend of the underdog, avoided making specific commitments on behalf of the civil rights of blacks, to appease his powerful southern allies. So bland was the Democratic party's 1944 platform on the issue of civil rights that the NAACP said sarcastically, "To call the section on the Negro a plank is a misnomer. It is best characterized as a splinter."

No one knew what to expect on civil rights issues from Harry S. Truman. When he unexpectedly assumed the presidency on April 12, 1945, Truman had been vice-president for only eighty-two days; before then he had been known as the senator from Missouri who had investigated war profiteers. Lacking the artfulness of his predecessor, Truman was not able simultaneously to command the loyalty of blacks and white southern politicians. Though the political ramifications did not become clear until the 1948 election, Truman cast his lot on December 5, 1946, when he appointed a President's Committee on Civil Rights to study the status of civil rights and civil liberties and to recommend new legislation. It was no accident that the committee of fifteen consisted entirely of moderate and liberals and included two Catholics, two Jews, two labor leaders, two blacks, two liberal southerners, and—perhaps to enhance its credibility—the president of General Electric as its chairman. In his memoirs, Truman wrote that he set up the committee "because of the repeated anti-minority incidents immediately after the war in which homes were invaded, property was destroyed, and a number of innocent lives were taken."

As a former senator, Truman knew that the chance of getting civil rights legislation through the Congress, with its southern committee chairmen, was nil. When the leadership of the Committee on Civil Rights asked him whether he wanted them only to make recommendations or to engage in "mass education as to our findings," the president told them that "the one thing he was interested in was in going to the public." In addition to documenting the extent of the problems, he told them "that the most practical and far-reaching aspect of our work would be whatever plans we devised for mass education of the public." The job of the committee, the president said, was to put before the American public an agenda for change, a list of particulars, and to begin the process of public education that must precede political and social change.

In late 1947, the Committee for Civil Rights delivered its report to the president. It was a concise documentation of civil rights violations, accompanied by specific proposals for governmental action. For the first time, a presidential commission declared that the problem of civil rights was not a Negro problem or a Jewish problem, but a national problem, a problem of bringing America's practice into congruence with its ideals. In prose that was simple and direct, the committee detailed the severity of discrimination in the United States:

- Six blacks had been lynched by mobs in 1946. Twenty-two people had been rescued from lynch mobs. All but one of the would-be victims were Negroes. Due to the attitudes of local police and juries, members of lynch mobs were rarely prosecuted, rarely arrested, rarely convicted.
- Police brutality was flagrant in the South. The police in some communities subjected prisoners to beatings, third-degree tactics, pistol whippings, and illegal searches.
- In some communities, prisoners could not get a fair trial, either because members of minority groups were systematically excluded from jury service or because the accused could not afford to hire legal counsel.
- The right to vote was restricted unconstitutionally in many states in order to prevent or minimize black participation. Some southern states, for example, had imposed a poll tax or had required prospective voters to interpret the state constitution to the satisfaction of local officials. Such devices kept the electorate small and unrepresentative; in the 1944 election, 18.3 percent of potential voters in the eight poll-tax states had voted, compared to 68.7 percent in the other forty states.
- Discrimination in the armed forces persisted despite proclamations to the contrary. Negroes were barred from enlistment in any branch of the Marine Corps except as stewards; 80 percent of Negro sailors were cooks or stewards; the army maintained a limit of 10 percent in all its sectors for Negroes. Only a tiny proportion of officers in any of the services were Negroes.
- Blacks were the victims of unfair employment practices and of wage discrimination. Whites and blacks with the same education were paid differently for the same work.
- Blacks were routinely excluded from hotels, restaurants, and other places of public accommodation.
- Health care facilities discriminated against Negroes. Many hospitals did not admit Negro patients or permit Negro doctors on their staff. Negro students were barred from most medical schools. "Medical schools graduate approximately 5,000 students a year, but only about 145 of these are Negro. And of these 145, 130 are from two Negro schools."

- School segregation, enforced by law in seventeen states and the District of Columbia, was manifestly unfair. "Whatever test is used—expenditure per pupil, teachers' salaries, the number of pupils per teacher, transportation of students, adequacy of school buildings and educational equipment, length of school term, extent of curriculum—Negro students are invariably at a disadvantage."

The committee unanimously recommended the elimination of segregation and discrimination based on race, color, creed, or national origin from all aspects of American life. It proposed a federal antilynching law; abolition of the poll tax; strengthening of the civil rights section of the Justice Department; federal protection of the right to vote; new legislation to end all discrimination in the armed forces; a ban on segregation and discrimination in employment, housing, health facilities, interstate transportation, and places of public accommodation.

Only two issues split the committee, and both were educational issues. While everyone agreed that segregation was wrong, the committee argued at length whether to recommend a ban on federal aid to racially segregated schools. Even as the committee was deliberating, the Congress was considering a program of federal aid to elementary and secondary schools that had a good chance of passing. The members of the committee realized that their recommendations might affect the fate of the bill before Congress. The committee had to choose whether to recommend that federal aid be equitably divided between black and white schools in the South or to recommend that no federal aid go to any segregated school. The choice was not that simple: only three years before, in 1944, a federal aid bill had been killed when conservative Republican Senator William Langer attached an amendment to deny federal aid to segregated schools; as he expected, the bill's southern supporters voted against it and defeated the bill. Because of the dire financial needs of southern schools, and especially black southern schools, the NAACP in 1947 was supporting federal aid so long as it was fairly apportioned between white and black schools.

The southern members of the committee argued that the South would reject federal aid rather than permit the federal government to dictate its way of life. Some nonsouthern members opposed federal sanctions because they believed that prejudice stemmed from inferior education and that no step should be endorsed that might retard the improvement of southern schools. To cut off funds from communities that were blighted by ignorance, worried one member, was to remove "the very means of redemption." Morris Ernst, a liberal lawyer from New York, led the fight for federal sanctions against segregated schools; he held that the committee would look foolish if it endorsed "segregation plus a lot more money." Others agreed, including Sadie Alexander, a black lawyer from Philadelphia, who objected to permitting the South "to set a pattern for the entire United States." The most telling argument came from Rabbi Roland B. Gittelsohn of New York:

I am deeply disturbed by this notion that by putting more money and better teachers into a segregated school system in the South you will thereby take an appreciable step toward the eventual elimination of segregation. You won't. Children don't learn from books, but from the life they are living, and the basic truth of a Southern educational system lies not in what you teach but in the fact that the white child knows that the colored child isn't good enough to go to school with him, and I don't care how much money you put into it, so long as you tell a white child, merely by implication, that the Negro child can't sit next to him in school, you are licked.

Channing Tobias, a black social worker, pointed out that a recommendation for sanctions against segregated schools might well cause the defeat of the federal aid bill, but he believed that he time had come "to say what is really in our hearts on this question of segregation and be willing to take what comes." And those who worried that the Congress would never pass federal sanctions were rebuked by James Carey, an official of the Congress of Industrial Organizations. Carey insisted that it was not the job of the committee to decide what was acceptable to the Congress, but to declare what was right: "If we could get a report and give it widespread publicity where people can see it, that this is the opinion of the people, of a cross section of the American society, it is the policy of the Federal Government, it goes way beyond what we expect to get even during the present Administration.... This represents our aspirations, and this is what we should seek." With an apologetic dissent from its two southern members, the committee endorsed the principle that no federal aid should be given to racially segregated schools.

The second issue that split the committee was whether, in admissions to educational institutions, there should be an absolute ban on discrimination based on race, color, creed, or national origin. No one favored racial or religious discrimination, but John Dickey, president of Dartmouth College, contended that educational institutions should have the right to take race, religion, and social background into account in order to have a diverse student body; he was especially interested in keeping a balance among students from different religious backgrounds at Dartmouth. Members who were associated with denominational schools worried that an absolute ban might destroy the character of their institutions. However, the black and Jewish members of the committee resolutely defended an absolute ban for all but denominational schools, since it would be impossible to determine whether an institution had discriminated for reasons of diversity or for reasons of bigotry. The final report recommended laws "prohibiting discrimination in the admission and treatment of students based on race, color, creed, or national origin," exempting denominational schools. The report noted: "There is a substantial division within the committee on this recommendation. A majority favors it."

Even before the committee issued its report, President Truman dramatically asserted his own civil rights views in an address to the NAACP on June 29, 1947. He was the first president ever to accept an invitation to speak to the NAACP. The night before he spoke, he wrote his sister: "I've got to make a speech to the Society for the Advancement of Colored People tomorrow and I wish I didn't have to make it. Mrs. R. and Walter White, Wayne Morse, Senator from Oregon, & your brother are the speakers.... Mamma won't like what I have to say because I wind up quoting Old Abe. But I believe what I say and I am hopeful we may implement it." Whatever his inner qualms, Truman delivered a forthright pledge to make the federal government the defender of the "rights and equalities of all Americans. And when I say all Americans— I mean all Americans." He stated that "every citizen in a truly democratic society" should have "the right to a decent home, the right to an education, the right to adequate medical care, the right to a worthwhile job, the right to an equal share in the making of public decisions through the ballot, and the right to a fair trial in a fair court." Truman won praise from the NAACP, the black press, and metropolitan newspapers in the North, but he was roundly criticized by the press in the South and the West, especially for his statement that everyone has the "right" to a home, a job, education, and medical care. These, said his critics, are to be earned, not guaranteed by government.

Truman made civil rights the centerpiece of his 1948 state of the union address to Congress. "Our first goal," he held, "is to secure fully the essential human rights of our citizens." He condemned the fact "that some of our citizens are still denied equal opportunity for education, for jobs and for economic advancement, and for the expression of their views at the polls. Most serious of all, some are denied equal protection under the laws. Whether discrimination is based on race, or creed, or color, or land of origin, it is utterly contrary to American ideals of democracy." Less than a month later, on February 2, 1948, Truman sent the Congress a special message on civil rights, incorporating the recommendations of his Committee on Civil Rights.

The president's advocacy of civil rights infuriated southern politicians. Senator James O. Eastland of Mississippi predicted that the South would withhold its votes in the presidential election and throw the election to the House of Representatives, where "a southern man would emerge as president." Others threatened to filibuster against the president's proposals. Southerners showed their contempt for Truman by walking out of the Democratic convention in 1948 and endorsing Governor Strom Thurmond of South Carolina as the "Dixiecrat" candidate for president. At the same time, the left wing of the Democratic party, irked by Truman's firm stand against Soviet expansionism in Europe, abandoned him to support Henry Wallace, the former vice-president, as the candidate of the Progressive party. Though Truman eked out a victory in 1948 against Republican Thomas Dewey, no one might reasonably have predicted that alienating both the right and the left wing of the party was a prescient political strategy.

Each year, in his State of the Union message, Truman proposed a civil rights program, and each year the southern-dominated Congress quietly killed it. But there were things he could do without the Congress. On July 26, 1948, he issued an executive order ending racial segregation in the armed forces and banning discrimination in federal employment. The Federal Housing Administration was directed to drop its ban on insuring homes in racially mixed neighborhoods. And Truman's Justice Department established a significant precedent by filing an amicus brief in the Supreme Court supporting the NAACP's attack on racially restrictive covenants in housing.

Through the work of the Committee on Civil Rights and by his own willingness to take a stand, President Truman set in motion a process of public education. In the struggle to resolve "the American dilemma," the contradiction between ideals and practices, the first requirement was to make the public aware of the dilemma. This was the tack of the Committee on Civil Rights. The value of its work—and of the president's doomed proposals—was to give legitimacy and encouragement to the growing movement for civil rights. Segregationists claimed that the nascent civil rights movement was led by agitators and Communists; the president of the United States said that its goals embodied the highest aspirations of the Constitution. In the decades ahead, events moved so quickly and public opinion shifted so decisively that the views of Truman and his Committee on Civil Rights came to sound commonplace, when in fact they had been uncommonly courageous.

The Atlanta Exposition Address, September 18, 1895

Booker T. Washington (1856–1915), who was born into slavery, founded the Tuskegee Normal and Industrial Institute in Alabama in 1881. At the Tuskegee Institute he emphasized industrial, skilled trade education rather than traditional college-level liberal arts studies. Washington pursued this policy because he believed that the majority of African Americans needed industrial and artisan skills to escape the sharecropper system of dependent agriculture in the post–Civil War South. He was able to influence many powerful conservative whites to support his program at the institute. Washington also founded the National Negro Business League in 1900. He owned several newspapers, and his ideas carried much weight among other Black-owned publishing enterprises of his day. Washington's most famous articulation of his educational philosophy was given to a business convention on September 18, 1895, in Atlanta, Georgia. This speech, called "The Atlanta Exposition Address," is reprinted in the following selection.

Washington was severely critiqued for his educational position, which focused on economic empowerment and practical skills and less so on intellectual empowerment. Black intellectual leader W. E. B. Du Bois was a notable critic of Washington's views, and he called for the development of an African American intellectual elite that would be able to argue and struggle for African American rights with the white American elite. Actually, many contemporary sociologists agree that both Washington's and Du Bois's social agendas for African American freedpersons were correct—both greater numbers of skilled Black workers *and* a Black American intelligentsia were necessary for African Americans to attain their constitutional rights in the late nineteenth and twentieth centuries.

Key Concept: practical education and "intercultural understanding" as the path to liberation

Booker T.
Washington

One-third of the population of the South is of the Negro race. No enterprise seeking the material, civil, or moral welfare of this section can disregard this element of our population and reach the highest success. I but convey to you, Mr. President and Directors, the sentiment of the masses of my race when I say that in no way have the value and manhood of the American Negro been more fittingly and generously recognized than by the managers of this magnificent Exposition at every stage of its progress. It is a recognition that will do more to cement the friendship of the two races than any occurrence since the dawn of freedom.

Not only this, but the opportunity here afforded will awaken among us a new era of industrial progress. Ignorant and inexperienced, it is not strange that in the first years of our new life we began at the top instead of at the bottom; that a seat in Congress or the State Legislature was more sought than real estate or industrial skill; that the political convention or stump speaking had more attractions than starting a dairy farm or truck garden.

A ship lost at sea for many days suddenly sighted a friendly vessel. From the mast of the unfortunate vessel was seen a signal: "Water, water, we die of thirst." The answer from the friendly vessel at once came back, "Cast down your bucket where you are." A second time the signal, "Water, water, send us water," ran up from the distressed vessel and was answered, "Cast down your bucket where you are." And a third and fourth signal for water was answered "Cast down your bucket where you are." The captain of the distressed vessel, at last heeding the injunction, cast down his bucket and it came up full of fresh, sparkling water from the mouth of the Amazon River.

To those of my race who depend on bettering their condition in a foreign land, or who underestimate the importance of cultivating friendly relations with the Southern white man who is their next-door neighbor, I would say: Cast down your bucket where you are; cast it down in making friends, in every manly way, of the people of all races by whom we are surrounded. Cast it down in agriculture, mechanics, in commerce, in domestic service, and in the professions. And in this connection it is well to bear in mind that whatever other sins the South may be called upon to bear, when it comes to business pure and simple, it is in the South that the Negro is given a man's chance in the commercial world, and in nothing is this Exposition more eloquent than in emphasizing this chance. Our greatest danger is that, in the great leap from slavery to freedom, we may overlook the fact that the masses of us are to live by the productions of our hands and fail to keep in mind that we shall prosper in the proportion as we learn to dignify and glorify common labor, and put brains and skill into the common occupations of life; shall prosper in proportion as we learn to draw the line between the superficial and the substantial, the ornamental gewgaws of life and the useful. No race can prosper till it learns that there is as much dignity in tilling a field as in writing a poem. It is at the bottom of life we must begin, and not at the top. Nor should we permit our grievances to overshadow our opportunities.

To those of the white race who look to the incoming of those of foreign birth and strange tongue and habits for the prosperity of the South, were I permitted I would repeat what I say to my own race, "Cast down your bucket where you are." Cast it down among the 8,000,000 Negroes whose habits you know, whose fidelity and love you have tested in days when to have proved treacherous meant the ruin of your firesides. Cast down your bucket among these people who have, without strikes and labor wars, tilled your fields, cleared your forests, builded your railroads and cities, and brought forth treasures from the bowels of the earth and helped make possible this magnificent representation of the progress of the South. Casting down your bucket among my people, helping and encouraging them as you are doing on these grounds, and, with education of head, hand and heart, you will find that they will buy your surplus land, make blossom the waste places in your fields, and run your factories.

While doing this, you can be sure in the future, as in the past, that you and your families will be surrounded by the most patient, faithful, law-abiding, and unresentful people that the world has seen. As we have proved our loyalty to you in the past, in nursing your children, watching by the sickbed of your mothers and fathers, and often following them with tear-dimmed eyes to their graves, so in the future, in our humble way, we shall stand by you with a devotion that no foreigner can approach, ready to lay down our lives, if need be, in defense of yours; interlacing our industrial, commercial, civil, and religious life with yours in a way that shall make the interests of both races one. In all things that are purely social we can be as separate as the fingers, yet one as the hand in all things essential to mutual progress.

There is no defense or security for any of us except in the highest intelligence and development of all. If anywhere there are efforts tending to curtail the fullest growth of the Negro, let these efforts be turned into stimulating, encouraging and making him the most useful and intelligent citizen. Effort or means so invested will pay a thousand percent interest. These efforts will be twice blessed—"blessing him that gives and him that takes."

There is no escape, through law of man or God, from the inevitable:

> The laws of changeless justice bind
> Oppressor with oppressed,
> And close as sin and suffering joined
> We march to fate abreast.

Nearly sixteen million hands will aid you in pulling the load upward, or they will pull against you the load downward. We shall constitute one-third and more of the ignorance and crime of the South, or one-third its intelligence and progress; we shall contribute one-third to the business and industrial prosperity of the South, or we shall prove a veritable body of death, stagnating, depressing, retarding every effort to advance the body politic.

Gentlemen of the Exposition: As we present to you our humble effort at an exhibition of our progress, you must not expect overmuch. Starting thirty years ago with ownership here and there in a few quilts and pumpkins and chickens (gathered from miscellaneous sources), remember: the path that has led us from these to the invention and production of agricultural implements, buggies, steam engines, newspapers, books, statuary, carving, paintings, the management of drugstores and banks, has not been trodden without contact with thorns and thistles. While we take pride in what we exhibit as a result of our independent efforts, we do not for a moment forget that our part in this exhibition would fall far short of your expectations but for the constant help that has come to our educational life, not only from the Southern states, but especially from Northern philanthropists who have made their gifts a constant stream of blessing and encouragement.

The wisest among my race understand that the agitation of questions of social equality is the extremest folly, and that progress in the enjoyment of all the privileges that will come to us must be the result of severe and constant struggle rather than of artificial forcing. No race that has anything to contribute to the markets of the world is long in any degree ostracized. It is important and right that all privileges of the laws be ours, but it is vastly more important that we be prepared for the exercise of those privileges. The opportunity to earn a dollar in a factory just now is worth infinitely more than the opportunity to spend a dollar in an opera house.

In conclusion, may I repeat that nothing in thirty years has given us more hope and encouragement and drawn us so near to you of the white race as this opportunity offered by the Exposition; and here bending, as it were, over the altar that represents the results of the struggles of your race and mine, both starting practically empty-handed three decades ago, I pledge that, in your effort to work out the great and intricate problem which God has laid at the doors of the South, you shall have at all times the patient, sympathetic help of my race. Only let this be constantly in mind that, while from representations in these buildings of the product of field, of forest, of mine, of factory, letters and art, much good will come—yet by far above and beyond material benefits, will be that higher good, that let us pray God will come, in a blotting out of sectional differences and racial animosities and suspicions, in a determination to administer absolute justice, in a willing obedience among all classes to the mandates of law. This, coupled with material prosperity, will bring into our beloved South a new heaven and a new earth.

Of Mr. Booker T. Washington and Others

W. E. B. (William Edward Burghardt) Du Bois (1868–1963) was one of the greatest African American intellectual leaders. In 1895 he became the first African American scholar to receive a Ph.D. from Harvard University. He cofounded the National Association for the Advancement of Colored People (NAACP) in 1909, and he was the founding editor of the NAACP magazine *Crisis*. Du Bois called the conference of African American leaders and scholars in 1905 that sparked the Niagara Movement, the civil rights movement that eventually produced the NAACP. He published many scholarly studies on the situation of African Americans. A great scholar and a valiant advocate for the civil liberties of all African Americans, Du Bois dedicated his life to the cause of human rights. He died on August 27, 1963, in Accra, Ghana, on the eve of the famous civil rights march and demonstration in Washington, D.C., to petition the U.S. Congress to pass a civil rights act to protect and enforce the constitutional rights of all persons (Congress did so in 1964).

A chronology of Du Bois's life as well as his political and literary activities is provided at the back of *The Souls of Black Folk* (Vintage Books, 1990), from which the following selection has been excerpted. In the selection, Du Bois critiques what he refers to as "the Atlanta Compromise" of his contemporary and African American spokesman Booker T. Washington as well as Washington's positions on the situation of African Americans. Du Bois advocates more college-level study opportunities for academically able African American students and argues for the enforcement of the constitutional rights of all African Americans. He argues that the policies of Washington and some other leaders of the African American community in the early 1900s did not go nearly far enough in defending the civil liberties of African Americans. Du Bois accuses Washington of encouraging a policy of racial "accommodation" that led black people to give up the struggle for political power, civil rights, and the higher education of black youth. He also contends that the policies of Washington and his supporters led to the disenfranchisement of blacks, the legal creation of a distinct status of civil inferiority for African Americans, and "the steady withdrawal of aid from institutions for the higher training of the Negro."

Key Concept: critique of the "Atlanta Compromise"

From birth till death enslaved; in word, in deed, unmanned!
Hereditary bondsmen! Know ye not
Who would be free themselves must strike the blow?

—Byron.

*E*asily the most striking thing in the history of the American Negro since 1876 is the ascendancy of Mr. Booker T. Washington. It began at the time when war memories and ideals were rapidly passing; a day of astonishing commercial development was dawning; a sense of doubt and hesitation overtook the freedmen's sons,—then it was that his leading began. Mr. Washington came, with a simple definite programme, at the psychological moment when the nation was a little ashamed of having bestowed so much sentiment on Negroes, and was concentrating its energies on Dollars. His programme of industrial education, conciliation of the South, and submission and silence as to civil and political rights, was not wholly original; the Free Negroes from 1830 up to wartime had striven to build industrial schools, and the American Missionary Association had from the first taught various trades; and Price and others had sought a way of honorable alliance with the best of the Southerners. But Mr. Washington first indissolubly linked these things; he put enthusiasm, unlimited energy, and perfect faith into this programme, and changed it from a by-path into a veritable Way of Life. And the tale of the methods by which he did this is a fascinating study of human life.

It startled the nation to hear a Negro advocating such a programme after many decades of bitter complaint; it startled and won the applause of the South, it interested and won the admiration of the North; and after a confused murmur of protest, it silenced if it did not convert the Negroes themselves.

To gain the sympathy and coöperation of the various elements comprising the white South was Mr. Washington's first task; and this, at the time Tuskegee was founded, seemed, for a black man, well-nigh impossible. And yet ten years later it was done in the word spoken at Atlanta: "In all things purely social we can be as separate as the five fingers, and yet one as the hand in all things essential to mutual progress." This "Atlanta Compromise" is by all odds the most notable thing in Mr. Washington's career. The South interpreted it in different ways: the radicals received it as a complete surrender of the demand for civil and political equality; the conservatives, as a generously conceived working basis for mutual understanding. So both approved it, and to-day its author is certainly the most distinguished Southerner since Jefferson Davis, and the one with the largest personal following.

Next to this achievement comes Mr. Washington's work in gaining place and consideration in the North. Others less shrewd and tactful had formerly essayed to sit on these two stools and had fallen between them; but as Mr. Washington knew the heart of the South from birth and training, so by singular insight he intuitively grasped the spirit of the age which was dominating the North. And so thoroughly did he learn the speech and thought of triumphant commercialism, and the ideas of material prosperity, that the picture of a lone black boy poring over a French grammar amid the weeds and dirt of a neglected home soon seemed to him the acme of absurdities. One wonders that Socrates and St. Francis of Assisi would say to this.

And yet this very singleness of vision and thorough oneness with his age is a mark of the successful man. It is as though Nature must needs make men narrow in order to give them force. So Mr. Washington's cult has gained unquestioning followers, his work has wonderfully prospered, his friends are legion, and his enemies are confounded. To-day he stands as the one recognized spokesman of his ten million fellows, and one of the most notable figures in a nation of seventy millions. One hesitates, therefore, to criticise a life which, beginning with so little, has done so much. And yet the time is come when one may speak in all sincerity and utter courtesy of the mistakes and shortcomings of Mr. Washington's career, as well as of his triumphs, without being thought captious or envious, and without forgetting that it is easier to do ill than well in the world.

The criticism that has hitherto met Mr. Washington has not always been of this broad character. In the South especially has he had to walk warily to avoid the harshest judgments,—and naturally so, for he is dealing with the one subject of deepest sensitiveness to that section. Twice—once when at the Chicago celebration of the Spanish-American War he alluded to the color-prejudice that is "eating away the vitals of the South," and once when he dined with President Roosevelt—has the resulting Southern criticism been violent enough to threaten seriously his popularity. In the North the feeling has several times forced itself into words, that Mr. Washington's counsels of submission overlooked certain elements of true manhood, and that his educational programme was unnecessarily narrow. Usually, however, such criticism has not found open expression, although, too, the spiritual sons of the Abolitionists have not been prepared to acknowledge that the schools founded before Tuskegee, by men of broad ideals and self-sacrificing spirit, were wholly failures or worthy of ridicule. While, then, criticism has not failed to follow Mr. Washington, yet the prevailing public opinion of the land has been but too willing to deliver the solution of a wearisome problem into his hands, and say, "If that is all you and your race ask, take it."

Among his own people, however, Mr. Washington has encountered the strongest and most lasting opposition, amounting at times to bitterness, and even to-day continuing strong and insistent even though largely silenced in outward expression by the public opinion of the nation. Some of this opposition is, of course, mere envy; the disappointment of displaced demagogues and the spite of narrow minds. But aside from this, there is among educated and thoughtful colored men in all parts of the land a feeling of deep regret, sorrow, and apprehension at the wide currency and ascendancy which some of Mr. Washington's theories have gained. These same men admire his sincerity of purpose, and are willing to forgive much to honest endeavor which is doing something worth the doing. They coöperate with Mr. Washington as far as they conscientiously can; and, indeed, it is no ordinary tribute to this man's tact and power that, steering as he must between so many diverse interests and opinions, he so largely retains the respect of all.

But the hushing of the criticism of honest opponents is a dangerous thing. It leads some of the best of the critics to unfortunate silence and paralysis of effort, and others to burst into speech so passionately and intemperately as to lose listeners. Honest and earnest criticism from those whose interests are most nearly touched,—criticism of writers by readers, of government by those governed, of leaders by those led,—this is the soul of democracy and the safeguard of modern society. If the best of the American Negroes receive by outer pressure a leader whom they had not recognized before, manifestly there is here a certain palpable gain. Yet there is also irreparable loss,—a loss of that peculiarly valuable education which a group receives when by search and criticism it finds and commissions its own leaders. The way in which this is done is at once the most elementary and the nicest problem of social growth. History is but the record of such group-leadership; and yet how infinitely changeful is its type and character! And of all types and kinds, what can be more instructive than the leadership of a group within a group?—that curious double movement where real progress may be negative and actual advance be relative retrogression. All this is the social student's inspiration and despair.

Now in the past the American Negro has had instructive experience in the choosing of group leaders, founding thus a peculiar dynasty which in the light of present conditions is worth while studying. When sticks and stones and beasts form the sole environment of a people, their attitude is largely one of determined opposition to and conquest of natural forces. But when to earth and brute is added an environment of men and ideas, then the attitude of the imprisoned group may take three main forms,—a feeling of revolt and revenge; an attempt to adjust all thought and action to the will of the greater group; or, finally, a determined effort at self-realization and self-development despite environing opinion. The influence of all of these attitudes at various times can be traced in the history of the American Negro, and in the evolution of his successive leaders.

Before 1750, while the fire of African freedom still burned in the veins of the slaves, there was in all leadership or attempted leadership but the one motive of revolt and revenge,—typified in the terrible Maroons, the Danish blacks, and Cato of Stono, and veiling all the Americas in fear insurrection. The liberalizing tendencies of the latter half of the eighteenth century brought, along with kindlier relations between black and white, thoughts of ultimate adjustment and assimilation. Such aspiration was especially voiced in the earnest sons of Phyllis, in the martyrdom of Attucks, the fighting of Salem and Poor, the intellectual accomplishments of Banneker and Derham, and the political demands of the Cuffes.

Stern financial and social stress after the war cooled much of the previous humanitarian ardor. The disappointment and impatience of the Negroes at the persistence of slavery and serfdom voiced itself in two movements. The slaves in the South, aroused undoubtedly by vague rumors of the Haytian revolt, made three fierce attempts at insurrection,—in 1800 under Gabriel in Virginia, in 1822 under Vesey in Carolina, and in 1831 again in Virginia under the terrible Nat Turner. In the Free States, on the other hand, a new and curious attempt at self-development was made. In Philadelphia and New York color-prescription led to a withdrawal of Negro communicants from white churches and the formation of a peculiar socio-religious institution among the Negroes known as the African Church,—an organization still living and controlling in its various branches over a million of men.

Walker's wild appeal against the trend of the times showed how the world was changing after the coming of the cotton-gin. By 1830 slavery seemed hopelessly fastened on the South, and the slaves thoroughly cowed into submission. The free Negroes of the North, inspired by the mulatto immigrants from the West Indies, began to change the basis of their demands; they recognized the slavery of slaves, but insisted that they themselves were freemen, and sought assimilation and amalgamation with the nation on the same terms with other men. Thus, Forten and Purvis of Philadelphia, Shad of Wilmington, Du Bois of New Haven, Barbadoes of Boston, and others, strove singly and together as men, they said, not as slaves; as "people of color," not as "Negroes." The trend of the times, however, refused them recognition save in individual and exceptional cases, considered them as one with all the despised blacks, and they soon found themselves striving to keep even the rights they formerly had of voting and working and moving as freemen. Schemes of migration and colonization arose among them; but these they refused to entertain, and they eventually turned to the Abolition movement as a final refuge.

Here, led by Remond, Nell, Wells-Brown, and Douglass, a new period of self-assertion and self-development dawned. To be sure, ultimate freedom and assimilation was the ideal before the leaders, but the assertion of the manhood rights of the Negro by himself was the main reliance, and John Brown's raid was the extreme of its logic. After the war and emancipation, the great form of Frederick Douglass, the greatest of American Negro leaders, still led the host. Self-assertion, especially in political lines, was the main programme, and behind Douglass came Elliot, Bruce, and Langston, and the Reconstruction politicians, and, less conspicuous but of greater social significance Alexander Crummell and Bishop Daniel Payne.

Then came the Revolution of 1876, the suppression of the Negro votes, the changing and shifting of ideas, and the seeking of new lights in the great night. Douglass, in his old age, still bravely stood for the ideas of his early manhood, —ultimate assimilation *through* self-assertion, and on no other terms. For a time Price arose as a new leader, destined, it seemed, not to give up, but to re-state the old ideals in a form less repugnant to the white South. But he passed away in his prime. Then came the new leader. Nearly all the former ones had become leaders by the silent suffrage of their fellows, had sought to lead their own people alone, and were usually, save Douglass, little known outside their race. But Booker T. Washington arose as essentially the leader not of one race but of two,—a compromiser between the South, the North, and the Negro. Naturally the Negroes resented, at first bitterly, signs of compromise which surrendered their civil and political rights, even though this was to be exchanged for larger chances of economic development. The rich and dominating North, however, was not only weary of the race problem, but was investing largely in Southern enterprises, and welcomed any method of peaceful coöperation. Thus, by national opinion, the Negroes began to recognize Mr. Washington's leadership; and the voice of criticism was hushed.

Mr. Washington represents in Negro thought the old attitude of adjustment and submission; but adjustment at such a peculiar time as to make his programme unique. This is an age of unusual economic development, and Mr. Washington's programme naturally takes an economic cast, becoming a gospel of Work and Money to such an extent as apparently almost completely to overshadow the higher aims of life. Moreover, this is an age when the more advanced races are coming in closer contact with the less developed races, and the race-feeling is therefore intensified; and Mr. Washington's programme practically accepts the alleged inferiority of the Negro races. Again, in our own land, the reaction from the sentiment of war time has given impetus to race-prejudice against Negroes, and Mr. Washington withdraws many of the high demands of Negroes as men and American citizens. In other periods of intensified prejudice all the Negro's tendency to self-assertion has been called forth; at this period a policy of submission is advocated. In the history of nearly all other races and peoples the doctrine preached at such crises has been that manly self-respect is worth more than lands and houses, and that a people who voluntarily surrender such respect, or cease striving for it, are not worth civilizing.

In answer to this, it has been claimed that the Negro can survive only through submission. Mr. Washington distinctly asks that black people give up, at least for the present, three things,—

- First, political power,
- Second, insistence on civil rights,
- Third, higher education of Negro youth,—

and concentrate all their energies on industrial education, the accumulation of wealth, and the conciliation of the South. This policy has been courageously and insistently advocated for over fifteen years, and has been triumphant for perhaps ten years. As a result of this tender of the palm-branch, what has been the return? In these years there have occurred:

1. The disfranchisement of the Negro.
2. The legal creation of a distinct status of civil inferiority for the Negro.
3. The steady withdrawal of aid from institutions for the higher training of the Negro.

These movements are not, to be sure, direct results of Mr. Washington's teachings; but his propaganda has, without a shadow of doubt, helped their speedier accomplishment. The question then comes: Is it possible, and probable, that nine millions of men can make effective progress in economic lines if they are deprived of political rights, made of servile caste, and allowed only the most meagre chance for developing their exceptional men? If history and reason give any distinct answer to these questions, it is an emphatic *No*. And Mr. Washington thus faces the triple paradox of his career:

1. He is striving nobly to make Negro artisans business men and property-owners; but it is utterly impossible, under modern competitive methods, for workingmen and property-owners to defend their rights and exist without the right of suffrage.

2. He insists on thrift and self-respect, but at the same time counsels a silent submission to civic inferiority such as is bound to sap the manhood of any race in the long run.
3. He advocates common-school and industrial training, and depreciates institutions of higher-learning; but neither the Negro common-schools, nor Tuskegee itself, could remain open a day were it not for teachers trained in Negro colleges, or trained by their graduates.

This triple paradox in Mr. Washington's position is the object of criticism by two classes of colored Americans. One class is spiritually descended from Toussaint the Savior, through Gabriel, Vesey, and Turner, and they represent the attitude of revolt and revenge; they hate the white South blindly and distrust the white race generally, and so far as they agree on definite action, think that the Negro's only hope lies in emigration beyond the borders of the United States. And yet, by the irony of fate, nothing has more effectually made this programme seem hopeless than the recent course of the United States toward weaker and darker peoples in the West Indies, Hawaii, and the Philippines,— for where in the world may we go and be safe from lying and brute force?

The other class of Negroes who cannot agree with Mr. Washington has hitherto said little aloud. They deprecate the sight of scattered counsels, of internal disagreement; and especially they dislike making their just criticism of a useful and earnest man an excuse for a general discharge of venom from smallminded opponents. Nevertheless, the questions involved are so fundamental and serious that it is difficult to see how men like the Grimkes, Kelly Miller, J. W. E. Bowen, and other representatives of this group, can much longer be silent. Such men feel in conscience bound to ask of this nation three things:

1. The right to vote.
2. Civic equality.
3. The education of youth according to ability.

They acknowledge Mr. Washington's invaluable service in counselling patience and courtesy in such demands; they do not ask that ignorant black men vote when ignorant whites are debarred, or that any reasonable restrictions in the suffrage should not be applied; they know that the low social level of the mass of the race is responsible for much discrimination against it, but they also know, and the nation knows, that relentless color-prejudice is more often a cause than a result of the Negro's degradation; they seek the abatement of this relic of barbarism, and not is systematic encouragement and pampering by all agencies of social power from the Associated Press to the Church of Christ. They advocate, with Mr. Washington, a broad system of Negro common schools supplemented by thorough industrial training; but they are surprised that a man of Mr. Washington's insight cannot see that no such educational system ever has rested or can rest on any other basis than that of the well-equipped college and university, and they insist that there is a demand for a few such institutions throughout the South to train the best of the Negro youth as teachers, professional men, and leaders.

This group of men honor Mr. Washington for his attitude of conciliation toward the white South; they accept the "Atlanta Compromise" in its broadest interpretation; they recognize, with him, many signs of promise, many men of high purpose and fair judgment, in this section; they know that no easy task has been laid upon a region already tottering under heavy burdens. But, nevertheless, they insist that the way to truth and right lies in straightforward honesty, not in indiscriminate flattery; in praising those of the South who do well and criticising uncompromisingly those who do ill; in taking advantage of the opportunities at hand and urging their fellows to do the same, but at the same time in remembering that only a firm adherence to their higher ideals and aspirations will every keep those ideals within the realm of possibility. They do not expect that the free right to vote, to enjoy civic rights, and to be educated, will come in a moment; they do not expect to see the bias and prejudices of years disappear at the blast of a trumpet; but they are absolutely certain that the way for a people to gain their reasonable rights is not by voluntarily throwing them away and insisting that they do not want them; that the way for a people to gain respect is not by continually belittling and ridiculing themselves; that, on the contrary, Negroes must insist continually, in season and out of season, that voting is necessary to modern manhood, that color discrimination is barbarism, and that black boys need education as well as white boys.

In failing thus to state plainly and unequivocally the legitimate demands of their people, even at the cost of opposing an honored leader, the thinking classes of American Negroes would shirk a heavy responsibility,—a responsibility to themselves, a responsibility to the struggling masses, a responsibility to the darker races of men whose future depends so largely on this American experiment, but especially a responsibility to this nation,—this common Fatherland. It is wrong to encourage a man or a people in evil-doing; it is wrong to aid and abet a national crime simply because it is unpopular not to do so. The growing spirit of kindliness and reconciliation between the North and South after the frightful differences of a generation ago ought to be a source of deep congratulation to all, and especially to those whose mistreatment caused the war; but if that reconciliation is to be marked by the industrial slavery and civic death of those same black men, with permanent legislation into a position of inferiority, then those black men, if they are really men, are called upon by every consideration of patriotism and loyalty to oppose such a course by all civilized methods, even though such opposition involves disagreement with Mr. Booker T. Washington. We have no right to sit silently by while the inevitable seeds are sown for a harvest of disaster to our children, black and white.

First, it is the duty of black men to judge the South discriminatingly. The present generation of Southerners are not responsible for the past, and they should not be blindly hated or blamed for it. Furthermore, to no class is the indiscriminate endorsement of the recent course of the South toward Negroes more nauseating than to the best thought of the South. The South is not "solid"; it is a land in the ferment of social change, wherein forces of all kinds are fighting for supremacy; and to praise the ill the South is to-day perpetrating is just as wrong as to condemn the good. Discriminating and broad-minded criticism is what the South needs,—needs it for the sake of her own white sons and daughters, and for the insurance of robust, healthy mental and moral development.

To-day even the attitude of the Southern whites toward the blacks is not, as so many assume, in all cases the same; the ignorant Southerner hates the Negro, the workingmen fear his competition, the money-makers wish to use him as a laborer, some of the educated see a menace in his upward development, while others—usually the sons of the masters—wish to help him to rise. National opinion has enabled this last class to maintain the Negro common schools, and to protect the Negro partially in property, life, and limb. Through the pressure of the money-makers, the Negro is in danger of being reduced to semi-slavery, especially in the country districts; the workingmen, and those of the educated who fear the Negro, have united to disfranchise him, and some have urged his deportation; while the passions of the ignorant are easily aroused to lynch and abuse any black man. To praise this intricate whirl of thought and prejudice is nonsense; to inveigh indiscriminately against "the South" is unjust; but to use the same breath in praising Governor Aycock, exposing Senator Morgan, arguing with Mr. Thomas Nelson Page, and denouncing Senator Ben Tillman, is not only sane, but the imperative duty of thinking black men.

It would be unjust to Mr. Washington not to acknowledge that in several instances he has opposed movements in the South which were unjust to the Negro; he sent memorials to the Louisiana and Alabama constitutional conventions, he has spoken against lynching, and in other ways has openly or silently set his influence against sinister schemes and unfortunate happenings. Notwithstanding this, it is equally true to assert that on the whole the distinct impression left by Mr. Washington's propaganda is, first, that the South is justified in its present attitude toward the Negro because of the Negro's degradation; secondly, that the prime cause of the Negro's failure to rise more quickly is his wrong education in the past; and, thirdly, that his future rise depends primarily on his own efforts. Each of these propositions is a dangerous half-truth. The supplementary truths must never be lost sight of: first, slavery and race-prejudice are potent if not sufficient causes of the Negro's position; second, industrial and common-school training were necessarily slow in planting because they had to await the black teachers trained by higher institutions,—it being extremely doubtful if any essentially different development was possible, and certainly a Tuskegee was unthinkable before 1880; and, third, while it is a great truth to say that the Negro must strive and strive mightily to help himself, it is equally true that unless his striving be not simply seconded, but rather aroused and encouraged, by the initiative of the richer and wiser environing group, he cannot hope for great success.

In his failure to realize and impress this last point, Mr. Washington is especially to be criticised. His doctrine has tended to make the whites, North and South, shift the burden of the Negro problem to the Negro's shoulders and stand aside as critical and rather pessimistic spectators; when in fact the burden belongs to the nation, and the hands of none of us are clean if we bend not our energies to righting these great wrongs.

The South ought to be led, by candid and honest criticism, to assert her better self and do her full duty to the race she has cruelly wronged and is still wronging. The North—her co-partner in guilt—cannot salve her conscience by plastering it with gold. We cannot settle this problem by diplomacy and suaveness, by "policy" alone. If worse come to worst, can the moral fibre of this country survive the slow throttling and murder of nine millions of men?

The black men of America have a duty to perform, a duty stern and delicate,—a forward movement to oppose a part of the work of their greatest leader. So far as Mr. Washington preaches Thrift, Patience, and Industrial Training for the masses, we must hold up his hands and strive with him, rejoicing in his honors and glorying in the strength of this Joshua called of God and of man to lead the headless host. But so far as Mr. Washington apologizes for injustice, North or South, does not rightly value the privilege and duty of voting, belittles the emasculating effects of caste distinctions, and opposes the higher training and ambition of our brighter minds,—so far as he, the South, or the Nation, does this,—we must unceasingly and firmly oppose them. By every civilized and peaceful method we must strive for the rights which the world accords to men, clinging unwaveringly to those great words which the sons of the Fathers would fain forget: "We hold these truths to be self-evident: That all men are created equal; that they are endowed by their Creator with certain unalienable rights; that among these are life, liberty, and the pursuit of happiness."

A Talk to Teachers

James Baldwin (1924–1987) was a widely known twentieth-century African American essayist, novelist, and playwright. Born and raised in the Harlem ghettos in New York City, he became one of the most eloquent voices in the struggle for civil rights in the United States. His works, which reflect his own experience as a Black American writer and which focus on themes relating to the struggle for human rights, include *Go Tell It on the Mountain* (1953), his first novel and a best-seller; the play *The Amen Corner* (1965); and a collection of essays entitled *Notes of a Native Son* (1955), which attracted much critical attention and public acceptance in both Europe and America. In November 1962 he wrote a long essay on the Black Muslim separatist movement and the civil rights struggle in general; it was republished as a book under the title *The Fire Next Time* (1963).

On October 16, 1963, Baldwin agreed to give a talk to approximately 200 New York City teachers at one of their professional in-service meetings. The topic he chose to speak on was "The Negro Child—His Self Image." Baldwin delivered the talk extemporaneously, but he permitted it to be recorded. Because Baldwin was a major voice in the civil rights struggle at the time, his remarks were published in the December 21, 1963, edition of *Saturday Review* under the title "A Talk to Teachers." The following selection is from that talk.

Key Concept: a child's right to critically challenge social reality

*L*et's begin by saying that we are living through a very dangerous time.... We are in a revolutionary situation, no matter how unpopular that word has become in this country. The society in which we live is desperately menaced, not by Khrushchev [premier of the Soviet Union], but from within. So any citizen of this country who figures himself as responsible—and particularly those of you who deal with the minds and hearts of young people—must be prepared to "go for broke." Or to put it another way, you must understand that in the attempt to correct so many generations of bad faith and cruelty, when it is operating not only in the classroom but in society, you will meet the most fantastic, the most brutal, and the most determined resistance. There is no point in pretending that this won't happen.

Now, ... I beg you to let me leave that and go back to what I think to be the entire purpose of education in the first place. It would seem to me that when a child is born, if I'm the child's parent, it is my obligation and my high duty to civilize that child. Man is a social animal. He cannot exist without a society. A society, in turn, depends on certain things which everyone within that society takes for granted. Now, the crucial paradox which confronts us here is that the whole process of education occurs within a social framework and is designed to perpetuate the aims of society. Thus, for example, the boys and girls who were born during the era of the Third Reich, when educated to the purposes of the Third Reich, became barbarians. The paradox of education is precisely this —that as one begins to become conscious one begins to examine the society in which he is being educated. The purpose of education, finally, is to create in a person the ability to look at the world for himself, to make his own decisions, to say to himself this is black or this is white, to decide for himself whether there is a God in heaven or not. To ask questions of the universe, and then learn to live with those questions, is the way he achieves his own identity. But no society is really anxious to have that kind of person around. What societies really, ideally, want is a citizenry which will simply obey the rules of society. If a society succeeds in this, that society is about to perish. The obligation of anyone who thinks of himself as responsible is to examine society and try to change it and to fight it—at no matter what risk. This is the only hope society has. This is the only way societies change.

Now, if what I have tried to sketch has any validity, it becomes thoroughly clear, at least to me, that any Negro who is born in this country and undergoes the American educational system runs the risk of becoming schizophrenic. On the one hand he is born in the shadow of the stars and stripes and he is assured it represents a nation which has never lost a war. He pledges allegiance to that flag which guarantees "liberty and justice for all." He is part of a country in which anyone can become President, and so forth. But on the other hand he is also assured by his country and his countrymen that he has never contributed anything to civilization—that his past is nothing more than a record of humiliations gladly endured. He is assured by the republic that he, his father, his mother, and his ancestors were happy, shiftless, watermelon-eating darkies who loved Mr. Charlie and Miss Ann, that the value he has as a black man is proven by one thing only—his devotion to white people. If you think I am exaggerating, examine the myths which proliferate in this country about Negroes.

Now all this enters the child's consciousness much sooner than we as adults would like to think it does. As adults, we are easily fooled because we are so anxious to be fooled. But children are very different. Children, not yet aware that it is dangerous to look too deeply at anything, look at everything, look at each other, and draw their own conclusions. They don't have the vocabulary to express what they see, and we, their elders, know how to intimidate them very easily and very soon. But a black child, looking at the world around him, though he cannot know quite what to make of it, is aware that there is a reason why his mother works so hard, why his father is always on edge. He is aware that there is some reason why, if he sits down in the front of the bus, his father or mother slaps him and drags him to the back of the bus. He is aware that there is some terrible weight on his parents' shoulders which menaces him. And it isn't long—in fact it begins when he is in school—before he discovers the shape of his oppression.

Let us say that the child is seven years old and I am his father, and I decide to take him to the zoo, or to Madison Square Garden, or to the U.N. Building, or to any of the tremendous monuments we find all over New York. We get into a bus and we go from where I live on 131st Street and Seventh Avenue downtown through the park and we get into New York City, which is not Harlem. Now, where the boy lives—even if it is a housing project—is in an undesirable neighborhood. If he lives in one of those housing projects of which everyone in New York is so proud, he has at the front door, if not closer, the pimps, the whores, the junkies—in a word, the danger of life in the ghetto. And the child knows this, though he doesn't know why.

I still remember my first sight of New York. It was really another city when I was born—where I was born. We looked down over the Park Avenue streetcar tracks. It was Park Avenue, but I didn't know what Park Avenue meant *downtown*. The Park Avenue I grew up on, which is still standing, is dark and dirty. No one would dream of opening a Tiffany's on that Park Avenue, and when you go downtown you discover that you are literally in the white world. It is rich —or at least it looks rich. It is clean—because they collect garbage downtown. There are doormen. People walk about as though they owned where they were —and indeed they do. And it's a great shock. It's very hard to relate yourself to this. You don't know what it means. You know—you know instinctively—that none of this is for you. You know this before you are told. And who is it for and who is paying for it? And why isn't it for you?

Later on when you become a grocery boy or messenger and you try to enter one of those buildings a man says, "Go to the back door." Still later, if you happen by some odd chance to have a friend in one of those buildings, the man says, "Where's your package?" Now this by no means is the core of the matter. What I'm trying to get at is that by this time the Negro child has had, effectively, almost all the doors of opportunity slammed in his face, and there are very few things he can do about it. He can more or less accept it with an absolutely inarticulate and dangerous rage inside—all the more dangerous because it is never expressed. It is precisely those silent people whom white people see every day of their lives—I mean your porter and your maid, who never say anything more than "Yes Sir" and "No Ma'am." They will tell you it's raining if that is what you want to hear, and they will tell you the sun is shining if *that* is what you want to hear. They really hate you—really hate you because in their eyes (and they're right) you stand between them and life. I want to come back to that in a moment. It is the most sinister of the facts, I think, which we now face.

There is something else the Negro child can do, too. Every street boy—and I was a street boy, so I know—looking at the society which has produced him, looking at the standards of that society which are not honored by anybody, looking at your churches and the government and the politicians, understands that this structure is operated for someone else's benefit—not for his. And there's no room in it for him. If he is really cunning, really ruthless, really strong—and many of us are—he becomes a kind of criminal. He becomes a kind of criminal because that's the only way he can live. Harlem and every ghetto in this city—

every ghetto in this country—is full of people who live outside the law. They wouldn't dream of calling a policeman. They wouldn't, for a moment, listen to any of those professions of which we are so proud on the Fourth of July. They have turned away from this country forever and totally. They live by their wits and really long to see the day when the entire structure comes down.

The point of all this is that black men were brought here as a source of cheap labor. They were indispensable to the economy. In order to justify the fact that men were treated as though they were animals, the white republic had to brainwash itself into believing that they were, indeed, animals and *deserved* to be treated like animals. Therefore it is almost impossible for any Negro child to discover anything about his actual history. The reason is that this "animal," once he suspects his own worth, once he starts believing that he is a man, has begun to attack the entire power structure. This is why America has spent such a long time keeping the Negro in his place. What I am trying to suggest to you is that it was not an accident, it was not an act of God, it was not done by well-meaning people muddling into something which they didn't understand. It was a deliberate policy hammered into place in order to make money from black flesh. And now, in 1963, because we have never faced this fact, we are in intolerable trouble.

The Reconstruction, as I read the evidence, was a bargain between the North and South to this effect: "We've liberated them from the land—and delivered them to the bosses." When we left Mississippi to come North we did not come to freedom. We came to the bottom of the labor market, and we are still there. Even the Depression of the 1930s failed to make a dent in Negroes' relationship to white workers in the labor unions. Even today, so brainwashed is this republic that people seriously ask in what they suppose to be good faith, "What does the Negro want?" I've heard a great many asinine questions in my life, but that is perhaps the most asinine and perhaps the most insulting. But the point here is that people who ask that question, thinking that they ask it in good faith, are really the victims of this conspiracy to make Negroes believe they are less than human.

In order for me to live, I decided very early that some mistake had been made somewhere. I was not a "nigger" even though you called me one. But if I was a "nigger" in your eyes, there was something about *you*—there was something *you* needed. I had to realize when I was very young that I was none of those things I was told I was. I was not, for example, happy. I never touched a watermelon for all kinds of reasons. I had been invented by white people, and I knew enough about life by this time to understand that whatever you invent, whatever you project, is you! So where we are now is that a whole country of people believe I'm a "nigger," and I *don't*, and the battle's on! Because if I am not what I've been told I am, then it means that *you're* not what you thought *you* were *either!* And that is the crisis.

It is not really a "Negro revolution" that is upsetting this country. What is upsetting the country is a sense of its own identity. If, for example, one managed to change the curriculum in all the schools so that Negroes learned more about themselves and their real contributions to this culture, you would be liberating not only Negroes, you'd be liberating white people who know nothing about their own history. And the reason is that if you are compelled to lie about one aspect of anybody's history, you must lie about it all. If you have to lie about my real role here, if you have to pretend that I hoed all that cotton just because I loved you, then you have done something to yourself. You are mad.

Now let's go back a minute. I talked earlier about those silent people—the porter and the maid—who, as I said, don't look up at the sky if you ask them if it is raining, but look into your face. My ancestors and I were very well trained. We understood very early that this was not a Christian nation. It didn't matter what you said or how often you went to church. My father and my mother and my grandfather and my grandmother knew that Christians didn't act this way. It was as simple as that. And if that was so there was no point in dealing with white people in terms of their own moral professions, for they were not going to honor them. What one did was to turn away, smiling all the time, and tell white people what they wanted to hear. But people always accuse you of reckless talk when you say this.

All this means that there are in this country tremendous reservoirs of bitterness which have never been able to find an outlet, but may find an outlet soon. It means that well-meaning white liberals place themselves in great danger when they try to deal with Negroes as though they were missionaries. It means, in brief, that a great price is demanded to liberate all those silent people so that they can breathe for the first time and *tell* you what they think of you. And a price is demanded to liberate all those white children—some of them near forty—who have never grown up, and who never will grow up, because they have no sense of their identity.

What passes for identity in America is a series of myths about one's heroic ancestors. It's astounding to me, for example, that so many people really appear to believe that the country was founded by a band of heroes who wanted to be free. That happens not to be true. What happened was that some people left Europe because they couldn't stay there any longer and had to go someplace else to make it. That's all. They were hungry, they were poor, they were convicts. Those who were making it in England, for example, did not get on the *Mayflower*. That's how the country was settled. Not by Gary Cooper. Yet we have a whole race of people, a whole republic, who believe the myths to the point where even today they select political representatives, as far as I can tell, by how closely they resemble Gary Cooper. Now this is dangerously infantile, and it shows in every level of national life. When I was living in Europe, for example, one of the worst revelations to me was the way Americans walked around Europe buying this and buying that and insulting everybody—not even out of malice, just because they didn't know any better. Well, that is the way they have always treated me. They weren't cruel, they just didn't know you were alive. They didn't know you had any feelings.

What I am trying to suggest here is that in the doing of all this for 100 years or more, it is the American white man who has long since lost his grip on reality. In some peculiar way, having created this myth about Negroes, and the myth about his own history, he created myths about the world so that, for example, he was astounded that some people could prefer Castro, astounded that there are people in the world who don't go into hiding when they hear the word "Communism," astounded that Communism is one of the realities of the twentieth century which we will not overcome by pretending that it does not exist. The political level in this country now, on the part of people who should know better, is abysmal.

The Bible says somewhere that where there is no vision the people perish. I don't think anyone can doubt that in this country today we are menaced—intolerably menaced—by a lack of vision.

It is inconceivable that a sovereign people should continue, as we do so abjectly, to say, "I can't do anything about it. It's the government." The government is the creation of the people. It is responsible to the people. And the people are responsible for it. No American has the right to allow the present government to say, when Negro children are being bombed and hosed and shot and beaten all over the deep South, that there is nothing we can do about it. There must have been a day in this country's life when the bombing of four children in Sunday School would have created a public uproar and endangered the life of a Governor Wallace. It happened here and there was no public uproar.

I began by saying that one of the paradoxes of education was that precisely at the point when you begin to develop a conscience, you must find yourself at war with your society. It is your responsibility to change society if you think of yourself as an educated person. And on the basis of the evidence—the moral and political evidence—one is compelled to say that this is a backward society. Now if I were a teacher in this school, or any Negro school, and I was dealing with Negro children, who were in my care only a few hours of every day and would then return to their homes and to the streets, children who have an apprehension of their future which with every hour grows grimmer and darker, I would try to teach them—I would try to make them know—that those streets, those houses, those dangers, those agonies by which they are surrounded, are criminal. I would try to make each child know that these things are the results of a criminal conspiracy to destroy him. I would teach him that if he intends to get to be a man, he must at once decide that he is stronger than this conspiracy and that he must never make his peace with it. And that one of his weapons for refusing to make his peace with it and for destroying it depends on what he decides he is worth. I would teach him that there are currently very few standards in this country which are worth a man's respect. That it is up to him to begin to change these standards for the sake of the life and the health of the country. I would suggest to him that the popular culture—as represented, for example, on television and in comic books and in movies—is based on fantasies created by very ill people, and he must be aware that these are fantasies that have nothing to do with reality. I would teach him that the press he reads is not as free as it says it is—and that he can do something about that, too. I would try to make him know that just as American history is longer, larger, more various, more beautiful, and more terrible than anything anyone has ever said about it, so is the world larger, more daring, more beautiful and more terrible, but principally larger—and that it belongs to him. I would teach him that he doesn't have to be bound by the expediencies of any given Administration, any given policy, any given time—that he has the right and the necessity to examine everything. I would try to show him that one has not learned anything about Castro when one says, "He is a Communist." This is a way of *not* learning something about

Castro, something about Cuba, something, in fact, about the world. I would suggest to him that he is living, at the moment, in an enormous province. America is not the world and if America is going to become a nation, she must find a way—and this child must help her to find a way—to use the tremendous potential and tremendous energy which this child represents. If this country does not find a way to use that energy, it will be destroyed by that energy.

Struggle for Public Policy: Black Children Since 1950

Meyer Weinberg (b. 1920) was a professor of history in the Graduate School of Education as well as director of the Center for Equal Education at Northwestern University. He has also been a professor of history at the City Colleges of Chicago and editor of the journal *Integrated Education.* Throughout his career, Weinberg has been a leader in the fight for human rights in education.

The selection that follows is from what many consider to be one of the most important books ever published on the history of race and education. The selection is from chapter 3, "Struggle for Public Policy: Black Children Since 1950," of Weinberg's *A Chance to Learn: The History of Race and Education in the United States* (Cambridge University Press, 1977). In it, Weinberg traces African Americans' struggle for freedom in the years just prior to the historic *Brown v. Board of Education of Topeka, Kansas,* decision in 1954 and the efforts to achieve school desegregation in the United States from *Brown* to the 1970s. He documents the historic leadership of Thurgood Marshall, chief counsel for the plaintiffs. He builds on the prior scholarship of African American scholars as well as on his close study of the arguments in the *Brown* decision and the historic events during and after the case. Weinberg's narrative embodies a convincing argument for social justice in America.

Key Concept: Black children and the struggle for equality of education

Midcentury marked a turning point in the history of black America. The movement for equality came under black leadership, embraced unprecedented numbers of Negroes, and became national in scope. A persistent black initiative forced a reformulation of public policies in education.

During the 1930s depression and discrimination had driven Negro living standards to new depths. Inequalities of schooling between black and white children in the South reached their widest extent in almost a century. Segregation spread in southern and northern cities. Yet a counter-movement began in the midst of despair. As earlier, political strength was a condition for impetus toward equality. In northern cities, the Negro vote became a counter for political change. New Deal welfare policies relieved significantly extensive unemployment among blacks. In 1936, in a wholesale switch away from the Republican party, Negroes became strong supporters of the Roosevelt administration. The emerging industrial union movement in the Congress of Industrial Organizations enrolled hundreds of thousands of blacks, giving "black and white workers a sense of common interest, of solidarity, that transcended racial lines."

World War II sped the process of transformation. Racial discrimination continued in employment, the armed forces, education, and public accommodations, but black protest was insistent. Membership in the NAACP grew almost ninefold between 1940 and 1946, from 50,556 to nearly 450,000. The group's branches increased threefold to 1,073. Negroes turned to demonstrative actions. The grandest of them was the projected March on Washington, organized in 1941 by A. Philip Randolph, a black labor leader. To head off the protest, President Roosevelt agreed to act against job discrimination and created by executive order the Fair Employment Practices Committee. "The Negro masses," as Dalfiume observes, "simply did not support a strategy of moderating their grievances for the duration of the war." Blacks hastened to point out parallels between Nazi racial doctrines and American racial practices.

In 1944, the U.S. Supreme Court struck down the "white primary" law of Texas, invalidating the single most important means of disfranchising the Negro voter. During the next dozen years, the number of registered Negro voters in the South rose nearly fivefold, from 250,000 to almost 1.25 million. The Negro vote seemed to be a significant element in the 1948 election of President Truman. A number of state and local measures were enacted on behalf of equal use of public accommodations and fair employment.

Southern schooling had undergone few important changes during the war. In 1946, Du Bois could write:

> The majority of Negro children in the United States, from 6 to 18, do not have the opportunity to learn to read and write. We know this is true in the country districts of Mississippi, Louisiana and a half dozen other southern states. But even in the towns and cities of the South, the Negro schools are so crowded and ill-equipped that no thorough teaching is possible.

TEACHER AND PARENT DEMANDS FOR EQUALIZATION

A new dynamic was introduced into black education when Negro teachers began taking on a new role during the late thirties and wartime. During the war, blacks became more numerous in the ranks of teachers in northern schools. Historically self-restrained from taking public action, even on behalf of their own group interests, they now began to respond publicly. They filed lawsuits demanding salary equalization with white teachers in a test of the doctrine of separate-but-equal. Courts responded almost uniformly in their favor. By 1948, of twenty-seven cases only four were lost. These victories introduced major strains into the structure of southern schools, based as they were on malappropriation of funds for whites that belonged to Negro students. If equal expenditures became a fact, white privilege would exist no longer.

The court victories engendered, in Jones's phrase, a "contagion" among black teachers throughout the South. State authorities moved quickly to create single salary schedules. They provided for state subsidies to those local school districts that pleaded an inability to meet the new requirement, lest impecunious districts be tempted to avoid creating expensive duplicate facilities by ending segregation.

Teacher equalization was often moderated by southern judges. On the one hand, they rejected school board complaints that they could not afford equalization; on the other hand, courts did not grant immediate relief to the teachers, but set up a time schedule over which equalization was to be achieved, thus, some believe, acting to coerce the Negro teachers into softening their demands.

School boards resorted to a "professional rating scale." Salaries were to be set in accordance with the judgment of the subject's supervisors, who presumably would employ defensible professional criteria. Black teachers' salaries most often turned out to be lower than their experience and training warranted. Court challenges to the new system were by and large fruitless. It proved almost impossible for the aggrieved to demonstrate that the assigned salary was set unprofessionally. To fend off suits by black teachers, one school district in Florida provided that any teacher dissatisfied with his or her placement could take the National Teacher Examination and permit the salary to be raised or lowered in accordance with the test score. The test was notorious among black teachers for its uncanny success in yielding low grades to Negro teachers. Consequently, few took up the dare.

The salary gap between black and white teachers narrowed nevertheless. In the dozen years after 1939, the average Negro salary increased from 52.5 percent to 87.2 percent of the average white salary. Black teachers' organizations had developed "a new aggressiveness" that paid off.

Black parents and, in some cases, students, also began to rebel against planned inequality and to demand equalization of facilities and programs. "At that time," NAACP counsel Thurgood Marshall recalled, "the best strategy seemed to be an attack against the segregation system by law suits seeking absolute and complete equalization of curricula, faculty, and physical equipment of the white and Negro schools on the theory that the extreme cost of maintaining two 'equal' school systems would eventually destroy segregation." A number of lawsuits were filed attacking material inequalities and asking for equalization although separate. Some cases were won; their number was not large but their import was. Perhaps 200 cases were filed against southern schools. Neither disfranchisement nor violence could be used to silence protest now. The currents of the time were against both. Southern state governments tried to deflect the movement by a rapid but highly spotty program of improvement of black school facilities.

Increased expenditure on black schools might put off one threat, but it intensified another:

A modernized physical plant and an increase in the quantity and quality of education mean greater diversity of offerings. Herein lies the danger and real significance of the new legal requirements affecting equality of educational opportunities at the physical and curriculum levels for the social system of the South. New offerings in the schools mean an increase in the number of professionally and technically trained persons at all levels—persons who, once trained, will enter the competitive labor market and thereby earn a greater share of the labor dollar.

Yet the white South of the 1940s and early 1950s was far from ready either to yield its privileges or invest seriously in equalization.

Over the period 1939–1951, in six southern states the black-white gap in current expenditures per pupil narrowed from 57.3 percent to 30.3 percent, although the absolute magnitude of the change was slight. The size of the gap in actual dollars was reduced from $53.85 to $50.12. Discrimination persisted. In seven southern states, by 1951, black children in metropolitan areas received only 76 percent of white allocations; in rural areas, 62 percent. In North Carolina, the figures were 95 and 79 percent; in Mississippi, 51 and 33 percent. Between 1940 and 1952, the value of black school buildings rose, reducing the black-white disparity from four-fifths to slightly more than one-half.

Mississippi, with at least one-tenth of all black children in the South, illustrated some of the dimensions of the challenge of equalization. During the 1953–1954 school year, 95 percent of all the one-teacher schools in the state were black schools. Nearly two-thirds of the state's black children attended schools with three or fewer teachers; only one-sixth of the white children attended such schools. Willie Morris said of the black schools in Yazoo City in 1948: "There were no school buses for Negroes, no indoor plumbing, and no central heating." In Attala County, James Meredith was going to school. "I walked to school over four miles each way, every day for eleven years," he said. "Throughout these years, the white school bus passed us each morning. There was no Negro school bus." By 1952, two years after Meredith graduated from high school, some black students were being bused in Mississippi, but many fewer, proportionately, than whites.

Late in 1953, Mississippi legislators began serious exploration of equalization. In 1954, Walter Sillers, speaker of the state house of representatives, acknowledged that "the cost to equalize will be high because in the past we actually have not maintained a dual system of schools, financially. We have maintained a white system."

Among black leaders there was a deep reluctance to abandon the effort to equalize separate schools. About 1948, recounts the historian Kelly, the matter of strategy was raised by Thurgood Marshall, chief counsel for the NAACP Legal Defense Fund: "At this stage of the game, . . . if the school boards in key southern states had shown a general disposition to accept any kind of gradualist program combining more adequate schools with some primary and secondary desegregation, the Association might well have agreed to cooperate, at least for a time." No such overtures were forthcoming, and so the legal attack turned in a new direction. Segregation, as the source of inequality, was to become the target of a sustained legal campaign.

Between 1938 and 1952, the U.S. Supreme Court decided six cases involving inequalities in higher education. These were *Gaines* (1938), *Sipuel* (1948), *Fisher* (1949), *Sweatt* (1950), *McLaurin* (1950), and *Gray* (1952). In each case, provisions for black students were found to be constitutionally objectionable. The Court shuttled between remedies of equalizing separate facilities and outright desegregation. In *McLaurin*, where a Negro was admitted to a previously all-white university, the plaintiff was forced to sit apart, near the door of a lecture room. The court held that this act of segregation of itself impaired McLaurin's equal opportunity to gain an education. This was a virtual declaration that segregation was incompatible with equal treatment. Lawyers for the NAACP Legal Defense Fund seized on the opening. In mid-1950, they began a wholesale attack on segregation as such in elementary and secondary school cases. Until this time, the LDF had argued such cases only on the basis of equalization of separate facilities.

The decision to challenge segregation was historic. In 1934, Horace Mann Bond concluded an important work on the education of black children without proposing that segregation be ended. Indeed, as he recalled later, in 1934 "the institution of racial segregation appeared to be an immutable feature of the American social order." Just sixteen years later, perspectives had altered sharply. A new sense of collective identity among Negroes had emerged from World War II. A readiness and a drive to protest against discrimination emboldened the NAACP to take a more forward position. Black teachers and parents in the South, even the rural South, drew lines with unprecedented daring. In 1954 Lewis found that Negroes as a whole were "developing a new sense of personal dignity and group pride... more akin to the pride of an integrating cultural minority than to pride as such." The managers of the segregated southern system were growing less secure in their conviction that segregation was the surest protection for their privileges.

The new legal strategy required for success close support by black communities. The earlier strategy of challenging unequal facilities in higher education drew very little community support. Few Negroes had been personally involved and, therefore, the effort seemed somewhat abstract. In the late 1940s, when the LDF and the NAACP turned to the common schools, community interest rose.

In Summerton, South Carolina, black parents in 1949 petitioned the school board to relieve severe overcrowding in the black high school. When no action resulted, an NAACP lawyer drew up a formal petition that was signed by 107 parents and children. After a period of inaction, in 1950 a formal lawsuit was entered, requesting not equal facilities but the end of segregated schools altogether. A year later, black high school students in Farmville, Virginia, carried on a strike against deplorable conditions at the school. At first the Negro Parent-Teacher Association supported demands for a new, although separate, high school. After an NAACP lawyer suggested the attack be on separation as such, parents agreed. The school board was petitioned to stop segregating. It refused. In May 1951, parents entered a lawsuit challenging segregation.

In Topeka, Kansas, black plaintiffs acknowledged material equality of black and white schools, but challenged segregation. And in Wilmington, Delaware, a state court granted parents' request that their children be admitted to a superior white school until both schools were equalized. In Washington, D.C., parents challenged the principle of segregation. All five cases were heard together by the U.S. Supreme Court in 1952–1955. They are known as the *School Segregation* cases.

The NAACP Legal Defense Fund, whose staff Marshall headed, represented the plaintiffs. Robert Carter, an LDF lawyer who handled the Topeka case and now a federal judge in New York, told the Court in 1952: "It is the gravamen of our complaint... that... we have been deprived of the equal protection of the laws where the statute requires appellants to attend public elementary schools on a segregated basis, because the act of segregation in and of itself denies them equal educational opportunities which the Fourteenth Amendment secures."

When counsel for the defendants demonstrated that various southern states were narrowing the racial gap in per student expenditures, LDF attorneys denied equality would ever be gained by this route. Thus, Spottswood Robinson explained that "even though Virginia could spend $26 millions—an enormous sum by Virginia standards—all that we succeed in doing is moving from a present 61 cents to 79 cents per Negro student for each dollar that is invested in buildings and sites for white students."

In the 1953 hearings, the NAACP submitted a long historical brief designed to show the role of segregated education in creating an official caste system in the United States:

> Controlling economic and political interests in the South were convinced that the Negro's subjugation was essential to their survival, and the Court in *Plessy* v. *Ferguson* had ruled that such subjugation through public authority was sanctioned by the Constitution.... Without the sanction of *Plessy* v. *Ferguson,* archaic and provincial notions of racial superiority could not have injured and disfigured an entire region for so long a time.

The rights of the aggrieved children "to learn and grow" and "to be treated as entire citizens of the society into which they have been born" were at stake. In the oral argument, LDF attorney James Nabrit inquired "whether under our Constitution the federal government is authorized to classify Negroes in the District of Columbia as untouchables for the purpose of educating them for living in a democracy."

On May 17, 1954, the Court handed down a unanimous opinion in *Brown* v. *Board of Education of Topeka* (347 U.S. 483). The central contention of the plaintiffs was upheld: "In the field of public education the doctrine of 'separate but equal' has no place. Separate educational facilities are inherently unequal.... We hold that the plaintiffs and others similarly situated ... are, by reason of the segregation complained of, deprived of equal protection of the laws guaranteed by the Fourteenth Amendment.

The court withheld any immediate orders regarding implementation. It announced that it would hold hearings later in the year before deciding upon specific measures of relief.

The *Brown* decision was hailed as initiating a new era in American history. Du Bois wrote: "I have seen the Impossible happen. It did happen on May 17, 1954." Much remained to be done against discrimination in travel, public accommodations, health, and elsewhere. Yet *Brown* was hailed as a "great victory," by black leaders and the black press, although Muse notes: "There was no dancing in the streets. The significance was not quickly grasped by the Negro masses."

As he had done so often in his long life, Du Bois summed up both sides of the black equation of anticipation and fear. In an address delivered in February 1955, he spoke of *Brown's* possible long-run effect on American democracy. The decision confronted "Negroes with a cruel dilemma." On the one hand, "they want their children educated. That is a must, else they continue in semislavery." On the other hand, "with successfully mixed schools they know what their children must suffer for years from southern white teachers, from white hoodlums who sit beside them and under school authorities from janitors to superintendents who hate and despise them. They know, dear God, how they know." He predicted that most of the best black teachers would lose their jobs "because they will not and cannot teach what many white folks will want taught."

A large cultural price for the end of segregation would have to be paid by blacks. Du Bois wrote: "They must eventually surrender race solidarity and the idea of American Negro culture to the concept of world humanity, above race and nation. This is the price of liberty. This is the cost of oppression."

"Eventually" was a long way off. Du Bois was by no means urging an end to a study of black history and culture. He wrote: "Much teaching of Negro history will leave the [desegregated] school and with it that brave story of Negro resistance. This teaching will be taught more largely in the home or in the church where, under current Christian custom, segregation by race and class will remain until the last possible moment." (Seven years earlier in the *Chicago Defender,* Du Bois had predicted that within another generation every American college and university would offer a standard course in Negro culture.)

In April 1955, the Supreme Court conducted a five-day hearing on the implementation of *Brown.* Nearly a year had elapsed since the decision. The Court had collected numerous suggestions from plaintiffs, defendants, and other interested parties, including attorneys general from each of the southern states.

The temper of the hearing was curious. Counsel for the plaintiffs was full of foreboding; the opposition was deferential but defiant. One issue was paramount: would the Court set a deadline for desegregation? Without a definite date, no specific commitment to action would follow.

Counsel for Clarendon County, South Carolina, warned: "I think if you ordered the trustees tomorrow to comply or else, that that would destroy the public school system of South Carolina." In Virginia, warned another lawyer, "an integrated system of public schools would require more than a court decree. It would require an evolutionary change in the attitude of people in Virginia, both Negro and white." The attorney general of Texas told the Court: "Texas loves its Negro people." His colleague added that "Texas enjoys harmonious relationships and has made excellent progress in economic, educational, and social advancement." Counsel for the District of Columbia informed the justices that "we have always had a school system which largely, though in two halves, was perfectly equal side by side." In reply to charges the South created and enforced a caste system, a North Carolina attorney explained: "Race consciousness is not race prejudice. It is not race hatred. It is not intolerance. It is a deeply ingrained awareness of a birthright held in trust for posterity."

These protestations of good faith and high moral ground, mixed with practical reminders of the power dominance of whites in the South, were expected by the LDF legal staff. What was disturbing was the possibility that the Court would be impressed by such arguments. In that case, the Court would effectively negate *Brown* by depending on the good faith of local authorities, who, in matters tinged by race, had historically demonstrated bad faith. *Brown* would, then, remain a vague declaration of general rights which no specific child could claim as a basis for action. An order that proclaimed gradualism as an operative principle would necessarily confer constitutional rights on some and withhold them from most others.

This problem had been anticipated even before the *Brown* proceedings started. In April 1952, Howard University held a national conference on "The Courts and Racial Integration in Education," attended by most, if not all, the LDF attorneys who later argued the *Brown* case before the Supreme Court. At the conference, James M. Nabrit, Jr., stressed that "the Constitution gives the Negro the fundamental right to enjoy *now* all benefits offered by the state, without any limitations based on race." Before the Court, during the first round of hearings late in 1952, the same point was made more than once. Jack Greenberg, an LDF attorney, held "that if constitutional rights are being denied our respondents, they are entitled to those rights as quickly as those rights can be made available." During the 1953 hearings, Thurgood Marshall told the Court that desegregation could be accomplished within a year: "If they don't have staff enough to do these administrative things, the sovereign states can hire more people to do it."

During the 1955 hearings, Marshall spoke extensively on the issue. He warned against allowing the pace of desegregation to be left up to the states, Should this happen, Marshall pointed out, "then the Negro in this country would be in a horrible shape. He, as a matter of fact, would be as bad, if not worse off than under the 'separate but equal' doctrine for this reason." District court judges would tend to accept school board pleas for more time, and the right to a desegregated education would be nullified. "This is a national Constitution," said Marshall. "There is no place for local option in our Constitution." Various justices continued to speak of the difficulties and complexities of desegregation. To this, Marshall replied, exasperated: "This Court is not dealing with the complexities, this Court is dealing with whether or not race can be used [in school assignments]."

Most of all, the plaintiffs wanted a definite court order installing desegregation in the litigated districts by September 1955. Marshall stated: "If we cannot get that, then we say that the least that would do us any good at all would be a decree which included four items: (1) That this Court make the clearest declaration that not only those statutes but others are in violation of the Fourteenth Amendment. We think it is necessary for that to be put in the decree. (2) That they start immediately to desegregate. (3) File reports. (4) That it must end at a certain day." Justice Frankfurter objected that the Court had to take into account "certain unalterable facts of life that cannot be changed even by this Court"; he referred to administrative problems. Marshall replied that gradual desegregation could never be effective. Further, he expressed shock "at arguments of the impotency of our government to enforce its Constitution." Without a decree that included a time limit, he concluded, "there will be no protection whatsoever for the decision of this Court rendered on May 17."

On the last day of the final hearing, in April 1955, Marshall repeated the plaintiffs' view, adding a charge of racism, although the target of the charge was not clear. "This time limit becomes a part of the effectiveness... of the May 17 decision," he told the Court. "But," he continued, "I don't believe any argument has ever been made to this Court to postpone the enforcement of a constitutional right." He then added: "The argument is never made until Negroes are involved." Essentially, only Negroes were being asked to forgo their rights.

The position of the national administration on a deadline was expressed in testimony by Solicitor General Simon E. Sobeloff. He opposed placing any general deadline at all in the final decree. On the other hand, he advocated instructing the district judges to inform school districts they must produce a plan within ninety days; extension could be given if necessary. "The thing ought not to be left hanging in the air indefinitely."

Seven weeks later the Supreme Court decided *Brown II* (349 U.S. 294). The cases were remanded to the respective U.S. District Courts to fashion specific decrees. "At stake," wrote the Court, "is the personal interest of the plaintiffs in admission to public schools as soon as practicable on a nondiscriminatory basis." Defendants, the Court held, will be required to "make a prompt and reasonable start toward full compliance." The district courts were to facilitate the admission of the plaintiffs "to public schools on a racially nondiscriminatory basis with all deliberate speed." The Supreme Court thus failed to set either a general deadline, as plaintiffs' lawyers had urged, or even a flexible deadline for the guidance of district judges.

In the retrospective opinion of at least one LDF lawyer, Robert L. Carter, *Brown II* was "a grave mistake." The clear implication of the deliberate speed formula "was movement toward compliance on terms that the white South could accept." In agreeing to less than immediate enforcement of every child's constitutional right, Carter wrote, "the Warren Court sacrificed individual and immediate vindication of the newly discovered right to desegregated education." Justice Hugo Black said much the same thing some years later. *Brown II* weakened *Brown I* in several respects; it strengthened it in none....

In many southern states, material inequality continued under segregation or token desegregation, while states spent tax moneys to fight desegregation and finance private white segregated schools. In Virginia, during 1961–1962, public funds amounting to $2,060,859 in tuition grants were transferred to white children who wished to avoid attending a desegregated school. In 1963–1964, Louisiana granted a total of $3,500,000. The transfer of public school property to private schools was authorized by law in seven states and tuition grants in eight states. Segregation was financed by public finds, thereby compelling "the Negro taxpayer to pay for insulting himself."

Before 1954, the myth of equal-though-separate was believed by few persons familiar with the facts of southern education. Yet direct evidence of comparative achievement disparities by race was not available. One reason for this is the earlier deliberate failure to gather statistics on Negro learning. In the public schools of the District of Columbia, for example, before 1954 achievement tests were given to white but not Negro children.

Texas, the largest southern state, was not untypical. In 1953–1954, the state's association of school administrators surveyed the quality of Texas education. Based on a study of 80 percent of the state's school children, the academic achievement of white pupils was ranked "very satisfactory"; that of Negro pupils was classed as "unsatisfactory." Governor Allen Shivers said "we still have a long way to go in obtaining separate but equal schools." In 1956, while three out of five white fourth-graders in Dallas were at or above grade level in reading achievement—the pivot of school success—only one of eight Negro children was so classified. In Houston during 1961 white first-graders averaged grade *B*; Negro first-graders averaged *C*. Three years later, 40 percent of the students in Houston's all-Negro Texas Southern University were taking, the school's dean of arts and sciences said, courses to supply them with knowledge they should have learned in high school. An investigator for the U.S. Commission on Civil Rights recalled, in 1964, that eight years earlier the average Negro eighth-grader in Houston had lagged behind the average white eighth-grader nearly a year and a half in spelling and three and a third years in reading (paragraph meaning). He did not report later data.

In Tennessee, the usual pattern held. Negro sixth-graders in Nashville were more than two years behind white children. Knoxville superintendent Thomas N. Johnson reported that Negro children were almost one and one-half years behind white children. In Memphis, Negro eighth-graders lagged two years and two months behind whites in achievement. A study for the U.S. Commission on Civil Rights commented that the state's educators frequently complained that Negro students lagged, on the average, from one and one-half to two grade levels.

The conclusion reached in 1962 by a similar study covering Virginia could apply more or less to the other southern states: "Negro education in Negro schools is not equal to the education provided whites, either in tangible aspects or, more importantly, in intangibles. Officially, very little is being done to improve the quality of this education. At present the educational opportunity of white and Negro children in the state is not [even] comparable."

During the years 1954–1964, southern educators in desegregated schools responded to achievement differentials by initiating or expanding ability grouping and tracking systems. This was the case in the District of Columbia, Saint Louis, Baltimore, and Wilmington, Delaware. When the tracking plan was first introduced for District of Columbia tenth graders in 1956, the 1,118 white and 2,822 black children were distributed as follows:

191

*Meyer
Weinberg*

College preparatory course
315 (86.7 percent) of whites
50 (13.7 percent) of blacks
Terminal course
685 (30.7 percent) of whites
1,453 (69.3 percent) of blacks
Basic course
158 (10.7 percent) of whites
1,319 (89.3 percent) of blacks

The college preparatory track was virtually all white; the basic track was overwhelmingly black. Little was tried to narrow the achievement gap, and less was accomplished. Before desegregation, the offering of special classes, including provisions for "slow learners," was common in the white schools of the District of Columbia, "but the Negro side of the school system had relatively few because of the lack of funds allocated for the purpose." School authorities claimed that tracking was a means of improving student performance by moving to higher tracks. Seven years after initiation of tracking, 96.9 percent of junior high school students in the District of Columbia were still in the track they had occupied two years earlier. . . .

THE LAW AND THE JUDICIARY

Neither *Brown* nor the Civil Rights Act of 1964 dealt with urban-style segregation. A common defense of northern school boards when charged with segregation during the 1950s and early 1960s was to point to residential segregation as the real culprit. Yet as one legal expert contended in 1965: "In every case of racially imbalanced schools sufficient responsibility can be ascribed to government to satisfy the requirement that stems from the equal protection clause's proscription of unequal treatment by government." No grand legal principle to this effect could have been proclaimed by any high court. Yet pragmatically, just such a structure of legal reasoning came into being by the opening of the 1970s. It took two main avenues: (1) state actions against so-called de facto segregation and (2) federal lower court actions against deliberate efforts to sustain de facto segregation.

During the decade after 1962, several northern states adopted legislative, judicial, or administrative standards that permitted or required the disestablishment of segregation, whatever its origin. The novelty lay in creating a positive obligation for school boards to desegregate, regardless of how the segregation originated. This was held by the supreme courts of California, Illinois, Massachusetts, Pennsylvania, and Washington. By administrative action, New York adopted the same policy. A number of other states adopted regulations that fell short of binding requirements.

In the federal courts, plaintiffs had the difficult assignment of proving conscious intent by school boards. Because the segregative techniques were often seemingly neutral, proving intent was not feasible.

CHAPTER 8 The Critical Perspective on the Struggle for Freedom in Education

8.1 PAULO FREIRE AND DONALDO MACEDO

Literacy and Critical Pedagogy

In the selection that follows, which is from *Literacy: Reading the Word and the World* (Bergin & Garvey, 1987), Paulo Freire and Donaldo Macedo demonstrate how achieving literacy is a political action and how people create the power to control their own lives through their own words—through their own expression of the contradictions and realities with which they have to deal in their cultural worlds. The authors argue that literacy "cannot be viewed as simply the development of skills aimed at acquiring the dominant standard language." They argue instead that a human being's decision to become literate is a choice to take power and control over his or her own life. They further state that literacy as a concept must be situated in the context of the struggle for human liberation from established systems of cultural reproduction. Literacy must involve the critical reexamination of all of a society's social arrangements and institutions on the part of those who choose to become literate.

194

*Chapter 8
The Critical
Perspective on
the Struggle for
Freedom
in Education*

Paulo Freire (1921–1997) was an educator in the Graduate Schools of Education at Harvard University. He also taught at the Catholic University of São Paulo, and he was a consultant to the World Council of Churches in Geneva, Switzerland. A pioneer in critical pedagogy whose theories on the social forces that prevent people from fulfilling their potentials have inspired a vast critical literature in the field of education, Freire helped to establish the Institute of Cultural Action (IDAC), and he participated in adult literacy campaigns in several Third World countries.

Donaldo Macedo (b. 1950) is an associate professor of linguistics at the University of Massachusetts–Boston. The book that Macedo coauthored with Freire and from which the following selection comes is considered a critical contribution to the struggle for human freedom.

Key Concept: literacy and human liberation

Within the last decade, the issue of literacy has taken on a new importance among educators. Unfortunately, the debate that has emerged tends to recycle old assumptions and values regarding the meaning and usefulness of literacy. The notion that literacy is a matter of learning the standard language still informs the vast majority of literacy programs and manifests its logic in the renewed emphasis on technical reading and writing skills.

... [L]iteracy cannot be viewed as simply the development of skills aimed at acquiring the dominant standard language. This view sustains a notion of ideology that systematically negates rather than makes meaningful the cultural experiences of the subordinate linguistic groups who are, by and large, the objects of its policies. For the notion of literacy to become meaningful it has to be situated within a theory of cultural production and viewed as an integral part of the way in which people produce, transform, and reproduce meaning. Literacy must be seen as a medium that constitutes and affirms the historical and existential moments of lived experience that produce a subordinate or a lived culture. Hence, it is an eminently political phenomenon, and it must be analyzed within the context of a theory of power relations and an understanding of social and cultural reproduction and production. By "cultural reproduction" we refer to collective experiences that function in the interest of the dominant groups, rather than in the interest of the oppressed groups that are the object of its policies. We use "cultural production" to refer to specific groups of people producing, mediating, and confirming the mutual ideological elements that emerge from and reaffirm their daily lived experiences. In this case, such experiences are rooted in the interests of individual and collective self-determination.

This theoretical posture underlies our examination of how the public school systems in the ex-Portuguese colonies in Africa have developed educational policies aimed at stamping out the tremendously high illiteracy rate inherited from colonialist Portugal. These policies are designed to eradicate the colonial educational legacy, which had as its major tenet the total de-Africanization of these people. Education in these colonies was discriminatory, mediocre, and based on verbalism. It could not contribute anything to national reconstruction because it was not constituted for this purpose. Schooling was antidemocratic in its methods, in its content, and in its objectives. Divorced from the reality of the country, it was, for this very reason, a school for a minority and thus against the majority.

Before the independence of these countries in 1975, schools functioned as political sites in which class, gender, and racial inequities were both produced and reproduced. In essence, the colonial educational structure served to inculcate the African[1] natives with myths and beliefs that denied and belittled their lived experiences, their history, their culture, and their language. The schools were seen as purifying fountains where Africans could be saved from their deep-rooted ignorance, their "savage" culture, and their bastardized language, which, according to some Portuguese scholars, was a corrupted form of Portuguese "without grammatical rules (they can't even be applied)."

This system could not help but reproduce in children and youth the profile that the colonial ideology itself had created for them, namely that of inferior beings, lacking in all ability.

On the one hand, schooling in these colonies served the purpose of deculturating the natives; on the other hand, it acculturated them into a predefined colonial model. Schools in this mold functioned "as part of an ideological state apparatus designed to secure the ideological and social reproduction of capital and its institutions, whose interests are rooted in the dynamics of capital accumulation and the reproduction of the labor force." This educated labor force in the ex-Portuguese colonies was composed mainly of low-level functionaries whose major tasks were the promotion and maintenance of the status quo. Their role took on a new and important dimension when they were used as intermediaries to further colonize Portuguese possessions in Africa. Thus, colonial schools were successful to the extent that they created a petit-bourgeois class of functionaries who had internalized the belief that they had become "white" or "black with white souls," and were therefore superior to African peasants, who still practiced what was viewed as barbaric culture.

This assimilation process penetrated the deepest level of consciousness, especially in the bourgeois class. For instance, with respect to becoming "white," we are reminded of an anecdote about a black Cape Verdian so preoccupied with his blackness that he paid a well-respected white Cape Verdian to issue him a decree proclaiming him white. The man jokingly wrote for him on a piece of paper "Dja'n branco dja," meaning "I have thereby been declared white."

After independence and in the reconstruction of a new society in these countries, schools have assumed as their major task the "decolonization of mentality," as it is termed by Aristides Pereira, and which Amilcar Cabral called the "re-Africanization of mentality." It is clear that both Pereira and Cabral were well aware of the need to create a school system in which a new mentality cleansed of all vestiges of colonialism would be formulated; a school system that would allow people to appropriate their history, their culture, and their language; a school system in which it was imperative to reformulate the programs of geography, history, and the Portuguese language, changing all the reading

196

Chapter 8
The Critical
Perspective on
the Struggle for
Freedom
in Education

texts that were so heavily impregnated with colonialist ideology. It was an absolute priority that students should study their own geography and not that of Portugal, the inlets of the sea and not Rio Tejo. It was urgent that they study their history, the history of the resistance of their people to the invader and the struggle for their liberation, which gave them back the right to make their own history—not the history of the kings of Portugal and the intrigues of the court.

The proposal to incorporate a radical pedagogy in schools has met a lukewarm reception in these countries. We want to argue that the suspicion of many African educators is deeply rooted in the language issue (African versus Portuguese) and has led to the creation of a neocolonialist literacy campaign under the superficially radical slogan of eliminating illiteracy in the new republics. The difficulties of reappropriating African culture have been increased by the fact that the means for such struggle has been the language of the colonizer. As we will argue . . . , the present literacy campaign in these nations concerns itself mainly with the creation of functional literates in the Portuguese language. No longer based on the cultural capital of subordinate Africans, the program has fallen prey to positivistic and instrumental approaches to literacy concerned mainly with the mechanical acquisition of Portuguese language skills. . . .

APPROACHES TO LITERACY

Almost without exception, traditional approaches to literacy have been deeply ingrained in a positivistic method of inquiry. In effect, this has resulted in an epistemological stance in which scientific rigor and methodological refinement are celebrated, while "theory and knowledge are subordinated to the imperatives of efficiency and technical mastery, and history is reduced to a minor footnote in the priorities of 'empirical' scientific inquiry." In general, this approach abstracts methodological issues from their ideological contexts and consequently ignores the interrelationship between the sociopolitical structures of a society and the act of reading. In part, the exclusion of social and political dimensions from the practice of reading gives rise to an ideology of cultural reproduction, one that views readers as "objects." It is as though their conscious bodies were simply empty, waiting to be filled by that word from the teacher. Although it is important to analyze how ideologies inform various reading traditions, . . . we will limit our discussion to a brief analysis of the most important approaches to literacy, linking them to either cultural reproduction or cultural production.

The Academic Approach to Reading

The purpose assigned to reading in the academic tradition is twofold. First, the rationale for this approach "derives from classical definitions of the well-educated man—thoroughly grounded in the classics, articulate in spoken and written expression, actively engaged in intellectual pursuits." This approach to reading has primarily served the interests of the elite classes. In this case, reading is viewed as the acquisition of predefined forms of knowledge and is organized around the study of Latin and Greek and the mastery of the great classical works. Second, since it would be unrealistic to expect the vast majority of society to meet such high standards, reading was redefined as the acquisition of reading skills, decoding skills, vocabulary development, and so on. This second rationale served to legitimize a dual approach to reading: one level for the ruling class and another for the dispossessed majority. According to Giroux (*Theory and Resistance*): "This second notion is geared primarily to working class students whose cultural capital is considered less compatible, and thus inferior in terms of complexity and value, with the knowledge and values of the dominant class."

This twofold academic approach to reading is inherently alienating in nature. On the one hand, it ignores the life experience, the history, and the language practice of students. On the other, it overemphasizes the mastery and understanding of classical literature and the use of literary materials as "vehicles for exercises in comprehension (literal and interpretative), vocabulary development, and word identification skills." Thus, literacy in this sense is stripped of its sociopolitical dimensions; it functions, in fact, to reproduce dominant values and meaning. It does not contribute in any meaningful way to the appropriation of working-class history, culture, and language.

The Utilitarian Approach to Reading

The major goal of the utilitarian approach is to produce readers who meet the basic reading requirements of contemporary society. In spite of its progressive appeal, such an approach emphasizes the mechanical learning of reading skills while sacrificing the critical analysis of the social and political order that generates the need for reading in the first place. This position has led to the development of "functional literates," groomed primarily to meet the requirements of our ever more complex technological society. Such a view is not simply characteristic of the advanced industrialized countries of the West; even within the Third World, utilitarian literacy has been championed as a vehicle for economic betterment, access to jobs, and increase of the productivity level. As it is clearly stated by UNESCO, "Literacy programs should preferably be linked with economic priorities. [They] must impart not only reading and writing, but also professional and technical knowledge, thereby leading to a fuller participation of adults in economic life."

This notion of literacy has been enthusiastically incorporated as a major goal by the back-to-basics proponents of reading. It has also contributed to the development of neatly packaged reading programs that are presented as the solution to difficulties students experience in reading job application forms, tax forms, advertisement literature, sales catalogs, labels, and the like. In general, the utilitarian approach views literacy as meeting the basic reading demand of an industrialized society. As Giroux points out:

Literacy within this perspective is geared to make adults more productive workers and citizens within a given society. In spite of its appeal to economic mobility,

198

*Chapter 8
The Critical
Perspective on
the Struggle for
Freedom
in Education*

functional literacy reduces the concept of literacy and the pedagogy in which it is suited to the pragmatic requirements of capital; consequently, the notions of critical thinking, culture and power disappear under the imperatives of the labor process and the need for capital accumulation.

Cognitive Development Approach to Reading

While the academic and utilitarian approaches to reading emphasize the mastery of reading skills and view the readers as "objects," the cognitive development model stresses the construction of meaning whereby readers engage in a dialectical interaction between themselves and the objective world. Although the acquisition of literacy skills is viewed as an important task in this approach, the salient feature is how people construct meaning through problem-solving processes. Comprehension of the text is relegated to a position of lesser importance in favor of the development of new cognitive structures that can enable students to move from simple to highly complex reading tasks. This reading process is highly influenced by the early work of John Dewey and has been shaped in terms of the development of Piagetian cognitive structures. Under the cognitive development model, reading is seen as an intellectual process, "through a series of fixed, value-free, and universal stages of development."

The cognitive development model thus avoids criticism of the academic and utilitarian views of reading and fails to consider the content of what is read. Instead, it emphasizes a process that allows students to analyze and critique issues raised in the text with an increasing level of complexity. This approach, however, is rarely concerned with questions of cultural reproduction. Since students' cultural capital—i.e., their life experience, history, and language—is ignored, they are rarely able to engage in thorough critical reflection, regarding their own practical experience and the ends that motivate them in order, in the end, to organize the findings and thus replace mere opinion about facts with an increasingly rigorous understanding of their significance.

The Romantic Approach to Reading

Like the cognitive development model, the romantic approach is based on an interactionist approach with a major focus on the construction of meaning; however, the romantic approach views meaning as being generated by the reader and not occurring in the interaction between reader and author via text. The romantic mode greatly emphasizes the affective and sees reading as the fulfillment of self and a joyful experience. One writer praised "the intimate reliving of fresh views of personality and life implicit in the work (of literature); the pleasure and release of tensions that may flow from such an experience . . . the deepening and broadening of sensitivity to the sensuous quality and emotional impact of day-to-day living."

In essence, the romantic approach to reading presents a counterpoint to the authoritarian modes of pedagogy which view readers as "objects." However, this seemingly liberal approach to literacy fails to make problematic class conflict, gender, or racial inequalities. Furthermore, the romantic model completely ignores the cultural capital of subordinate groups and assumes that all people have the same access to reading, or that reading is part of the cultural capital of all people. This failure to address questions of cultural capital or various structural inequalities means that the romantic model tends to reproduce the cultural capital of the dominant class, to which reading is intimately tied. It is presumptuous and naive to expect a student from the working class, confronted and victimized by myriad disadvantages, to find joy and self-affirmation through reading alone. But more important is the failure of the romantic tradition to link reading to the asymmetrical relations of power within the dominant society, relations of power that not only define and legitimate certain approaches to reading but also disempower certain groups by excluding them from such a process.

We have argued thus far that all of these approaches to literacy have failed to provide a theoretical model for empowering historical agents with the logic of individual and collective self-determination. While these approaches may differ in their basic assumptions about literacy, they all share one common feature: they all ignore the role of language as a major force in the construction of human subjectivities. That is, they ignore the way language may either confirm or deny the life histories and experiences of the people who use it. This becomes clearer in our analysis of the role of language in the literacy programs.

THE ROLE OF LANGUAGE IN LITERACY

... Educators must develop radical pedagogical structures that provide students with the opportunity to use their own reality as a basis of literacy. This includes, obviously, the language they bring to the classroom. To do otherwise is to deny students the rights that lie at the core of the notion of an emancipatory literacy. The failure to base a literacy program on the native language means that oppositional forces can neutralize the efforts of educators and political leaders to achieve decolonization of mind. Educators and political leaders must recognize that "language is inevitably one of the major preoccupations of a society which, liberating itself from colonialism and refusing to be drawn into neo-colonialism, searches for its own recreation. In the struggle to re-create a society, the reconquest by the people of their own world becomes a fundamental factor." It is of tantamount importance that the incorporation of the students' language as the primary language of instruction in literacy be given top priority. It is through their own language that they will be able to reconstruct their history and their culture.

In this sense, the students' language is the only means by which they can develop their own voice, a prerequisite to the development of a positive sense of self-worth. As Giroux elegantly states, the students' voice "is the discursive means to make themselves 'heard' and to define themselves as active authors of their world." The authorship of one's own world, which would also imply one's own language, means what Mikhail Bakhtin defines as "retelling a story in one's own words."

Chapter 8
The Critical
Perspective on
the Struggle for
Freedom
in Education

Although the concept of voice is fundamental in the development of an emancipatory literacy, the goal should never be to restrict students to their own vernacular. This linguistic constriction inevitably leads to a linguistic ghetto. Educators must understand fully the broader meaning of student's "empowerment." That is, empowerment should never be limited to what Arnowitz describes as "the process of appreciating and loving oneself." In addition to this process, empowerment should also be a means that enables students "to interrogate and selectively appropriate those aspects of the dominant culture that will provide them with the basis for defining and transforming, rather than merely serving, the wider social order." This means that educators should understand the value of mastering the standard dominant language of the wider society. It is through the full appropriation of the dominant standard language that students find themselves linguistically empowered to engage in dialogue with the various sectors of the wider society. What we would like to reiterate is that educators should never allow the students' voice to be silenced by a distorted legitimation of the standard language. The students' voice should never be sacrificed, since it is the only means through which they make sense of their own experience in the world.

... Educators must develop an emancipatory literacy program informed by a radical pedagogy so that the students' language will cease to provide its speakers the experience of subordination and, moreover, may be brandished as a weapon of resistance to the dominance of the standard language.

As we stated earlier, the linguistic issues raised [here] are not limited to developing countries of Africa and Latin America. The asymmetrical power relations in reference to language use are also predominant in highly industrialized societies. For instance, the U.S. English movement in the United States headed by the ex-California senator S. I. Hayakawa points to a xenophobic culture that blindly negates the pluralistic nature of U.S. society and falsifies the empirical evidence in support of bilingual education, as has been amply documented. These educators ... fail to understand that it is through multiple discourses that students generate meaning of their everyday social contexts. Without understanding the meaning of their immediate social reality, it is most difficult to comprehend their relations with the wider society.

By and large, U.S. English proponents base their criticism of bilingual education on quantitative evaluation results, which are "the product of a particular model of social structure that gear the theoretical concepts to the pragmatics of the society that devised the evaluation model to begin with." That is, if the results are presented as facts determined by a particular ideological framework, these facts cannot in themselves get us beyond that framework. We would warn educators that these evaluation models can provide answers that are correct and nevertheless without truth. A study that concludes that linguistic minority students in the United States perform way below other mainstream students in English is correct, but such an answer tells us very little about the material conditions with which these linguistic- and racial-minority students work in the struggle against racism, educational tracking, and the systematic negation of their histories. ...

We believe that the answer lies not in the technical questions of whether English is a more elaborate and viable language of instruction. This position would point to an assumption that English is in fact a superior language. We want to propose that the answer rests in a full understanding of the ideological elements that generate and sustain linguistic, racial, and sex discrimination. . . .

The new literacy programs must be largely based on the notion of emancipatory literacy, in which literacy is viewed "as one of the major vehicles by which 'oppressed' people are able to participate in the sociohistorical transformation of their society." In this view, literacy programs should be tied not only to mechanical learning of reading skills but, additionally, to a critical understanding of the overall goals for national reconstruction. Thus, the reader's development of a critical comprehension of the text, and the sociohistorical context to which it refers, becomes an important factor in our notion of literacy. The act of learning to read and write, in this instance, is a creative act that involves a critical comprehension of reality. The knowledge of earlier knowledge, gained by the learners as a result of analyzing praxis in its social context, opens to them the possibility of a new knowledge. The new knowledge reveals the reason for being that is behind the facts, thus demythologizing the false interpretations of these same facts. Thus, there is no longer any separation between thought-language and objective reality. The reading of a text now demands a reading within the social context to which it refers.

Literacy, in this sense, is grounded in a critical reflection on the cultural capital of the oppressed. It becomes a vehicle by which the oppressed are equipped with the necessary tools to reappropriate their history, culture, and language practices. It is, thus, a way to enable the oppressed to reclaim "those historical and existential experiences that are devalued in everyday life by the dominant culture in order to be both validated and critically understood."

NOTES

1. By African we mean to refer to African natives belonging to African countries that were colonized by Portugal. For the sake of economy of terms, we have selected this term, but we want to point out that we are aware of the great linguistic and cultural diversity that exists in Africa.

Radical Excesses and Post-Modernism

"Postmodernism" and "deconstructionism" are two leading concepts in the critical theoretical debate over the social purposes of education. The postmodernist movement was founded by Jacques Derrida and Michel Foucault. Derrida used the term *deconstruction* to make the point that all human knowledge is situated in a matrix, or web, of racial, cultural, gender, and social class relations. Postmodernists tend to believe that reason itself is politicized in such a matrix to the extent that people always reason from some politicized situation in life. Postmodernists also maintain that dominant social class, gender, and cultural forces in society exercise effective control over the lives of subordinate social groups, such as cultural minorities, women, and low-income or unemployed persons. When postmodernists turn to educational issues, they argue that teachers must play a socially transformative role in their classrooms by helping students to "deconstruct" the dominant group's vision of social reality and justice and to replace dominant conceptions of knowledge with visions of social reality based on their own experience of it.

In the following selection, Benjamin R. Barber explores the assumptions of critical theory and attacks them from a liberal perspective. Barber is concerned that postmodernism and deconstructionism may become new orthodoxies whose adherents will resist fundamental questioning of their theoretical framework. This selection illustrates the advantages of critical, reasoned analysis of ideas.

Barber (b. 1939) is the Walt Whitman Professor of Political Science and director of the Walt Whitman Center for the Culture and Politics of Democracy at Rutgers University. *An Aristocracy of Everyone: The Politics of Education and the Future of America* (Oxford University Press, 1992), from which the following selection is taken, is his eighth book.

Key Concept: a critique of pedagogical radicals and present-day progressive educators

*T*raditional orthodoxies have too often been replaced with new counter-orthodoxies, no less noxious for being novel, no less inimical to democracy for being offered on behalf of the powerless. Orthodoxy cannot be fought with counterorthodoxy. The challenge is to overcome not to replace dogma, and this requires a critical spirit. I have argued that too many critics of political correctness have drawn a phony picture of neutrality that is oblivious to the realities of power in the modern school and university—particularly when seen from the perspective of the powerless. But pedagogical radicals at times outcaricature their critics and have themselves been oblivious to several of the most insidious modern sophistries, including a species of reductionism that lurks in their own "deconstruction" of traditional academic rationality. They have sometimes aceeded to the temptation to intimidate, to suppress, and to silence not merely the powerful without but the doubtful within. They have been quick to assert as dogma convictions they do not wish to see subjected to critical questioning. And they have all too easily confounded their psychic longing for values with an actual argument on behalf of values.

Powerlessness is a justification for rebellion, but it is not a license for mindlessness. The reality of being without a voice can become part of a good argument, but it is not the same thing as a good argument; it certainly does not exempt the powerless and the voiceless from the obligation to offer good reasons. Indeed, this is precisely why there is both a need and a right to be heard—a right secured only through an education in liberty. This right, however, is not necessarily the same thing as the right to stop others from talking or the right to cease listening. Reason can be a smoke screen for interest, but the argument that it is a smoke screen itself depends on reason—or we are caught up in an endless regression in which each argument exposing the dependency of someone else's argument on arbitrariness and self-interest is in turn shown to be self-interested and arbitrary.

Let us consider the principal sins of the present generation of progressive educators justifiably concerned with the future of democracy—sins more of exaggeration than of attitude. Some of the problem is plain old silliness: the utterly serious and therefore utterly comical insistence on certain campuses that "seminars" be called "ovulars" or the caricatured transformation of Christopher Columbus from a silent movie saint into a silent movie villain, to be known henceforth exclusively as a torturer, plunderer, and proto-imperialist. The instinct of the sympathetic moderate here can only be to cry, "Whoa! Slow down!" In traversing the terra infirma of modern education, I have expressed a cautious solidarity with the progressives who have devoted themselves to institutionalizing in the schools the 1960's critique of establishment education of the 1990s. Yet by trying to negotiate several sharp curves at too great a velocity, some seem in recent years to have skidded off the tracks. In their understandable haste to arrive at more democratic schools, their grasp on the meaning of democracy has sometimes looked shaky. In their devotion to a public education that can encompass a new and radically heterogenous American public, their feel for the public character of public education has been weakened. Impatience has prompted them to travel at reckless speeds; and so, at what we might fancifully call the curve of critical doubt, they have plunged into a gorge of hyperskepticism, where every argument turns relentlessly on itself and where the demand to ground values reasonably becomes a relativization of all values. At the sharp turn of difference, they have fallen into the ravine of hyperpluralism, where overdifferentiation destroys the possibility of integration and community.

204

Chapter 8
The Critical
Perspective on
the Struggle for
Freedom
in Education

I want to examine here these two perils of the current reform movement. Doubt is a powerful vehicle of learning, but moving at too high a speed can also undermine the process. Diversity is a condition of freedom for all, but when it runs off the rails it can rob the "all" of common identity and ultimately destroy the liberty of individuals.

HYPERSKEPTICISM: PRUDENT DOUBT OR FATAL NIHILISM?

All thoughtful inquiry, and hence all useful education, starts with questioning. All usable knowledge, and thus all practical science, starts with the provisional acceptance of answers. Education is a dialectic in moderation in which probing and accepting, questioning and answering, must achieve a delicate balance. Stories must be told, queried, retold, revised, questioned, and retold still again— much as the American story has been. In periods of rebellion, academic no less than social, when challenging authority means questioning answers, there is an understandable tendency toward skepticism, even cynicism. Michael Wood has characterized Jacques Derrida's approach to method as "a patient and intelligent suspicion," which is a useful description of one moment in a student's democratic education.

The methodologies deployed by critics of power and convention in the academy do not always find the dialectical center, however, and are subject to distortion by hyperbole. Sometimes they seem to call for all questions and no answers, all doubt and no provisional resting places. This radicalism has many virtues as scholarship, but as pedagogy far fewer. In its postmodern phase, where the merely modern is equated with something vaguely reactionary and post-modernism means a radical battering down of all certainty, this hyperskeptical pedagogy can become self-defeating.

Skepticism is an essential but slippery and thus dangerously problematic teaching tool. It demystifies and decodes; it denies absolutes; it cuts through rationalization and hypocrisy. Yet it is a whirling blade, an obdurate reaper hard to switch off at will. It is not particularly discriminating. It doesn't necessarily understand the difference between rationalization and reason, since its effectiveness depends precisely on conflating them. It can lead to a refusal to judge or to take responsibility or to impose norms on conduct. If, as Derrida has insisted, "the concept of making a charge itself belongs to the structure of phallogocentrism" (the use of reason and language as forms of macho domination), there can be no responsibility, no autonomy, no morals, no freedom. Like a born killer who may be a hero in wartime but, unable to discriminate between war and peace, becomes a homocidal maniac when the war ends for everyone else, radical skepticism lacks a sense of time and place, a sense of elementary propriety.

The questions this poses for pedagogy are drawn in the recondite language of literary postmodernism and deconstruction, but are of the first importance for education. Does the art of criticism doom the object of critical attention to displacement by the self-absorbed critic? In other words, does criticizing books replace reading them? Can the art of questioning be made self-limiting, or do critics always become skeptics? Are skeptics in turn doomed by their negative logic to be relativists? Must relativists melt down into nihilists? Conservatives have worried that this particularly slippery slope cannot be safely traversed at all, and thus have worried about a pedagogy that relies on a too-critical mode of radical questioning. They prefer to think of education as instilling the right values and teaching authoritative bodies of knowledge to compliant students for whom learning is primarily a matter of absorbing information. When these conservatives appeal to the ancients, it is the rationalist Plato to whom they turn, rather than the subversive Socrates.

Yet pedagogical progressives actually confirm the conservatives' fears when they themselves tumble happily down the slope, greasing it as they go with an epistemology that denies the possibility of any stopping place, any objectivity, any rationality, any criterion of reasonableness or universalism whatsoever. Asked to choose between dogma and nihilism, between affirming hegemonic authority and denying all authority, including the authority of reason, of science, and of open debate, what choice does the concerned teacher have but despair? Where she seeks a middling position, she is offered orthodoxy or nihilism. Where she seeks moderation in her students—a respect for rationality but an unwillingness to confound it with or measure it by somebody's power, or eloquence, or status—she is informed that all appeals to rationality are pretense....

There is little new or surprising in skepticism's consuming appetite. Cynicism has been a tendency of philosophy from the start, and its inclination to move from intelligent suspicion to wholesale paranoia is well documented. In *The Republic* Socrates had to contend with Thrasymachus, who saw behind every claim on behalf of truth or justice a sneaky rationalization of somebody's stealthily concealed interest. Socrates showed that Thrasymachus started with a prudent if furtive suspicion but ended as a moral bankrupt, a sellout to the brute argument of force, unable to defend any notion of virtue or justice. For many of the same reasons, the Sophists of ancient Athens who followed Thrasymachus were understood to be tireless interrogators who could ask, "Yes, but why?" until people with beliefs dropped of exhaustion or surrendered, running out of reasonable "becauses" long before their tormentors ran out of probing "whys."

From their earliest encounters with belief (the claims of subjectivity), knowledge (the claims of intersubjectivity), and truth (the claims of objectivity), pedagogy and scholarship have tried to balance the need to ask questions with the need to offer well-grounded if tentative answers. Since an answer is at least a provisional suspension of questioning, it interrupts the critical process and also suspends the critical element in learning. But unless questioning stops and is at some point provisionally satisfied, there is no knowledge worth the name—neither subjective beliefs, intersubjective values, nor objective truths (however small the *t* in truth).

The pedagogy of questioning naturally and properly takes the standpoint of suspicion. It looks behind appearances and beneath surfaces, and thus has a penchant for reductionism: turning the immediate into the mediated, turning the observed into the intuited, turning apparent universals into actual particu-

206

*Chapter 8
The Critical
Perspective on
the Struggle for
Freedom
in Education*

lars, turning putative reasons into sham rationalizations, turning claims to truth into rationalizations of interest—looking always for a concealed reality behind *prima facie* events.... To reductionists, things are never quite what they seem. Suspicious of truth as an external "empirical" thing or an inherently meaningful text or an uncontested object, they reduce such entities to the conditions (psychological, historical, material) by which they are produced and the interests of those who produce them.

The author of a book, argues Foucault, a reductionist here who sees behind the smoke screen of "reason" a hundred hidden varieties of coercion, is not some vessel of art or creative genius but merely "an ideological product." A book is less a work of literature imbued with truth and beauty or with standards to which human conduct might be made to conform (the old-fashioned view) than a product of its readers or its critics; an emanation of the class, gender, and status of the background that produced the writer or his audience. As David Hume, skeptic and critic of objectivist ethics, said long before deconstruction seized on such arguments, a value is not a symbol for some objective right or eternal good, it is merely a token of someone's preference. To say "It is good" is merely a disguised way of saying "I like it." And whereas (when we allow that objective standards exist) we can presumably assess and argue rationally about human conduct, preferences are purely subjective, and all we can say about them is that at most they exist. The assertion "Cruelty is good" takes a form inviting debate and argument, and may elicit the counterassertion "No, it is evil," which can in turn be debated in historical, moral, and philosophical terms. On the other hand, the descriptive sentence "Cruelty feels good to me" cannot be contested at all other than in terms of its descriptive accuracy ("Does it *really* feel good to you?"). To someone who says "I like being cruel," neither "No, you don't" nor "But cruelty is evil" is an appropriate response. The reductive language of what philosophers call "noncognitivism" makes ethics radically subjective, and it soon vanishes as a subject of moral discourse....

Reducing supposed objective goods to subjective preferences and reducing claims about truth to statements about power and interest are two related forms of a very ancient and very useful but also very risky skepticism. For millennia, both skepticism and reductionism lived as parasites off the host philosophy—which, fortunately, had its own affirmative business to attend to (understanding human conduct in an often unintelligible cosmos). In the last hundred years or so, these two have more or less consumed the philosophical tradition that sustained them. The same thing has happened in literature, as the critic came first to deny the meaning of literature, then to displace it with the activities of the critics. Criticism is now seemingly severed from literature in many universities, leading and independent existence as literary theory in English departments that teach not literature and the art of reading, but theory and the art of criticism. Social scientists and humanists in many other departments, especially those understandably dissatisfied with traditional academe and its spurious appeals to neutrality and universalism, are taking their cue from literary theorists and deploying reductive post-modern critiques against the establishment. This has certain virtues as a tactic but ultimately is poor strategy and bad pedagogy.

... As Edmund Burke once noted, those who destroy everything are certain to remedy some grievance. The annihilation of all values will undoubtedly rid us of hypocritical ones or the ones misused by hypocrites. We can prevent the powerful from using reason to conceal their hegemony by burning the cloak—extirpating reason from political and moral discourse. However, those who come after can hardly complain that they feel naked or that their discourse, absent such terms as reason, legitimacy, and justice, seems incapable of establishing an affirmative pedagogy or a just politics.

Just how crucially such seemingly abstruse issues impact on actual college curricula is unpleasantly evident in this approving portrait of literature and culture in a recent issue of the *Bulletin of the American Association of University Professors*:

> Cultural studies moves away from "history of ideas" to a contested history of struggles for power and authority, to complicated relations between "center" and "margin," between dominant and minority positions. Literature is no longer investigated primarily as the masterworks of individual genius, but as a way of designating specialized practices of reading and writing and cultural production.... The renaming of "literature" as "culture" is thus not just a shift in vocabulary. It marks a rethinking of what is experienced as cultural materials ... [including] media, MTV, popular culture, newspapers, magazines, advertising, textbooks, and advice materials. But the shift also marks the movement away from the study of an "object" to the study of a practice, the practice called "literary study" or "artistic production," the practice of criticism.

How slippery this particular slope has become! What begins as a sound attempt to show that art is produced by real men and women with agendas and interests attached to things like their gender, race, and economic status ends as the nihilistic denial of art as object. What beings as a pedagogically useful questioning of the power implications of truth ends as the cynical subverting of the very possibility of truth. What begins as a prudent unwillingness to accept at face value "objective" knowledge, which is understood to be, at least in part, socially constructed, ends as the absurd insistence that knowledge is exclusively social and can be reduced entirely to the power of those who produce it. What begins as an educationally provocative inquiry into the origins of literature in the practice of literary production ends in the educationally insidious annihilation of literature and its replacement by criticism—the practice, it turns out ever so conveniently, of those asking the questions! Thus does the whirling blade of skepticism's latest reductive manifestations, post-modernism and deconstruction, cut and cut and go on cutting until there is nothing left. Thus does the amiable and pedagogically essential art of criticism somehow pass into carnage.

As epistemology, this is what post-moderns would, in their mimitable jargon, call logocidal—deadly to reason and discourse. As pedagogy it is suicidal, above all to those already deprived of power and voice by the social forms and educational strategies supposedly being deconstructed. It is hard to tell what service a teacher does a ninth grader just learning to read books when she informs him that there is no difference between Emily Dickinson and MTV, both

208

*Chapter 8
The Critical
Perspective on
the Struggle for
Freedom
in Education*

being simply cultural products of interested artisans pushing their particular ideological interests. To make his point about the relativism of cultural values, Houston A. Baker, the current president of the Modern Language Association, tells us there is no more difference between high culture and pop culture than between a hoagie and a pizza. What he means is that there is no more difference between Shakespeare and Virginia Woolf than between Virginia Woolf and a pepperoni slice with extra cheese. This is to say, as John Stuart Mill quipped about Jeremy Bentham's reductionist utilitarianism, that there is no difference between pushpin and poetry.

These are more than theoretical points: Rutgers has offered social science courses not only on film but on MTV, and Duke University teaches Louis L'Amour alongside Shakespeare and George Eliot, not because popular writing deserves a place in the curriculum along with high culture (it does), but in the belief that the distinction between pop and high culture is spurious, an invention of elites trying to maintain their cultural hegemony. Yet without the aspiration to excellence, however contested the end products, "culture" loses its normative and directing power and becomes a cipher; no distinctions can be made between the "culture of pinball machines," "the drug culture," and "skinhead culture," on the one hand, and "Italian Renaissance culture," "the culture of Benin civilization," and "Harlem Renaissance culture," on the other....

Like all fundamental political and social terms, culture is inherently and necessarily normative. That is why we argue about it, why it is contested. That is what makes multiculturalism worth debating. To annul the power of the word "culture" as a standard of human organization, aesthetic and intellectual evolution, and general excellence does nothing to enhance cultural pluralism or learning in the name of liberty and respect. On the contrary, it creates the impression that there are no standards of excellence whatsoever other than the bogus claims advanced by elites.

The confusion of multiculturalists on this question is evident in their ambivalence over whether to take some significant credit for Western civilization by showing its roots in Egyptian and African sources (thereby paying tribute to its many achievements), as does Martin Bernal in *Black Athena,* or to reject it altogether in favor of a radical "Afrocentric" view that celebrates Africa and subjects Western culture to a not so benign neglect, as scholars like Molefi Asante have done. If Western culture manifests certain virtues, if culture implies standards (however contested) and is more than just a collection of artifacts, then the sources of "Western" civilization are worth fighting over. If not, why bother contest their origins at all?

Sometimes multiculturalists want it both ways, sounding a little like the storied defense attorney who, without taking a breath, managed to argue, "My client is innocent, your honor; he never took the jewels, and besides, he didn't know they belonged to anyone, and anyway they were fake." With the same all-encompassing logic, the Afrocentric multiculturalist at times seems to say, "Western civilization is worthless, dangerous, a colonizing imperium with pretended virtues it never lives up to; and besides, it was originally *OUR* creation, a product of an Egypt we can prove was Black, and anyway Black Africa had a great culture of its own, which we can see reflected in the values of so-called Western civilization *IT* actually produced." Critics have suggested that Afrocentrists are not really multiculturalists at all, but monocultural zealots of a civilization other than Europe's. Perhaps a response in keeping with the moderation offered earlier would be to see Afrocentrism as a stage on the way to a more genuine multiculturalism, itself a stage on the way to appreciating America as a culture defined precisely by its diversity and multiculturalism. This eliminates the harsh attack on Western culture, which is of more use to conservative critics looking to dismiss multiculturalism than to multicultured educators.

Conservatives (who surely have to be congratulating themselves privately on their good fortune in being tossed so splendid a provocation!) have repeatedly expressed their horror over the Stanford march led by the Reverend Jesse Jackson not so long ago in which students protesting traditional curricula chanted, "Hey, hey, ho, ho, Western Culture has got to go!" (although it was the course labeled as such rather than the generic entity they were protesting). As new expressions of anti-Western monocultural intolerance, such slogans are reprehensible. But they are also implicit in the reductionist perspective, which denies "culture" any status other than that of "ideological product." By transforming normative truths subject to rational debate that are embodied in the books, conventions, and institutions that constitute a civilization into an unwholesome product of vested interests, the skeptic undermines not civilization but civility, not rationalization but reason, not dogma but the possibility of consensus and thus community. Along the way, in impugning the inherent authority of the idea of culture, he also manages to impugn the authority of the non-Western civilizations to which his multiculturalism supposedly pays homage.

Questioning should challenge objectivity but also be capable of redeeming it. Criticism finds its pedagogical legitimacy in its powers of redemption: the power to save virtue from hypocrisy, truth from its counterfeits, reason from rationalization. Anything else pushes skepticism over the brink and gives to subjectivism the aspect of narcissism. In philosophy, this narcissism is called solipsism, a term suggesting a self so absorbed in the mysteries of its capacity to sense and make sense (or nonsense) of the world that it ceases to perceive anything but itself. This is a matter of the eye being distracted from the object to which the finger points to the finger itself, until the whole world resembles nothing so much as a finger.

... [A]dvocates of the new hyperskepticism... are genuine reformers struggling against the dogmas of what they see as a hypocritical establishment. They seek more equality, more justice, better education for all. They want not just to expose the hypocrisies of power, but to tame and equalize it. They want to reclaim true justice from its hypocritical abusers. They chase shadows in the valley of cynicism but trust they are on the path that leads to redemption.

Yet the instruments of revolution they have chosen are more suited to the philosophical terrorist than the pedagogical reformer. Radical skepticism, reductionism, solipsism, nihilism, subjectivism, and cynicism will not help American women gain a stronger voice in the classroom; will not lift Americans of color from the prison of ignorance and despair to which centuries of oppression, broken families, and ghettoized schools have relegated them; will not provide a firm value foundation for the young in equality, citizenship, and justice. How

210

*Chapter 8
The Critical
Perspective on
the Struggle for
Freedom
in Education*

can such reformers think they will empower the voiceless by proving that voice is always a function of power? How can they believe the ignorant will be rescued from illiteracy by showing that literacy is an arbitrary form of cultural imperialism? How do they think the struggle for equality and justice can be waged with an epistemology that denies standing to reasons and normative rational terms such as justice and equality?

... [R]eason is an ideal that can teach us how to live in comity and free ourselves from the incivility that always attends reasons' failure. When reason is polluted by interest and power, the remedy is not to jettison but to cleanse it. The remedy for hypocrisy is not less but more reason. Rationalization is evidence of reason abused, not proof that there is no reason. The object of questioning is to test and strengthen rather than to annihilate the idea of the rational.

Education is a training in the middle way between the dogmatic belief in absolutes and the cynical negation of all belief. On the fringes where dogma or nihilism prevail, force is always master. Well-taught students learn to suspect every claim to truth and then to redeem truth provisionally by its capacity to withstand pointed questioning. They learn that somewhere between Absolute Certainty and Permanent Doubt there is a point of balance that permits knowledge to be provisionally accepted and applied (science, modestly understood, for example) and allows conduct to be provisionally evaluated in a fashion that makes ethics, community, and democracy possible. There is much illusion in this fragile middle ground. Civilization, Yeats reminded us, it tied together by a hoop of illusion. It would be dangerous to pretend that the illusion is real, but it is fatal to dispense with it altogether. Justice and democracy are the illusions that permit us to live in comity. Truth and knowledge are the illusions that permit us to live commodiously. Art and literature are the illusions that make commodious living worthwhile. Deconstruction may rid us of all our illusions and thus seem a clever way to think, but it is no way at all to live.

The educator's art is to prompt questions that expose our illusions and at the same time to tether illusion to provisional moorings. The teacher must know how to arouse but also how to mollify the faculty of doubt. Her special art is moderation. She will question whether the statements "This is good! This is beautiful! This is justice!" mean something more than "I control the discourse! I define art! I am justice." But her aim will be to distinguish the counterfeit from the real rather than to expunge the very ideas of the good, the beautiful, and the right. There are illusions and there are illusions. "We the People" as a description of a slave-holding society is an illusion that needs to be exposed; "We the People" as an aspiration that permitted, even encouraged, the eventual abolition of slavery is an illusion worth keeping, even worth fighting for, along with such illusions as natural right and human reason on which the concept relies. The ability to discern the difference between these two forms of illusion is what good education teaches. Such judgment can come neither from inculcating fixed canons nor from deconstructing all canons.

The educator cannot teach when offered only the choice between dogma and nothingness; between orthodoxy and meaninglessness; between someone's covert value hegemony and the relativism of all values. The first business of educational reformers in schools and universities—multiculturalists, feminists, progressives—ought to be to sever their alliance with esoteric post-modernism; with literary metatheory (theory about theory); with fun-loving, self-annihilating hyperskepticism. As pedagogy these intellectual practices court catastrophe.... They give to people whose very lives depend on the right choices a lesson in the impossibility of judgment. They tell emerging citizens looking to legitimize their preferences for democracy that there is no intellectually respectable way to ground political legitimacy.

*Benjamin R.
Barber*

Women and Education

9.1 ELIZABETH CADY STANTON

Eighty Years and More (1815–1897): Reminiscences of Elizabeth Cady Stanton

Elizabeth Cady Stanton (1815–1902) was a leader in the fight for women's rights in the United States. Along with Lucretia Mott and others, Stanton led the call for the Seneca Falls (New York) Convention, which convened on July 19–20, 1848. This event is credited as being the official launching of the organized women's rights movement in the United States. Stanton read a "Declaration of Sentiments" before the Seneca Falls Convention, in which she listed the wrongs inflicted on women by then-existing laws and customs. She demanded suffrage and property rights for women as well as the right of women to divorce for good cause.

In the following selection from Stanton's autobiography, *Eighty Years and More (1815–1897): Reminiscences of Elizabeth Cady Stanton* (T. Fisher Unwin, 1898), we see the beginnings of her commitment as a girl and as a young woman to engage in the struggle for the rights of women. Her writing captures the spirit of her time and of her schooling.

Key Concept: education of girls in the nineteenth century

When I was eleven years old, two events occurred which changed considerably the current of my life. My only brother, who had just graduated from Union College, came home to die. A young man of great talent and promise, he was the pride of my father's heart. We early felt that this son filled a larger place in our father's affections and future plans than the five daughters together. Well do I remember how tenderly he watched my brother in his last illness, the sighs and tears he gave vent to as he slowly walked up and down the hall, and, when the last sad moment came, and we were all assembled to say farewell in the silent chamber of death, how broken were his utterances as he knelt and prayed for comfort and support. I still recall, too, going into the large darkened parlor to see my brother, and finding the casket, mirrors, and pictures all draped in white, and my father seated by his side, pale and immovable. As he took no notice of me, after standing a long while, I climbed upon his knee, when he mechanically put his arm about me and, with my head resting against his beating heart, we both sat in silence, he thinking of the wreck of all his hopes in the loss of a dear son, and I wondering what could be said or done to fill the void in his breast. At length he heaved a deep sigh and said: "Oh, my daughter, I wish you were a boy!" Throwing my arms about his neck, I replied: "I will try to be all my brother was."

Then and there I resolved that I would not give so much time as heretofore to play, but would study and strive to be at the head of all my classes and thus delight my father's heart. All that day and far into the night I pondered the problem of boyhood. I thought that the chief thing to be done in order to equal boys was to be learned and courageous. So I decided to study Greek and learn to manage a horse. Having formed this conclusion I fell asleep. My resolutions, unlike many such made at night, did not vanish with the coming light. I arose early and hastened to put them into execution. They were resolutions never to be forgotten—destined to mold my character anew. As soon as I was dressed I hastened to our good pastor, Rev. Simon Hosack, who was always early at work in his garden.

"Doctor," said I, "which do you like best, boys or girls?"

"Why, girls, to be sure; I would not give you for all the boys in Christendom."

"My father," I replied, "prefers boys; he wishes I was one, and I intend to be as near like one as possible. I am going to ride on horseback and study Greek. Will you give me a Greek lesson now, doctor? I want to begin at once."

"Yes, child," said he, throwing down his hoe, "come into my library and we will begin without delay."

He entered fully into the feeling of suffering and sorrow which took possession of me when I discovered that a girl weighed less in the scale of being than a boy, and he praised my determination to prove the contrary. The old grammar which he had studied in the University of Glasgow was soon in my hands, and the Greek article was learned before breakfast.

Then came the sad pageantry of death, the weeping of friends, the dark rooms, the ghostly stillness, the exhortation to the living to prepare for death, the solemn prayer, the mournful chant, the funeral cortège, the solemn, tolling bell, the burial. How I suffered during those sad days! What strange undefined fears of the unknown took possession of me! For months afterward, at the twilight hour, I went with my father to the new-made grave. Near it stood two tall poplar trees, against one of which I leaned, while my father threw himself on the grave, with outstretched arms, as if to embrace his child. At last the frosts and storms of November came and threw a chilling barrier between the living and the dead, and we went there no more.

During all this time I kept up my lessons at the parsonage and made rapid progress. I surprised even my teacher, who thought me capable of doing anything. I learned to drive, and to leap a fence and ditch on horseback. I taxed every power, hoping some day to hear my father say: "Well, a girl is as good as a boy, after all." But he never said it. When the doctor came over to spend the evening with us, I would whisper in his ear: "Tell my father how fast I get on," and he would tell him, and was lavish in his praises. But my father only paced the room, sighed, and showed that he wished I were a boy; and I, not knowing why he felt thus, would hide my tears of vexation on the doctor's shoulder.

Soon after this I began to study Latin, Greek, and mathematics with a class of boys in the Academy, many of whom were much older than I. For three years one boy kept his place at the end of the class, and I always stood next. Two prizes were offered in Greek. I strove for one and took the second. How well I remember my joy in receiving that prize. There was no sentiment of ambition, rivalry, or triumph over my companions, nor feeling of satisfaction in receiving this honor in the presence of those assembled on the day of the exhibition. One thought alone filled my mind. "Now," said I, "my father will be satisfied with me." So, as soon as we were dismissed, I ran down the hill, rushed breathless into his office, laid the new Greek Testament, which was my prize, on his table and exclaimed: "There, I got it!" He took up the book, asked me some questions about the class, the teachers, the spectators, and, evidently pleased, handed it back to me. Then, while I stood looking and waiting for him to say something which would show that he recognized the equality of the daughter with the son, he kissed me on the forehead and exclaimed, with a sigh, "Ah, you should have been a boy!"

My joy was turned to sadness. I ran to my good doctor. He chased my bitter tears away, and soothed me with unbounded praises and visions of future success. He was then confined to the house with his last illness. He asked me that day if I would like to have, when he was gone, the old lexicon, Testament, and grammar that we had so often thumbed together. "Yes, but I would rather have you stay," I replied, "for what can I do when you are gone?" "Oh," said he tenderly, "I shall not be gone; my spirit will still be with you, watching you in all life's struggles." Noble, generous friend! He had but little on earth to bequeath to anyone, but when the last scene in his life was ended, and his will was opened, sure enough there was a clause saying: "My Greek lexicon, Testament, and grammar, and four volumes of Scott's commentaries, I will to Elizabeth Cady." I never look at these books without a feeling of thankfulness that in childhood I was blessed with such a friend and teacher. . . .

An important event in our family circle was the marriage of my oldest sister, Tryphena, to Edward Bayard of Wilmington, Delaware. He was a graduate of Union College, a classmate of my brother, and frequently visited at my father's house. At the end of his college course, he came with his brother Henry to study law in Johnstown. A quiet, retired little village was thought to be a good place in which to sequester young men bent on completing their education, as they were there safe from the temptations and distracting influences of large cities. In addition to this consideration, my father's reputation made his office a desirable resort for students, who, furthermore, not only improved their opportunities by reading Blackstone, Kent, and Story, but also by making love to the Judge's daughters. We thus had the advantage of many pleasant acquaintances from the leading families in the country, and, in this way, it was that four of the sisters eventually selected most worthy husbands.

Though only twenty-one years of age when married, Edward Bayard was a tall, fully developed man, remarkably fine looking, with cultivated literary taste and a profound knowledge of human nature. Warm and affectionate, generous to a fault in giving and serving, he was soon a great favorite in the family, and gradually filled the void made in all our hearts by the loss of the brother and son.

My father was so fully occupied with the duties of his profession, which often called him from home, and my mother so weary with the cares of a large family, having had ten children, though only five survived at this time, that they were quite willing to shift their burdens to younger shoulders. Our eldest sister and her husband, therefore, soon became our counselors and advisers. They selected our clothing, books, schools, acquaintances, and directed our reading and amusements. Thus the reins of domestic government, little by little, passed into their hands, and the family arrangements were in a manner greatly improved in favor of greater liberty for the children.

The advent of Edward and Henry Bayard was an inestimable blessing to us. With them came an era of picnics, birthday parties, and endless amusements; the buying of pictures, fairy books, musical instruments and ponies, and frequent excursions with parties on horseback. Fresh from college, they made our lessons in Latin, Greek, and mathematics so easy that we studied with real pleasure and had more leisure for play. Henry Bayard's chief pleasures were walking, riding, and playing all manner of games, from jack-straws to chess, with the three younger sisters, and we have often said that the three years he passed in Johnstown were the most delightful of our girlhood. . . .

As my father's office joined the house, I spent there much of my time, when out of school, listening to the clients stating their cases, talking with the students, and reading the laws in regard to woman. In our Scotch neighborhood many men still retained the old feudal ideas of women and property. Fathers, at their death, would will the bulk of their property to the eldest son, with the proviso that the mother was to have a home with him. Hence it was not unusual for the mother, who had brought all the property into the family, to be made an unhappy dependent on the bounty of an uncongenial daughter-in-law and a dissipated son. The tears and complaints of the women who came to my father for legal advice touched my heart and early drew my attention to the injustice and cruelty of the laws. As the practice of the law was my father's business, I could not exactly understand why he could not alleviate the sufferings of these women. So, in order to enlighten me, he would take down his books and show me the inexorable statutes. The students, observing my interest, would amuse themselves by reading to me all the worst laws they could find, over which I would laugh and cry by turns. One Christmas morning I went into the office to show them, among other of my presents, a new coral necklace and bracelets. They all admired the jewelry and then began to tease me with hypothetical cases of future ownership. "Now," said Henry Bayard, "if in due time you should be my wife, those ornaments would be mine; I could take them and lock them up, and you could never wear them except with my permission. I could even exchange them for a box of cigars, and you could watch them evaporate in smoke."

With this constant bantering from students and the sad complaints of the women, my mind was sorely perplexed. So when, from time to time, my attention was called to these odious laws, I would mark them with a pencil, and becoming more and more convinced of the necessity of taking some active measures against these unjust provisions, I resolved to seize the first opportunity, when alone in the office, to cut every one of them out of the books; supposing my father and his library were the beginning and the end of the law. However, this mutilation of his volumes was never accomplished, for dear old Flora Campbell, to whom I confided my plan for the amelioration of the wrongs of my unhappy sex, warned my father of what I proposed to do. Without letting me know that he had discovered my secret, he explained to me one evening how laws were made, the large number of lawyers and libraries there were all over the State, and that if his library should burn up it would make no difference in woman's condition. "When you are grown up, and able to prepare a speech," said he, "you must go down to Albany and talk to the legislators; tell them all you have seen in this office—the sufferings of these Scotchwomen, robbed of their inheritance and left dependent on their unworthy sons, and, if you can persuade them to pass new laws, the old ones will be a dead letter." Thus was the future object of my life foreshadowed and my duty plainly outlined by him who was most opposed to my public career when, in due time, I entered upon it.

Until I was sixteen years old, I was a faithful student in the Johnstown Academy with a class of boys. Though I was the only girl in the higher classes of mathematics and the languages, yet, in our plays, all the girls and boys mingled freely together. In running races, sliding downhill, and snowballing, we made no distinction of sex. True, the boys would carry the school books and pull the sleighs up hill for their favorite girls, but equality was the general basis of our school relations. I dare say the boys did not make their snowballs quite so hard when pelting the girls, nor wash their faces with the same vehemence as they did each other's, but there was no public evidence of partiality. However, if any boy was too rough or took advantage of a girl smaller than himself, he was promptly thrashed by his fellows. There was an unwritten law and public sentiment in that little Academy world that enabled us to study and play together with the greatest freedom and harmony.

From the academy the boys of my class went to Union College at Schenectady. When those with whom I had studied and contended for prizes for five years came to bid me good-by, and I learned of the barrier that prevented me from following in their footsteps—"no girls admitted here"—my vexation and mortification knew no bounds. I remember, now, how proud and handsome the boys looked in their new clothes, as they jumped into the old stage coach and drove off, and how lonely I felt when they were gone and I had nothing to do, for the plans for my future were yet undetermined. Again I felt more keenly than ever the humiliation of the distinctions made on the ground of sex.

My time was now occupied with riding on horseback, studying the game of chess, and continually squabbling with the law students over the rights of women. Something was always coming up in the experiences of everyday life, or in the books we were reading, to give us fresh topics for argument. They would read passages from the British classics quite as aggravating as the laws. They delighted in extract from Shakespeare, especially from "The Taming of the Shrew," an admirable satire in itself on the old common law of England. I hated Petruchio as if he were a real man. Young Bayard would recite with unction the famous reply of Milton's ideal woman to Adam: "God thy law, thou mine." The Bible, too, was brought into requisition. In fact it seemed to me that every book taught the "divinely ordained" headship of man; but my mind never yielded to this popular heresy.

GIRLHOOD

Mrs. Willard's Seminary at Troy was the fashionable school in my girlhood, and in the winter of 1830, with upward of a hundred other girls, I found myself an active participant in all the joys and sorrows of that institution. When in family council it was decided to send me to that intellectual Mecca, I did not receive the announcement with unmixed satisfaction, as I had fixed my mind on Union College. The thought of a school without boys, who had been to me such a stimulus both in study and play, seemed to my imagination dreary and profitless.

The one remarkable feature of my journey to Troy was the railroad from Schenectady to Albany, the first ever laid in this country. The manner of ascending a high hill going out of the city would now strike engineers as stupid to the last degree. The passenger cars were pulled up by a train, loaded with stones, descending the hill. The more rational way of tunneling through the hill or going around it had not yet dawned on our Dutch ancestors. At every step of my journey to Troy I felt that I was treading on my pride, and thus in a hopeless frame of mind I began my boarding-school career. I had already studied everything that was taught there except French, music, and dancing, so I devoted myself to these accomplishments. As I had a good voice I enjoyed singing, with a guitar accompaniment, and, having a good ear for time, I appreciated the harmony in music and motion and took great delight in dancing. The large house, the society of so many girls, the walks about the city, the novelty of everything made the new life more enjoyable than I had anticipated. To be sure I missed the boys, with whom I had grown up, played with for years, and later measured by intellectual powers with, but, as they became a novelty, there was new zest in occasionally seeing them. After I had been there a short time, I heard a call one day: "Heads out!" I ran with the rest and exclaimed, "What is it?" expecting to see a giraffe or some other wonder from Barnum's Museum. "Why, don't you see those boys?" said one. "Oh," I replied, "is that all? I have seen boys all my life." When visiting family friends in the city, we were in the way of making the acquaintance of their sons, and as all social relations were strictly forbidden, there was a new interest in seeing them. As they were not allowed to call upon us or write notes, unless they were brothers or cousins, we had, in time, a large number of kinsmen.

There was an intense interest to me now in writing notes, receiving calls, and joining the young men in the streets for a walk, such as I had never known when in constant association with them at school and in our daily amusements. Shut up with girls, most of them older than myself, I heard many subjects discussed of which I had never thought before, and in a manner it were better I had never heard. The healthful restraint always existing between boys and girls in conversation is apt to be relaxed with either sex alone. In all my intimate association with boys up to that period, I cannot recall one word or act for criticism, but I cannot say the same of the girls during the three years I passed at the seminary in Troy. My own experience proves to me that it is a grave mistake to send boys and girls to separate institutions of learning, especially at the most impressible age. The stimulus of sex promotes alike a healthy condition of the intellectual and the moral faculties and gives to both a development they never can acquire alone.

Mrs. Willard, having spent several months in Europe, did not return until I had been at the seminary some time. I well remember her arrival, and the joy with which she was greeted by the teachers and pupils who had known her before. She was a splendid-looking woman, then in her prime, and fully realized my idea of a queen. I doubt whether any royal personage in the Old World could have received her worshipers with more grace and dignity than did this far-famed daughter of the Republic. She was one of the remarkable women of that period, and did a great educational work for her sex. She gave free scholarships to a large number of promising girls, fitting them for teachers, with a proviso that, when the opportunity arose, they should, in turn, educate others....

After the restraints of childhood at home and in school, what a period of irrepressible joy and freedom comes to us in girlhood with the first taste of liberty. Then is our individuality in a measure recognized and our feelings and opinions consulted; then we decide where and when we will come and go, what we will eat, drink, wear, and do. To suit one's own fancy in clothes, to buy what one likes, and wear what one chooses is a great privilege to most young people. To go out at pleasure, to walk, to ride, to drive, with no one to say us nay or question our right to liberty, this is indeed like a birth into a new world of happiness and freedom. This is the period, too, when the emotions rule us, and we idealize everything in life; when love and hope make the present an ecstasy and the future bright with anticipation.

Then comes that dream of bliss that for weeks and months throws a halo of glory round the most ordinary characters in every-day life, holding the strongest and most common-sense young men and women in a thraldom from which few mortals escape. The period when love, in soft silver tones, whispers his first words of adoration, painting our graces and virtues day by day in living colors in poetry and prose, stealthily punctuated ever and anon with a kiss or fond embrace. What dignity it adds to a young girl's estimate of herself when some strong man makes her feel that in her hands rest his future peace and happiness! Though these seasons of intoxication may come once to all, yet they are seldom repeated. How often in after life we long for one more such rapturous dream of bliss, one more season of supreme human love and passion!

After leaving school, until my marriage, I had the most pleasant years of my girlhood. With frequent visits to a large circle of friends and relatives in various towns and cities, the monotony of home life was sufficiently broken to make our simple country pleasures always delightful and enjoyable. An entirely new life now opened to me. The old bondage of fear of the visible and the invisible was broken and, no longer subject to absolute authority, I rejoiced in the dawn of a new day of freedom in thought and action.

My brother-in-law, Edward Bayard, ten years my senior, was an inestimable blessing to me at this time, especially as my mind was just then opening to the consideration of all the varied problems of life. To me and my sisters he was a companion in all our amusements, a teacher in the higher departments of knowledge, and a counselor in all our youthful trials and disappointments. He was of a metaphysical turn of mind, and in the pursuit of truth was in no way trammeled by popular superstitions. He took nothing for granted and, like Socrates, went about asking questions. Nothing pleased him more than to get a bevy of bright young girls about him and teach them how to think clearly and reason logically.

One great advantage of the years my sisters and myself spent at the Troy Seminary was the large number of pleasant acquaintances we made there, many of which ripened into lifelong friendships. From time to time many of our classmates visited us, and all alike enjoyed the intellectual fencing in which my brother-in-law drilled them. He discoursed with us on law, philosophy, political economy, history, and poetry, and together we read novels without number. The long winter evenings thus passed pleasantly, Mr. Bayard alternatively talking and reading aloud Scott, Bulwer, James, Cooper, and Dickens, whose works were just then coming out in numbers from week to week, always leaving us in suspense at the most critical point of the story. Our readings were varied with recitations, music, dancing, and games. . . .

As I had become sufficiently philosophical to talk over my religious experiences calmly with my classmates who had been with me through the Finney revival meetings, we all came to the same conclusion—that we had passed through no remarkable change and that we had not been born again, as they say, for we found our tastes and enjoyments the same as ever. My brother-in-law explained to us the nature of the delusion we had all experienced, the physical conditions, the mental processes, the church machinery by which such excitements are worked up, and the impositions to which credulous minds are necessarily subjected. As we had all been through that period of depression and humiliation, and had been oppressed at times with the feeling that all our professions were arrant hypocrisy and that our last state was worse than our first, he helped us to understand these workings of the human mind and reconciled us to the more rational condition in which we now found ourselves. He never grew weary of expounding principles to us and dissipating the fogs and mists that gather over young minds educated in an atmosphere of superstition.

We had a constant source of amusement and vexation in the students in my father's office. A succession of them was always coming fresh from college and full of conceit. Aching to try their powers of debate on graduates from the Troy Seminary, they politely questioned all our theories and assertions. However, with my brother-in-law's training in analysis and logic, we were a match for any of them. Nothing pleased me better than a long argument with them on woman's equality, which I tried to prove by a diligent study of the books they read and the games they played. I confess that I did not study so much for a love of the truth or my own development, in these days, as to make those young men recognize my equality. I soon noticed that, after losing a few games of chess, my opponent talked less of masculine superiority. Sister Madge would occasionally rush to the defense with an emphatic "Fudge for these laws, all made by men! I'll never obey one of them. And as to the students with their impertinent talk of superiority, all they need is such a shaking up as I gave the most disagreeable one yesterday. I invited him to take a ride on horseback. He accepted promptly, and said he would be most happy to go. Accordingly I told Peter to saddle the toughest-mouthed, hardest-trotting carriage horse in the stable. Mounted on my swift pony, I took a ten-mile canter as fast as I could go, with that superior being at my heels calling, as he found breath, for me to stop, which I did at last and left him in the hands of Peter, half dead at his hotel, where he will be laid out, with all his marvelous masculine virtues, for a week at least. Now do not waste your arguments on these prigs from Union College. Take each, in turn, the ten-miles' circuit on 'Old Boney' and they'll have no breath left to prate of woman's inferiority. You might argue with them all day, and you could not make them feel so small as I made that popinjay feel in one hour. I knew 'Old Boney' would keep up with me, if he died for it, and that my escort could neither stop nor dismount, except by throwing himself from the saddle."

"Oh, Madge!" I exclaimed; "what will you say when he meets you again?"

"If he complains, I will say 'the next time you ride see that you have a curb bit before starting.' Surely, a man ought to know what is necessary to manage a horse, and not expect a woman to tell him."

Our lives were still further varied and intensified by the usual number of flirtations, so called, more or less lasting or evanescent, from all of which I emerged, as from my religious experiences, in a more rational frame of mind. We had been too much in the society of boys and young gentlemen, and knew too well their real character, to idealize the sex in general. In addition to our own observations, we had the advantage of our brother-in-law's wisdom. Wishing to save us as long as possible from all matrimonial entanglements, he was continually unveiling those with whom he associated, and so critically portraying their intellectual and moral condition that it was quite impossible, in our most worshipful moods, to make gods of any of the sons of Adam.

However, in spite of all our own experiences and of all the warning words of wisdom from those who had seen life in its many phases, we entered the charmed circle at last, all but one marrying into the legal profession, with its odious statute laws and infamous decisions. And this, after reading Blackstone, Kent, and Story, and thoroughly understanding the status of the wife under the old common law of England, which was in force at that time in most of the States of the Union.

9.2 AMERICAN ASSOCIATION OF UNIVERSITY WOMEN

How Schools Shortchange Girls

The American Association of University Women (AAUW) is an organization of college and university graduates that was founded in 1881 to work for the advancement of women. In 1990 the AAUW Educational Foundation's Eleanor Roosevelt Fund commissioned the Wellesley College Center for Research on Women to do an in-depth study and to report on the treatment of girls from early childhood through grade 12. The completed study, which is based on the analysis of several years of empirical research on the status of girls in American schools, was published in 1992. *The AAUW Report: How Schools Shortchange Girls* will be a major source of reliable information on how girls are treated in school for several years to come. The data in the report are to be used to help advise educators and government policymakers on educational policy issues relating to equality of educational opportunities for girls and young women in school.

The selection that follows is from the AAUW's executive summary of their findings, and it includes the association's recommendations for action to improve the quality of opportunities for girls and young women in school. There are many implications for educational policymakers and for classroom teachers in the findings of the AAUW report. The call for gender fairness in the education of all American children is in earnest. The report's recommendations, such as that girls be taught assertive and affiliative skills as well as verbal and mathematical skills, cover several areas of concern.

Key Concept: gender equity in the schools

*F*or those who believe that equitable education for all young Americans is the greatest source of a nation's strength, The AAUW Report: How Schools Shortchange Girls, will not be reassuring. Commissioned by the AAUW Educational Foundation and developed by the Wellesley College Center for Research on Women, the study challenges the common assumption that girls and boys are treated equally in our public schools.

Ironically, AAUW's first national study—undertaken in 1885—was initiated to dispel the commonly accepted myth that higher education was harmful to women's

221

health. This latest report presents the truth behind another myth—that girls and boys receive equal education.

While most of us are painfully aware of the crisis in American education, few understand or acknowledge the inequities that occur daily in classrooms across the country. Didn't we address that problem in Title IX of the 1972 Education Amendments, which prohibits discrimination in educational institutions receiving federal funds? Many of us worked hard to ensure that this legislation would be passed. Its passage, however, did not solve the problem.

This report is a synthesis of all the available research on the subject of girls in school. It presents compelling evidence that girls are not receiving the same quality, or even quantity, of education as their brothers.

The implications of the report's findings are enormous. Women and children are swelling the ranks of the poor, at great cost to society. Yet our education policymakers are failing to address the relationship between education and the cycle of poverty. The shortchanging of girls is not even mentioned in the current educational restructuring debate.

A well-educated work force is essential to the country's economic development, yet girls are systematically discouraged from courses of study essential to their future employability and economic well-being. Girls are being steered away from the very courses required for their productive participation in the future of America, and we as a nation are losing more than one-half of our human potential. By the turn of the century, two out of three new entrants into the work force will be women and minorities. This work force will have fewer and fewer decently paid openings for the unskilled. It will require strength in science, mathematics, and technology—subjects girls are still being told are not suitable for them.

The AAUW Report presents a base for a new and enlightened education policy —a policy that will ensure that this nation will provide the best possible education for all its children. It provides policymakers with impartial data on the ways in which our school system is failing to meet the needs of girls and with specific strategies that can be used to effect change. The wealth of statistical evidence must convince even the most skeptical that gender bias in our schools is shortchanging girls—and compromising our country.

The AAUW Educational Foundation is proud to present The AAUW Report: How Schools Shortchange Girls, *made possible through the generosity of the many supporters of the Eleanor Roosevelt Fund. This report is destined to add a new dimension to the education debate. The evidence is in, and the picture is clear: shortchanging girls—the women of tomorrow—shortchanges America.*

—Alice McKee, President
AAUW Educational Foundation

WHY A REPORT ON GIRLS?

The invisibility of girls in the current education debate suggests that girls and boys have identical educational experiences in school. Nothing could be further from the truth. Whether one looks at achievement scores, curriculum design, or teacher-student interaction, it is clear that sex and gender make a difference in the nation's public elementary and secondary schools.

The educational system is not meeting girls' needs. Girls and boys enter school roughly equal in measured ability. Twelve years later, girls have fallen behind their male classmates in key areas such as higher-level mathematics and measures of self-esteem. Yet gender equity is still not a part of the national debate on educational reform.

Neither the *National Education Goals* issued by the National Governors Association in 1990 nor *America 2000*, the 1991 plan of the President and the U.S. Department of Education to "move every community in America toward these goals," makes any mention of providing girls equitable opportunities in the nation's public schools. Girls continue to be left out of the debate—despite the fact that for more than two decades researchers have identified gender bias as a major problem at all levels of schooling.

Schools must prepare both girls and boys for full and active roles in the family, the community, and the work force. Whether we look at the issues from an economic, political, or social perspective, girls are one-half of our future. We must move them from the sidelines to the center of the education-reform debate.

A critical step in correcting educational inequities is identifying them publicly. The *AAUW Report: How Schools Shortchange Girls* provides a comprehensive assessment of the status of girls in public education today. It exposes myths about girls and learning, and it supports the work of the many teachers who have struggled to define and combat gender bias in their schools. The report challenges us all—policymakers, educators, administrators, parents, and citizens—to rethink old assumptions and act now to stop schools from shortchanging girls.

Our public education system is plagued by numerous failings that affect boys as negatively as girls. But in many respects girls are put at a disadvantage simply because they are girls. *The AAUW Report* documents this in hundreds of cited studies.

When our schools become more gender-fair, education will improve for all our students—boys as well as girls—because excellence in education cannot be achieved without equity in education. By studying what happens to girls in school, we can gain valuable insights about what has to change in order for each student, every girl and every boy, to do as well as she or he can.

WHAT THE RESEARCH REVEALS

What Happens in the Classroom?

- Girls receive significantly less attention from classroom teachers than do boys.

- African American girls have fewer interactions with teachers than do white girls, despite evidence that they attempt to initiate interactions more frequently.
- Sexual harassment of girls by boys—from innuendo to actual assault—in our nation's schools is increasing.

A large body of research indicates that teachers give more classroom attention and more esteem-building encouragement to boys. In a study conducted by Myra and David Sadker, boys in elementary and middle school called out answers eight times more often than girls. When boys called out, teachers listened. But when girls called out, they were told to "raise your hand if you want to speak." Even when boys do not volunteer, teachers are more likely to encourage them to give an answer or an opinion than they are to encourage girls.

Research reveals a tendency, beginning at the preschool level, for educators to choose classroom activities that appeal to boys' interests and to select presentation formats in which boys excel. The teacher-student interaction patterns in science classes are often particularly biased. Even in math classes, where less-biased patterns are found, psychologist Jacquelynne Eccles reports that select boys in each math class she studied received particular attention to the exclusion of all other students, female and male.

Teaching methods that foster competition are still standard, although a considerable body of research has demonstrated that girls—and many boys as well—learn better when they undertake projects and activities cooperatively rather than competitively.

Researchers, including Sandra Damico, Elois Scott, and Linda Grant, report that African American girls have fewer interactions with teachers than do white girls, even though they attempt to initiate interactions more often. Furthermore, when African American girls do as well as white boys in school, teachers often attribute their success to hard work while assuming that the white boys are not working up to their potential.

Girls do not emerge from our schools with the same degree of confidence and self-esteem as boys. The 1990 AAUW poll, *Shortchanging Girls, Shortchanging America,* documents a loss of self-confidence in girls that is twice that for boys as they move from childhood to adolescence. Schools play a crucial role in challenging and changing gender-role expectations that undermine the self-confidence and achievement of girls.

Reports of boys sexually harassing girls in schools are increasing at an alarming rate. When sexual harassment is treated casually, as in "boys will be boys," both girls and boys get a dangerous, damaging message: "girls are not worthy of respect; appropriate behavior for boys includes exerting power over girls."

What Do We Teach Our Students?

- The contributions and experiences of girls and women are still marginalized or ignored in many of the textbooks used in our nation's schools.

- Schools, for the most part, provide inadequate education on sexuality and healthy development despite national concern about teen pregnancy, the AIDS crisis, and the increase of sexually transmitted diseases among adolescents.
- Incest, rape, and other physical violence severely compromise the lives of girls and women all across the country. These realities are rarely, if ever, discussed in schools.

Curriculum delivers the central message of education. It can strengthen or decrease student motivation for engagement, effort, growth, and development through the images it gives to students about themselves and the world. When the curriculum does not reflect the diversity of students' lives and cultures, it delivers an incomplete message.

Studies have shown that multicultural readings produced markedly more favorable attitudes toward nondominant groups than did the traditional reading lists, that academic achievement for all students was linked to use of non-sexist and multicultural materials, and that sex-role stereotyping was reduced in students whose curriculum portrayed males and females in nonstereotypical roles. Yet during the 1980s, federal support for reform regarding sex and race equity dropped, and a 1989 study showed that of the ten books most frequently assigned in public high school English courses only one was written by a woman and none by members of minority groups.

The "evaded" curriculum is a term coined in this report to refer to matters central to the lives of students that are touched on only briefly, if at all, in most schools. The United States has the highest rate of teenage childbearing in the Western industrialized world. Syphilis rates are now equal for girls and boys, and more teenage girls than boys contract gonorrhea. Although in the adult population AIDS is nine times more prevalent in men than in women, the same is not true for young people. In a District of Columbia study, the rate of HIV infection for girls was almost three times that for boys. Despite all of this, adequate sex and health education is the exception rather than the rule.

Adolescence is a difficult period for all young people, but it is particularly difficult for girls, who are far more likely to develop eating disorders and experience depression. Adolescent girls attempt suicide four to five times as often as boys (although boys, who choose more lethal methods, are more likely to be successful in their attempts).

Perhaps the most evaded of all topics in schools is the issue of gender and power. As girls mature they confront a culture that both idealizes and exploits the sexuality of young women while assigning them roles that are clearly less valued then male roles. If we do not begin to discuss more openly the ways in which ascribed power—whether on the basis of race, sex, class, sexual orientation, or religion—affects individual lives, we cannot truly prepare our students for responsible citizenship.

How Do Race/Ethnicity and Socioeconomic Status Affect Achievement in School?

- Girls from low-income families face particularly severe obstacles. Socioeconomic status, more than any other variable, affects access to school resources and educational outcomes.
- Test scores of low-socioeconomic-status girls are somewhat better than for boys from the same background in the lower grades, but by high school these differences disappear. Among high-socioeconomic-status students, boys generally outperform girls regardless of race/ethnicity.
- Too little information is available on differences among various groups of girls. While African Americans are compared to whites, or boys to girls, relatively few studies or published data examine differences by sex *and* race/ethnicity.

All girls confront barriers to equal participation in school and society. But minority girls, who must confront racism as well as sexism, and girls from low-income families face particular severe obstacles. These obstacles can include poor schools in dangerous neighborhoods, low teacher expectations, and inadequate nutrition and health care.

Few studies focus on issues affecting low-income girls and girls from minority groups—unless they are pregnant or drop out of school. In order to develop effective policies and programs, a wide range of issues—from course-taking patterns to academic self-esteem—require further examination by sex, race/ethnicity, and socioeconomic status.

How Are Girls Doing in Math and Science?

- Differences between girls and boys in math achievement are small and declining. Yet in high school, girls are still less likely than boys to take the most advanced courses and be in the top-scoring math groups.
- The gender gap in science, however, is *not* decreasing and may, in fact, be increasing.
- Even girls who are highly competent in math and science are much less likely to pursue scientific or technological careers than are their male classmates.

Girls who see math as "something men do" do less well in math than girls who do not hold this view. In their classic study, Elizabeth Fennema and Julia Sherman reported a drop in both girls' math confidence and their achievement in the middle school years. The drop in confidence *preceded* the decline in achievement.

Researcher Jane Kahle found that boys come to science classes with more out-of-school familiarity and experience with the subject matter. This advantage is furthered in the classroom. One study of science classrooms found that 79 percent of all student-assisted science demonstrations were carried out by boys.

We can no longer afford to disregard half our potential scientists and science-literate citizens of the next generation. Even when girls take math and science courses and do well in them, they do not receive the encouragement they need to pursue scientific careers. A study of high school seniors found that 64 percent of the boys who had taken physics and calculus were planning to major in science and engineering in college, compared to only 18.6 percent of the girls who had taken the same subjects. Support from teachers can make a big difference. Studies report that girls rate teacher support as an important factor in decisions to pursue scientific and technological careers.

Tests: Stepping Stones or Stop Signs?

- Test scores can provide an inaccurate picture of girls' and boys' abilities. Other factors such as grades, portfolios of student work, and out-of-school achievements must be considered in addition to test scores when making judgments about girls' and boys' skills and abilities.
- When scholarships are given based on the Scholastic Aptitude Test (SAT) scores, boys are more apt to receive scholarships than are girls who get equal or slightly better high school grades.
- Girls and boys with the same Math SAT scores do not do equally well in college—girls do better.

In most cases tests reflect rather than cause inequities in American education. The fact that groups score differently on a test does not necessarily mean that the test is biased. If, however, the score differences are related to the validity of the test—for example, if girls and boys know about the same amount of math but boys' test scores are consistently and significantly higher—then the test is biased.

A number of aspects of a test—beyond that which is being tested—can affect the score. For example, girls tend to score better than boys on essay tests, boys better than girls on multiple-choice items. Even today many girls and boys come to a testing situation with different interests and experiences. Thus a reading-comprehension passage that focuses on baseball scores will tend to favor boys, while a question testing the same skills that focuses on child care will tend to favor girls.

Why Do Girls Drop Out and What Are the Consequences?

- Pregnancy is not the only reason girls drop out of school. In fact, less than half the girls who leave school give pregnancy as the reason.
- Dropout rates for Hispanic girls vary considerably by national origin: Puerto Rican and Cuban American girls are more likely to drop out than are boys from the same cultures or other Hispanic girls.
- Childhood poverty is almost inescapable in single-parent families headed by women without a high school diploma: 77 percent for whites and 87 percent for African Americans.

In a recent study, 37 percent of the female dropouts compared to only 5 percent of the male dropouts cited "family-related problems" as the reason they left high school. Traditional gender roles place greater family responsibilities on adolescent girls than on their brothers. Girls are often expected to "help out" with caretaking responsibilities; boys rarely encounter this expectation.

However, girls as well as boys also drop out of school simply because they do not consider school pleasant or worthwhile. Asked what a worthwhile school experience would be, a group of teenage girls responded, "School would be fun. Our teachers would be excited and lively, not bored. They would act caring and take time to understand how students feel.... Boys would treat us with respect. If they run by and grab your tits, they would get into trouble."

Women and children are the most impoverished members of our society. Inadequate education not only limits opportunities for women but jeopardizes their children's—and the nation's—future.

Ecstasy: Teaching and Learning Without Limits

The following selection, which is from *Teaching to Transgress: Education as the Practice of Freedom* (Routledge, 1994), captures the spirit and imagination of a truly committed feminist scholar and teacher. It speaks well to the issues confronting aspiring young women artists and scholars while addressing the possibilities of committed teaching for affirmative learning experiences for both women and men. The selection is a testimony to the possibilities of teaching to enhance students' faith in themselves and their work. It is an autobiographical account entailing true engagement in critical thinking about teaching.

The author of *Teaching to Transgress,* bell hooks (she prefers to sign her name with lowercase letters), addresses the key concept of "engaged pedagogy"—teaching with commitment to one's bravest hopes. Hooks speaks to the heavy personal emotional stresses produced by a teacher's commitment to impassioned teaching without limits. In her concept of "engaged pedagogy," she advocates intellectual as well as emotional involvement of the teacher with the students in the classroom. She addresses the issue of creativity in teachers and asserts that engaged teachers try to spark creative dialogue between themselves and their students. She believes that engaged teachers must be concerned about the lives of their students beyond the classroom setting.

Hooks is the Distinguished Professor of English at City College in New York City. She taught for several years at Oberlin College in Ohio, where she earned great regard from her students. She is an actively publishing feminist scholar whose ideas speak to the affirmation and fulfillment of the aspirations of all persons.

Key Concept: "engaged pedagogy"

O n a gorgeous Maine summer day, I fell down a hill and broke my wrist severely. As I was sitting in the dirt, experiencing the most excruciating pain, more intense than any I had ever felt in my life, an image flashed across the screen of my mind. It was one of me as a young girl falling down another hill. In both cases, my falling was related to challenging myself to move beyond limits.

As a child it was the limits of fear. As a grown woman, it was the limits of being tired—what I call "bone weary." I had came to Skowhegan to give a lecture at a summer art program. A number of nonwhite students had shared with me that they rarely have any critique of their work from scholars and artists of color. Even though I felt tired and very sick, I wanted to affirm their work and their needs, so I awakened early in the morning to climb the hill to do studio visits.

Skowhegan was once a working farm. Old barns had been converted into studios. The studio I was leaving, after having had an intense discussion with several young black artists, female and male, led into a cow pasture. Sitting in pain at the bottom of the hill, staring in the face of the black female artist whose studio door I had been trying to reach, I saw such disappointment. When she came to help me, she expressed concern, yet what I heard was another feeling entirely. She really needed to talk about her work with someone she could trust, who would not approach it with racist, sexist, or classist prejudice, someone whose intellect and vision she could respect. That someone did not need to be me. It could have been any teacher. When I think about my life as a student, I can remember vividly the faces, gestures, habits of being of all the individual teaches who nurtured and guided me, who offered me an opportunity to experience joy in learning, who made the classroom a space of critical thinking, who made the exchange of information and ideas a kind of ecstasy.

Recently, I worked on a program at CBS on American feminism. I and other black women present were asked to name what we felt helps enable feminist thinking and feminist movement. I answered that to me "critical thinking" was the primary element allowing the possibility of change. Passionately insisting that no matter what one's class, race, gender, or social standing, I shared my beliefs that without the capacity to think critically about our selves and our lives, none of us would be able to move forward, to change, to grow. In our society, which is so fundamentally anti-intellectual, critical thinking is not encouraged. Engaged pedagogy has been essential to my development as an intellectual, as a teacher/professor because the heart of this approach to learning is critical thinking. Conditions of radical openness exist in any learning situation where students and teachers celebrate their abilities to think critically, to engage in pedagogical praxis.

Profound commitment to engaged pedagogy is taxing to the spirit. After twenty years of teaching, I have begun to need time away from the classroom. Somehow, moving around to teach at different institutions has always prevented me from having that marvelous paid sabbatical that is one of the material rewards of academic life. This factor, coupled with commitment to teaching, has meant that even when I take a job that places me on a part-time schedule, instead of taking time away from teaching, I lecture elsewhere. I do this because I sense such desperate need in students—their fear that no one really cares whether they learn or develop intellectually.

My commitment to engaged pedagogy is an expression of political activism. Given that our educational institutions are so deeply invested in a banking system, teachers are more rewarded when we do not teach against the grain. The choice to work against the grain, to challenge the status quo, often has negative consequences. And that is part of what makes that choice one that is not politically neutral. In colleges and universities, teaching is often the least valued of our many professional tasks. It saddens me that colleagues are often suspicious of teachers whom students long to study with. And there is a tendency to undermine the professorial commitment of engaged pedagogues by suggesting that what we do is not as rigorously academic as it should be. Ideally, education should be a place where the need for diverse teaching methods and styles would be valued, encouraged, seen as essential to learning. Occasionally students feel concerned when a class departs from the banking system. I remind them that they can have a lifetime of classes that reflect conventional norms.

Of course, I hope that more professors will seek to be engaged. Although it is a reward of engaged pedagogy that students seek courses with those of us who have made a wholehearted commitment to education as the practice of freedom, it is also true that we are often overworked, our classes often overcrowded. For years, I envied those professors who taught more conventionally, because they frequently had small classes. Throughout my teaching career my classes have been too large to be as effective as they could be. Over time, I've begun to see that departmental pressure on "popular" professors to accept larger classes was also a way to undermine engaged pedagogy. If classes became so full that it is impossible to know students' names, to spend quality time with each of them, then the effort to build a learning community fails. Throughout my teaching career, I have found it helpful to meet with each student in my classes, if only briefly. Rather than sitting in my office for hours waiting for individual students to choose to meet or for problems to arise, I have preferred to schedule lunches with students. Sometimes, the whole class might bring lunch and have discussion in a space other than our usual classroom. At Oberlin, for instance, we might go as a class to the African Heritage House and have lunch, both to learn about different places on campus and gather in a setting other than our classroom.

Many professors remain unwilling to be involved with any pedagogical practices that emphasize mutual participation between teacher and student because more time and effort are required to do this work. Yet some version of engaged pedagogy is really the only type of teaching that truly generates excitement in the classroom, that enables students and professors to feel the joy of learning.

I was reminded of this during my trip to the emergency room after falling down that hill. I talked so intensely about ideas with the two students who were rushing me to the hospital that I forgot my pain. It is this passion for ideas, for critical thinking and dialogical exchange that I want to celebrate in the classroom, to share with students.

Talking about pedagogy, thinking about it critically, is not the intellectual work that most folks think is hip and cool. Cultural criticism and feminist theory are the areas of my work that are most often deemed interesting by students and colleagues alike. Most of us are not inclined to see discussion of pedagogy as central to our academic work and intellectual growth, or the practice of teaching as work that enhances and enriches scholarship. Yet it has been the mutual interplay of thinking, writing and sharing ideas as an intellectual and teacher that creates whatever insights are in my work. My devotion to that interplay keeps me teaching in academic settings, despite their difficulties.

When I first read *Strangers in Paradise: Academics from the Working Class*, I was stunned by the intense bitterness expressed in the individual narratives. This bitterness was not unfamiliar to me. I understood what Jane Ellen Wilson meant when she declared, "The whole process of becoming highly educated was for me a process of losing faith." I have felt that bitterness most keenly in relation to academic colleagues. It emerged from my sense that so many of them willingly betrayed the promise of intellectual fellowship and radical openness that I believe is the heart and soul of learning. When I moved beyond those feelings to focus my attention on the classroom, the one place in the academy where I could have the most impact, they became less intense. I became more passionate in my commitment to the art of teaching.

Engaged pedagogy not only compels me to be constantly creative in the classroom, it also sanctions involvement with students beyond that setting. I journey with students as they progress in their lives beyond our classroom experience. In many ways, I continue to teach them, even as they become more capable of teaching me. The important lesson that we learn together, the lesson that allows us to move together within and beyond the classroom, is one of mutual engagement.

I could never say that I have no idea of the way students respond to my pedagogy; they give me constant feedback. When I teach, I encourage them to critique, evaluate, make suggestions and interventions as we go along. Evaluations at the end of a course rarely help us improve the learning experience we share together. When students see themselves as mutually responsible for the development of a learning community, they offer constructive input.

Students do not always enjoy studying with me. Often they find my courses challenge them in ways that are deeply unsettling. This was particularly disturbing to me at the beginning of my teaching career because I wanted to be liked and admired. It took time and experience for me to understand that the rewards of engaged pedagogy might not emerge during a course. Luckily, I have taught many students who take time to reconnect and share the impact of our working together on their lives. Then the work I do as a teacher is affirmed again and again, not only by the accolades extended to me but by the career choices students make, their habits of being. When a student tells me that she struggled with the decision to do corporate law, joined such and such a firm, and then at the last minute began to reconsider whether this was what she felt called to do, sharing that her decision was influenced by the courses she took with me, I am reminded of the power we have as teachers as well as the awesome responsibility. Commitment to engaged pedagogy carries with it the willingness to be responsible, not to pretend that professors do not have the power to change the direction of our students' lives.

... After twenty years of teaching, I can confess that I am often most joyous in the classroom, brought closer here to the ecstatic than by most of life's experiences.

The American Constitutional Tradition and Education

Chapter 10 The Struggle for Civil Liberty in the Schools 235

On the Internet . . .

Sites appropriate to Part Four

The National Clearinghouse for ESL Literacy Education (NCLE), an adjunct ERIC Clearinghouse at the Center for Applied Linguistics (CAL), is the only national clearinghouse focusing on literacy education—including family literacy, workplace literacy, and native language literacy—for adults and out-of-school youth learning English as a second language (ESL). NCLE's mission is to provide timely information about adult ESL literacy education.

        http://www.cal.org/ncle/

This site provides a brief history leading up to the famous segregation case *Plessy v. Ferguson,* the majority opinion of Justice Billings Brown, and the dissenting opinion of Justice John Marshall Harlan.

        http://civnet.org/teaching/basic/part6/
          33.htm

This news story from DailyXPress, the online product of The Daily Press, is from May 17, 1954, and includes immediate reactions from politicians and others following the decision of *Brown v. Board of Education of Topeka, Kansas.*

        http://www.dailyxpress.com/dp100/
          desegre.htm

The Struggle for Civil Liberty in the Schools

10.1 U.S. SUPREME COURT

Brown v. Board of Education of Topeka, Kansas

In 1954 the United States Supreme Court issued a truly historic, constitutionally groundbreaking interpretation of the meaning of the "equal protection of the laws" clause of the Fourteenth Amendment to the Constitution of the United States. In the decision of *Brown v. Board of Education of Topeka, Kansas*, the Court held that "in the field of public education the doctrine of 'separate but equal' has no place. Separate educational facilities are inherently unequal." Seventeen states had used the "separate but equal" principle first enunciated in *Plessy v. Ferguson* (1896) to pass laws requiring the segregation of students of differing racial backgrounds in the public schools of those states. The *Brown* decision declared such segregation unconstitutional. What gave even greater historical importance to *Brown* was that the Court found "for Linda Brown and *all similarly situated persons*" (emphasis added by editor). This phrase made the decision a class action decision, the first time the "equal protection of the laws" clause was applied to all segregated persons.

In the years following the *Brown* decision, Hispanic Americans, Native Americans, Asian Americans, and all American women benefited from the powerful, clear finding for "Linda Brown and all similarly situated persons." Furthermore, during the 20 years after *Brown*, laws were passed by Congress that improved the educational opportunities of *all* Americans.

Key Concept: educational equality

*M*r. Chief Justice Warren delivered the opinion of the Court.

These cases come to us from the States of Kansas, South Carolina, Virginia, and Delaware. They are premised on different facts and different local conditions, but a common legal question justifies their consideration together in this consolidated opinion.

In each of the cases, minors of the Negro race, through their legal representatives, seek the aid of the courts in obtaining admission to the public schools of their community on a nonsegregated basis. In each instance, they had been denied admission to schools attended by white children under laws requiring or permitting segregation according to race. This segregation was alleged to deprive the plaintiffs of the equal protection of the laws under the Fourteenth Amendment. In each of the cases other than the Delaware case, a three-judge federal district court denied relief to the plaintiffs on the so-called "separate but equal" doctrine announced by this Court in *Plessy* v. *Ferguson*.... Under that doctrine, equality of treatment is accorded when the races are provided substantially equal facilities even though these facilities be separate. In the Delaware case, the Supreme Court of Delaware adhered to that doctrine, but ordered that the plaintiffs be admitted to the white schools because of their superiority to the Negro schools.

The plaintiffs contend that segregated public schools are not "equal" and cannot be made "equal," and that hence they are deprived of the equal protection of the laws. Because of the obvious importance of the question presented, the Court took jurisdiction. Argument was heard in the 1952 Term, and reargument was heard this Term on certain questions propounded by the Court.

Reargument was largely devoted to the circumstances surrounding the adoption of the Fourteenth Amendment in 1868. It covered exhaustively consideration of the Amendment in Congress, ratification by the states, then existing practices in racial segregation, and the views of proponents and opponents of the Amendment. This discussion and our own investigation convince us that, although these sources cast some light, it is not enough to resolve the problem with which we are faced. At best, they are inconclusive. The most avid proponents of the post–War Amendments undoubtedly intended them to remove all legal distinctions among "all persons born or naturalized in the United States." Their opponents, just as certainly were antagonistic to both the letter and the spirit of the Amendments and wished them to have the most limited effect. What others in Congress and the state legislatures had in mind cannot be determined with any degree of certainty.

An additional reason for the inconclusive nature of the Amendment's history, with respect to segregated schools, is the status of public education at that time. In the South, the movement toward free common schools, supported by general taxation, had not yet taken hold. Education of white children was largely in the hands of private groups. Education of Negroes was almost nonexistent, and practically all of the race were illiterate. In fact, any education of Negroes was forbidden by law in some states. Today, in contrast, many Negroes have achieved outstanding success in the arts and sciences as well as in the business and professional world. It is true that public education had already advanced further in the North, but the effect of the Amendment on Northern States was generally ignored in the congressional debates. Even in the North, the conditions of public education did not approximate those existing today. The curriculum was usually rudimentary; ungraded schools were common in rural areas; the school term was but three months a year in many states; and compulsory school attendance was virtually unknown. As a consequence, it is not surprising that there should be so little in the history of the Fourteenth Amendment relating to its intended effect on public education.

In the first cases in this Court construing the Fourteenth Amendment, decided shortly after its adoption, the Court interpreted it as proscribing all state-imposed discriminations against the Negro race. The doctrine of "separate but equal" did not make its appearance in this court until 1896 in the case of *Plessy* v. *Ferguson, supra,* involving not education but transportation. American courts have since labored with the doctrine for over half a century. In this Court, there have been six cases involving the "separate but equal" doctrine in the field of public education. In *Cumming* v. *County Board of Education* ... and *Gong Lum* v. *Rice* ... , the validity of the doctrine itself was not challenged. In more recent cases, all on the graduate school level, inequality was found in that specific benefits enjoyed by white students were denied to Negro students of the same educational qualifications. *Missouri* ex rel. *Gaines* v. *Canada; Sipuel* v. *Oklahoma; Sweatt* v. *Painter; McLaurin* v. *Oklahoma State Regents.* In none of these cases was it necessary to reexamine the doctrine to grant relief to the Negro plaintiff. And in *Sweatt* v. *Painter, supra,* the Court expressly reserved decision on the question whether *Plessy* v. *Ferguson* should be held inapplicable to public education.

In the instant cases, that question is directly presented. Here, unlike *Sweatt* v. *Painter,* there are findings below that the Negro and white schools involved have been equalized, or are being equalized, with respect to buildings, curricula, qualifications and salaries of teachers, and other "tangible" factors. Our decision, therefore, cannot turn on merely a comparison of these tangible factors in the Negro and white schools involved in each of the cases. We must look instead to the effect of segregation itself on public education.

In approaching this problem, we cannot turn the clock back to 1868 when the Amendment was adopted, or even to 1896 when *Plessy* v. *Ferguson* was written. We must consider public education in the light of its full development and its present place in American life throughout the Nation. Only in this way can it be determined if segregation in public schools deprives these plaintiffs of the equal protection of the laws.

Today, education is perhaps the most important function of state and local governments. Compulsory school attendance laws and the great expenditures for education both demonstrate our recognition of the importance of education to our democratic society. It is required in the performance of our most basic public responsibilities, even service in the armed forces. It is the very foundation of good citizenship. Today it is a principal instrument in awakening the child to cultural values, in preparing him for later professional training, and in helping him to adjust normally to his environment. In these days, it is doubtful that any child may reasonably be expected to succeed in life if he is denied the opportunity of an education. Such an opportunity, where the state has undertaken to provide it, is a right which must be made available to all on equal terms.

We come then to the question presented: Does segregation of children in public schools solely on the basis of race, even though the physical facilities and other "tangible" factors may be equal, deprive the children of the minority group of equal educational opportunities? We believe that it does.

In *Sweatt* v. *Painter, supra,* in finding that a segregated law school for Negroes could not provide them equal educational opportunities, this Court relied in large part on "those qualities which are incapable of objective measurement but which make for greatness in a law school." In *McLaurin* v. *Oklahoma State Regents, supra,* the Court, in requiring that a Negro admitted to a white graduate school be treated like all other students, again resorted to intangible considerations: " ... his ability to study, to engage in discussions and exchange views with other students, and, in general, to learn his profession." Such considerations apply with added force to children in grade and high schools. To separate them from others of similar age and qualifications solely because of their race generates a feeling of inferiority as to their status in the community that may affect their hearts and minds in a way unlikely ever to be undone. The effect of this separation on their educational opportunities was well stated by a finding in the Kansas case by a court which nevertheless felt compelled to rule against the Negro plaintiffs:

> Segregation of white and colored children in public schools has a detrimental effect upon the colored children. The impact is greater when it has the sanction of the law; for the policy of separating the races is usually interpreted as denoting the inferiority of the Negro group. A sense of inferiority affects the motivation of a child to learn. Segregation with the sanction of law, therefore, has a tendency to retard the educational and mental development of Negro children and to deprive them of some of the benefits they would receive in a racially integrated school system.

Whatever may have been the extent of psychological knowledge[1] at the time of *Plessy* v. *Ferguson,* this finding is amply supported by modern authority. Any language in *Plessy* v. *Ferguson* contrary to this finding is rejected.

We conclude that in the field of public education the doctrine of "separate but equal" has no place. Separate educational facilities are inherently unequal.

Therefore, we hold that the plaintiffs and others similarly situated for whom the actions have been brought are, by reason of the segregation complained of, deprived of the equal protection of the laws guaranteed by the Fourteenth Amendment. This disposition makes unnecessary any discussion whether such segregation also violates the Due Process Clause of the Fourteenth Amendment.

Because these are class actions, because of the wide applicability of this decision, and because of the great variety of local conditions, the formulation of decrees in these cases presents problems of considerable complexity. On reargument, the consideration of appropriate relief was necessarily subordinated to the primary question—the constitutionality of segregation in public education. We have now announced that such segregation is a denial of the equal protection of the laws. In order that we may have the full assistance of the parties in formulating decrees, the cases will be restored to the docket, and the parties are requested to present further argument.

NOTES

1. The decision in *Brown* v. *Board of Education* was justified in part on psychological and sociological grounds. This line of argument helped Chief Justice Warren obtain a unanimous decision, but it did not provide the strongest legal foundation for attacking segregation.

Twenty Years After "Brown": Where Are We Now?

Marian Wright Edelman is president of the Children's Defense Fund and a well-known scholar on the history of school desegregation since *Brown v. Board of Education of Topeka, Kansas* (1954). In 1974 she published an excellent synthesis and interpretation of United States Supreme Court decisions of several key cases that established the interpretive parameters for what the Court had meant in *Brown*. She also published an earlier version of her scholarship on school desegregation, "Southern School Desegregation: 1954–1973," *The Annals of the American Academy of Political and Social Science* (vol. 407, 1973, pp. 32–42). Edelman has led a distinguished life of leadership and example in the cause of human rights, and she is widely recognized for her efforts.

The selection that follows, which is from the *New York University Education Quarterly* (Summer 1974), was published 20 years after the initial *Brown* decision. Edelman's call for action for social justice in the field of education is as necessary and meaningful today as it was in 1974. In interpreting the first 20 years after *Brown,* she argues that effective racial integration is the most just manner through which to ensure equality of educational opportunity.

Key Concept: school integration

*I*n May of 1954, rewarding the hope and toil of decades, the Supreme Court's decision in *Brown v. Board of Education* seemed a great, transforming event. (1) A great event it was. Whether it would work the transformation it promised remained to be seen. For, after all, the Fourteenth Amendment itself had promised much but accomplished little over almost a century.

In the spring of 1964, a decade after *Brown* and a decade ago, the achievement of school desegregation seemed almost as far off as ever. We asked ourselves: When will the law be enforced? When will the law be obeyed? But, behind those questions lay another: What *was* the law? Without a clear under-standing of what the law was—and without a solid political coalition to rally behind a clear view of the law—enforcement and obedience could only become more problematic.

That was the situation on the tenth anniversary of *Brown*. And, I believe, that is the situation today, on the twentieth anniversary. Despite all of the progress during the intervening years, we are standing at a crossroads again, where the future is opaque and the tasks before us difficult.

DOES DESEGREGATION REQUIRE INTEGRATION?

The comparison with 1964 is instructive. At that time, concerned with enforce-ment and obedience, we lawyers focused on the Supreme Court's "all deliberate speed" formula. There was much debate about the chain of causation. Had the Court's formula opened the door for—indeed, encouraged—Southern re-sistance and federal foot-dragging? Or, was Southern resistance and federal inaction inevitable at first? Was "all deliberate speed" a corruption of the rule of law, or was it a statesmanlike recognition that desegregation could only be a slow process? (2) This debate on *Brown's* tenth anniversary was interesting; but, in a way, it missed a basic problem underlying the lack of progress in the fifties and early sixties.

The problem was that for ten long years the Supreme Court had not de-cided even one major case to define just what school "desegregation" meant. "All deliberate speed" was all the less speedy because no one knew what we were supposed to be inching toward. The effect was corrosive.

In 1955, only one year after *Brown*, a Southern federal court had raised the most central issue, going to the heart of school desegregation. In the case of *Briggs v. Elliott* (3), a District Court in South Carolina had argued that the Constitution forbids segregation but "does not require integration." *Brown*, ac-cording to the *Briggs* court, did not imply that a state must "mix persons of different races in the schools or ... deprive them of the right of choosing the schools they attend." One might have thought the Supreme Court would re-spond. But it did not. In 1958, it convened a special session to announce that, whatever the resistance, a judicial desegregation order must be obeyed. (4) But what sort of desegregation were the lower courts entitled to order? The Court did not say. It maintained its silence up to 1964.

Finally, in the year of *Brown's* tenth anniversary, it did signal that the time for delay had run out (5); and a year later it stated that "delays in desegregating school systems are no longer tolerable." (6) But, still, it gave no real clue what "desegregating school systems" implied.

With no lead to follow, and with no answer to the issue posed in *Briggs v. Elliott*, the lower courts did little for ten years. They issued decrees permitting a few token, though courageous, black children voluntarily to attend "white" schools. And they struck down the most egregious Southern pupil placement laws that preserved the segregatory assignment system. But no affirmative duty to integrate was put in their place.

By 1964, a conservative scholar, Alexander Bickel, could predict that "the end result of desegregation" would simply be "a school system in which there is residential zoning, either absolute or modified by some sort of choice or transfer scheme." The most ever to be expected, he said, was that Southern school districts would settle "into conditions of substantial *de facto* segregation, alleviated by a number of successful integrated situations. In other words, essentially Northern conditions.... This," he concluded, "is the likely—and anticlimactic —outcome of all the litigating and striving." (2)

The years between 1964 and 1974 would seem to have proved Bickel wrong. The Supreme Court has spoken at last. Freedom-of-choice plans in the South have been swept aside and effective dismantling of formally dual school systems has been mandated by *Green v. County School Board.* (7) And both busing and assignment on an explicitly integrative basis—cutting across neighborhood lines—have been upheld in *Swann v. Charlotte-Mecklenburg Board of Education* as reasonable means to achieve that end. (8)

It might seem, then, that we have solved the problem of what *is* law. We might suppose that the central issue has now been resolved: Integration *is* required in America. It might appear, once again, that the only remaining problem is one of enforcement and obedience to the law.

BREAKDOWN IN ENFORCEMENT

Without doubt, enforcement and obedience are major problems now. They no longer stem from the "all deliberate speed" formula. That formula was finally buried in 1969 in *Alexander v. Holmes County Board of Education.* (9) Rather, delay 1974-style stems from federal government foot-dragging—even hostility. It is not an altogether unfamiliar phenomenon. During *Brown's* first ten years, we felt the deadening effect of President Eisenhower's refusal even to endorse the principle of desegregation and President Kennedy's excessive caution in the face of pressure from Southern Democrats. But, in the middle and late sixties, we learned what an important, powerful weapon enforcement by the federal government can be. Vigorous court action by the Justice Department and, particularly, vigorous endorsement of desegregation guidelines by the Department of Health, Education and Welfare under the Civil Rights Act of 1964, boosted by the Elementary and Secondary Education Act of 1965 pouring large sums of federal aid into local school coffers, helped to produce the first really substantial progress toward school desegregation in the South. Now that the Nixon Administration has cut back enforcement across the board, the chilling effect is all too plain. (10)

One solution might be to exert new pressure on the now-vulnerable Administration to mend its ways. Another might be to invoke more vigorously the Supreme Court's *Alexander* decision, repudiating Justice Department requests for delay in enforcing court decrees. Yet another solution might be to implement the recent District Court decision in *Adams v. Richardson*, ordering the Department of Health, Education and Welfare to resume desegregation enforcement under the 1964 Civil Rights Act. (11) All of these efforts focusing on enforcement are important. But the present problem is deeper than that.

The present breakdown in enforcement and obedience to the law is tied—as it was in 1964—to a new and troubling uncertainty as to the substance of the law. What is uncertain is the extent of applicability of the principles originally set forth in *Brown v. Board of Education.* The law grows incrementally, by analogy to past cases, with little regard for overriding principle. But, if that is the case, the growth of the law may be stopped at any point. And, today, as new and different issues of school desegregation present themselves, some question whether *Brown* still has the life left in it to meet them. For the principles of *Brown* appear almost as susceptible to limitation as to expansion.

One might ask: How can that be? Hasn't *Briggs v. Elliott* been discredited? Hasn't it been held that desegregation demands effective integration? The answer is: Yes, those paramount issues of the sixties have been resolved. But they were resolved in the context of Southern school districts, very recently separated by law into "white" schools and "black" schools. It has been established that unconstitutional segregation must be remedied by integration. But the issue we face now is a more basic one: What *is* unconstitutional segregation?

The problem lies not just in the familiar distinction between *de jure* and *de facto* segregation. It is a problem of having had to spend too long just beginning to dismantle the most egregious forms of school segregation. Anything seems tame by comparison. And now it is being suggested that the job is finished. New questions assume key importance. What does *de jure* segregation mean in the North? How blatant must it be? How long do its effects last? Are we approaching a time when courts will say that the "taint"—even in the South—has been dissipated and that the remedy of affirmative integration is no longer required? Is anything short of the most extreme form of segregation really harmful to children? If the harm is not so great, should the remedy be less strict?

There are those who say that *Brown v. Board of Education* suggests no answer to these questions, that *Brown* is now "obsolete." (12) And there are those who would declare that America's schools have been "desegregated" without being fully integrated. Thus the prediction by Professor Bickel ten years ago—that we would end up with the nationwide institution of *de facto* school segregation—has still to be finally disproved.

Once again, as the Supreme Court draws back from "activism" and as the civil rights coalition of the sixties comes apart, the law threatens to come unhinged. It is our job to put it right once more, to build the doctrine we once thought secure, and, in my view, to reestablish integration in our schools as the basic goal.

I recognize that there are those, black and white, who quarrel with this goal. As one who grew up in segregated and unequal schools, themselves the product of power inequities between whites and blacks grounded in the deep racism still pervasive in all America, I hold the strong view that real integration is the best goal and the best strategy for achieving nondiscriminatory, quality, and responsive education for black children and all children. I reject bargaining off constitutional rights for other necessary steps toward building a good educational system for our children including community control and "compensatory" educational measures which black and white parents should demand for the good of their youngsters anyway. We should never forget the power and political realities with which we live and the problem posed to segregation of resources and power along with segregation of schools. Those people who have resisted real integration have also fought equalization and will fight empowerment of minority communities to control their own lives, which they are entitled to do regardless of segregation or desegregation. While desegregation is not *the* answer to all the difficult problems of schooling today—inequitable financing schemes, misclassification and tracking, unresponsive and sometimes hostile teachers are some others—can there be doubt that the root of some of these problems is founded in the racial (and class) discrimination which *Brown* attempted to address?...

SEGREGATION BY MANIPULATION

Yet the definition of *de jure* segregation is probably the most unsettled aspect of desegregation doctrine today. Often, integrationists seek to short-circuit this problem. They argue that courts should simply hold now that all *de facto* segregation is unconstitutional, making the definition of *de jure* segregation unimportant.

This approach offers the great advantage of clarity. In time, we may hope that it will prevail. But, at present, such a holding would require a great doctrinal and psychological leap. For years, lower courts have refused to go so far, so fast. The Supreme Court has not only avoided the issue; recently, when the claim was presented in far too sweeping form, it summarily rejected it. Thus the game of defining *de jure* segregation, in my opinion, must be played through to its conclusion.

For the time being, there is no need even to concede the validity of the *de jure/de facto* distinction. Indeed, there is no such thing as *de facto* school segregation of the pure type. Governmental involvement of one sort or another can usually be found in the history of segregated residential patterns; and, after all, it is a governmental agency that bases school assignments on neighborhoods *known* to be segregated-in-fact. (14) What we face are varying kinds and degrees of governmental responsibility for assignment by race. Until the Court rigidly confines the meaning of *de jure* segregation to *certain* kinds and degrees of governmental responsibility, *de facto* segregation has no meaning of its own. And, until that time, there is no reason to ask the courts to take the leap of declaring all *de facto* segregation unconstitutional. At present, the Court has not so confined the meaning of *de jure* segregation. And yet it has defined it in such a way that confusion and uncertainty now prevail and will for some while.

For nineteen years after *Brown*, the Court heard argument only in cases from school districts that had very recently been openly segregated by statute. *De jure* segregation in that context was too clear to be questioned. Finally, just last year, the Court took a case from the North, from Denver. In the *Keyes* case, it began at long last to define the broader meaning of *de jure* segregation. Its decision was important not only for the North. It also could be controlling in cases from the South if it is ever held that the "taint" of Southern segregation by statute has been dissipated.

What the Court did in *Keyes* was barely to inch forward from the Southern paradigm of *de jure* segregation. Specifically the Court held that segregation-in-fact is unconstitutional if it is the product of "segregatory intent" on the part of governmental authorities. Some thought this is a victory. For the Court went beyond the pure form of Southern segregation. But the formula of "segregatory intent" presents all sorts of problems. It is itself hard to define. And, depending on its definition, it may be difficult to prove and narrow in impact.

Despite the lack of a recently mandated statutory segregation and despite protestations that the Denver school board was simply following a "neutral" neighborhood school policy, the Court held that sufficient "segregatory intent" had been shown in the board's "manipulations" of its neighborhood policy to increase the segregation than would have resulted from a truly "neutral" approach.

The occasions for "manipulation" of a neighborhood policy are present every time any school board draws a zoning line, or locates a new school, or determines the size of a new school, or closes an old school, or adopts a voluntary transfer plan. (13) The *Keyes* opinion recognizes most of these occasions, and more. Certainly, the myriad decisions involved in administering a neighborhood school policy offer litigators many opportunities for investigation and many opportunities to make a showing of *de jure* segregation.

But what kind of showing? Is it enough, for example, simply to show that the location of new schools *resulted* in increased segregation? Must that result have been *foreseeable* or *known* to the school board? Or must there be a showing of a *desire* for increased segregation—a conscious segregatory policy—underlying such "manipulative" decisions? If so, can it be inferred from a pattern of decisions producing segregatory results? Or must it be proved independently?

If particular "manipulations" of a neighborhood policy can be explained *only* as serving a segregatory purpose, "segregatory intent" would seem clear. But what if they can be explained as serving other purposes as well? That probably is the most typical case. Is an inference of "segregatory intent" still possible? Must the segregatory purpose be "dominant"?

The *Keyes* opinion raises all these problems, but does not resolve any of them conclusively. For, in a way, *Keyes* was an easy case for the Supreme Court. The District Court had already found that the Denver school board had pursued a "policy of deliberate racial segregation" in one section of the city. That finding was not contested; and the Supreme Court did not examine it. Rather, the Court simply held that once there has been such a finding as to one part of the city, the burden is on the school board to show that it did not act with "segregatory intent" in the rest of the city and that the board could not meet its burden at that stage simply by showing that its actions served some end in addition to segregation. But the Court said nothing about how litigants may make the crucial, initial showing of "deliberate" segregation.

Thus *Keyes* does not close the door to nationwide integration. Nor does it open the door wide. At best, *Keyes* leaves it swinging ajar, uneasily and uncertainly. In the short run—and, in matters of school desegregation, that unfortunately means the next five or ten years—litigators will have to press carefully for an elaboration of the *Keyes* standard that is both clear and expansive.

DEFINITION OF SEGREGATIVE INTENT
TIED TO RESULTS

There is one dialectic that will confront our efforts, whether in the short-run attempt to expand the meaning of *de jure* segregation or in the long-run assault on the citadel of *de facto* segregation, once defined. That is the dialectic of fairness in rules of selection versus fairness in fact.

The rhetoric of equal protection law, as applied to racial discrimination, has purported to separate the two rigidly. It has focused largely on fairness in governmental rules of selection—rules of selection for juries, for voting rights, for employment, for use of public facilities, for school assignments. Courts have suggested that so long as those rules of selection are held to be fair, it is improper to inquire into their results. So long as the rule used to select jurors is fair, courts will not concern themselves with the actual representation of minorities. So long as the rule used to select employees is fair, courts will not worry about the number of minority employees hired. And so long as the actions that determine school assignments are fair—or, in *Keyes*, are not infected by "segregatory intent"—courts insist that they will not mandate actual integration.

In theory, this rigid distinction corresponds to the powerful American ideology of equal opportunity. But, in practice, the distinction is untenable. The fairness of a rule of selection—whether for juries or employment or school assignments—cannot be assessed in total blindness to results achieved.

In the law of employment discrimination, it has repeatedly been held that a showing of a discriminatory effect is enough to establish, *prima facie,* that the criteria used for hiring are discriminatory. And, in the law of jury discrimination, it has been held that even though a rule of selection may appear fair on its face, a court must look to the results it achieves to determine if it is being applied discriminatorily. In the law of school desegregation, too, the courts have examined the results of apparently "neutral" policies of school assignment, at least in Southern school districts once segregated by statute. They must be urged to do so in all cases. (14)

It is the task of litigators now to persuade the courts that the element of "segregatory intent" is something that can be inferred from results, as well as proved independently. More importantly, we must persuade the courts that the very meaning of "segregatory intent" is tied to the actual segregation resulting from governmental action. "Segregatory intent" must be broader than the *desire* for segregation. We are not dealing with first degree murder cases. We should not be looking for "malice aforethought." The Constitution, after all, is meant to protect, not to punish.

In other areas of the law, more comparable to constitutional law, one is held to "intend" particular results if he simply *knew* that those results would follow his act. Such knowledge is inferred if a reasonable man would have been substantially certain that the results would, in fact, occur. Similarly, it should be enough to show "segregatory intent" that increased segregation was substantially certain to follow a "manipulation" of a neighborhood school policy, and that any reasonable member of the school board should have known it. Such a showing usually would not be too difficult. (15)

Such a definition of "segregatory intent" may have a more sweeping impact than the *Keyes* Court had in mind. If the Court were to accept it, it might feel that it must balance the harm done by the intended, increased segregation against the value of other intended results of the particular "manipulation" of the neighborhood policy. But such a balancing act would lead us directly to the basic issue of *de facto* segregation. For once a court starts balancing segregation against other values as those, for example, allegedly served by a neighborhood policy, it matters little whether it is dealing with the *increased* segregation resulting from a "manipulation" of the policy or with the basic segregation inherent in the policy itself.

We should endeavor to lead the courts through this step-by-step progression to the basic issue at stake. If, in the end, defining *de jure* segregation becomes more a matter of weighing the costs and benefits of the *results* of a neighborhood policy than a matter of searching out "segregatory intent," that is entirely appropriate.

Violations of the First Amendment rights need not generally be "intentional" before they are unconstitutional. Nor Fourth Amendment rights. Nor Fifth Amendment rights. Why should the right to the equal protection of the laws under the Fourteenth Amendment be somehow different? When the courts apply the equal protection clause to apportionment laws, they do not look for "intent" to discriminate against certain voters. Rather, they look to the extent of the inequality that *results* from the apportionment laws. Why should *racial* discrimination be treated more leniently?

In time, then, if all goes well, the question of "intention" may drop away. For, in view of residential patterns in our cities, segregation is the substantially certain result of any neighborhood policy. By *Brown's* thirtieth anniversary, the Court may see that its job, finally, is to decide whether the values served by a neighborhood school policy justify the resulting segregation. Our job will be to show that there can be no such justification. I feel strongly that there is not. . . .

THE PROBLEM OF REMEDY

But even if we do manage to establish that the "taint" of segregation is not soon dissipated, that *de jure* segregation is not confined to narrowly "intentional" segregatory acts, and that a segregated education is indeed an inferior education, we shall face one last uncertainty at the core of desegregation law. This is the uncertainty of remedy. Unlike the others, this one is not the product of anything the Supreme Court has yet said or done. Rather, it is the product of something the Court did not do and of what one fears the Court may do in the future.

In a word, the problem of remedy may be the problem of busing. Busing—or rather a particular kind of busing (of white children to black schools, of too many black children to white schools)—is not very popular today. Even though we have spent ever increasing energy and resources getting more buses for more children every decade, totally unrelated to desegregation, the present opposition to it stems from a more basic opposition to further integration or from a dislike of sending one's children to a "distant," "unfamiliar," and often "inferior" school (the fact that usually gives rise to the necessity to desegregate in the first place). After all, you cannot expect our children to suffer what "their" children are forced to suffer! The fact is that "busing" has become a symbol, a separate political issue of its own, created by the Southerners with Mr. Nixon's help, to achieve the basic end of resegregating the nation's schools. It drove liberal politicians in 1972 to speak the language of "quality education," as if it were irreconcilable or separable from nondiscriminatory or desegregated education! And it may have contributed to the now-tattered mandate the President received that year. If the Court, as is said, "follows the election returns," the busing remedy may be in for trouble. Because busing is *not* a separate issue, but is tied to the only possibility for real desegregation, the effect of a pull-back by the Court could be devastating.

Since the *Green* decision in 1968 the Court had held that, once a condition of *de jure* school segregation or its "vestiges" are found in a school district, the remedy must be a total one, a "root and branch" dismantling of the segregated system. In *Swann,* the Court held that this remedy could include busing, within the reasonable discretion of the trial judge. Both *Green* and *Swann* arose in Southern school districts that had recently been openly and thoroughly segregated by statute. Last year, in the *Keyes* decision, the Court took a major step forward despite the election returns. It held that the "root and branch" remedial requirement, including busing, applies no less in a Northern city where *de jure* segregation is the result of many, discrete segregatory "manipulations," rather than of a statutory "dual system."

One might think, after *Keyes,* that the busing remedy presents no separate doctrinal problems. That may be correct—insofar as it is established that "root and branch" desegregation must follow any finding of *de jure* segregation. But must "root and branch" desegregation include busing? And how much busing must there be?

When we step back for a moment, we see a troubling uncertainty in the very decision once hailed as a great victory: *Swann v. Charlotte-Mecklenburg Board of Education.* The Court there stated that desegregation plans "cannot be limited to the walk-in school." It required that transportation of students at least be considered. But it did not *require* any particular degree of busing. To the contrary, it suggested a vague, uncertain *limit* on the busing remedy.

The limit on the remedy, the *Swann* Court said, "will vary with many factors," including the time and distance to be traveled, the directness of the route, and the age of the students. "The reconciliation of competing values," it said, "is . . . a difficult task with many sensitive facets but fundamentally no more so than remedial measures courts of equity have traditionally employed." This left matters somewhat up in the air. But, within months, the author of the *Swann* opinion—Chief Justice Burger—was complaining publicly that the opinion had been read too broadly. He said, in a memorandum opinion, that a desegregation plan might "trespass the limits on school bus transportation indicated in *Swann*" and suggested that a most important limit was that of time to be traveled to school. (16)

The transportation time sanctioned in *Swann* was about one hour roundtrip. Lower courts have upheld plans involving similarly limited traveling time. But no one can be sure whether one hour is an outer limit or not. It is not clear how serious a limitation this might be, as I suspect that most of the busing in the nation falls within this reasonable limit and practice. Contrary to the misinformation and fears inflamed by opponents of desegregation, courts have not been ordering busing in amounts which broke with past practice or which could be considered unreasonable. Even in the metropolitan remedy proposed in Richmond, in only one of the six sub-districts would busing time have reached one hour. I would, nonetheless, like the time flexibility to remain and not have rigid lines drawn. After all, there is precedent for much longer busing time stemming from efforts to maintain segregation.

The Court's decision not to decide on clear guidelines for the busing remedy—but just the same to insist that there are limits—may have put some desegregation plans into doubt and may have influenced another non-decision by the Court: its equally-divided silence in the Richmond metropolitan cross-district busing case. (17) Of course, the Court is considering this issue again this year in the Detroit case. (18) One hopes that the opinion it issues may not simply compound the current confusion.

That there is confusion and that it could end up limiting, rather than expanding, opportunities for school integration was made clear in Mr. Justice Powell's separate opinion in last year's *Keyes* decision. He agreed that busing is "one tool of school desegregation"; but, he said, the "crucial issue is when, under what circumstances, and to what extent such transportation may appropriately be ordered." He then argued that tight restrictions should be imposed in the future, raising the spectre of "white flight" and even questioning the use of a "root and branch" remedy for separate, discrete segregative acts.

We may be walking on a minefield in the dark. But, if we look and not leap too far, we should be able to expect success. For, so long as we hold the courts to the obligation of "root and branch" desegregation, the busing remedy will be indispensable and no arbitrary limits can be imposed on it. If, on the other hand, the courts abandon the standard of "root and branch" desegregation, then all desegregation's future may be extremely difficult.

AFFIRMATIVE ACTION

Perhaps not too difficult. There is still the possibility of voluntary action by particular local communities to adopt plans for "root and branch" dismantling of even *de facto* school segregation. Many communities have taken such action. The lower state and federal courts have unanimously upheld their action. The

Supreme Court has not spoken. In *Swann,* it did strongly indicate that voluntary desegregation, using "benign" racial classifications and busing, is permissible. But not until this very year did it even take a case involving such classifications.

The case, of course, is *DeFunis v. Odegaard.* (19) It involves an affirmative effort by a state law school to admit minority students. It may be distinguishable from voluntary school desegregation. But the basic principles involved are the same.

The DeFunis case is important in one other respect which should be mentioned in closing. It revealed for all to see that the civil rights coalition of the sixties may be coming apart. But it should not be surprising that the willingness to share and sacrifice becomes thinner the closer one's own perceived interests are affected. Civil rights groups, educators, some unions, some Jewish groups, and many other organizations supported the state law school's affirmative admissions program. But the AFL-CIO, several Jewish groups, and a few "ethnic" organizations and some academics opposed it in amicus briefs to the Court.

If, in fact, the coalition of the sixties does break apart, the effect could be more devastating than any of the doctrinal uncertainties I have discussed up to now. There is no simple preventive medicine to be applied. The issues of the seventies *are* difficult ones for many who supported civil rights before. The danger simply shows that our task now is less a legal one than a political and leadership one.

If the sixties were the time of eradicating egregious segregation, the seventies are the time of seeking real equality. This will be much harder because it involves an equalization of sacrifice in order to overcome the past inequality of sacrifice imposed on some minorities. It may even mean that some individuals may have a more difficult time in the process during the interim of trying to ensure fairness in the process for all groups and all individuals. It also means that many institutions, unusually timid in the past, who have condemned and practiced overt or covert discrimination, must go beyond adopting paper policies to implementing affirmative programs to desegregate that will be controversial. But any reform, racial or nonracial, is controversial. What is needed is nondefensive leadership with a commitment to real equality.

This account of the state of school desegregation on *Brown's* twentieth anniversary may not be encouraging. Some might prefer to celebrate the achievements of the past ten years and leave developments in the next ten for discussion at the thirtieth anniversary. But, if that occasion, ten years hence, is to be a pleasant one, we must realistically assess where we stand now, perhaps stressing the dangers. For, if we are to avoid them, we must first see them clearly.

The *Quarterly* was unable to grant the author's request for use of full legal citations in the published version of her paper. Cases are noted only at the point of first reference, and the initial page of the proceedings is provided. References to related legal principals established by the courts are omitted. However, interested readers may request a copy of Mrs. Edelman's original manuscript containing complete citation.

—Editor [of *New York University Education Quarterly*]

1. Brown v. Board of Education, 347 U.S. 483 (1954).

2. H. H. Quint, *Profile in Black and White,* Westport, Conn.: Greenwood, 1973; A. Bickel, "The Decade of School Desegregation: Progress and Prospects," *Columbia Law Review* 64 (1964): 193–229.

3. Briggs v. Elliott, 132 F. Supp. 776 (E.D.S.C. 1955).

4. Cooper v. Aaron, 358 U.S. 1 (1958).

5. Griffin v. Prince Edward County Board of Education, 377 U.S. 218 (1964).

6. Bradley v. School Board of Richmond, 382 U.S. 103 (1965).

7. Green v. County School Board, 391 U.S. 450 (1968).

8. Swann v. Charlotte-Mecklenburg Board of Education, 402 U.S. 1 (1971).

9. Alexander v. Holmes County Board of Education, 396 U.S. 19 (1969).

10. See Marian W. Edelman, "Southern School Desegregation, 1954–1973: A Judicial-Political Overview," *Annals of the American Academy of Political and Social Science* 407 (1973): 32–42.

11. Adams v. Richardson, 351 F. Supp. 636 (D.D.C. 1972).

12. E.g., A. Bickel, *The Supreme Court and the Idea of Progress,* New York: Harper & Row, 1970.

13. See O. M. Fiss, "Racial Imbalance in the Public Schools: The Constitutional Concepts," *Harvard Law Review* 78 (1964): 564–617.

14. Just this Term, the Court indicated that it would look to results in the context of a Northern city: Mayor of Philadelphia v. Educational Equality League, 42 U.S.L.W. 4405 (1975).

15. See O. M. Fiss, "The Charlotte-Mecklenburg Case—Its Significance for Northern School Desegregation," *University of Chicago Law Review* 38 (1971): 697–709; Note, "School Desegregation after Swann: A Theory of Government Responsibility," *University of Chicago Law Review* 39 (1972): 421–447.

16. Winston Salem/Forsyth County Board of Education v. Scott, 404 U.S. 1221 (1971).

17. Bradley v. School Board of Richmond, 412 U.S. 937 (1973).

18. Milliken v. Bradley, cert. granted, 42 U.S.L.W. 3306 (11/20/73).

19. DeFunis v. Odegaard, cert. granted, 42 U.S.L.W. 3129 (9/11/73).

A Better Chance to Learn: Bilingual-Bicultural Education

In May 1975 the United States Commission on Civil Rights issued a thoroughly documented, in-depth statement on the history of the education of language minority students in the United States and on how the struggle of language minority students to achieve equality of educational opportunity is linked to the broader struggle for equality in the field of education. The commission specifically discussed the direct relationship between the United States Supreme Court decision in *Brown v. Board of Education of Topeka, Kansas* (1954) and various federal court decisions involving the educational rights of limited English proficiency (LEP) students. The commission's document was distributed to all public school districts that had or were putting into place either bilingual educational programs or English as a Second Language programs for language minority children. This document, *A Better Chance to Learn: Bilingual-Bicultural Education* (Clearinghouse Publication 51, May 1975), is excerpted in the following selection. In it, the commission clarifies how the Supreme Court decision in *Lau v. Nichols* (1975) is based on Fourteenth Amendment "equal protection of the laws" precedents, which had led the Court to declare in *Brown* that segregated schools are "inherently unequal." The historical precedents for bilingual educational programs in the United States are also reviewed in the document.

Key Concept: bilingual education

INTRODUCTION

No public institution has a greater or more direct impact on future opportunity than the school. Between the ages of 6 and 16, American children spend much of their time in school. Early educational success or failure dictates to a large extent a student's expectations for the future, including whether he or she will seek postsecondary education and thus have a wide range of economic options available following formal schooling. The importance of an equal opportunity to public education was underscored in the case of *Brown* v. *Board of Education* and was followed in the 1960's by civil rights activity to end segregated schools. Similarly, much of the effort to overcome discrimination against limited or non-English speaking persons in the 1970's has been focused on schools.

The term "language minority" is used in this report to refer to persons in the United States who speak a non-English native language and who belong to an identifiable minority group of generally low socioeconomic status. Such language minority groups—including Mexican Americans, Puerto Ricans, Native Americans, and Asian Americans—have been subject to discrimination and limited opportunity. The emphasis given attainment of an education places them at a further disadvantage, since the public school does not appear to have met the needs of language minority groups.

Not only have many language minority children been subject to segregated education, low teacher expectations, cultural incompatibility with dominant culture-oriented curricula, and the educational neglect experienced by minority children in general, many also face a unique and equally severe form of discrimination which results from lack of proficiency in the language of instruction. In January 1974, the Supreme Court affirmed in *Lau* v. *Nichols* that school districts are compelled under Title VI of the Civil Rights Act of 1964 to provide children who speak little or no English with special language programs which will give them an equal opportunity to an education. The form such assistance should take is the subject of debate among educators, concerned language minority parents, and others.

There is little disagreement that learning English is essential to economic and social mobility in this monolingual English speaking society. The main controversy surrounds the issue of how language minority children can be taught English in a manner so that they do not fall so far behind in subject matter instruction that they cannot recover. Questions also have been raised concerning what methods are best for teaching English to language minority students; whether the learning of English alone will equalize educational opportunity and what role, if any, should be played by the native language and culture in the educational process.

Bilingual bicultural education is instruction using the native language and culture as a basis for learning subjects until second language skills have been developed sufficiently; it is the most widely discussed of approaches to providing language minority children with an equal educational opportunity. On the one hand, it has been hailed as a sound educational approach that overcomes the incompatibility between language minority students and the monolingual English public school. On the other, it has been criticized as failing to provide language minority students with sufficient English skills and as fostering ethnic separateness.

In this report, the Commission examines the extent to which bilingual bicultural education is an effective educational approach for increasing the opportunity of language minority students. In undertaking this study, the Commission assessed the educational principles behind bilingual bicultural education but did not analyze findings from existing bilingual bicultural programs, since few reliable evaluation data are available.

Because of the Commission's civil rights jurisdiction, this report concentrates primarily on bilingual bicultural education as a means for overcoming a denial of equal educational opportunity. However, another valuable objective of bilingual bicultural education is the enrichment of the education of children of all socioeconomic levels and racial/ethnic groups through learning two languages and two cultures....

THE NEED TODAY

Although the height of immigration has long since passed, a large proportion of Americans still have a native language that is other than English. According to the 1970 census, 33.2 million Americans, or roughly 16 percent of the population, speak a language other than English as a native tongue. Spanish, German, and Italian speakers are the most numerous, in that order. Spanish is the only one of the three which has experienced substantial growth in the number of speakers since 1940, largely owing to increased immigration from Latin America.

Although persons of Mexican origin are native to the Southwest, the number of Spanish speaking persons in this country has grown noticeably since 1920. In the 1920's two factors contributed to a major influx of Mexican immigrants: a socially disruptive revolution in Mexico and the agricultural development of the Southwest United States and the subsequent need for labor. Between 1920 and 1973, 1,480,887 or more than 60 percent of all Mexican immigrants came to the United States.

Similarly, since 1920, Puerto Ricans have migrated in greater numbers, stimulated by the crowded living and bad economic conditions of Puerto Rico and the need in urban areas for low-paid, unskilled workers. The Puerto Rican migration swelled from 7,000 in 1920 to 852,061 in 1970.

Between 1920 and 1973, 215,778 Central Americans and 487,925 South Americans immigrated to this country. By 1973, Spanish origin persons numbered 9,072,602 nationwide and constituted the second largest minority group in the United States at roughly 4.4 percent of the total American population.

Immigration continues to be a major source for increasing the size of American language minority communities. Asian groups, for example, have experienced rapid increases in size since restrictive legislation barring or limiting their entry was repealed. In the less than 10 years since 1965, when all immigration quotas were liberalized, 654,736 or more than one-third of all Asian immigrants since 1820 have entered the United States. In 1973 more Asians immigrated than any other group. Other language minority groups, including Italians, Greeks, French Canadians, and Portuguese, have been part of a steady stream of language minorities coming to this country.

The 1970 census estimates that 31 percent of the 760,572 Native Americans counted speak a Native American tongue as their first language. Unlike the other groups, the survival of Native American languages is primarily the result of their continued use by existing groups and geographic isolation, rather than of replenishment through immigration.

Although precise data are not available on the numbers of limited or non-English speaking children currently in school, at the present time, the U.S. Office of Education estimates that at least 5 million need special language programs. The Census Bureau reports that 4.5 million Spanish speaking children under 20 years of age speak Spanish at home. An estimated 259,830 Asian American children speak little or no English, and some 56,493 Native American children speak a Native American language as a first language.

Unlike earlier non-English speaking children in this country, these children face an increasingly technical, skills-oriented society. There has been a shift in jobs from manual labor to skilled occupations. Although there is no direct correlation between years of schooling and ability to perform many jobs, educational level has become one frequently employed means of differentiating job applicants from one another.

Educators have known for many years that language minority children have difficulty succeeding in English monolingual schools. As early as 1930 it was documented that, in Texas, overageness and dropout rates were higher for Mexican American children than for either black or white students, and that most Mexican American children never progressed beyond third grade. In addition, while approximately 95 percent of Anglo children were enrolled in schools, only 50 percent of Mexican American children were. The causes were considered at the time to include lack of English language knowledge, low socioeconomic status, and inaccurate measuring instruments.

Although some scattered attempts were made to improve the education of Mexican American children from 1920–1940, no large scale effort was undertaken to alter the effects of education on them. A number of questions were raised about the education of non-English speaking children, including whether children would suffer less language handicap in school if first instruction in reading were in their native language. In the 1940's one researcher called for action to be taken by the Texas Department of Education, teacher training institutions, and schools to better meet the needs of Spanish speaking students. In 1946, the First Regional Conference on the Education of Spanish-speaking People in the Southwest was held in Austin, Texas. Recommendations included an end to segregated schools for Spanish speaking children, improved teacher training, and more efficiency in teaching English.

That public education continued to neglect the needs of language minority students for another 20 years is evident in the fact that recommendations of the 1964 Orange County Conference on the Education of Spanish Speaking Children and Youth were almost identical to those developed 18 years before. Nearly three decades after the First Regional Conference on the Education of Spanish-speaking People compiled information on the difficulties experienced by Mexican American students, the U.S. Commission on Civil Rights conducted a five-year Mexican American education study. It revealed that problems of segregation, teacher training, and language difficulty are still severe for Mexican American students in the five Southwestern States. In addition, the Commission's State Advisory Committees have examined the problems of Puerto Ricans, Native Americans, and Asian Americans. All of these studies document the continuing failure of public schools to provide language minority children with a meaningful education.

Compared with the median number of 12.0 school years completed for whites, the median is 8.1 for Mexican Americans, 8.6 for Puerto Ricans, 9.8 for Native Americans, and 12.4 for Asian Americans. The Commission's Mexican American Education Study shows that 40 percent of Mexican Americans who enter first grade never complete high school. As of 1972, the drop out rate for Puerto Ricans in New York City from 10th grade to graduation was 57 percent. In New England, 25 percent of the Spanish speaking student population had been retained in grade for at least 3 years; 50 percent, for at least 2 years. Only 12 percent were found to be in the correct grade for their age group. The dropout rate for Native Americans in the Southwest between grades 9 and 12 is 30.6 percent. For Navajos, the largest Native American tribe, the median educational level achieved is fifth grade.

Academic achievement scores recorded for language minority groups in the 1966 Coleman report show that they lag significantly behind majority group Americans. By the 12th grade the Mexican American student is 4.1 years behind the national norm in math achievement; 3.5, in verbal ability; and 3.3, in reading. The Puerto Rican student is 4.8 years behind the national norm in math; 3.6, in verbal ability; and 3.2, in reading. The Asian American student is 0.9 years behind the norm in math; 1.6, in verbal ability; and 1.6, in reading. Studies indicate that the longer language minority students stay in school the further they fall behind their classmates in grade level achievements. On tests of general information—including humanities, social sciences, and natural sciences —the median 12th grade score is 43.3 for Mexican Americans, 41.7 for Puerto Ricans, 44.7 for Native Americans, and 49.0 for Asian Americans as compared to a median score of 52.2 for whites.

In the 1960's there was a growing recognition that language minority children needed some manner of special assistance if they were to have an opportunity to succeed in school. Where efforts were made to provide such assistance, they usually took the form of supplemental English language development, or what is commonly known as the English as a Second Language (ESL) approach. In 1968, the Bilingual Education Act provided funds to support a few bilingual programs, which were to use the children's native language and culture for instruction while they were learning English. Since 1971, Massachusetts, Texas, Illinois, and New Jersey have enacted mandatory bilingual education laws.

The first expression of Executive policy in the area of equal educational opportunity for language minority students came in 1970 when the Department of Health, Education, and Welfare (HEW) issued its May 25 memorandum, which required federally-funded school districts to provide assistance for language minority children. The memorandum indicated that failure to provide such assistance, where needed, would be considered a violation of Title VI of the Civil Rights Act of 1964.

In *Lau* v. *Nichols,* the Supreme Court affirmed that interpretation of Title VI's scope, stating:

> Under these state-imposed standards there is no equality of treatment merely by providing students with the same facilities, textbooks, teachers, and curriculum; for students who do not understand English are effectively foreclosed from any meaningful education.

Basic English skills are at the very core of what these public schools teach. Imposition of a requirement that, before a child can effectively participate in the educational program, he must already have acquired those basic skills is to make a mockery of public education. We know that those who do not understand English are certain to find their classroom experiences wholly incomprehensible and in no way meaningful.

... It seems obvious that the Chinese-speaking minority receives less benefits than the English-speaking majority from respondents' school system which denies them a meaningful opportunity to participate in the educational program ...

Both HEW and the Supreme Court declined to prescribe for school districts the type of assistance program which would provide language minority children with equal benefits in the attainment of an education, leaving the ultimate decision to the local districts themselves. Many school districts are faced with determining what constitutes that equality of educational opportunity. If we assume that the goal of public education is to provide basic skills and knowledge needed for participation in American society, then equal educational opportunity means that all students should have the same chance to acquire those skills and knowledge. In considering ESL and bilingual bicultural education— the two major approaches to meeting the needs of language minority children— it is important, therefore, to examine their overall potential for providing such an education.

CONCLUSION

The Commission's basic conclusion is that bilingual bicultural education is the program of instruction which currently offers the best vehicle for large numbers of language minority students who experience language difficulty in our schools.

Many language minority children, including Mexican Americans, Puerto Ricans, Native Americans, and Asian Americans, face two obstacles in attaining an education. Not only may they be the target of discrimination because they belong to identifiable minority groups, they also may not understand English well enough to keep up with their English speaking counterparts.

Under *Lau* v. *Nichols,* the Supreme Court has held that school districts receiving Federal funds cannot discriminate against children of limited or non-English speaking ability by denying them the language training they need for meaningful participation in the educational process. In this report, the Commission has examined whether the bilingual bicultural education approach is an effective means of providing that opportunity. Primary emphasis was placed on the educational principles which support the use of the native language in educating children, in nurturing positive self concept, and in developing proficiency in English. However, consideration was also given the effect on successful learning of the attitudes toward language minority groups in this country.

PART FIVE

Testing and Assessment of Learning

Chapter 11 Testing and the Critical Response Test   261

Chapter 12 The Cognitive Revolution in Learning   295

On the Internet . . .

Sites appropriate to Part Five

This page provides links to sites that contain information on Benjamin S. Bloom's Taxonomy of Educational Objectives.

> http://www.voicenet.com/~reevesk/
> bloom.html

This site, sponsored by the North Central Regional Educational Laboratory, offers links to three NCREL essays on student assessment and lists assessment resources recommended by the National Research Centers.

> http://www.ncrel.org/sdrs/areas/assmnt.htm

Design Based Education: K-12, a project of the Graduate Program in Industrial Design and the Art Education Department of the University of the Arts in Philadelphia.

> http://www.uarts.edu/~arts/DK12home.html

This site contains a number of links to information, organizations, and resources that epitomize John Dewey's vision of ideal education.

> http://www.goddard.edu/students/
> progressive-education/ped.htm

CHAPTER 11 Testing and the Critical Response Test

11.1 BENJAMIN S. BLOOM ET AL.

The Nature and Development of the Taxonomy

Benjamin S. Bloom (b. 1913) was a pioneer in the development of the categorization of educational objectives. During his long career at the University of Chicago, he conducted ongoing research on mastery learning with children and young adults. His work became the basis for behavioral objectives in instruction. Bloom has published a number of works on learning, including *Every Kid Can: Learning for Mastery* (College/University Press, 1973) and *Handbook on Formative and Summative Evaluation of Student Learning* (McGraw-Hill, 1971), coedited with J. Thomas Hastings and George F. Madaus. Bloom's work on mastery learning as well as his taxonomy of educational objectives in the cognitive domain have had enormous impact on the testing and measurement of school learning in the United States.

Bloom worked with a committee composed of members of the American Educational Research Association to produce *Taxonomy of Educational*

Objectives, Handbook I: Cognitive Domain (David McKay, 1956). This became the conceptual basis for the development of behavioral objectives in
American curriculum and instruction in the 1970s and 1980s. Although this
taxonomy was first published in 1956, its use in the development of instructional objectives really did not begin to achieve widespread acceptance by
American educators until the late 1960s. The following selection, which
is from *Taxonomy of Educational Objectives, Handbook I,* introduces the
reader to the overall structure of the taxonomy in the cognitive domain.

Key Concept: cognitive objectives of instruction and evaluation

THE TAXONOMY AS A CLASSIFICATION DEVICE

The major purpose in constructing a taxonomy of educational objectives is
to facilitate communication. In our original consideration of the project we
conceived of it as a method of improving the exchange of ideas and materials among test workers, as well as other persons concerned with educational
research and curriculum development. For instance, the use of the taxonomy
as an aid in developing a precise definition and classification of such vaguely
defined terms as "thinking" and "problem solving" would enable a group of
schools to discern the similarities and differences among the goals of their
different instructional programs. They could compare and exchange tests and
other evaluative devices intended to determine the effectiveness of these programs. They could, therefore, begin to understand more completely the relation
between the learning experiences provided by these various programs and the
changes which take place in their students.

Set at this level, the task of producing a taxonomy, that is, a classification of
educational outcomes, is quite analogous to the development of a plan for classifying books in a library. Or, put more abstractly, it is like establishing symbols
for designating classes of objects where the members of a class have something
in common. In a library these symbols might be the words "fiction" and "nonfiction" and would apply to classes of books having something in common. If
the problem is essentially one of finding new symbols for the classes, any set of
symbols, numbers, nonsense syllables, or words could be used. Thus, we could
have used the symbols "F" and "NF" for fiction and nonfiction. Further, since
the symbols selected are not intended to convey that one class is of a higher order than another or that there is any particular relationship between the classes,
they can be selected in very arbitrary fashion. The labels "fiction" and "nonfiction" do not imply that the one class of book is better, more abstract, or more
complex than the other kind.

Of course, such a classification procedure cannot be a private fantasy since
it is of value only if used by the workers who wish to communicate with each
other. Thus, the classifications "fiction" and "nonfiction" are of value only if li-
brarians use them. Acceptance of such classifications by potential users is likely
to be facilitated if the class names are terms which are reasonably familiar to
them and if these terms are given precise and usable definitions. Thus, one

might expect more ready acceptance of a library classification scheme if he took such a term as "fiction," which is already in use, and defined it so that any competent librarian would easily be able to determine which books fit the classification.

In summary then, the major task in setting up any kind of taxonomy is that of selecting appropriate symbols, giving them precise and usable definitions, and securing the consensus of the group which is to use them. Similarly, developing a classification of educational objectives requires the selection of an appropriate list of symbols to represent all the major types of educational outcomes. Next, there is the task of defining these symbols with sufficient precision to permit and facilitate communication about these phenomena among teachers, administrators, curriculum workers, testers, educational research workers, and others who are likely to use the taxonomy. Finally, there is the task of trying the classification and securing the consensus of the educational workers who wish to use the taxonomy.

WHAT IS TO BE CLASSIFIED

Before one can build a classification scheme, it must be clear what it is that is to be classified. This is not much of a problem when one is classifying books. But descriptions of curricula are set up on such different bases as descriptions of teacher behavior, descriptions of instructional methods, and descriptions of intended pupil behaviors. As achievement testers and educational research workers, the major phenomena with which we are concerned are the changes produced in individuals as a result of educational experiences. Such changes may be represented by the global statements of the educational objectives of an educational unit, or they may be represented by the actual description of the student behaviors which are regarded as appropriate or relevant to the objectives. Objectives may also be inferred from the tasks, problems, and observations used to test or evaluate the presence of these behaviors.

We are of the opinion that although the objectives and test materials and techniques may be specified in an almost unlimited number of ways, the student behaviors involved in these objectives can be represented by a relatively small number of classes. Therefore, the taxonomy is designed to be a classification of the student behaviors which represent the intended outcomes of the educational process. It is assumed that essentially the same classes of behavior may be observed in the usual range of subject-matter content, at different levels of education (elementary, high school, college), and in different schools. Thus, a single set of classifications should be applicable in all these instances.

It should be noted that we are not attempting to classify the instructional methods used by teachers, the ways in which teachers relate themselves to students, or the different kinds of instructional materials they use. We are not attempting to classify the particular subject matter or content. What we are classifying is the *intended behavior* of students—the ways in which individuals are to act, think, or feel as the result of participating in some unit of instruction.

(Only such of these intended behaviors as are related to mental acts or thinking are included in the part of the taxonomy developed in this Handbook.)

It is recognized that the *actual behaviors* of the students after they have completed the unit of instruction may differ in degree as well as in kind from the *intended behaviors* specified by the objectives. That is, the effects of instruction may be such that the students do not learn a given skill to the desired level of perfection; or, for that matter, they may not develop the intended skill to any degree. This is a matter of grading or evaluating the goodness of the performance. The emphasis in the Handbook is on obtaining evidence on the extent to which desired and intended behaviors have been learned by the student. It is outside the scope of the task we set ourselves to properly treat the matter of determining the appropriate value to be placed on the different degrees of achievement of the objectives of instruction.

It should also be noted that the intended behaviors specified by educational objectives do not include many of the behaviors which psychologists are interested in classifying and studying. One reason is that the intended behaviors represent the social goals imposed upon youngsters by their society or culture. Thus, the intended or desired behaviors included in educational objectives usually do not include undesirable or abnormal behaviors which are socially disapproved. Similarly, certain natural or unsocialized behaviors which might be of interest to psychologists may fall outside the categories of the taxonomy.

Our present studies of the affective area have indicated that the selective nature of intended behaviors will be even more apparent there than in the cognitive domain. The fact that we include objectives which specify social and emotional adjustment as a part of the affective domain points up this fact.

GUIDING PRINCIPLES

Since the determination of classes and their titles is in some ways arbitrary, there could be an almost infinite number of ways of dividing and naming the domains of educational outcomes. To guide us in our selection of a single classification system and to make the product more readily understood and used, we established certain guiding principles. First, since the taxonomy is to be used in regard to existing educational units and programs, we are of the opinion that the major distinctions between classes should reflect, in large part, the distinctions teachers make among student behaviors. These distinctions are revealed in the ways teachers state educational objectives. They are also found in their curricular plans, their instructional material, and their instructional methods. To the extent it was possible, the subdivisions of the taxonomy are intended to recognize these distinctions.

A second principle is that the taxonomy should be logically developed and internally consistent. Thus, each term should be defined and used in a consistent way throughout the taxonomy. In addition, each category should permit logical subdivisions which can be clearly defined and further subdivided to the extent that appears necessary and useful.

A third principle is that the taxonomy should be consistent with our present understanding of psychological phenomena. Those distinctions which are psychologically untenable, even though regularly made by teachers, would be avoided. Further, distinctions which seem psychologically important, even though not frequently made in educational objectives, would be favorably considered for inclusion. Perhaps it should be reiterated that, since the taxonomy deals only with educationally intended behavior, it falls considerably short of being a classification scheme for all psychological phenomena.

A fourth principle is that the classification should be a purely descriptive scheme in which every type of educational goal can be represented in a relatively neutral fashion. Thus, the Dewey decimal classification system for libraries describes all the classes of books. It does not indicate the value or quality of one class as compared with another, nor does it specify the number and kind of books any particular library should possess. Similarly, to avoid partiality to one view of education as opposed to another, we have attempted to make the taxonomy neutral by avoiding terms which implicitly convey value judgments and by making the taxonomy as inclusive as possible. This means that the kinds of behavioral changes emphasized by *any* institution, educational unit, or educational philosophy can be represented in the classification. Another way of saying this is that any objective which describes an intended behavior should be classifiable in this system. On the other hand, the taxonomy will probably include a greater variety of behaviors than those emphasized by any one school, course, or educational philosophy. Thus, one course might have objectives classifiable in four of the categories, another in only three of the categories, and so on.

In one sense, however, the taxonomy is not completely neutral. This stems from the already-noted fact that it is a classification of intended behaviors. It cannot be used to classify educational plans which are made in such a way that either the student behaviors cannot be specified or only a single (unanalyzed) term or phrase such as "understanding," or "desirable citizen," is used to describe the outcomes. Only those educational programs which can be specified in terms of intended student behaviors can be classified.

DEVELOPING THE TAXONOMY

Keeping in mind the aforementioned principles, we began work by gathering a large list of educational objectives from our own institutions and the literature. We determined which part of the objective stated the behavior intended and which stated the content or object of the behavior. We then attempted to find divisions or groups into which the behaviors could be placed. We initially limited ourselves to those objectives commonly referred to as knowledge, intellectual abilities, and intellectual skills. (This area, which we named the cognitive domain, may also be described as including the behaviors: remembering; reasoning; problem solving; concept formation; and, to a limited extent, creative thinking.) We proceeded to divide the cognitive objectives into subdivisions from the simplest behavior to the most complex. We then attempted to find ways of defining these subdivisions in such a way that all of us working with the material could communicate with each other about the specific objectives as well as the testing procedures to be included.

We have not succeeded in finding a method of classification which would permit complete and sharp distinctions among behaviors.... There are two basic views. First, we were again made aware of what any teacher knows—two boys may appear to be doing the same thing; but if we analyze the situation, we find they are not. For example, two students solve an algebra problem. One student may be solving it from memory, having had the identical problem in class previously. The other student has never met the problem before and must reason out the solution by applying general principles. We can only distinguish between their behaviors as we analyze the relation between the problem and each student's background of experience. This then introduces a new aspect of the classification problem, namely, the experiential backgrounds of the students to whom the objective is to apply.... [T]his may be a very important factor in using the taxonomy to classify test exercises.

A second difficulty in classification results from the fact that the more complex behaviors include the simpler behaviors. If we view statements of educational objectives as intended behaviors which the student shall display at the end of some period of education, we can then view the process of one of change. As teachers we intend the learning experiences to change the student's behavior from a simpler type to another more complex one which in some ways at least will include the first type.

One may take the Gestalt point of view that the complex behavior is more than the sum of the simpler behaviors, or one may view the complex behavior as being completely analyzable into simpler components. But either way, so long as the simpler behaviors may be viewed as components of the more complex behaviors, we can view the educational process as one of building on the simpler behavior. Thus, a particular behavior which is classified in one way at a given time may develop and become integrated with other behaviors to form a more complex behavior which is classified in a different way. In order to find a single place for each type of behavior, the taxonomy must be organized from simple to complex classes of behavior. Furthermore, for consistency in classification, a rule of procedure may be adopted such that a particular behavior is placed in the most complex class which is appropriate and relevant.

But, having specified that the classes shall be arranged from simple to complex, we have exceeded the simple classification scheme which called primarily for a series of categories without order or rank. The next section addresses itself to this problem.

THE PROBLEM OF A HIERARCHY—
CLASSIFICATION VERSUS TAXONOMY

We have so far used the terms "classification" and "taxonomy" more or less interchangeably. It is necessary, however, that we examine the relationship between these terms because, strictly speaking, they are not interchangeable. Taxonomies, particularly Aristotelian taxonomies, have certain structural rules which exceed in complexity the rules of a classification system. While a classification scheme may have many arbitrary elements, a taxonomy scheme may not. A taxonomy must be so constructed that the order of the terms must correspond to some "real" order among the phenomena represented by the terms. A classification scheme may be validated by reference to the criteria of communicability, usefulness, and suggestiveness; while a taxonomy must be validated by demonstrating its consistency with the theoretical views in research findings of the field it attempts to order.

As educators and specialists in research, we are interested in a long-term inquiry into the nature of the phenomena with which we deal, and no simple set of terms and definitions by itself really is a satisfactory tool in making this inquiry. We need a method of ordering phenomena such that the method of ordering reveals significant relationships among the phenomena. This is the basic problem of a taxonomy—to order phenomena in ways which will reveal some of their essential properties as well as the interrelationships among them. Members of the taxonomy group spent considerable time in attempting to find a psychological theory which would provide a sound basis for ordering the categories of the taxonomy. We reviewed theories of personality and learning but were unable to find a single view which, in our opinion, accounted for the varieties of behaviors represented in the educational objectives we attempted to classify. We were reluctantly forced to agree with Hilgard[1] that each theory of learning accounts for some phenomena very well but is less adequate in accounting for others. What is needed is a larger synthetic theory of learning than at present seems to be available. We are of the opinion that our method of ordering educational outcomes will make it possible to define the range of phenomena for which such a theory must account. The taxonomy also uses an order consistent with research findings and it should provide some clues as to the nature of the theory which may be developed. This is an extremely complex problem; and although it has probably not been solved completely satisfactorily, it is the opinion of the writers that we have made some progress toward a solution.

As the taxonomy is now organized, it contains six major classes:

1.00 Knowledge

2.00 Comprehension

3.00 Application

4.00 Analysis

5.00 Synthesis

6.00 Evaluation

The classes of Bloom's taxonomy are defined in an appendix in the original source. The following are abbreviated definitions of the six classes:

1.00 Knowledge: *the recall of specifics and universals, the recall of methods and processes, or the recall of a pattern, structure, or setting.*

2.00 Comprehension: *the lowest level of understanding, in which the individual has a basic understanding or apprehension such that he or she knows what is being communicated without necessarily relating it to other material or seeing its fullest implications.*

3.00 Application: *the use of abstractions in particular and concrete situations; abstractions may be in the form of general ideas, rules of procedures, generalized methods, or technical principles, ideas, and theories that must be remembered and applied.*

4.00 Analysis: *the breakdown of a communication into its constituent elements or parts such that the relative hierarchy of ideas is made clear or the relations between the ideas expressed are made explicit.*

5.00 Synthesis: *the putting together of elements and parts so as to form a whole; this involves the process of working with pieces, parts, elements, etc., and arranging and combining them in such a way as to constitute a pattern or structure that was not clearly there before.*

6.00 Evaluation: *judgments about the value of material and methods for given purposes; quantitative and qualitative judgments about the extent to which material and methods satisfy criteria, which could be provided for the student*

Although it is possible to conceive of these major classes in several different arrangements, the present one appears to us to represent something of the hierarchical order of the different classes of objectives. As we have defined them, the objectives in one class are likely to make use of and be built on the behaviors found in the preceding classes in this list. . . .

Our attempt to arrange educational behaviors from simple to complex was based on the idea that a particular simple behavior may become integrated with other equally simple behaviors to form a more complex behavior. Thus our classifications may be said to be in the form where behaviors of type A form one class, behaviors of type AB form another class, while behaviors of type ABC form still another class. If this is the real order from simple to complex, it should be related to an order of difficulty such that problems requiring behavior A alone should be answered correctly more frequently than problems requiring AB. We have studied a large number of problems occurring in our comprehensive examinations and have found some evidence to support this hypothesis. Thus, problems requiring knowledge of specific facts are generally answered correctly more frequently than problems requiring a knowledge of the universals and abstractions in a field. Problems requiring knowledge of principles and concepts are correctly answered more frequently than problems requiring both knowledge of the principle and some ability to apply it in new situations. Problems requiring analysis and synthesis are more difficult than problems requiring comprehension. Scatter plots of the performances of individuals on one test composed of items at a simple level in the taxonomy against their performances on another test composed of items at a more complex level in the taxonomy show that it is more common to find that individuals have low scores on complex problems and high scores on the less complex problems than the reverse. Our evidence on this is not entirely satisfactory, but there is an unmistakable trend pointing toward a hierarchy of classes of behavior which is in accordance with our present tentative classification of these behaviors.

While we have been primarily concerned with the cognitive domain, we have done some thinking about the classification versus taxonomy problem as it applies to all the domains. The arrangement of behaviors from simple to complex and the differentiation of behaviors into three domains—the cognitive, the psychomotor, and the affective—were made primarily from an educational viewpoint. That is, these are the distinctions which teachers make in the development of curriculum and teaching procedures. We as educational testers also make similar distinctions. As we examine the classification system so far developed, however, we note an additional dimension not usually considered in educational and teaching procedures. One of the major threads running through all the taxonomy appears to be a scale of consciousness or awareness. Thus, the behaviors in the cognitive domain are largely characterized by a rather high degree of consciousness on the part of the individual exhibiting the behavior, while the behaviors in the affective domain are much more frequently exhibited with a low level of awareness on the part of the individual. Further, in the cognitive domain especially, it appears that as the behaviors become more complex, the individual is more aware of their existence. We are of the opinion that this applies to the other domains as well. Clearly there is no precise scale of consciousness which may be used to test these speculations. However, some of our research on the thought processes involved in problem solving[2] indicates that students are able to give more complete reports of their attack on a problem as the problem becomes more complex, that is, as the problem is classified in the more complex classes of intellectual abilities and skills.

If the level of consciousness can be demonstrated to be an important dimension in the classification of behavior, it would pose a great range of problems and point to a whole new set of relationships which would be of interest to researchers in the field of educational psychology. One might hope that it would provide a basis for explaining why behaviors which are initially displayed with a high level of consciousness become, after some time and repetition, automatic or are accompanied by a low level of consciousness. Perhaps this would provide a partial basis for explaining why some learning, especially of the affective behaviors, is so difficult. Perhaps it will also help to explain the extraordinary retention of some learning—especially of the psychomotor skills.

1. Hilgard, E. R., *Theories of Learning* (Century Psychology Series), New York: Appleton-Century-Crofts, 1948.
2. Bloom, B. S., and Broder, Lois, *Problem-solving processes of college students* (A Supplementary Educational Monograph), Chicago: University of Chicago Press, Summer, 1950.

11.2 DAVID R. KRATHWOHL, BENJAMIN S. BLOOM, AND BERTRAM B. MASIA

Affective Domain

David R. Krathwohl, in collaboration with Benjamin S. Bloom and Bertram B. Masia, developed a classification scheme for educational objectives in the affective (emotional) domain. In the following selection from *Taxonomy of Educational Objectives, Handbook II: Affective Domain* (David McKay, 1964), which presents a section from the book's very important fourth chapter, Krathwohl, Bloom, and Masia discuss the relationships between the cognitive and the affective domains of human behavior and how these interrelationships impact on the task of preparing or evaluating affective behavior. The authors emphasize that the cognitive and affective domains are linked, not autonomous (independent) dimensions of behavior.

Krathwohl, currently a professor emeritus at Syracuse University in Syracuse, New York, was teaching at Michigan State University when *Taxonomy of Educational Objectives, Handbook II* was published. Bloom and Masia both held academic appointments at the University of Chicago at that time.

Key Concept: affective educational objectives

Internalization as It Appears in the Taxonomy Structure

The process of internalization can be described by summarizing the continuum at successive levels as they appear in the *Affective Domain Taxonomy*. The process begins when the attention of the student is captured by some phenomenon, characteristic, or value. As he pays attention to the phenomenon, characteristic, or value, he differentiates it from the others present in the perceptual field. With differentiation comes a seeking out of the phenomenon as he gradually attaches emotional significance to it and comes to value it. As the process unfolds he relates this phenomenon to other phenomena to which he responds that also have value. This responding is sufficiently frequent so that he comes to react regularly, almost automatically, to it and to other things like it. Finally the values are interrelated in a structure or view of the world, which he brings as a "set" to new problems.

Even from this abstract description it can be seen that the internalization process represents a continuous modification of behavior from the individual's being aware of a phenomenon to a pervasive outlook on life that influences all his actions.

While this description of the process seemed reasonably satisfactory, if a hierarchical structure was to be provided and more adequate description of the process developed, it was clear that the continuum needed to be divided into steps or stages. In so far as possible, when this was done, the breaking points between steps were located where there appeared to be some kind of transition, such as the addition of a new component or kind of activity. Since the boundaries of the categories are completely arbitrary and can be defended only on pragmatic grounds, it is possible that later work may suggest that other breaking points would be more satisfactory. The divisions between major categories have proved quite useful in the analysis of objectives. We feel more sure of the major divisions than of the subcategories, some of which appear to be easier to delineate than others.

The steps in the process and their description... are reviewed here to acquaint the reader with them and to show the parallel between the description of internalization which has been developed and the steps and levels into which it has been arbitrarily divided.

We begin with the individuals being aware of the stimuli which initiate the affective behavior and which form the context in which the affective behavior occurs. Thus, the lowest category is 1.0 *Receiving.* It is subdivided into three categories. At the 1.1 *Awareness* level, the individual merely has his attention attracted to the stimuli (e.g., he develops some consciousness of the use of shading to portray depth and lighting in a picture).[1] The second subcategory, 1.2 *Willingness to receive,* describes the state in which he has differentiated the stimuli from others and is willing to give it his attention (e.g., he develops a tolerance for bizarre uses of shading in modern art). At 1.3 *Controlled or selected attention* the student looks for the stimuli (e.g., he is on the alert for instances where shading has been used both to create a sense of three-dimensional depth and to indicate the lighting of the picture; or he looks for picturesque words in reading).

At the next level, 2.0 *Responding,* the individual is perceived as responding regularly to the affective stimuli. At the lowest level of responding, 2.1 *Acquiescence in responding,* he is merely complying with expectations (e.g., at the request of his teacher, he hangs reproductions of famous paintings in his dormitory room; he is obedient to traffic rules). At the next higher level, 2.2 *Willingness to respond,* he responds increasingly to an inner compulsion (e.g., voluntarily looks for instances of good art where shading, perspective, color, and design have been well used, or has an interest in social problems broader than those of the local community). At 2.3 *Satisfaction in response* he responds emotionally as well (e.g., works with clay, especially in making pottery for personal pleasure). Up to this point he has differentiated the affective stimuli; he has begun to seek them out and to attach emotional significance and value to them.

As the process unfolds, the next levels of 3.0 *Valuing* describe increasing internalization, as the person's behavior is sufficiently consistent that he comes to hold a value: 3.1 *Acceptance of a value* (e.g., continuing desire to develop the ability to write effectively and hold it more strongly), 3.2 *Preference for a value* (e.g., seeks out examples of good art for enjoyment of them to the level where he behaves so as to further this impression actively), and 3.3 *Commitment* (e.g., faith in the power of reason and the method of experimentation).

As the learner successively internalizes values he encounters situations for which more than one value is relevant. This necessitates organizing the values into a system, 4.0 *Organization*. And since a prerequisite to interrelating values is their conceptualization in a form which permits organization, this level is divided in two: 4.1 *Conceptualization of a value* (e.g., desires to evaluate works of art which are appreciated, or to find out and crystallize the basic assumptions which underlie codes of ethics) and 4.2 *Organization of a value system* (e.g., acceptance of the place of art in one's life as one of dominant value, or weighs alternative social policies and practices against the standards of public welfare).

Finally, the internalization and the organization processes reach a point where the individual responds very consistently to value-laden situations with an interrelated set of values, a structure, a view of the world. The *Taxonomy* category that describes this behavior is 5.0 *Characterization by a value or value complex,* and it includes the categories 5.1 *Generalized set* (e.g., views all problems in terms of their aesthetic aspects, or readiness to revise judgments and to change behavior in the light of evidence) and 5.2 *Characterization* (e.g., develops a consistent philosophy of life).

Stripped of their definitions, the category and subcategory titles appear in sequence as follows:

1.0 Receiving (attending)
   1.1 Awareness
   1.2 Willingness to receive
   1.3 Controlled or selected attention
2.0 Responding
   2.1 Acquiescence in responding
   2.2 Willingness to respond
   2.3 Satisfaction in response
3.0 Valuing
   3.1 Acceptance of a value
   3.2 Preference for a value
   3.3 Commitment (conviction)
4.0 Organization
   4.1 Conceptualization of a value
   4.2 Organization of a value system
5.0 Characterization by a value or value complex
   5.1 Generalized set
   5.2 Characterization

Relation of the Affective-Domain Structure to Common Affective Terms

... [T]he analysis of such commonly used terms as interest, attitude, appreciation, and value showed each of them to have a wide range of meanings. When we examined the range of meanings for any one term and compared this range to the *Taxonomy* structure we found that each term generally took on meanings over a section of the internalization continuum. Figure 1 illustrates this.

Thus, objectives were found where interpretation of the term "interest" ranged all the way from the student's being aware that a phenomenon exists to

FIGURE 1

*The Range of Meaning Typical of Commonly Used Affective Terms
Measured Against the Taxonomy Continuum*

the behavior of avidly seeking a phenomenon. This is shown in Figure 1 by the line marked "Interest" extending from the *Taxonomy* category of 1.1 *Awareness* to 3.2 *Preference for a value.* Apparently the term "interest" typically describes behavior that would be classified at the lower levels of the *Taxonomy.* Rarely would it be interpreted as describing a behavior we would describe as *Commitment* or higher.

Interpretation of the term "appreciation" as it appears in objectives shows that it may refer to such simple behavior as the person's being willing to attend to certain aspects of a phenomenon, to his feeling a response to some stimulus, or to his showing a preference for certain behavior or stimuli. Thus, appreciation would not be interpreted typically as including the behaviors at the lowest levels of the *Taxonomy* nor at the highest. The line in Figure 1 shows the segment of the continuum which appears to include the bulk of its range of meanings.[2]

Similarly when we examined the range of interpretations given to the terms "attitude" and "value" in educational objectives, we found they ranged from situations where the student was expected to display a particular behavior, especially with a certain amount of emotion (enthusiasm, warmth, or even disgust, if appropriate), to situations in which he might go out of his way to display the value or to communicate to others about it. Thus the lines in Figure 1 for these terms extend from 2.2 *Willingness to respond* to 4.1 *Conceptualization of a value.*

The term "adjustment" appeared to take on a range of meanings, from a simple display of appropriate behavior in social interaction to the interrelation of one aspect of self to another—one's outlook on life. Thus, the line indicating its range of meanings extends from 2.2 *Willingness to respond* through 5.2 *Characterization.* It has the widest potential range of meanings of any of the terms, extending nearly across the entire range of taxonomic categories.

Several points with respect to this figure are worth noting. All the terms overlap one another in meaning in the middle range of the *Taxonomy* continuum. No specificity can be gained by replacing one term by another in this range, and possibilities for confusion are great.

A corollary of this observation is that no term (e.g., attitude) uniquely describes its entire segment of the continuum. Every term is overlapped by at least one other term for a major portion of that part of the continuum it describes.

Only the terms "interest" and "adjustment," at the lower and upper extremes, are not overlapped by another term for a portion of the continuum they include. In the objectives we have analyzed, "interest" appears to be used more often to describe behavior toward the middle range of the continuum than where it might be used with unique meaning, at the lowest extreme. "Adjustment," on the other hand, most frequently does refer in these objectives to the more complex kinds of behavior described in the upper levels of the *Taxonomy* to which it alone extends. In this respect, despite the range over which it is used, in its most frequent application it is intended to have a nearly unique meaning.

Finally, the figure indicates the increase in precision which it is hoped that the use of the affective continuum can achieve if its terms replace those in common use. For instance, the behavior involved in an "interest" objective could be given increased specificity if the objective were defined by placing it in one of the eight *Taxonomy* categories typically embraced by the term "interest." . . .

THE RELATION OF THE AFFECTIVE TO THE COGNITIVE DOMAIN

There has been much research on and logical analysis of the relation of cognitive to affective behavior, particularly the attainment of affective goals by cognitive means. We hope that the development of the *Affective Domain Taxonomy* will stimulate further research and thought on the relation between it and the cognitive domain....

The Fundamental Unity of the Organism

The fact that we attempt to analyze the affective area separately from the cognitive is not intended to suggest that there is a fundamental separation. There is none. As Scheerer puts it, "... behavior may be conceptualized as being embedded in a cognitive-emotional-motivational matrix in which no true separation is possible. No matter how we slice behavior, the ingredients of motivation-emotion-cognition are present in one order or another" (Scheerer, 1954, p. 123)....

Thus James, a forerunner of modern psychology, admits a fundamental unity of affective and cognitive behavior but proceeds to a fragmenting analysis showing how one is involved in the other. That this kind of reasoning continues is indicated by Rokeach, a contemporary psychologist who, also realizing the unity, shows how the one domain is involved in the other. This is what we, too, have done in developing the *Taxonomy*. Our problem has been (recognizing the arbitrariness of our conceptualization) to gain a perspective of our task essential to the formulating of a useful framework.

The Arbitrariness of Classification Schemes

Every classification scheme is an abstraction which arbitrarily makes divisions among phenomena solely for the convenience of the user, more particularly to emphasize some special characteristic of the phenomena of importance to the user. Some of these divisions seem "natural," since they correspond to differences which are readily perceived in the phenomena categorized. In other instances, the differences may be much more difficult to perceive and thus seem more arbitrary. One may find both "natural" and quite arbitrary classifications within the same framework, depending upon the nature of the phenomenon to be classified and what is important to the person using the framework. To the biochemist, the dichotomy between the physical and the biological sciences is extremely arbitrary, and there is nothing "natural" about it, though this division may be highly useful and "natural" to the administrators of a large university.

The arbitrariness of the *Taxonomy* structure is at once apparent in, among other things,[3] its division of the realm of educational goals into three domains: cognitive, affective, and psychomotor. These seem to be "natural" divisions, since teachers and educators have more or less traditionally divided their objectives into these categories, either explicitly or implicitly. It is hoped that the divisions within each of the domains will also seem "natural," once the reader is familiar with them. We have tried to make the breaks between categories at what appeared to be the "natural" places without attempting to force a correspondence between domains. Whether this permits the most useful and meaningful analysis remains for the user to judge.... The increasing use of the *Taxonomy's* already published portion encourages us to believe that this kind of analysis has proved useful and meaningful and that this second portion may prove to be of worth as well.

David R. Krathwohl et al.

With full recognition of the arbitrariness of the *Taxonomy's* division between cognitive and affective behavior, we may find it helpful to examine the way teachers' statements of objectives split cognitive from affective behavior, and then how the cognitive domain is related to the affective in terms of the particular categories used in this taxonomic analysis.

The Affective Component of Cognitive Objectives

The "garden variety" of objectives concentrates on specifying behavior in only one domain at a time. No doubt this results from the customarily analytic approaches to building curricula. Only occasionally do we find a statement like "The student should learn to analyze a good argument with pleasure." Such a statement suggests not only the cognitive behavior but also the affective aspect that accompanies it. In spite of the lack of explicit formulation, however, nearly all cognitive objectives have an affective component if we search for it. Most instructors hope that their students will develop a continuing interest in the subject matter taught. They hope that their students will have learned certain attitudes toward the phenomena dealt with or toward the way in which problems are approached. But they leave these goals unspecified. This means that many of the objectives which are classified in the cognitive domain have an implicit but unspecified affective component that could be concurrently classified in the affective domain. Where such an attitude or interest objective refers, as it most often does, to the content of the course as a whole or at least to a sizable segment of it, it may be most convenient to specify it as a separate objective. Many such affective objectives—the interest objective, for example—become the affective components of all or most of the cognitive objectives in the course. The affective domain is useful in emphasizing the fact that affective components exist and in analyzing their nature. Perhaps by its very existence it will encourage greater development of affective components of cognitive objectives.

It is possible that a different affective objective accompanies every cognitive objective in a course.[4] Were this a common situation, the present form of the *Taxonomy* would be unwieldy, for it would require a dual categorization of each objective. While the present state of the art of curriculum development suggests that the latter concern is by no means immediate, this is not a possibility to be discarded.

The relation of cognitive to affective objectives as conceived by teachers is mirrored in the relations of the taxonomies of the two domains. We turn next to this matter.

TABLE 1

1. The cognitive continuum begins with the student's recall and recognition of *Knowledge* (1.0),	1. The affective continuum begins with the student's merely *Receiving* (1.0) stimuli and passively attending to it. It extends through his more actively attending to it,
2. it extends through his *Comprehension* (2.0) of the knowledge,	2. his *Responding* (2.0) to stimuli on request, willingly responding to these stimuli, and taking satisfaction in this responding,
3. his skill in *Application* (3.0) of the knowledge that he comprehends,	3. his *Valuing* (3.0) the phenomenon or activity so that he voluntarily responds and seeks out ways to respond,
4. his skill in *Analysis* (4.0) of situations involving this knowledge, his skill in *Synthesis* (5.0) of this knowledge into new organizations,	4. his *Conceptualization* (4.1) of each value responded to,
5. his skill in *Evaluation* (6.0) in that area of knowledge to judge the value of material and methods for given purposes.	5. his *Organization* (4.2) of these values into systems and finally organizing the value complex into a single whole, a *Characterization* (5.0) of the individual.

Relations Between the Taxonomy Categories of the Two Domains

When one looks for relations between the subcategories of the two domains one finds that they clearly overlap. This overlap is implicit in [Table 1, which presents] descriptions of roughly parallel steps in the two continua. The terms set in italic are used as heads of divisions in the *Taxonomy* of the cognitive or affective domains. Their category numbers are given in parentheses.

The most apparent places at which the affective domain meets the cognitive domain in this description are at steps 1, 4, and 5. Setting the two domains parallel, as we have done to facilitate the examination of the relationship, suggests a much closer level-to-level correspondence than actually exists, however. Let us examine this correspondence, taking steps 1, 4, and 5, and 2 and 3 in that order.

STEP 1. The first point of close parallelism between the domains is at step 1, where "receiving" a phenomenon, or attending to it to some extent, corresponds to having "knowledge" of the phenomenon. But the emphasis in 1.0 *Receiving* is different from that in 1.0 *Knowledge* in that we are less concerned with memory and retrieval on demand. There is a relation, however, for certainly attending to a phenomenon is prerequisite to knowing about it. Further, only as one is willing to attend to a phenomenon will he learn about it.

On first glance, one might assume that "receiving" would always refer to awareness of certain information, and thus its parallel in the cognitive domain would always be the *Knowledge* category (e.g., the simple awareness of the way perspective is portrayed in a painting). While frequently true, this is not necessarily the case. Thus, *Receiving* includes the objective "Listens to music with some discrimination as to its mood and meaning and with some recognition of the contributions of various musical elements and instruments to the total effect." This certainly involves 2.0 *Comprehension,* the second category of the cognitive continuum, and probably 3.0 *Application* and 4.0 *Analysis,* the third and fourth levels of it. On looking over the objectives in the lowest levels of the affective domain, however, this is about as high a level in the cognitive continuum as one finds implied by the cognitive concomitants of these affective objectives.

But whatever the behavior specified in the lowest level in the affective domain, it is almost a certainty that one could interpret the objective so that, except for the fact that it is a building stone for more complex affective objectives, the objective might be restated so as to be classified in the cognitive domain. Some of our critics have argued that we should have begun the affective domain with 2.0 *Responding,* because of the heavily cognitive nature of this bottom category. But the fact that this behavior is a necessary first step to building objectives higher in the affective-domain hierarchy is the reason—an important one—for its being included as the bottom rung in the affective domain. Further, the emphasis in "receiving" is different from that of "knowledge," stressing, as is proper for an affective category, the volitional aspects of the knowing act.

STEPS 4 AND 5.   A second point of apparent close contact between the affective and cognitive domains is the correspondence in the upper levels of the two continua at steps 4 and 5. Here the behavior described by the affective domain is at least in part cognitive, as the student conceptualizes a value to which he has been responding, and this value is in turn integrated and organized into a system of values which comes eventually to characterize the individual. Such objectives would appear to require, at the very least, the ability to 2.0 *Comprehend,* for the student must translate his behavior into a set of verbal terms describing the value involved. In some instances this might call for the student to 4.0 *Analyze* the common value element from a series of activities or situations in which he has been involved and to 5.0 *Synthesize* this commonality into a value which encompasses all of them. The ability to organize and interrelate values into systems must certainly call for the ability to 4.0 *Analyze,* as it is described in the cognitive domain, and the development of new value complexes also most likely involves the ability to 5.0 *Synthesize.* Further, the ability to balance values against one another, which is implied by the very highest affective categories, implies capability for 6.0 *Evaluation* as it is defined in the cognitive domain. For example, "Judges problems and issues in terms of situations, issues, purposes, and consequences involved rather than in terms of fixed, dogmatic precepts or emotionally wishful thinking" (Part II, p. 184).

It is possible, however, that in everyday behavior much of this balancing of values is at a semiconscious intuitive level rather than at the rational, objective, conscious, level implied by 6.0 *Evaluation* in the cognitive domain. Such semiconscious behavior is described in the affective domain by category 5.1 *Generalized Set,* where the behavior is so internalized that it is displayed almost automatically, without conscious consideration. On the surface, this makes the affective domain appear to extend further than the cognitive in the sense that it describes a behavior so deeply internalized that it is automatic. No such behavior appears in the cognitive continuum.

But one could argue that some cognitive evaluation behavior ought also to be that well learned. Indeed, one may question whether such regularity of behavior is not implicit in most cognitive and affective objects at all *Taxonomy* levels. In general, in both the cognitive and affective domains the regularity of behavior is measured, not in terms of the *Taxonomy* level of behavior, but as such regularity affects the test score. Given a test which includes a variety of situations in which the observed behavior should be displayed if learned or internalized, the regularity with which it is displayed across these situations is reflected in the person's score. At the top level of the affective domain we happen to have specified a level of behavior which is so well learned, so deeply internalized, that it is automatic.

In this sense, at the 5.1 *Generalized Set* level we have described a kind of behavior which can be attained only with complete regularity, and the level of performance required in scoring is implicit in the behavior description. (This is the only category in the *Taxonomy* which so specifies the score performance for achievement of that level.) It was included because affective objectives were found which described this regularity of the behavior. Certain affective objectives have made explicit a complete regularity and automaticity of response which may also be implied in many cognitive objectives. Thus a discrepancy wherein the affective domain appears to extend beyond the cognitive domain can be reconciled on careful examination. The overlap between the two domains at this level appears to be real.

STEPS 2 AND 3.   In the middle portions of the affective continuum the individual begins to respond to the stimuli, at first on request (2.1 *Acquiescence in responding*), then increasingly on his own volition to the point where he is actively seeking instances in which he may respond (3.3 *Commitment*). These are not unrelated to the cognitive domain, but the nature of the relation is much less easily specified. The range of cognitive behavior corresponding to this portion of the affective continuum appears to cover a wide portion of the cognitive domain. But in all the affective behavior the cognitive element is present and implied. For example, in the lowest level of this portion, in the subcategory 2.1 *Acquiescence in responding,* we find the objective "Willingness to comply with health regulations." This objective implies that at least there is comprehension of these regulations and the ability to apply them to new situations; both of these are cognitive behaviors. At the highest level of this middle range of the continuum, in the subcategory 3.3 *Commitment,* we find the objective "Devotion to those ideas and ideals which are the foundation of democracy." This objective in turn implies cognitive behaviors such as the ability to analyze situations in order to determine how the ideas and ideals apply in a given situation.

It can be noted that throughout this analysis of the five steps there is some tendency for the cognitive counterpart of a low-level objective to come from the lower levels of the affective continuum and for objectives at the upper level of the affective continuum to have upper-level cognitive counterparts.

From the analysis above it appears that at all levels of the affective domain, affective objectives have a cognitive component, and one can find affective components for cognitive objectives. But lest this relationship appear more obvious than it really is, it should be noted that the examples of objectives in the preceding discussion were chosen so as to make the relation clear. We could have chosen affective-domain objectives for which the cognitive component is much more obscure; for instance, "Enjoyment of worship" or "Responds emotionally to a work of art." While we could recognize a cognitive component in such objectives, we should clearly be less certain to secure agreement among educators about the most appropriate cognitive behavior to accompany the affective behavior. Though undoubtedly there is some cognitive component in every affective objective, its nature is much more easily seen in some instances than in others.

Other Relationships Between the Cognitive and Affective Domains...

Cognitive Objectives as Means to Affective Goals.   The fact that our learning research and theories focus largely on cognitive behavior is an indication that we feel we know better how to handle the cognitive domain. Moving from the cognitive domain to the affective thus tends to be the preferred orientation. Attitudes, and even feelings, for example, tend to be defined in cognitive terms. James, in the quotation cited earlier in this chapter, defined feeling as a kind of knowing. Asch (1952) stated that an "attitude contains a more or less coherent ordering of data... an organization of experience and data with reference to an object" (p. 580). Rhine (1958) surveyed the definitions of attitudes by outstanding psychologists and concluded that the common element is the essence of what is generally meant by a concept. He therefore defined an attitude as a concept with an evaluative component and proceeded to explain attitude formation in the cognitive terms usually reserved for concept formation. As he pointed out, this approach could make attitudes more amenable to laboratory scrutiny, one indication of why this approach to the affective domain is preferred.

Rokeach, as already noted, saw a basic congruence between the cognitive and affective systems. He stated further, "... although our approach to belief systems, including esthetic ones, is a purely cognitive one... if the assumption is correct that every emotion has its cognitive counterpart, then we should be able to reach down into the complexities of man's emotional life via a study of his cognitive processes.... If we know something about the way a person relates himself to the world of ideas we may also be able to say in what way he relates himself to the world of people and to authority" (Rokeach, 1960, p. 8).

Similarly, Rosenberg (1956) examined attitudes in terms of cognitive structure. Noting the relations between cognitive and affective components, he argued that a tendency to respond to an object with positive or negative affect is "accompanied by a cognitive structure made up of beliefs about the potentialities of that object for attaining or blocking the realization of valued states"

(p. 367). He further argued that both the direction of the affect—whether it is positive or negative with reference to the object—and the strength of the affect are correlated with the content of the associated cognitive structure. Here again we see the affective component made a function of cognitive components which are more easily dealt with, thus permitting manipulation of the affective by the cognitive.

Festinger (1957) and Heider (1958), among others, have propounded so-called "balance theories" which provide another approach to the study of affective changes as a result of cognitive behavior. Festinger, in his theory of cognitive dissonance, described the motivating effect of disharmonious or dissonant states in cognition. He defined cognition so broadly as to include affectively tinged states such as opinions and beliefs as well as cognitive states of knowledge. Thus his theory easily bridges the cognitive-affective distinction and cannot be seen as one which manipulates cognitive behavior (in its usual sense) alone. But Festinger did describe the effects of changes in knowledge on affective behavior, and this represents one kind of approach to affective behavior through cognition.

The careful observer of the classroom can see that the wise teacher as well as the psychological theorist uses cognitive behavior and the achievement of cognitive goals to attain affective goals. In many instances she does so more intuitively than consciously. In fact, a large part of what we call "good teaching" is the teachers' ability to attain affective objectives through challenging the students' fixed beliefs and getting them to discuss issues.

In some instances teachers use cognitive behavior not just as a means to affective behavior but as a kind of prerequisite. Thus appreciation objectives are often approached cognitively by having the student analyze a work of art so that he will come to understand the way in which certain effects are produced —the nuances of shading to produce depth, color to produce emotional tone, etc. Such analysis on a cognitive level, when mastered, may be seen as learning necessary for "truly" appreciating a work of art.

In other instances teachers use cognitive behavior and cognitive goals as a means to multiple affective ends. This occurs especially in areas where the problem of indoctrination arises. Cognitive behavior may be used to indoctrinate points of view and to build attitudes and values. Indeed, we do this shamelessly in the aesthetic fields, where we want our students to learn to recognize "good" poetry, painting, architecture, sculpture, music, and so on. But in most areas of the curriculum we have a horror of indoctrinating the student with any but our most basic core values (we cannot always agree on the nature of these core values, the court cases on religion in the schools are an example). In most instances where indoctrination is avoided, we seek to have the student take his own position with respect to the issue. Thus a discussion may result in the development of a variety of "correct" positions and attitudes with respect to the area of concern, rather than in a single type of behavioral outcome as when a cognitive objective has been achieved. This also occurs where there are conflicts in values within our own culture. For example, the problems of honesty vs. dishonesty vs. "white lies," or of competition vs. cooperation, usually result in a variety of acceptable solutions, each a function of the situation in which such a conflict arises.

There are some instances where the cognitive route to affective achievement has resulted in learning just the opposite of that intended. Thus the infamous example of the careful and detailed study of "good" English classics, which was intended to imbue us with a love of deathless prose, has in many instances alienated us from it instead. Emphasis on very high mastery of one domain may in some instances be gained at the expense of the other.

Similarly, ... emphasis on one domain may tend to drive out the other. New courses often start with a careful analysis of both cognitive and affective objectives. But we feel more comfortable in teaching for cognitive than for affective objectives. Our drive for subject-matter mastery and the ever-increasing amount of knowledge available gives us more and more subject matter to cover. Further, our preference for approaching affective achievement through the attainment of cognitive objectives tends to focus attention on these cognitive goals as ends in themselves without our determining whether they are actually serving as means to an affective end. Over time the emphasis in most courses tends more and more to concentrate on the cognitive objectives at the expense of the affective ones. This erosion may be inevitable, but it could be lessened or stopped if we were conscious of its action. One of the major uses of *Handbook I: Cognitive Domain* has been to provide a basis for showing the current overwhelming emphasis on knowledge objectives at the expense of the development of skills and abilities in using that knowledge. Similarly, the development of *Handbook II: Affective Domain* should help to highlight the current emphasis on cognitive objectives at the expense of the affective.

Affective Objectives as Means to Cognitive Goals. From the previous discussion it seems clear that the cognitive approach to affective objectives is a frequently traveled route. What about the reverse? One of the main kinds of affective-domain objectives which are sought as means to cognitive ends is the development of interest or motivation. As viewed from the cognitive pole, the student may be treated as an analytic machine, a "computer" that solves problems. In contrast, viewed from the affective pole, we take greater cognizance of the motivation, drives, and emotions that are the factors bringing about achievement of cognitive behavior.

Obviously motivation is critical to learning and thus is one of the major ways in which the affective domain is used as a means to the cognitive. The large number of interest objectives indicates the importance of this aspect of the learning situation. The influence of hedonic tone on memory and learning is also important: children are more likely to learn and remember material for which they have a positive feeling. Note for instance the prevalence of girls who dislike mathematics and so cannot learn it, as well as boys who dislike school in general and do poorly. Though these "likes" may be produced by role expectancies, it is the internalized preferences which produce the effect.

Where educational objectives are involved we are almost always concerned with positive affect, with leading rather than driving the student into learning. But there are some school situations where negative affect is used to prevent certain behaviors from occurring and to facilitate cognitive learning. Such is the use of negative affect (fear of punishment, for instance) rather than the attempt to attain affective objectives as means to cognitive ends. In some instances social pressure may be exerted to change a student's position or viewpoint. We recognized that occasionally the school will have affective goals of this kind when we provided category 2.1 *Acquiescence in responding* but noted that this was a rarely used category.

Both the theoretical and experimental literature suggest that this is not an easy route to cognitive change. Both Kelman's (1958) model and Jahoda (1956) point to the likelihood that persons may outwardly comply under such situations but inwardly remain unchanged. Festinger's (1957) theory of cognitive dissonance posits that severe external threat or pressure represents a justification to the individual for engaging in behavior contrary to his beliefs, so that there is less need to reduce the dissonance caused by his engaging in this behavior under the threat conditions. Where the threat is mild, there is less justification for engaging in the behavior, and we can thus expect more change in private opinion to reduce the dissonance. Experimentation by Festinger and Carlsmith (1959) backs up this theoretical prediction. It appears that certain threatening school climates could actually defeat teachers' attempts to bring about both cognitive and affective learning.

But, as already noted, more often our motivation results from positive affect. Increasingly this is taking the form of building upon the method of self-discovery as a means of fostering interest in learning material. In thus enhancing curiosity and exploratory activity we may be building upon a basic drive. White (1959), giving careful consideration to previous literature on motivation and to recent experimentation on curiosity and the attractiveness of novel stimuli, posits a drive for competency, a need for a feeling of efficacy. He suggests that curiosity, exploratory behavior, manipulation, and general activity bring man in contact with his environment and make him more competent to deal with it. White's competency drive underlies these and similar activities. Few of us have recognized that with discovery-type objectives we may have been building on a basic drive.

Discovery-type material, such as that going into the University of Illinois School Mathematics Program, uses the affective effects of self-discovery as a means of simultaneously achieving the goals of mastery of the material and developing interest in it. This corresponds to what Bruner (1960) points to as an important goal in our new curricula. He suggests that we must increase "the inherent interest of the materials taught, giving the student a sense of discovery, translating what we say into thought forms appropriate to the child and so on. What this amounts to is developing in the child an interest in what he is learning and with it an appropriate set of attitudes and values about intellectual activities in general" (p. 73). This suggestion, that we build in a set of attitudes toward learning and the value of learning, represents another of the all-encompassing goals of most curricula. It is another common way in which attainment of the affective goal is a means to the facilitation of cognitive learning.

Simultaneous Achievement of Cognitive and Affective Goals. In some instances it is impossible to tell whether the affective goal is being used as a means to a cognitive goal or vice versa. It is a chicken and egg proposition. Perhaps it is fairest to say they are both being sought simultaneously. . . .

In some instances the joint seeking of affective and cognitive goals results in curricula which use one domain as the means to the other on a closely-knit alternating basis. Thus a cognitive skill is built and then used in rewarding situations so that affective interest in the task is built up to permit the next cognitive task to be achieved, and so on. Perhaps it is analogous to a man scaling a wall using two step ladders side by side, each with rungs too wide apart to be conveniently reached in a single step. One ladder represents the cognitive behaviors and objectives, the other the affective. The ladders are so constructed that the rungs of one ladder fall between the rungs of the other. The attainment of some complex goal is made possible by alternately climbing a rung on one ladder, which brings the next rung of the other ladder within reach. Thus alternating between affective and cognitive domains, one may seek a cognitive goal using the attainment of a cognitive goal to raise interest (an affective goal). This permits achievement of a higher cognitive goal, and so on. . . .

Summary

This really only scratches the surface of what is undoubtedly a very complex relationship between the cognitive and affective domains. We still have much to learn about it. But the fact should be clear that the two domains are tightly intertwined. Each affective behavior has a cognitive-behavior counterpart of some kind and vice versa. An objective in one domain has a counterpart in the opposite domain, though often we do not take cognizance of it. There is some correlation between the *Taxonomy* levels of an affective objective and its cognitive counterpart. Each domain is sometimes used as a means to the other, though the more common route is from the cognitive to the affective. Theory statements exist which permit us to express one in terms of the other and vice versa.

Our split between the affective and cognitive domains is for analytical purposes and is quite arbitrary. Hopefully the analysis of the two domains will have heuristic value so that we may better understand the nature of each as well as the relationship of one to the other.

NOTES

1. This same objective is successively modified to carry it through many of the levels of the continuum.
2. Appreciation is sometimes interpreted to mean that the student can describe that aspect of a phenomenon (e.g., a dance) that he appreciates. In this respect the line should extend to 4.1 *Conceptualization of a value*. Yet, rarely does an appreciation objective connote a commitment to a value.
3. We could, for example, cite as arbitrary the insistence that educational goals are most meaningfully stated as student behaviors rather than teacher activities. But this aspect is less relevant to the chapter topic.
4. This is not to imply that the full range from 1.1 to 5.2 of affective behaviors would apply to every cognitive objective, however. This matter is explored further in the next section.

Assessment and the Morality of Testing

Grant P. Wiggins is a nationally recognized expert in the development and implementation of performance assessments. He is president of the Center on Learning, Assessment and School Structure and a senior associate with the National Center on Education and the Economy. He is a special consultant on assessment for the Coalition of Essential Schools, and he has published many articles on school reform in such journals as *Phi Delta Kappan* and *Educational Leadership.*

In the selection that follows, which is from *Assessing Student Performance: Exploring the Purpose and Limits of Testing* (Jossey-Bass, 1993), Wiggins discusses individualized approaches to assessment of student achievement. He believes that teachers and students can work as allies rather than as adversaries in developing models for assessing student progress. Wiggins raises the point that at both the kindergarten and the doctoral dissertation levels of study, students are encouraged to be creative and original, yet from the first grade through at least the beginning of the undergraduate years, students are judged mostly by their scores on standardized and short-answer tests. Wiggins then argues for the development of improved models for determining how student progress is to be assessed. He raises moral and ethical issues regarding how student achievement should be assessed, and he asserts that because the student is the primary client in all assessment, the assessment process needs to be developed in order to improve student performance and not just to monitor it.

Wiggins contends that there needs to be procedural due process rights for students to raise questions about how they are assessed and how they can question the means or content of assessment. Students, he argues, need to be able to cross-examine the results of assessment and to make their case regarding assessment. He therefore proposes the development of and offers his own version of an "Assessment Bill of Rights" for students.

Key Concept: Assessment Bill of Rights

People write the history of experiments on those born blind, on wolf-children, or those under hypnosis. But who will write the more general, more fluid, but also more determinant history of the "examination"—its rituals, its methods, its characters and their roles, its play of questions and answers, its systems of marking and classification? For in this slender technique are to be found a whole domain of knowledge, a whole type of power.

—Michel Foucault[1]

Consider, for a moment, one unorthodox "examination" strategy that now exists within our educational world. In this form of assessment, the challenges are not at all standardized; indeed, they are by design fully personalized, allowing each student free rein as to topic, format, and style. And although students are not subject to uniform tasks required of all, no one thinks this lack of uniformity is odd or "soft." Contrary to common practice, this test is never secret: the assessment is centered on students' intellectual interests and the thoughtfulness with which those ideas are pursued. Students are assessed on how well knowledge and interest are crafted into products and performances of their own design. No student must "earn" this right to create projects and works of one's choosing; this is an assumed right.

The setting for such assessment is mainstream, not "alternative." Nonetheless, the schedule in support of such assessment is out of the ordinary, designed to suit the learner's, not the teacher's pace; each student is assessed only when ready. Instead of having an adversarial relationship, teacher and student are allies. The teacher is the student's guide through the challenges of the assessment, not an enemy to be "psyched out." The assessor is in fact *obligated* to understand the student's point of view in order to validly assess the student's grasp of things—a far cry from the typical "gotcha!" test.

Perhaps by now you have guessed the locale of such scenes: many kindergartens and graduate schools throughout our country. At both extremes of the school career, we deemphasize one-shot uniform testing in favor of a careful assessment, from different perspectives, of the student's own projects. We focus more on the student's ability to extend or play with ideas than on the correctness of answers to generic questions. Each piece of work, be it a drawing or a dissertation, is examined—often through dialogue—for what it reveals about the learner's habits of mind and ability to create meaning, not his or her "knowledge" of "facts." At the beginning and end of formal education, we understand that intellectual accomplishment is best judged through a "subjective" but rigorous interaction of mind and mind. Since performance based on one's own inquiry is being measured, test "security" is a moot issue. The essential aim behind this kind of tactful examining can be expressed as a question: Do the student's particular ideas, arguments, and products *work*—that is, do the work-products effectively and gracefully achieve the student's intention?

During the bulk of schooling, unfortunately, the story is far different. From first grade through at least the beginning (and often the end) of the undergraduate years in college, standardized and short-answer tests—and the mentality that they promote—are dominant. Students are tested not on the way they use, extend, or criticize "knowledge" but on their ability to generate a superficially correct response on cue. They are allowed one attempt at a test that they know nothing about until they begin taking it. For their efforts, they receive—and are judged by—a single numerical score that tells them little about their current level of progress and gives them no help in improving. The result is, as Lauren and Daniel Resnick, researchers and heads of the New Standards Project, have written, that American students are the "most tested but least examined" in the world.[2]

BETTER ASSESSMENT, NOT BETTER TESTING

But "read me well!" as Nietzsche asked of his readers in the preface to *Dawn*. This book is not a (predictable) critique of multiple-choice tests. On the contrary, *we have the tests we deserve,* including the tests that teachers design and give. The stubborn problems in assessment reform have to do with a pervasive thoughtlessness about testing and a failure to understand the relationship between assessment and learning. We have the tests we deserve because we are wont to reduce "assessment" to "testing" and to see testing as *separate* from learning—something you do expediently, once, after the teaching is over, to see how students did (usually for *other* people's benefit, not the performer's). Standardized multiple-choice tests thus represent an extreme version of an endemic problem: under these unspoken premises, it is inevitable that we come to rely on the most simple, efficient, and trivial tasks that can be reliably used. Saving time and labor becomes a paramount design virtue and causes every designer to rely on simple, quickly employed, and reusable (hence "secure") items.

The willingness by faculties to machine-score a local test or refer student answers to a key devised for quick marking during a faculty meeting reveals that teachers too, not just professional test makers, think that human judgment is an unnecessary extravagance in sound assessment. "But we teach so many students! What else can we do?" Why not see it the other way around? Why have the band director, debate coach, science fair judge, play director, and volley-ball coach not succumbed to the same thoughtless or fatalistic expediency? Because they understand that the "test" of performance *is* the course, not something you do *after* it. Because they understand that both validity and reliability of judgment about complex performance depend upon many pieces of information gained over many performances. If our thoughtless assessment practices are going to change, we need to do more than simply replace traditional forms of "test" (multiple-choice) with new forms of "test" ("performance" or "portfolio"); we need to change the fundamental relationship between tester and student.

Let me put this more forcefully ... : *tests are intrinsically prone to sacrifice validity to achieve reliability and to sacrifice the student's interests for the test maker's.* All testing involves compromise. Tasks are simplified and decontextualized for the sake of precision in scoring. Limits are placed on the student's access to resources. Standardization establishes a distance between tester and student: the student can neither adapt the question to personal style nor question the questioner (a right, one would think, in a modern society, and something we would encourage in a more personal educational relationship). ...

This [selection] offers a philosophy of assessment based upon a basic and decidedly more modern and unfatalistic principle: because the *student* is the primary client of all assessment, assessment should be designed to *improve* performance, not just monitor it. Any modern testing (including testing used for accountability) must ensure that the primary client for the information is well served.

But any philosophy of student assessment depends upon more than a value statement as to what assessment "should" be. A philosophy should lay out a coherent and thorough position describing how the theory and practice of testing and assessment should be best understood. Any philosophy of assessment must therefore provide a set of justified principles to serve as criteria for "testing the test."... How would such criteria differ from technical standards (those already established by psychometricians, for example)? The simple answer is that the tester's standards can tell us only when tests are sound or unsound, not when we should and should not test. To answer the latter question, we need to raise questions normally not raised in such discussions: When is testing apt, and when is it not? What should happen when the interests of test makers, test users, and test takers diverge? How should schools and districts establish safeguards against the harm of excessive testing and inadequate assessment? These are questions crying out for consideration.

These questions are pressing not merely because we are in the midst of unparalleled debate about testing and schooling. A logically prior question has never been adequately considered in the testing debates: Are the primary client's interests served by testing? As I hope to show, a preponderance of testing (as opposed to assessment) is *never* in the student's interests, whether we use multiple-choice or performance-based tests. Because a test, by its design, is an artifice whose audience is an outsider, whose purpose is ranking, and whose methods are reductionist and insensitive.

Our habits run too deep for mere technical scrutiny. The questionable practices used in testing are not rational, no matter how ubiquitous; they cannot be understood on technical or policy grounds alone. Our "modern" testing systems are built upon an ancient human urge to perpetuate a "marking and classification" system, in Michel Foucault's words. (Stephen Jay Gould's history of intelligence testing in *The Mismeasure of Man* makes clear how easily ethnocentric assumptions infected the testing but were hidden by the methods.[3]) Our tests, as the... opening quote from Foucault suggests, still reflect premodern views about the student's (unequal) relationship to the examiner (and hence premodern views about the student's rights). The "rituals" and "roles" of the examination are rooted in a medieval world of inquisitions and class distinctions. The examiner's "methods," then as now, prevent the student from questioning the tester about the questions, the methods, or the results—especially because of "secure" testing, a legacy of the secretive methods employed by medieval guilds. The use of such chicanery as "distracters" on tests and win-lose grading systems are among many practices that mark the testing relationship as morally imbalanced.

When our sole aim is to measure, the child is invariably treated as an object by *any* test, a theme to which I will repeatedly return. The educative role of genuine assessment is always at risk if by *test* we mean a process in which we insist upon *our* questions, *our* timing, and *our* imposed constraints on resources and prior access to the questions and in which we see *our* scoring and reporting needs as paramount. When we isolate the learner's "knowledge" from the learner's character in a test, we no longer feel an obligation to get to know the assessee well (or even to pursue the meaning of an answer). It is no longer obligatory to worry whether we have provided students with the opportunity to have their achievements thoroughly examined and documented; it is no longer obligatory to construct opportunities for them to show what they can do (or, at the very least, to sign off on the results).

There is an *inescapable* moral dimension, in other words, to the assessment relationship—a dimension that we ignore. In school testing as we have always known it, that relationship is inherently tilted in favor of the tester. The tenor of the relationship has little to do with what *kind* of test we use and everything to do with the manner in which testing and other assessment methods treat the student, as we shall see in the chapters that follow. A philosophy of assessment in which student interests are viewed as primary would have us ask, What approaches to assessment are most respectful?

Respectful may seem like an odd word to use in talking about quizzes, tests, exams, grades, and the like, but it is the most apt word with which to initiate the rethinking of our deep-seated habits about testing. The assessor either respects or disrespects the student by the manner in which the relationship is conducted. It is respectful, for example, to be open with people about your intent and methods; a steady dose of secure tests must then be disrespectful and off-putting. It is respectful to allow people to explain themselves when we think that they have erred or when we do not understand their answer. Tests that provide no opportunity for students to supply a rationale for answers reveal that what they think and why they think it is unimportant. It is respectful to give people timely, accurate, and helpful feedback on their "effect," yet most tests provide the student with nothing more than a score—and often weeks later. It is respectful to give people ample opportunity to practice, refine, and master a task that we wish them to do; yet secure, one-shot tests prevent the efficacy that comes from cycles of model/practice/feedback/refine.

The assessment relationship can thus range from being one of complete mutual respect—through ongoing responsiveness, flexibility, patience, and a capacity for surprise in our questioning and follow-up—to one in which the student is only "tested" (and is thus treated as an object), through the imposition of tasks and procedures that provide the student (and teacher, in the case of externally designed tests) with no opportunity to enter the conversation.

... [T]here is undoubtedly a risk in drawing upon the language and logic of morality (and epistemology) in discussing student assessment and testing, because to do so may appear either naive or unhelpful to those who must address the pressing problems of testing and school reform. Nonetheless, it is essential that we take the risk. *Any use of power and its limits involves moral questions and moral consequences, and testers have extraordinary and often unilateral power.* Thus nothing could be more practical than to develop procedures whereby the logically prior questions about the purposes and effects of assessment and testing are thoroughly considered and codified into intelligent policies and practices.

Every test, every grade affects the learner. Every dull test—no matter how technically sound—affects the learner's future initiative and engagement. No, even saying it this way does not do justice to the consequences of our testing practices: every test *teaches* the student. It teaches the student what kinds of questions educators value, it teaches the student what kind of answers we value (correct merely? justified? chosen from our list? constructed by the student?), it teaches the student about intellectual relationship, and it teaches the student how much we respect student thinking.

TOWARD AN ASSESSMENT BILL OF RIGHTS

We might, then, think of sound assessment and the appropriate use of tests along the lines of the modern judiciary or our own Bill of Rights. Due process is essential in good assessment, just as it is in legal proceedings. What counts as evidence must be acceptable not only to disinterested judges but also to such interested parties as the student and the student's teachers. The student/teacher should have not only the right of appeal but the right to question the questioner (to "cross-examine") and to present other kinds of evidence—in short, to make one's case. (That these rights sound fantastic and impossible, though they are routinely granted in the U.S. higher-education system and the K–12 systems of other countries, shows how far we have come in valuing efficiency over effectiveness, "measurement" over education.)

Cronbach makes explicit what is usually implicit in this regard: "The tester enters into a contract with the person tested. In former days the understanding was left vague. The tester is now expected to be frank and explicit...." Cronbach offers some general guidelines about problematic practices ("Scores that will have an important effect on the person's future should be reported in understandable form," "A procedure for challenging a test report should be available and the test taker should be informed of the procedure," and so on) but warns that "such principles are not easily put into practice."[4]

But demanding that the tester be more "frank and explicit" is not enough. The power is still so unequally distributed and the methods used by the test maker are so arcane that the student (and the teacher, when the tests are external) has no real opportunity to understand the proceedings. As in the legal model, there ought to be not only an appeals process for testing and assessment decisions (as there often is in special education decisions, for example) but also "cross-examination" of test makers as to the compromises and limitations of the test design and the meaningfulness of the scores.

Local educators need greater guidance and more helpful decision-making structures as they attempt to balance the inherently competing interests of test giver and test taker. It is *never* in the student's interests for test questions and answer sheets to remain secure not only before but after administration, yet test companies and teachers have thus far successfully lobbied to retain the right to protect their product and save themselves time and money.

Principles for the conduct of assessment that put the student's rights on a moral par with the technical needs of psychometricians and the policy needs of school-board and community members are long overdue. I know of only a handful of school districts that have testing and assessment policies. And policy makers, educators, classroom teachers, and district administrators need significant help in "testing" the tests—help that takes the typical complaints beyond the merely personal to the principled.

More formal and powerful help could perhaps come from a genuinely disinterested national organization set up to review tests and test-maker claims, modeled along the lines of Underwriters' Laboratory or the Federal Trade Commission—an idea offered by Haney and Madaus and others as a more appropriate venue than the de facto one of courts of law: "[We call for] the establishment of an independent auditing agency that would, without vested interest, evaluate tests and testing programs that profoundly affect the lives of examinees."[5] Legislation may well be part of the solution. In a recent article on what should be done at the federal level to prevent testing-related abuses, Michel Feuer, Kathleen Fulton, and Patricia Morrison of the Congressional Office of Technology Assessment made a similar pitch: Congress might "focus on various proposals to certify, regulate, oversee, or audit tests," including the establishment of an oversight agency.[6]

Feuer, Fulton, and Morrison also argue Congress should "require or encourage school districts to develop and publish a testing policy."[7] Each school district ought to, at the very least, state the permissible uses of such morally problematic practices as test security, scoring work on a curve, the use of nonarticulated and generic tests, the failure to require consistent grading among teachers for the same work, and so on—practices discussed throughout this book. These policies would do more than state the values of the institution; they would provide a local procedure for ensuring that assessment practices of both students and educators were publicly scrutinized, discussed, justified, and improved. Regional service agencies and federally funded educational labs and centers might also be asked to serve as a clearinghouse for policy statements and for guidelines in their formulation.

Here is a sample set of guiding principles from the New Zealand Department of Education:[8]

Principles of Assessment for Better Learning

1. The interests of the students shall be paramount. Assessment shall be planned and implemented in ways which maximize benefits for students, while minimizing any negative effects on them.
2. The primary purpose of assessment shall be to provide information which can be used to identify strengths and to guide improvement. In other words, it should suggest actions which may be taken to improve the educational development of students and the quality of educational programmes.
3. Assessment information should not be used for judgmental or political purposes if such use would be likely to cause harm to students or to the effectiveness of teachers or schools.

4. Every effort should be made to ensure that assessment and evaluation procedures are fair to all.
5. Community involvement is essential to the credibility and impact of assessment and evaluation processes. All parties with a direct interest should have an opportunity to contribute fully. Self-assessment is the appropriate starting point.
6. Careful consideration should be given to the motivational effects of assessment and evaluation practices.
7. In the assessment of intellectual outcomes, substantial attention should be devoted to more sophisticated skills such as understanding of principles, applying skill and knowledge to new tasks, and investigating, analyzing, and discussing complex issues and problems.
8. Emphasis should be given to identifying and reporting educational progress and growth, rather than to comparisons of individuals or schools.
9. The choices made in reporting assessment information largely determine the benefit or harm resulting from the information. For this reason, the selection, presentation, and distribution of information must be controlled by the principles outlined previously.

My own view is that, while these principles represent an important step toward protecting the student, they are too diffuse as stated. I would prefer that school systems develop an Assessment Bill of Rights to protect the inherently vulnerable student from the harms that testing easily leads to. It would be supported by explicit audit or oversight policies to ensure that the rights were protected. Here is my rough draft of such a set of rights:

Assessment Bill of Rights

All students are entitled to the following:

1. Worthwhile (engaging, educative, and "authentic") intellectual problems that are validated against worthy "real-world" intellectual problems, roles, and situations
2. Clear, apt, published, and consistently applied teacher criteria in grading work and published models of excellent work that exemplifies standards
3. Minimal secrecy in testing and grading
4. Ample opportunities to produce work that they can be proud of (thus, ample opportunity in the curriculum and instruction to monitor, self-assess, and self-correct their work)
5. Assessment, not just tests: multiple and varied opportunities to display and document their achievement, and options in tests that allow them to play to their strengths
6. The freedom, climate, and oversight policies necessary to question grades and test practices without fear of retribution

7. Forms of testing that allow timely opportunities for students to explain or justify answers marked as wrong but that they believe to be apt or correct

8. Genuine feedback: usable information on their strengths and weaknesses and an accurate assessment of their long-term progress toward a set of exit-level standards framed in terms of essential tasks

9. Scoring/grading policies that provide incentives and opportunities for improving performance and seeing progress against exit-level and real-world standards

I am sorry to report that the idea of an Assessment Bill of Rights has been attacked by more than a few teachers when I have offered it in workshops. Some have actually angrily called for a *prior* list of student responsibilities (though I do not recall such a list in our Constitution). Perhaps nothing better illustrates why these rights are deserving of formal protection, given the uneven balance of moral power in both the testing and teaching relationships as traditionally defined. The implicit hypocrisy in the position of these teachers is easily made explicit when one asks them whether they would be willing to endure a professional performance appraisal conducted under the same conditions as student testing.

NOTES

1. M. Foucault, *Discipline and Punish* (New York: Vintage Books, 1979), pp. 184–185. Translation Copyright © 1977 by Alan Sheridan.

2. D. P. Resnick and L. B. Resnick, "Standards, Curriculum, and Performance: A Historical and Comparative Perspective," *Educational Researcher* 14 (1985): 5–21.

3. S. J. Gould, *The Mismeasure of Man* (New York: W. W. Norton, 1981).

4. Cronbach, *Essentials of Psychological Testing*, pp. 74–75.

5. Haney and Madaus, *The Evolution of Ethical and Technical Standards for Testing*, p. 34.

6. M. Feuer, K. Fulton, and P. Morrison, "Better Tests and Testing Practices: Options for Policy Makers," *Phi Delta Kappan* 74 (1993): 530–533, p. 532.

7. Ibid.

8. Department of Education, *Assessment for Better Learning: A Public Discussion Document* (Wellington, New Zealand: Department of Education, 1989).

CHAPTER 12 The Cognitive Revolution in Learning

12.1 ANN L. BROWN ET AL.

Learning, Remembering, and Understanding

The selection that follows explores two foundational concepts in the cognitivist tradition in the psychology of learning and human development: metacognition and self-regulation. Metacognition deals with how we acquire strategies for learning, remembering, understanding, and problem solving. The concept of self-regulation is important in understanding how we learn to master strategies for achieving "executive" (self) control over those cognitive processes whereby we learn how to apply old and newly acquired knowledge to the problems that we encounter in life.

The following selection is an excerpt from chapter 2, "Learning, Remembering, and Understanding," of Paul H. Mussen, ed., *Handbook of Child Psychology, vol. 3: Cognitive Development,* 4th ed. (John Wiley, 1983). The chapter represents the efforts of Ann L. Brown and her colleagues to summarize the development of research on human learning, remembering, and understanding that had taken place since the 1960s. This source has had a very extensive impact on thought regarding human learning from a cognitive perspective. The authors of this selection are prominent cognitive researchers. The senior author, Brown, developed her ideas and understandings of metacognition so that she could inquire into how students can learn to become consciously aware of learning strategies they can use and practice to meet the challenges of school learning and to remember and use what they learn.

Brown grew up in England and studied psychology at the University of London. Although she was schooled in the behaviorist tradition, she began to study the cognitive approach to the psychology of learning and human development after moving to the United States in 1968. She did research on the teaching of reading and developed her pioneering insight into the concept of metacognition. She currently teaches and performs research on student learning in schools at the University of California, Berkeley. She has also held teaching positions at the University of Sussex in England and at the University of Illinois, and in 1994 she gave the Presidential Address before the annual meeting of the American Education Research Association (AERA).

Key Concept: metacognition and self-regulation

A TETRAHEDRAL FRAMEWORK FOR EXPLORING PROBLEMS OF LEARNING

The majority of developmental memory research conducted in the late 1960s and throughout the 1970s led to the establishment of a fairly detailed picture of how the child becomes a school expert, that is, how the young learner acquires academic skills and comes to know how to learn deliberately. To illustrate the current state of our knowledge, we would like to introduce the diagram in Figure 1. At first glance this seems like a simple model, particularly in comparison with the elaborate flow diagrams favored by modern cognitive psychologists, who were imprinted on the computer in their formative years. Unfortunately, as is often the case in psychology, the simple model becomes more complex on closer examination, it does, however, provide a useful aid to help us remember the major factors that should be taken into account when considering any aspect of learning. We would like to stress that not only should we, the psychologists, consider the tetrahedral nature of the learning process but also that this is exactly what expert learners come to consider when they design their own plans for learning (Flavell & Wellman, 1977; also see *Metacognition, Executive Control...*).

There are a minimum of four factors that comprise the learner-in-context, and these factors interact in nontrivial ways. The four factors are: (1) the learner's activity, (2) the characteristics of the learner, (3) the nature of the materials to be learned, and (4) the criterial task. Because of the sheer weight of empirical evidence, we will give only a few illustrations of the types of factors that have been considered under each of these rubrics and then provide selected examples of the essentially interactive nature of the model.

Learning Activities

The activities that the learner engages in are a prime determinant of efficiency. Some systematic activities that learners use are referred to as strategies, although what is strategic and what is not has not been made particularly clear in the literature....

FIGURE 1

*An Organizational Framework for Exploring Questions
About Learning*

Ann L. Brown
et al.

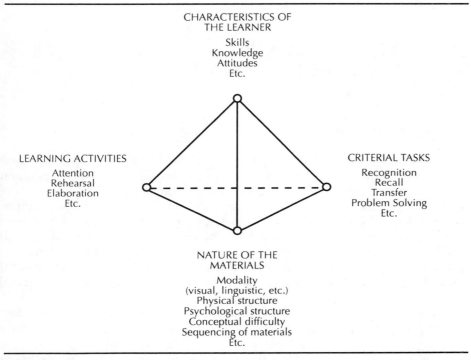

CHARACTERISTICS OF
THE LEARNER
Skills
Knowledge
Attitudes
Etc.

LEARNING ACTIVITIES
Attention
Rehearsal
Elaboration
Etc.

CRITERIAL TASKS
Recognition
Recall
Transfer
Problem Solving
Etc.

NATURE OF THE
MATERIALS
Modality
(visual, linguistic, etc.)
Physical structure
Psychological structure
Conceptual difficulty
Sequencing of materials
Etc.

Adapted from Jenkins, 1979, and Bransford, 1979.

Strategies are part of the knowledge base and, therefore, could be classified as a characteristic of the learner within the model. But the learner's activities are not necessarily synonymous with the strategies available in the knowledge base. Learners can access strategies or any other form of knowledge to help learning, but they need not. Having knowledge, of any kind, does not necessitate using it effectively....

One of the most established facts is the active strategic nature of a great deal of learning in older children. During the 1960s and 1970s, developmental psychologists provided a rich picture of the development of strategies for learning and remembering as well as quite convincing evidence that efficient performance in a wide variety of tasks is in large part dependent on the appropriate activities the subject engages in, either on his own volition when trained to do so or even when tricked into doing so by means of a cunning incidental orienting task. As children mature, they gradually acquire a basic repertoire of strategies, first as isolated task-dependent actions, but gradually these may evolve into flexible, and to some extent generalizable, skills. With extensive use, strategic intervention may become so dominant that it takes on many of the characteristics of automatic and unconscious processing (Shiffrin & Schneider, 1977). Under instructions to remember, the mature learner employs a variety of acquisition and retrieval strategies that are not readily available to the developmentally less mature individual. . . .

METACOGNITION, EXECUTIVE CONTROL, SELF-REGULATION, AND OTHER EVEN MORE MYSTERIOUS MECHANISMS[1]

What Is Metacognition?

In this section, we will describe some of the historical roots and discuss the current status of the fashionable but complex concept of metacognition and other topics with which it shares a family resemblance. Various forms of metacognition have appeared in the literature and some of these instantiations are puzzling and mysterious. For example, Marshall and Morton (1978) refer to the mechanism that permits the detection and correction of errors in speech production as an EMMA—even more mysterious apparatus; it is a mechanism that could be an optional extra. We will argue that far from being an optional extra, the processes that have recently earned the title metacognitive are central to learning. . . .

Knowledge about cognition refers to the relatively stable, statable, often fallible, and late-developing information that human thinkers have about their own cognitive processes and those of others (Flavell & Wellman, 1977). This form of knowledge is relatively *stable*. One would expect that knowledge of pertinent facts about a domain, for example, memory (that it is fallible, that it is severely limited for short-term verbatim retention, etc.), would be a permanent part of one's naive theory on the topic. This form of knowledge is often *statable*, in that one can reflect on the cognitive processes involved and discuss them with others. Of course, this form of knowledge is often *fallible*, in that the child (or adult for that matter) can perfectly well know certain facts about cognition that are not true. Naive psychology is not always empirically supportable. Finally, this type of knowledge is usually assumed to be *late developing*, in that it requires that learners step back and consider their own cognitive processes as objects of thought and reflection (Flavell & Wellman, 1977).

The second cluster of activities dubbed metacognitive in the developmental literature consists of those used to regulate and oversee learning. These processes include *planning* activities prior to undertaking a problem (predicting outcomes, scheduling strategies, various forms of vicarious trial and error, etc.), *monitoring* activities during learning (testing, revising, rescheduling one's strategies for learning), and *checking* outcomes (evaluating the outcome of any strategic actions against criteria of efficiency and effectiveness). It has been assumed that these activities are not necessarily statable, somewhat unstable, and relatively age independent, that is, task and situation dependent (Brown, 1978, 1980, in press-a).

Although knowledge and regulation of cognition are incestuously related, the two forms of activity have quite different roots and quite different attendant problems. The tension generated by the use of the same term, metacognition, for the two types of behavior is well illustrated by the fact that even the leading proponents in the field tend to answer questions about the nature of metacognition with, "It depends." Is metacognition late developing? It depends on the type of knowledge or process to which one refers. Is metacognition conscious? It depends....

Self-Regulation

Any active learning process involves continuous adjustments and fine tuning of action by means of self-regulating processes and "other even more mysterious" mechanisms (Marshall & Morton, 1978). Psychologists interested in mechanisms of growth and change have traditionally been concerned with such self-regulating processes. Of course, substantial contributions are made by external agents.... But even without external pressure, human thinkers "play" with thinking (Gardner, 1978), that is, subject their own thought processes to examination and treat their own thinking as an object of thought. Similarly, learners regulate and refine their own actions, sometimes in response to feedback concerning errors, but often in the absence of such feedback. Indeed, even if the system with which one is experimenting is adequate, active learners will improve upon their original production (Karmiloff-Smith, 1979a, 1979b).

Recently, the term metacognition has been extended to encompass such regulatory functions as error detection and correction (Brown & DeLoache, 1978; Clark, in press), but the historical roots of such concepts can be found in most of the major developmental theories....

Given space limitations, we will concentrate here primarily on relatively recent Genevan research on self-regulatory mechanisms in children's thinking and on the growing emphases in developmental psycholinguistics on error correction, systematization, and metalinguistic awareness.

PIAGET'S THEORY OF REGULATION.   In the latter part of his career, the transformational period (Riegel, 1975), Piaget became more and more interested in mechanisms of learning and the influence of both conscious and unconscious regulatory functions in promoting conceptual change. Again, owing to space restrictions, we cannot begin to describe the complex theory of Piaget's latter years.... Briefly (and probably too simplistically), Piaget distinguished between three primary types of self-regulation: autonomous, active, and conscious.

Autonomous regulation is an inherent part of any knowing act; learners continually regulate their performance, fine tuning and modulating actions, however small the learner and however simple the action (Bruner, 1973; Koslowski & Bruner, 1972). *Active regulation* is more akin to trial and error, where the learner is engaged in constructing and testing theories-in-action (Karmiloff-Smith & Inhelder, 1974/1975). Under the guidance of a powerful theory-in-action, the learner tests a current theory via concrete actions that produce tangible results. Not until a much later stage can the learner mentally construct and reflect upon the hypothetical situations that would confirm or refute a current theory without the need for active regulation. *Conscious regulation* involves the mental formulation of hypotheses capable of being tested via imaginary counterexamples or confirmatory evidence.

Consciousness first emerges as the child becomes capable of reflecting upon her own actions in the presence of the actual event. At this initial stage, consciousness is tied to concrete action but does not direct it. The child's "reactions remain elementary, the subject is likely to distort conceptualizations of what he observes, instead of recording it without modification." Such distortion can be quite dramatic. For example, having witnessed an event that is contrary to a tenaciously held belief, the "subject contests the unexpected evidence of his own eyes and thinks that he sees what he predicted would happen" (Piaget, 1976, p. 340).

At the most mature level, which Piaget would prefer to restrict to the stage of formal operations, the entire thinking process can be carried out on the mental plane. The learner can consciously invent, test, modify, and generalize theories and discuss these operations with others. . . .

In brief, the developmental progression is from unconscious autonomous regulation to active regulation but in the absence of anything more than a "fleeting consciousness." The beginning of conscious reflection occurs when the child is capable of considering her actions and describing them to others, albeit sometimes erroneously. The mature level of reflected abstraction, however, is characterized by conscious processes that can be carried out exclusively on the mental plane. Mature learners can create imaginary worlds and theories to explain actions and reactions within them. Such theories can be confirmed or refuted by means of the further construction of mental tests, conflict trials, or thought experiments that extend the limits of generality of the theory. This is the essence of scientific reasoning and the end state for a Piagetian development progression of "child as scientist." . . .

METAPROCEDURAL REORGANIZATION AND SYSTEMATIZATION. Piaget's colleagues, Inhelder and Karmiloff-Smith, have introduced another concept relevant to this discussion of self-regulation, that of *metaprocedural reorganization* (Karmiloff-Smith, 1979a; Karmiloff-Smith & Inhelder, 1974/1975). The basic idea is that learning within a domain follows a predictable sequence that is characterized by internal pressure to systematize, consolidate, and generalize knowledge. The prototypical microgenetic sequence is that the child first works on developing an adequate partial theory for a salient aspect of the problem space; the partial theory is practiced and perfected until it is fully operational. Only when the partial theory is consolidated and functioning efficiently can the child step back and consider the system as a whole. Typically, the child will develop several juxtaposed theories adequate for various parts of the problem space, each theory operating in isolation from the other. Once the procedures are functioning well, the next stage of development is possible and the child "steps up" and reconsiders the problem-space metaprocedurally. Once children become aware of the discrepancies or contradictions resulting from the simultaneous existence of several different partial theories, they begin attempts to reconcile the differences and obviate contradictions resulting from the juxtaposition (Inhelder et al., 1974).

A concrete example might help to clarify this complicated theoretical notion. Karmiloff-Smith and Inhelder (1974/1975) asked 4- to 9-year-old children to balance rectangular wooden blocks on a narrow metal rod fixed to a larger piece of wood. Length blocks had their weight evenly distributed, and the correct solution was to balance the blocks at the geometric center. With weight blocks, the weight of each "side" varied either conspicuously (by gluing a large square block to one end of the base rectangular block) or inconspicuously (by inserting a hidden weight into a cavity on one end of the rectangular block).

At first, the children made the blocks balance by brute trial and error, using proprioceptive information to guide action. Behavior was purely directed at the goal of balancing. This ploy was obviously successful; the children balanced each block in turn. There was no attempt to examine the properties of the objects that led to balance and no attempt to subject each block to a test of a unified theory.

This early errorless, but unanalyzed, phase was supplanted by the emergence of strong theories-in-action. These theories were directed at uncovering the rules governing balance in the miniature world of these particular blocks. Unfortunately, they were incomplete rules that produced errors. A common early theory developed by the children was to concentrate exclusively on the geometric center and attempt to balance all blocks in this fashion. This works for unweighted blocks. When the theory did not result in balance, the blocks involved were discarded as exceptions ("impossible to balance").

After this theory was well established and working well for length blocks, the children became discomforted by the number of, and regularity of, the errors. A new juxtaposed theory was then developed for the conspicuous weight blocks. For these, the children compensated for the weight that was obviously added to one end and adjusted the point of balance accordingly. For a time, however, length and weight were considered independently. Length blocks were solved by the geometric center rule and conspicuous weight blocks were solved by the rule of estimate weight first and then compensate. Inconspicuous weight problems still generated errors; they looked identical to the unweighted blocks and were, therefore, subjected to the dominant geometric center rule. When they did not conform to the theory they were discarded as anomalies that were "impossible to balance." The children's verbal responses reflected these juxtaposed solutions, with exclusively length justifications given for unweighted blocks and weight justifications given for conspicuously weighted blocks.

Gradually and reluctantly, the children entered the period of metaprocedural reorganization, which was only possible when both their juxtaposed procedures were working smoothly. Now, the young theorists were made uncomfortable by the remaining exceptions to their own rules and began to seek a rule for them. In so doing, a metaprocedural reorganization was induced that resulted in a single rule for all blocks. The children abandoned the simple theories and reorganized the problem space so that a single unifying theory predominated. Now, the children paused before balancing any block and roughly assessed the point of balance. Verbal responses reflected their consideration of both length and weight, for example, "You have to be careful, sometimes it's just as heavy on each side and so the middle is right, and sometimes it's heavier on one side." *After* inferring the probable point of balance, and only then, did the child place the block on the bar.

There are three main points to note about this example: first, there is the finding of a developmental lull or even a seemingly retrogressive stage when errors predominate. Initially, the children made no errors; all blocks were balanced. But, during the quest for a comprehensive theory of balance, the children generated partially adequate procedures that resulted in errors. Only when the unifying theory was discovered did the children revert to perfect performance. If errors alone formed the data base, a U-shaped developmental growth curve would be apparent (Strauss & Stavey, in press). Actually, what was happening was that the children were analyzing the problem space to generate a theory that would incorporate all the blocks. In so doing, they made what looked like errors but what were often tests of the existing partial theory.

A second main point is that metaprocedural reorganization leading to a "stepping up" in theory complexity is only possible when the partially adequate, juxtaposed systems are well established (see also Siegler, 1981). It is essential that the child gain control of simple theories in her quest for a more complex and more adequate theory. Karmiloff-Smith and Inhelder refer to this as creative simplification:

> The construction of false theories or the over-generalization of limited ones are in effect productive processes. Overgeneralization, a sometimes derogatory term, can be looked upon as the *creative simplification* of a problem by ignoring some of the complicating factors (such as weight in our study). This is implicit in the young child's behavior but could be intentional in the scientist's. Overgeneralization is not just a means to simplify but also to unify; it is then not surprising that the child and the scientist often refuse counterexamples since they complicate the unification process. However, to be capable of unifying positive examples implies that one is equally capable of attempting to find a unifying principle to cover counterexamples... [there is] a general tendency to construct a powerful, yet often inappropriate hypothesis which [learners] try to verify rather than refute. This temporarily blinds the [learner] to counterexamples which should actually suffice to have them reject their hypothesis immediately. (Karmiloff-Smith & Inhelder, 1974/1975, p. 209)

Progress comes only when the inadequate partial theory is well established and the learner is free to attempt to extend the theory to other phenomena. In this way, the theorists, be they children or scientists, are able to discover new properties that, in turn, make it possible for new theories to be constructed.

The third main point is that metaprocedural reorganization is not solely a response to external pressure or failure but rather occurs spontaneously when the child has developed well-functioning procedures that are incomplete but adequate for the task at hand. It is not failure that directs the change but success, success that the child wishes to extend throughout the system....

LEVELS OF SELF-REGULATION.   In this brief and oversimplified synopsis of latter-day Genevan psychology and language-acquisition data, a central place in theoretical speculation is afforded to the concept of self-regulation; there is basic agreement that self-regulatory functions are integral to learning and are central mechanisms of growth and change. Similarly, in the emergent field of metacognition, the notion of self-regulatory mechanisms has a central place (Brown & DeLoache, 1978).

All agree that there are many degrees of self-regulation and that self-regulation is essential for any knowing act. It is important to note, however, that a sharp distinction is made in both theories of language acquisition and in Genevan psychology, a sharp distinction that has not been made as clearly in the metacognitive literature. The distinction is between conscious awareness and direction of thought versus self-correction and regulation that can proceed below this level.

Piaget (1976, 1978) distinguishes sharply between active regulation as part of any knowing act and conscious regulation and direction of thought, the keystone of formal operations. The first process is age independent, even the young learner succeeds in action by regulating, correcting, and refining his current theories. Some form of error correction must be part of any active learning attempt, even very young children are capable of regulating their activities by means of a systematic procedure of error detection and correction. For example, in a recent study, DeLoache, Sugarman, and Brown (1981) observed young children (24 to 42 months) as they attempted to assemble a set of nesting cups. Children in this age range did not differ in the likelihood of their attempting to correct a set of nonseriated cups. They did, however, differ in their strategies for correction.

The most primitive strategy, used frequently by children below 30 months, was brute force. When a large cup was placed on a smaller one, the children would press down hard on the nonfitting cup. Variants of brute pressure were twisting and banging, but the same principle held—the selected cup will fit if only one can press hard enough. Older children also used the brute-force approach, but only after an unsuccessful series of maneuvers; for them, it appeared to be a last resort.

A second strategy initiated by some of the younger subjects was that of trying an alternative. After placing two nonfitting cups together, the child removed the top cup and did one of two things. He either looked for an alternative base for the nonfitting cup or he tried an alternative top for the original base. Both ploys involve minimal restructuring and necessitate considering the relation between only two cups at any one time. The third characteristic ploy of children below 30 months was to respond to a cup that would not fit into a partially completed set of cups by dismantling the entire set and starting again.

Older children (30 to 42 months) faced with a nonfitting cup engaged in strategies that involved consideration of the entire set of relations in the stack. For example, one sophisticated strategy was insertion; the children took apart the stack at a point that enabled them to insert the new cup in its correct position. A second strategy, reversal, was also shown by older children. After placing two nonfitting cups together, the child would *immediately* reverse the relation between them (5/4 immediately switched to 4/5).

The rapidly executed reversal strategy was not shown by the younger group. Some young children would repeatedly assemble, for example, cups 4 to 1, starting with 4 as a base and then inserting 3, 2, and 1. Then, they encountered the largest cup, that is, 5 and attempted to insert it on top of the completed partial stack, pressing and twisting repeatedly. When brute force failed, they would dismantle the whole stack and start again. Similarly, having assembled 1, 2, 4, and 5 and then encountering 3, the younger children's only recourse was to begin again. . . .

The DeLoache et al. (1981) study of self-correction in young children is used as one example (see also Koslowski & Bruner, 1972) of the obvious fact that even very young children correct their errors while solving a problem. Of more interest is the demonstration that the child's error-correction strategies provide us with a window through which to view the child's theories-in-action. The very processes used to correct errors reflect the level of understanding the child has of the problem space. Similarly, developmental psycholinguists have argued that production errors are most informative, "the tongue slips into patterns" (Nooteboom, 1969). Such errors reveal a great deal about the organization of the semantic knowledge of the speaker (Bowerman, in press; Clark, in press). . . .

Beyond Cold Cognition

. . . Virtually everything we have discussed so far involves what many would call the "cold cognitive" aspect of learning (Zajonc, 1980). But there are other dimensions to learning that are extremely important; for example, people have feelings about particular learning tasks and about themselves as learners that can have pervasive effects on their performance (Bransford, 1979; Brown, 1978; Henker, Whalen, & Hinshaw, 1980; Holt, 1964). Some individuals may be convinced of their inability to learn mathematics for example (Tobias, 1978) or of their incapacity to solve certain types of problems. Some children actively resist learning because their peers think it inappropriate or demeaning (McDermott, 1974) or because of their own diagnosis of personal incompetency. A particularly sweeping self-diagnosis was given by Daniel, a learning disabled 10-year-old, who worked with the first author. Upon encountering his first laboratory task, Daniel volunteered this telling comment: "Is this a memory thing?" (it wasn't)—"Didn't they tell you I can't do this stuff?"—"Didn't they tell you I don't have a memory?" Given this devastating estimate of his own ability, it is not surprising that Daniel would be diagnosed as passive, even resistant in situations that he classified as tests of his nonexistent faculty. It would take many sessions of systematically mapping out the specific nature of his memory problem and providing feedback about just where the problem was acute but also where there were no problems at all before Daniel could derive a more realistic evaluation of his learning problem and, as a consequence, would be willing to attempt active learning strategies to overcome a recognized problem.

It is by no means difficult, therefore, to imagine ways that negative feelings about a task or about oneself can affect learning. Nor is it surprising that people tend to avoid situations that tap their areas of weakness, thus conspiring to provide themselves with less practice in areas where it is most needed. Teachers inadvertently conspire to help students do this by, for example, addressing questions to students capable of answering and passing by those that need help to save everyone embarrassment. For example, recent observations of reading groups (Au, 1980; McDermott, 1978) have shown that good and poor readers are not treated equally. Good readers are questioned about the meaning behind what they are reading, asked to evaluate and criticize material, and so on. By contrast, poor readers receive primarily drill in pronunciation and decoding. Rarely are they given practice in qualifying and evaluating their comprehension (Au, 1980). There is considerable evidence that teachers give less experience in this learning mode to those who, because of their lack of prior experience, need it most (Gumperz & Hernandez-Chavez, 1972).

A plausible emotional block to effective learning involves an inefficient use of limited attention because a significant amount of cognitive effort is being directed to self-defeating, anxiety-producing self-evaluation. If learners focus on thoughts, such as "I can't do this" or "I'm going to fail again," they will not be able to attend to the details of the actual problem. Such negative ideation (Meichenbaum, 1977) can have a paralyzing effect on learning (*Dweck, vol. IV, chap. 8*).

Another related block to learning includes a lack in the confidence necessary to debug one's own errors. Some learners may not be sufficiently secure to enable them to tolerate mistakes; hence, they may ignore any errors they make or forget about them as quickly as possible (Bransford, 1979; Holt, 1964). Others may refuse to take the risk of responding incorrectly and, hence, be deprived of valuable feedback. It seems clear that the cold cognitive aspects of learning are only part of a much larger system that influences development; indeed, the purely cognitive aspects may be less primary than we like to think they are.

Beyond Isolated Cognition

In this last section, we would like to stress that learning is not only a less purely cognitive activity than we often suppose but it is also a less individual activity than might be readily apparent from a consideration of learning studies.... Here we will discuss only one issue to illustrate the importance of social mediation in learning. We will concentrate on tutors as agents of change in cognitive development....

Many of the activities employed by effective mediators are specifically focused on cold cognitive aspects of instruction, on particular concepts, factual knowledge, or strategies for example. But effective mediators do much more than impart cognitive lore. They encourage children, try to help them stay on task, express joy at the child's accomplishments, and so forth. Learning proceeds smoothly when child and mediator are in synchrony (Schaffer, 1977, 1979). But it is often very difficult to establish and maintain this synchrony; many of the moves made by effective mediators are designed to do just this.

To give one example, a side benefit of the zone-of-proximal-development testing procedures being developed (Brown & Ferrara, in press; Campione et al., in press) is that of increasing the child's feelings of competence. The procedure is such that if children fail to solve a problem unaided, they are given a set of increasingly explicit hints toward solution. The interactive and collaborative value of the adult/child relationship is such that the children believe that they are collaborating in the problem-solving process. Even when the adult provides such explicit clues that the answer is virtually given to the children, the prior collaboration leads the children to maintain faith in their own vital part in the learning solution. They seem to feel they have worked toward a solution that they eventually discover for themselves (Brown & Ferrara, in press). . . .

Mediators vary in how effectively they can establish the necessary empathy so that learning can occur. The present authors have had the opportunity to observe videotapes of Feuerstein (1980) working with academically less successful adolescents. Feuerstein is a gifted clinician, a cognitive therapist, if you will. He does a great deal of prompting to help children improve their approaches to various academic problems, but this is only part of his function; many of the moves that he makes are designed to alter the child's general reactions to the situation and the task. For example, one child faced with her first figural analogy problem said, in an extremely agitated and whiney voice: "I can't do that! I'm not used to that kind of problem." Feuerstein's response was: "Of course you can't do it—*yet*. Nobody can do things well until they have learned them. You can *learn* to do these problems, and I'm going to help you learn to do them." The girl did indeed learn to solve the problems (much to her amazement as well as that of her parents); furthermore, the session ended with the girl demanding to be given more problems when Feuerstein decided that it was time to stop. . . .

There is an ever-present conflict faced by mediators, a conflict between their humanitarian side and their cold cognitive side. Mediators hesitate to push too hard for fear of making learners anxious and unhappy (sometimes rebellious perhaps). But the failure to push at all may protect the child from learning something new. Effective learning environments are those where the humanitarian and cold cognitive side of mediators are not in direct conflict. Many of the moves made by successful mediators can be viewed as attempts to create and maintain a balance between these two dimensions. If the balance is not developed and maintained, effective mediation does not occur.

There are many things that mediators do intuitively that eventually need to become part of a comprehensive theory of learning. When working with less successful students who are anxious about being tested, an effective mediator may adapt the role of helper or benefactor rather than tester. There are other common ploys that enhance learning. For example, rather than emphasizing the student's ability (or inability) to remember information one can focus on the degree to which the material is easy or difficult. Students, then, focus on evaluating the material rather than themselves and are open to suggestions concerning methods of making difficult materials easier to learn. Similarly, the ability to detect errors in one's own work and then make revisions can be viewed as a positive achievement rather than a sign of failure.

One of the most important aspects of effective mediation may involve procedures that enable children to experience a sense of mastery, that let them see that they have some control over learning situations, and that systematic analysis can lead to successful performance. An important outcome of such mediation may be a more positive attitude toward the general task of learning and problem solving and toward one's self as a learner. These outcomes may be as important as number of problems solved successfully, although one would hope that they would be positively correlated. Successful mediation involves much more than the act of dispensing pearls of cognitive wisdom. Successful researchers in cognitive development implicitly know this, of course, and use the information to design effective experiments and training studies; but it is important to move this knowledge from the domain of lab lore to the domain of theory. If we do not, we may be ignoring some of the most important influences on development that exist. The emotional cannot be divorced from the cognitive nor the individual from the social.

Ann L. Brown
et al.

Teaching Thinking and Problem Solving

John Bransford is a prominent cognitive psychologist whose many books and articles on cognitive learning have been well received within the academic community of cognitive psychologists. He has published research with Ann L. Brown, Barry Stein, and several other cognitive researchers, and he is the coauthor, with Stein, of *The Ideal Problem Solver: A Guide to Improving Thinking, Learning, and Creativity* (W. H. Freeman, 1984).

In the selection that follows, which is from "Teaching Thinking and Problem Solving," *American Psychologist* (October 1986), Bransford and his colleagues review some of the research on human thinking and problem solving that psychologists in the cognitive tradition have undertaken. The authors take the position that students need to be taught specific strategies for solving problems as well as specific knowledge bases, which students should be taught to consciously organize for problem-solving purposes. Bransford et al. discuss some of the major findings from two types of cognitive research on human learning: studies of individuals who are experts in particular areas of knowledge, and studies of the general and specific strategies used by persons to develop metacognitive skills. The authors provide an excellent overview of the concept of metacognition, and they agree with other major researchers in cognitive psychology that the idea of metacognition is central to the search for how human beings can be taught to be expert learners. Finally, Bransford et al. predict the direction of future research in this area of study.

Key Concept: teaching thinking and problem-solving skills

*T*he topic of teaching thinking and problem solving is currently receiving a great deal of attention. One reason is that increasingly fast-paced changes in society make it necessary for people to think for themselves and to solve novel problems (Simon, 1980); another is that assessments of student achievement suggest that today's students may be failing to develop effective thinking and problem-solving skills (e.g., National Assessment of Educational Progress, 1983).

Books such as Mann's (1979) history of cognitive process training remind us that the goal of teaching thinking and problem solving is not unique to the 1980s. Attempts to achieve this goal have been espoused for centuries and have stimulated a variety of suggestions for increasing thinking. Many have focused on the need to develop "mental discipline" by subjecting students to the rigors of learning difficult subjects such as mathematics and Latin. Mann (1979) cited Plato's arguments: "Arithmetic stirs up him who is by nature sleepy and dull, and makes him quick to learn, retentive, and shrewd. He makes progress quite beyond his natural powers" (p. 125). Similar ideas were espoused by Sir Francis Bacon, who favored the study of mathematics as a remedy to students' lack of attention (Mann, 1979, p. 13). In the 1800s, many educators argued that the study of Latin would develop the mental discipline necessary to learn in any domain.

Research conducted during the 1940s and 1950s (e.g., Dunker, 1945; Katona, 1940; Wertheimer, 1959), and especially during the 1970s and 1980s, goes considerably beyond a general emphasis on "mental discipline" as the active ingredient underlying effective thinking and problem solving. Our goal in this article is to discuss some of the relevant research and to consider its implications for the issue of teaching thinking and problem solving. Our major emphasis is on the need for both (a) general problem solving strategies and (b) specific knowledge that is organized in ways that are appropriate for individual needs....

The Concept of Metacognition

[R]esearchers who have studied differences in approaches to learning have tried to work with materials that require knowledge that is potentially available to participants. The goal of the research has been to assess the degree to which people spontaneously utilize knowledge previously acquired. Results ... have led to a number of researchers to argue that people's ability to use what they know—to access task-relevant information—is an important hallmark of intelligence (e.g., A. Brown & Campione, 1981; Butterfield & Belmont, 1977; Sternberg, 1980, 1984). This concern with the utilization of previously acquired knowledge has led to an emphasis on the concept of executive or metacognitive processes (e.g., A. Brown, 1977; A. Brown & DeLoache, 1978; Flavell, 1979; Flavell & Wellman, 1977; Scardamalia & Bereiter, 1985).

An important methodological tool for exploring the role of metacognition has been the training study (A. Brown et al., 1983). Researchers have provided individuals with different types of learning opportunities and assessed the effects on mastery tasks and transfer tasks. In a discussion of this literature, A. Brown, Campione, and Day (1981) noted that different types of teaching environments have strong effects on transfer. Many of the training studies that have resulted in failures of transfer involved what A. Brown and her colleagues called *blind training*. Individuals were taught to use strategies but were not helped to understand why they were useful and when they might be used.

A. Brown and her colleagues differentiated blind training from informed training and from informed training plus self-control. In informed training, students are helped to understand when and why to use various strategies. The informed plus self-control training adds the opportunity to practice strategies and monitor their effects.

Experiments conducted by other investigators also provide evidence that an emphasis on executive or metacognitive processes can result in improvements in thinking and problem solving. Data from several studies illustrate how such training can increase learning (e.g., Paris, Cross, & Lipson, in press; Paris & Jacobs, in press; Wong 1980, 1982; Wong & Sawatsky, 1984). Similarly, work by Lodico, Ghatala, Levin, Pressley, and Bell (in press) illustrates how executive training can help children learn to select and evaluate new strategies. Furthermore, work in the areas of writing (Bereiter & Scardamalia, 1985; Flower & Hayes, 1980) and mathematical problem solving (Schoenfeld, 1982, 1983, 1985) provides evidence for the importance of a metacognitive or executive approach to teaching. An exciting implication of these studies is that it may be possible to help people improve their abilities to think and learn in a wide variety of domains. Researchers have also studied the types of early social environments that facilitate the development of the types of skills that enable children to learn in formal educational settings. Heath's (1983) work is particularly relevant here.

RELATIONSHIPS BETWEEN EXECUTIVE PROCESSES AND SPECIFIC KNOWLEDGE

... [I]n most studies, relationships between training in executive processes and in specific knowledge are confounded. For example, although research illustrating the advantages of "informed" training on transfer emphasizes the effects on metacognitive processes (e.g., A. Brown et al., 1983), it seems clear that this type of training also affects the nature and organization of the knowledge acquired by learners. The acts of (a) informing them about uses of strategies and (b) allowing them to practice and evaluate the effects, help students "conditionalize" their knowledge.... [S]uch knowledge organizations increase the probability that relevant information will be accessed when needed. By placing more emphasis on the systematic development of well-organized knowledge in addition to executive processes, it may be possible to increase considerably the speed with which people can become able to think effectively in a variety of knowledge-rich domains (see also N. Stein, in press).

Take the example of deciding whether to buy a soft-top jeep. Recently, one of the authors bought one after weighing the pleasure of open-air summer rides against the inconveniences of drafty winter rides and having to raise the top manually. Three days later, when the radio was stolen, the oversight of not considering the soft-top jeep's vulnerability to theft became apparent.

There are several ways to think about the preceding shortcomings in thinking about the jeep. At one level we can fault the individual's attempts to systematically search memory in order to access relevant categories for evaluation. Our decision maker may have been too impulsive and hence prematurely ended his memory search. On the other hand, something needs to guide one's search of memory.... The ability to search selectively should be affected by the organization or representation of knowledge. For example, the knowledge representation of a person who has owned a soft-top jeep that was broken into will have information such as "easily accessible to burglars" linked directly to jeep. Because of this organization of the knowledge base, failures to assess such information should be much less likely to occur.

Metacognition and Teaching

Research on both metacognitive, or control, processes and domain-specific knowledge has important implications for teaching thinking and problem solving. Consider first the emphasis on metacognition. Analyses of a number of existing programs for teaching thinking and problem solving suggest that they vary with respect to their emphasis on metacognitive or executive processes (e.g., see Chipman, Segal, & Glaser, 1985; Segal, Chipman, & Glaser, 1985; Tuma & Reif, 1980). Programs such as Instrumental Enrichment (Feuerstein et al., 1980), Philosophy for Children (Lipman, 1985), Analytic Reasoning (Lochhead, 1985), Intelligence Applied (Sternberg, 1986), Patterns of Problem Solving (Rubenstein, 1975, 1980), and Guided Design (e.g., Wales & Stager, 1977) place a heavy emphasis on the importance of helping students analyze their current problem-solving processes and learn about themselves as learners. Similarly, researchers in the area of science education have emphasized the importance of helping students develop a conceptual and practical understanding of scientific reasoning and inquiry skills rather than merely memorize scientific facts (e.g., Aarons, 1984a, 1984b; Lawson, 1985; Renner & Lawson, 1973). In contrast, many descriptions of attempts to teach thinking by programming computers in *Logo* (e.g., Papert, 1980, 1985) place little explicit emphasis on the need to systematically help students reflect on their approaches to programming and to think about these activities as instances of more general problem-solving strategies. Some researchers argue that this lack of explicit focus on metacognitive processes may be a major reason why evidence of general effects of *Logo* programming on thinking ability have proved to be so difficult to find (e.g., Bransford, Stein, Delclos, & Littlefield, 1986; Delclos, Littlefield, & Bransford, 1985; Pea & Kurland, 1984).

An especially promising aspect of metacognitive approaches to teaching is that they can be used to transform basic fact- and skill-oriented activities into lessons involving thinking. For example, Hasselbring, Goin, and Bransford (1985) discussed work with math-delayed fifth and sixth graders who were working on arcade-like software designed to give them practice at basic addition problems such as 7 + 8. The arcade program awarded points for speed and accuracy. All the students wanted to increase their scores. However, most had little idea of how to "debug" their current approaches to the game. For example, the vast majority paid little attention to the fact that they often counted on their fingers and hence could not significantly increase their speed until they moved from productive to reproductive strategies (Greeno, 1978). Furthermore, students knew the answers to some problems (e.g., 5 + 5) and hence needed to memorize answers to only a subset of the problems. Nevertheless, they did not spontaneously attempt to identify the set of problems that would be most beneficial for them to practice at home. With specific guidance from the teacher, the students were prompted to view the arcade game as a problem-solving situation, and they were helped to debug their current approaches to the problem of increasing their scores. Without the teaching, it is doubtful that the students would have taken a "higher order thinking" approach to the development of "lower order" skills (for additional discussion of the role of teaching in the development of problem-solving abilities, see Collins & Stevens, 1982; Feuerstein et al., 1980; Vygotsky, 1978; Wertsch, 1979; Wood, 1980).

Systematic Approaches to Knowledge Acquisition

Programs that emphasize metacognitive or executive processes do not necessarily attempt to develop well-organized knowledge structures that can function as tools for problem solving. For example, Feuerstein et al.'s (1980) Instrumental Enrichment program is purposely designed to involve problem situations that do not presuppose a great deal of content knowledge. The use of these types of problems can be very important, especially for building confidence among students who have had a number of failure experiences in academic settings (for example, see Covington, 1985; Dweck & Elliott, 1983). However, Feuerstein et al. also emphasized the need to "bridge" from the Instrumental Enrichment exercises to specific areas such as mathematics, reading, and so forth (for example, see Bransford, Stein, Arbitman-Smith, & Vye, 1985). Nevertheless, it can often be difficult for teachers to bridge to other areas—especially if these are being taught by different teachers. Because of this, one can often find evidence for positive effects of Instrumental Enrichment in the context of everyday tasks such as planning a field trip yet see much less evidence in the context of achievement tests—tests that generally presuppose the availability of rich knowledge domains (for example, Arbitman-Smith, Haywood, & Bransford, 1985).

Programs such as Philosophy for Children (e.g., Lipman, 1985) and Guided Design (Wales & Stager, 1977) provide prototypes for teaching thinking in the context of domains such as science, art, engineering, and so forth. There certainly seems to be room for more approaches such as these. In mathematics, for example, evidence suggests that children often make a variety of systematic errors because they rather blindly learn procedures rather than understand how the information being presented simplifies the solution to important, real-world problems (e.g., J. Brown & Burton, 1978; Clement, 1982; Resnick, in press; Sleeman, 1983; Soloway, Lochhead, & Clement, 1982). Similarly, students learning science are often asked to memorize information about density, displacement, and so forth yet are not helped to understand its value for interpreting everyday situations and for solving problems. They therefore acquire facts rather than conceptual tools (e.g., Bransford, in press; Bransford, Sherwood, & Sturdevant, in press; di Sessa, 1982; Lochhead & Clement, 1979; Perkins, in press).

Theories of access should provide an important framework for helping students learn to think and solve problems. For example, it seems clear that instruction that emphasizes memory for a variety of facts and definitions (a large number of introductory courses fit this definition) will *seem* effective if we simply test students on this information. However, data reviewed in the present article suggest that this information will generally remain inert even though it is relevant for various problems.

DIRECTIONS FOR FUTURE RESEARCH

Overall, it seems clear that research on thinking and problem solving is thriving and is producing information that has important implications for teaching. The results of this research also suggest some issues that seem particularly fruitful to explore.

One set of issues centers around the concept of gaining access to previously acquired knowledge. We noted earlier that different ways of presenting information had powerful effects on the degree to which relevant knowledge was accessed when it was needed. Experimental paradigms such as those used by Gick and Holyoak (1980, 1983) can provide important information about access. Work on the architecture of cognition and on the role of different knowledge representations (e.g., J. Anderson, 1983; Simon, 1980) should provide the basis for well-articulated theories about conditions under which access occurs.

An emphasis on access also highlights the role of perceptual learning and pattern recognition. Simon (1980) noted this by pointing out the importance of helping problem solvers learn to differentiate problem types and the relation of different problem types to solutions. The research illustrating more sophisticated performance of learners and problem solvers in familiar compared to unfamiliar domains also supports the idea that perceptual learning may play an important role in problem solving. The Gibsons (e.g., Gibson, 1969, 1982; Gibson & Gibson, 1955) emphasized that perceptual learning involves differentiating the features and dimensions in situations where there is variation and learning the significance of those variations to the problem at hand. Many teaching activities fail to educate students' attention to the relevant features that are critical to solving different problems and problem types, and research is needed to determine how to educate attention. Teaching often involves telling learners the relevant information and asking them to combine it in some way to arrive at a problem situation. For example, students may be asked to solve word problems in arithmetic for which they are poor at differentiating parts of the problem situation that are numerically relevant from those that are irrelevant to its solution (Littlefield & Rieser, 1985).

Teaching without a systematic emphasis on perceptual learning can account for access failures that lead to poor generalization of learning. For example, clinical psychology students often learn to diagnose psychological syndromes by reading case descriptions. However, many case descriptions suggest situations (e.g., the client is "anxious" and somewhat "hostile") that represent outputs of an expert's pattern-recognition process. Therefore, students who can correctly diagnose clinical syndromes from verbally stated symptoms in the classroom may fail to transfer that diagnostic skill to actual interview situations where the symptoms are not stated so clearly. Recent advances in interactive videotape and videodisc technology make available rapid access and review of video (e.g., Bransford, Sherwood, & Hasselbring, 1985). This technology can be used to study how perceptual experiences within specific domains can be arranged to supplement traditional instruction and facilitate transfer to new domains.

In addition to research on access and perceptual learning, we expect to see more work that combines an emphasis on general metacognitive and domain-specific knowledge. For example, consider the exciting work of Palincsar and Brown (1984) on the use of reciprocal teaching to increase reading comprehension. This type of instruction might produce even more powerful effects if it were carried out in a semantically rich problem-solving context that enabled children to see how the information in each of their stories or passages could be used to solve problems in this context. Similarly, global problem-solving contexts might be used to provide more continuity to each child's day so that mathematics, reading, writing, and other subjects are all seen as relevant to the same contextual domain (e.g., Bransford, Sherwood, & Hasselbring, 1985).

Finally, we expect to see more research on the nature of cognitive development. We noted earlier that knowledge-base alternatives to stage theories are beginning to flourish. These new alternatives have important implications for educational practice. For example, they focus on the need to assess children's initial conceptions of concepts and principles so that misconceptions can be corrected (e.g., Carey, 1985), and they provide important information about ways in which tasks might be made manageable to children at different developmental levels (e.g., Gelman & Baillargeon, 1983). Furthermore, research on both micro- and macrodevelopment should help us understand the kinds of "natural learning conditions" that facilitate problem solving. For example, whereas many courses in thinking are taught in terms of piecemeal, workbooklike tasks, it is not clear that these types of experiences result in the types of knowledge representations that support understanding, access, and transfer (e.g., Lipman, 1985; Palincsar & Brown, 1984; N. Stein, in press). Research on this issue should be especially helpful to educators who want to help students learn to think and learn.

12.3 HOWARD GARDNER AND JOSEPH WALTERS

A Rounded Version

In the selection that follows, which is from *Multiple Intelligences: The Theory in Practice* (Basic Books, 1993), Howard Gardner and Joseph Walters discuss the multiple forms of intelligent human behavior. They begin by stating that an intelligence involves the use of problem-solving skills or making things that are of importance to people in particular cultural settings or groups. The problem-solving skill permits individuals to approach situations with a goal-oriented frame of reference and to develop strategies or plans for achieving their goals. Gardner and Walters argue that our understanding of intelligence must be pluralized to take into account the many ways in which people demonstrate insightful understanding and performance. The authors' view of the nature of "intelligence" departs from the traditional view of the nature of intelligence developed by behaviorist psychologists in the early decades of the twentieth century.

After defining intelligence, Gardner and Walters identify and describe the seven intelligences that fit their definition. They provide a brief biographical sketch of a famous or proficient user of each type of intelligence and then elaborate on how and why that person is representative of its use. The seven intelligences identified are musical intelligence, bodily-kinesthetic intelligence, logical-mathematical intelligence, linguistic intelligence, spatial intelligence, interpersonal intelligence, and intrapersonal intelligence.

Gardner is a professor of human development in the Harvard Graduate School of Education. His book *Frames of Mind: The Theory of Multiple Intelligences* (Basic Books, 1983), which won the Best Book Award from the American Psychological Association in 1984, explains in greater depth his theories about intelligence. Walters coauthored the chapter of *Multiple Intelligences* from which this selection was excerpted.

Key Concept: multiple intelligences

WHAT CONSTITUTES AN INTELLIGENCE?

The question of the optimal definition of intelligence looms large in our inquiry. Indeed, it is at the level of this definition that the theory of multiple intelligences diverges from traditional points of view. In a traditional view, intelligence is defined operationally as the ability to answer items on tests of intelligence. The inference from the test scores to some underlying ability is supported by statistical techniques that compare responses of subjects at different ages; the apparent correlation of these test scores across ages and across different tests corroborates the notion that the general faculty of intelligence, *g*, does not change much with age or with training or experience. It is an inborn attribute or faculty of the individual.

Multiple intelligences theory, on the other hand, pluralizes the traditional concept. An intelligence entails the ability to solve problems or fashion products that are of consequence in a particular cultural setting or community. The problem-solving skill allows one to approach a situation in which a goal is to be obtained and to locate the appropriate route to that goal. The creation of a *cultural* product is crucial to such functions as capturing and transmitting knowledge or expressing one's views or feelings. The problems to be solved range from creating an end for a story to anticipating a mating move in chess to repairing a quilt. Products range from scientific theories to musical compositions to successful political campaigns.

MI theory is framed in light of the biological origins of each problem-solving skill. Only those skills that are universal to the human species are treated. Even so, the biological proclivity to participate in a particular form of problem solving must also be coupled with the cultural nurturing of that domain. For example, language, a universal skill, may manifest itself particularly as writing in one culture, as oratory in another culture, and as the secret language of anagrams in a third.

Given the desire of selecting intelligences that are rooted in biology, and that are valued in one or more cultural settings, how does one actually identify an "intelligence"? In coming up with our list, we consulted evidence from several different sources: knowledge about normal development and development in gifted individuals; information about the breakdown of cognitive skills under conditions of brain damage; studies of exceptional populations, including prodigies, idiots savants, and autistic children; data about the evolution of cognition over the millenia; cross-cultural accounts of cognition; psychometric studies, including examinations of correlations among tests; and psychological training studies, particularly measures of transfer and generalization across tasks. Only those candidate intelligences that satisfied all or a majority of the criteria were selected as bona fide intelligences. A more complete discussion of each of these criteria for an "intelligence" and the seven intelligences that have been proposed so far, is found in *Frames of mind* (1983). This book also considers how the theory might be disproven and compares it to competing theories of intelligence.

In addition to satisfying the aforementioned criteria, each intelligence must have an identifiable core operation or set of operations. As a neurally based computational system, each intelligence is activated or "triggered" by certain kinds of internally or externally presented information. For example, one core of musical intelligence is the sensitivity to pitch relations, whereas one core of linguistic intelligence is the sensitivity to phonological features.

An intelligence must also be susceptible to encoding in a symbol system—a culturally contrived system of meaning, which captures and conveys important forms of information. Language, picturing, and mathematics are but three nearly worldwide symbol systems that are necessary for human survival and productivity. The relationship of a candidate intelligence to a human symbol system is no accident. In fact, the existence of a core computational capacity anticipates the existence of a symbol system that exploits that capacity. While it may be possible for an intelligence to proceed without an accompanying symbol system, a primary characteristic of human intelligence may well be its gravitation toward such an embodiment.

THE SEVEN INTELLIGENCES

Having sketched the characteristics and criteria of an intelligence, we turn now to a brief consideration of each of the seven intelligences. We begin each sketch with a thumbnail biography of a person who demonstrates an unusual facility with that intelligence. These biographies illustrate some of the abilities that are central to the fluent operation of a given intelligence. Although each biography illustrates a particular intelligence, we do not wish to imply that in adulthood intelligences operate in isolation. Indeed, except for abnormal individuals, intelligences always work in concert, and any sophisticated adult role will involve a melding of several of them. Following each biography we survey the various sources of data that support each candidate as an "intelligence."

Musical Intelligence

When he was three years old, Yehudi Menuhin was smuggled into the San Francisco Orchestra concerts by his parents. The sound of Louis Persinger's violin so entranced the youngster that he insisted on a violin for his birthday and Louis Persinger as his teacher. He got both. By the time he was ten years old, Menuhin was an international performer (Menuhin, 1977).

Violinist Yehudi Menuhin's musical intelligence manifested itself even before he had touched a violin or received any musical training. His powerful reaction to that particular sound and his rapid progress on the instrument suggest that he was biologically prepared in some way for that endeavor. In this way evidence from child prodigies supports our claim that there is a biological link to a particular intelligence. Other special populations, such as autistic children who can play a musical instrument beautifully but who cannot speak, underscore the independence of musical intelligence.

A brief consideration of the evidence suggests that musical skill passes the other tests for an intelligence. For example, certain parts of the brain play important roles in perception and production of music. These areas are characteristically located in the right hemisphere, although musical skill is not as clearly "localized," or located in a specifiable area, as language. Although the particular susceptibility of musical ability to brain damage depends on the degree of training and other individual differences, there is clear evidence for "amusia" or loss of musical ability.

Music apparently played an important unifying role in Stone Age (paleolithic) societies. Birdsong provides a link to other species. Evidence from various cultures supports the notion that music is a universal faculty. Studies of infant development suggest that there is a "raw" computational ability in early childhood. Finally, musical notation provides an accessible and lucid symbol system.

In short, evidence to support the interpretation of musical ability as an "intelligence" comes from many different sources. Even though musical skill is not typically considered an intellectual skill like mathematics, it qualifies under our criteria. By definition it deserves consideration; and in view of the data, its inclusion is empirically justified.

Bodily-Kinesthetic Intelligence

Fifteen-year-old Babe Ruth played third base. During one game his team's pitcher was doing very poorly and Babe loudly criticized him from third base. Brother Mathias, the coach, called out, "Ruth, if you know so much about it, YOU pitch!" Babe was surprised and embarrassed because he had never pitched before, but Brother Mathias insisted. Ruth said later that at the very moment he took the pitcher's mound, he KNEW he was supposed to be a pitcher and that it was "natural" for him to strike people out. Indeed, he went on to become a great major league pitcher (and, of course, attained legendary status as a hitter) (Connor, 1982).

Like Menuhin, Babe Ruth was a child prodigy who recognized his "instrument" immediately upon his first exposure to it. This recognition occurred in advance of formal training.

Control of bodily movement is, of course, localized in the motor cortex, with each hemisphere dominant or controlling bodily movements on the contra-lateral side. In right-handers, the dominance for such movement is ordinarily found in the left hemisphere. The ability to perform movements when directed to do so can be impaired even in individuals who can perform the same movements reflexively or on a nonvoluntary basis. The existence of specific *apraxia* constitutes one line of evidence for a bodily-kinesthetic intelligence.

The evolution of specialized body movements is of obvious advantage to the species, and in humans this adaptation is extended through the use of tools. Body movement undergoes a clearly defined developmental schedule in children. And there is little question of its universality across cultures. Thus it appears that bodily-kinesthetic "knowledge" satisfies many of the criteria for an intelligence.

The consideration of bodily-kinesthetic knowledge as "problem solving" may be less intuitive. Certainly carrying out a mime sequence or hitting a tennis ball is not solving a mathematical equation. And yet, the ability to use one's body to express an emotion (as in a dance), to play a game (as in a sport), or to create a new product (as in devising an invention) is evidence of the cognitive features of body usage. The specific computations required to solve a particular bodily-kinesthetic *problem*, hitting a tennis ball, are summarized by Tim Gallwey:

At the moment the ball leaves the server's racket, the brain calculates approximately where it will land and where the racket will intercept it. This calculation includes the initial velocity of the ball, combined with an input for the progressive decrease in velocity and the effect of wind and after the bounce of the ball. Simultaneously, muscle orders are given: not just once, but constantly with refined and updated information. The muscles must cooperate. A movement of the feet occurs, the racket is taken back, the face of the racket kept at a constant angle. Contact is made at a precise point that depends on whether the order was given to hit down the line or cross-court, an order not given until after a split-second analysis of the movement and balance of the opponent.

To return an average serve, you have about one second to do this. To hit the ball at all is remarkable and yet not uncommon. The truth is that everyone who inhabits a human body possesses a remarkable creation (Gallwey, 1976).

Logical-Mathematical Intelligence

In 1983 Barbara McClintock won the Nobel prize in medicine or physiology for her work in microbiology. Her intellectual powers of deduction and observation illustrate one form of logical-mathematical intelligence that is often labeled "scientific thinking." One incident is particularly illuminating. While a researcher at Cornell in the 1920s McClintock was faced one day with a problem: while *theory* predicted 50 percent pollen sterility in corn, her research assistant (in the "field") was finding plants that were only 25 to 30 percent sterile. Disturbed by this discrepancy, McClintock left the cornfield and returned to her office where she sat for half an hour, thinking:

> Suddenly I jumped up and ran back to the (corn) field. At the top of the field (the others were still at the bottom) I shouted "Eureka, I have it! I know what the 30% sterility is!" ... They asked me to prove it. I sat down with a paper bag and a pencil and I started from scratch, which I had not done at all in my laboratory. It had all been done so fast; the answer came and I ran. Now I worked it out step by step— it was an intricate series of steps—and I came out with [the same result]. [They] looked at the material and it was exactly as I'd said it was; it worked out exactly as I had diagrammed it. Now, why did I know, without having done it on paper? Why was I so sure? (Keller, 1983, p. 104).

This anecdote illustrates two essential facts of the logical-mathematical intelligence. First, in the gifted individual, the process of problem solving is often remarkably rapid—the successful scientist copes with many variables at once and creates numerous hypotheses that are each evaluated and then accepted or rejected in turn.

The anecdote also underscores the *nonverbal* nature of the intelligence. A solution to a problem can be constructed *before* it is articulated. In fact, the solution process may be totally invisible, even to the problem solver. This need not imply, however, that discoveries of this sort—the familiar "Aha!" phenomenon —are mysterious, intuitive, or unpredictable. The fact that it happens more frequently to some people (perhaps Nobel prize winners) suggests the opposite. We interpret this as the work of the logical-mathematical intelligence.

Along with the companion skill of language, logical-mathematical reasoning provides the principal basis for IQ tests. This form of intelligence has been heavily investigated by traditional psychologists, and it is the archetype of "raw intelligence" or the problem-solving faculty that purportedly cuts across domains. It is perhaps ironic, then, that the actual mechanism by which one arrives at a solution to a logical-mathematical problem is not as yet properly understood.

This intelligence is supported by our empirical criteria as well. Certain areas of the brain are more prominent in mathematical calculation than others. There are idiots savants who perform great feats of calculation even though they remain tragically deficient in most other areas. Child prodigies in mathematics abound. The development of this intelligence in children has been carefully documented by Jean Piaget and other psychologists.

Linguistic Intelligence

At the age of ten, T. S. Eliot created a magazine called "Fireside" to which he was the sole contributor. In a three-day period during his winter vacation, he created eight complete issues. Each one included poems, adventure stories, a gossip column, and humor. Some of this material survives and it displays the talent of the poet (see Soldo, 1982).

As with the logical intelligence, calling linguistic skill an "intelligence" is consistent with the stance of traditional psychology. Linguistic intelligence also passes our empirical tests. For instance, a specific area of the brain, called "Broca's Area," is responsible for the production of grammatical sentences. A person with damage to this area can understand words and sentences quite well but has difficulty putting words together in anything other than the simplest of sentences. At the same time, other thought processes may be entirely unaffected.

The gift of language is universal, and its development in children is strikingly constant across cultures. Even in deaf populations where a manual sign language is not explicitly taught, children will often "invent" their own manual language and use it surreptitiously! We thus see how an intelligence may operate independently of a specific input modality or output channel.

Spatial Intelligence

Navigation around the Caroline Islands in the South Seas is accomplished without instruments. The position of the stars, as viewed from various islands, the weather patterns, and water color are the only sign posts. Each journey is broken into a series of segments; and the navigator learns the position of the stars within each of these segments. During the actual trip the navigator must envision mentally a reference island as it passes under a particular star and from that he computes the number of segments completed, the proportion of the trip remaining, and any corrections in heading that are required. The navigator cannot *see* the islands as he sails along; instead he maps their locations in his mental "picture" of the journey (Gardner, 1983).

Spatial problem solving is required for navigation and in the use of the notational system of maps. Other kinds of spatial problem solving are brought to bear in visualizing an object seen from a different angle and in playing chess. The visual arts also employ this intelligence in the use of space.

Evidence from brain research is clear and persuasive. Just as the left hemisphere has, over the course of evolution, been selected as the site of linguistic processing in right-handed persons, the right hemisphere proves to be the site most crucial for spatial processing. Damage to the right posterior regions causes impairment of the ability to find one's way around a site, to recognize faces or scenes, or to notice fine details.

Patients with damage specific to regions of the right hemisphere will attempt to compensate for their spacial deficits with linguistic strategies. They will try to reason aloud, to challenge the task, or even make up answers. But such nonspatial strategies are rarely successful.

Blind populations provide an illustration of the distinction between the spatial intelligence and visual perception. A blind person can recognize shapes by an indirect method: running a hand along the object translates into length of time of movement, which in turn is translated into the size of the object. For the blind person, the perceptual system of the tactile modality parallels the visual modality in the seeing person. The analogy between the spatial reasoning of the blind and the linguistic reasoning of the deaf is notable.

There are few child prodigies among visual artists, but there are idiots savants such as Nadia (Selfe, 1977). Despite a condition of severe autism, this preschool child made drawings of the most remarkable representational accuracy and finesse.

Interpersonal Intelligence

With little formal training in special education and nearly blind herself, Anne Sullivan began the intimidating task of instructing a blind and deaf seven-year-old Helen Keller. Sullivan's efforts at communication were complicated by the child's emotional struggle with the world around her. At their first meal together, this scene occurred:

> Annie did not allow Helen to put her hand into Annie's plate and take what she wanted, as she had been accustomed to do with her family. It became a test of wills —hand thrust into plate, hand firmly put aside. The family, much upset, left the dining room. Annie locked the door and proceeded to eat her breakfast while Helen lay on the floor kicking and screaming, pushing and pulling at Annie's chair. After half an hour Helen went around the table looking for her family. She discovered no one else was there and that bewildered her. Finally, she sat down and began to eat her breakfast, but with her hands. Annie gave her a spoon. Down on the floor it clattered, and the contest of wills began anew (Lash, 1980, p. 52).

Anne Sullivan sensitively responded to the child's behavior. She wrote home: "The greatest problem I shall have to solve is how to discipline and control her without breaking her spirit. I shall go rather slowly at first and try to win her love."

In fact, the first "miracle" occurred two weeks later, well before the famous incident at the pumphouse. Annie had taken Helen to a small cottage near the family's house, where they could live alone. After seven days together, Helen's personality suddenly underwent a profound change—the therapy had worked:

> My heart is singing with joy this morning. A miracle has happened! The wild little creature of two weeks ago has been transformed into a gentle child (p. 54).

It was just two weeks after this that the first breakthrough in Helen's grasp of language occurred; and from that point on, she progressed with incredible speed. The key to the miracle of language was Anne Sullivan's insight into the *person* of Helen Keller.

Interpersonal intelligence builds on a core capacity to notice distinctions among others; in particular, contrasts in their moods, temperaments, motivations, and intentions. In more advanced forms, this intelligence permits a skilled adult to read the intentions and desires of others, even when these have been hidden. This skill appears in a highly sophisticated form in religious or political leaders, teachers, therapists, and parents. The Helen Keller–Anne Sullivan story suggests that this interpersonal intelligence does not depend on language.

All indices in brain research suggest that the frontal lobes play a prominent role in interpersonal knowledge. Damage in this area can cause profound personality changes while leaving other forms of problem solving unharmed—a person is often "not the same person" after such an injury.

Alzheimer's disease, a form of presenile dementia, appears to attack posterior brain zones with a special ferocity, leaving spatial, logical, and linguistic computations severly impaired. Yet, Alzheimer's patients will often remain well groomed, socially proper, and continually apologetic for their errors. In contrast, Pick's disease, another variety of presenile dementia that is more frontally oriented, entails a rapid loss of social graces.

Biological evidence for interpersonal intelligence encompasses two additional factors often cited as unique to humans. One factor is the prolonged childhood of primates, including the close attachment to the mother. In those cases where the mother is removed from early development, normal interpersonal development is in serious jeopardy. The second factor is the relative importance in humans of social interaction. Skills such as hunting, tracking, and killing in prehistoric societies required participation and cooperation of large numbers of people. The need for group cohesion, leadership, organization, and solidarity follows naturally from this.

Intrapersonal Intelligence

In an essay called "A Sketch of the Past," written almost as a diary entry, Virginia Woolf discusses the "cotton wool of existence"—the various mundane events of life. She contrasts this "cotton wool" with three specific and poignant memories from her childhood: a fight with her brother, seeing a particular flower in the garden, and hearing of the suicide of a past visitor:

> These are three instances of exceptional moments. I often tell them over, or rather they come to the surface unexpectedly. But now for the first time I have written

them down, and I realize something that I have never realized before. Two of these moments ended in a state of despair. The other ended, on the contrary, in a state of satisfaction.

The sense of horror (in hearing of the suicide) held me powerless. But in the case of the flower, I found a reason; and was thus able to deal with the sensation. I was not powerless.

Though I still have the peculiarity that I receive these sudden shocks, they are now always welcome; after the first surprise, I always feel instantly that they are particularly valuable. And so I go on to suppose that the shock-receiving capacity is what makes me a writer. I hazard the explanation that a shock is at once in my case followed by the desire to explain it. I feel that I have had a blow; but it is not, as I thought as a child, simply a blow from an enemy hidden behind the cotton wool of daily life; it is or will become a revelation of some order; it is a token of some real thing behind appearances; and I make it real by putting it into words (Woolf, 1976, pp. 69–70).

This quotation vividly illustrates the intrapersonal intelligence—knowledge of the internal aspects of a person: access to one's own feeling life, one's range of emotions, the capacity to effect discriminations among these emotions and eventually to label them and to draw upon them as a means of understanding and guiding one's own behavior. A person with good intrapersonal intelligence has a viable and effective model of himself or herself. Since this intelligence is the most private, it requires evidence from language, music, or some other more expressive form of intelligence if the observer is to detect it at work. In the above quotation, for example, linguistic intelligence is drawn upon to convey intrapersonal knowledge; it embodies the interaction of intelligences, a common phenomenon to which we will return later.

We see the familiar criteria at work in the intrapersonal intelligence. As with the interpersonal intelligence, the frontal lobes play a central role in personality change. Injury to the lower area of the frontal lobes is likely to produce irritability or euphoria; while injury to the higher regions is more likely to produce indifference, listlessness, slowness, and apathy—a kind of depressive personality. In such "frontal-lobe" individuals, the other cognitive functions often remain preserved. In contrast, among aphasics who have recovered sufficiently to describe their experiences, we find consistent testimony: while there may have been a diminution of general alertness and considerable depression about the condition, the individual in no way felt himself to be a different person. He recognized his own needs, wants, and desires and tried as best he could to achieve them.

The autistic child is a prototypical example of an individual with impaired intrapersonal intelligence; indeed, the child may not even be able to refer to himself. At the same time, such children often exhibit remarkable abilities in the musical, computational, spatial, or mechanical realms.

Evolutionary evidence for an intrapersonal faculty is more difficult to come by, but we might speculate that the capacity to transcend the satisfaction of instinctual drives is relevant. This becomes increasingly important in a species not perennially involved in the struggle for survival.

In sum, then, both interpersonal and intrapersonal faculties pass the tests of an intelligence. They both feature problem-solving endeavors with significance for the individual and the species. Interpersonal intelligence allows one to understand and work with others; intrapersonal intelligence allows one to understand and work with oneself. In the individual's sense of self, one encounters a melding of inter- and intra-personal components. Indeed, the sense of self emerges as one of the most marvelous of human inventions—a symbol that represents all kinds of information about a person and that is at the same time an invention that all individuals construct for themselves.

SUMMARY: THE UNIQUE CONTRIBUTIONS OF THE THEORY

As human beings, we all have a repertoire of skills for solving different kinds of problems. Our investigation has begun, therefore, with a consideration of these problems, the contexts they are found in, and the culturally significant products that are the outcome. We have not approached "intelligence" as a reified human faculty that is brought to bear in literally any problem setting; rather, we have begun with the problems that humans *solve* and worked back to the "intelligences" that must be responsible.

Evidence from brain research, human development, evolution, and cross-cultural comparisons was brought to bear in our search for the relevant human intelligences: a candidate was included only if reasonable evidence to support its membership was found across these diverse fields. Again, this tack differs from the traditional one: since no candidate faculty is *necessarily* an intelligence, we could choose on a motivated basis. In the traditional approach to "intelligence," there is no opportunity for this type of empirical decision.

We have also determined that these multiple human faculties, the intelligences, are to a significant extent *independent*. For example, research with brain-damaged adults repeatedly demonstrates that particular faculties can be lost while others are spared. This independence of intelligences implies that a particularly high level of ability in one intelligence, say mathematics, does not require a similarly high level in another intelligence, like language or music. This independence of intelligences contrasts sharply with traditional measures of IQ that find high correlations among test scores. We speculate that the usual correlations among subtests of IQ tests come about because all of these tasks in fact measure the ability to respond rapidly to items of a logical-mathematical or linguistic sort; we believe that these correlations would be substantially reduced if one were to survey in a contextually appropriate way the full range of human problem-solving skills.

Until now, we have supported the fiction that adult roles depend largely on the flowering of a single intelligence. In fact, however, nearly every cultural role of any degree of sophistication requires a combination of intelligences. Thus, even an apparently straightforward role, like playing the violin, transcends a reliance on simple musical intelligence. To become a successful violinist requires bodily-kinesthetic dexterity and the interpersonal skills of relating to an audience and, in a different way, choosing a manager; quite possibly it involves an intrapersonal intelligence as well. Dance requires skills in bodily-kinesthetic, musical, interpersonal, and spatial intelligences in varying degrees. Politics requires an interpersonal skill, a linguistic facility, and perhaps some logical aptitude. Inasmuch as nearly every cultural role requires several intelligences, it becomes important to consider individuals as a collection of aptitudes rather than as having a singular problem-solving faculty that can be measured directly through pencil-and-paper tests. Even given a relatively small number of such intelligences, the diversity of human ability is created through the differences in these profiles. In fact, it may well be that the "total is greater than the sum of the parts." An individual may not be particularly gifted in any intelligence; and yet, because of a particular combination or blend of skills, he or she may be able to fill some niche uniquely well. Thus it is of paramount importance to assess the particular combination of skills that may earmark an individual for a certain vocational or avocational niche.

Howard Gardner and Joseph Walters

PART SIX

Society, Culture, and Education

Chapter 13 Social Change 329

Chapter 14 Culture and Education 346

On the Internet . . .

Sites appropriate to Part Six

New Horizons for Learning offers resources for learning
organizations, translating research and theory into workable
solutions for contemporary learning organizations. This site
focuses on the theory of multiple intelligences.

    http://www.newhorizons.org/bibmishelf.html

Children's Express is an on-line magazine created "by kids
and for everyone." The staff at CE are all under 16 years old
and from various urban locations throughout the United
States. This is an interview with Jonathan Kozol conducted by
the CE staff.

    http://www.ce.org/topnews/kozol.htm

Harvard Project Zero, a research group at the Harvard
Graduate School of Education, has investigated the
development of learning processes in children and adults for
30 years. Today, Project Zero is building on this research to
help create communities of reflective, independent learners; to
enhance deep understanding within disciplines; and to
promote critical and creative thinking.

    http://pzweb.harvard.edu/HPZpages/
      History.html

CHAPTER 13 Social Change

13.1 JOHN DEWEY

Education and Social Change

The Social Frontier was a very important publishing forum for the ideas of progressive-liberal scholars in American education from 1934 to 1944. During its brief history, *The Social Frontier* published many important essays by William Heard Kilpatrick, Goodwin Watson, Harold Rugg, and many other prominent liberal scholars in the fields of teacher education and social foundations of education. John Dewey was a regular contributor to this journal. Dewey's view was that schools have an important role in forging any society's future.

In the following selection, which is from "Education and Social Change," *The Social Frontier* (May 1937), Dewey uses one of his favorite rhetorical techniques: He gives the reader three clearly different arguments; he then phrases two of them so as to lead the reader to support the one he prefers. Dewey delivers in this essay a stirring defense of democracy as well as of freedom of information and communication in schools as a way to better prepare students for social change.

Dewey (1859–1952) was a professor of philosophy at Columbia University. His many publications include *Democracy and Education: An Introduction to the Philosophy of Education* (Macmillan, 1916) and *How We Think: A Restatement of the Relation of Reflective Thinking to the Educative Process* (D. C. Heath, 1933).

Key Concept: schools and social change

*U*pon certain aspects of my theme there is nothing new to be said. Attention has been continually called of late to the fact that society is in process of change, and that the schools tend to lag behind. We are all familiar with the pleas that are urged to bring education in the schools into closer relation with the forces that are producing social change and with the needs that arise from these changes. Probably no question has received so much attention in educational discussion during the last few years as the problem of integration of the schools with social life. Upon these general matters, I could hardly do more than reiterate what has often been said.

Nevertheless, there is as yet little consensus of opinion as to what the schools can do in relation to the forces of social change and how they should do it. There are those who assert in effect that the schools must simply reflect social changes that have already occurred, as best they may. Some would go so far as to make the work of schools virtually parasitic. Others hold that the schools should take an active part in *directing* social change, and share in the construction of a new social order. Even among the latter there is, however, marked difference of attitude. Some think the schools should assume this directive role by means of indoctrination; others oppose this method. Even if there were more unity of thought than exists, there would still be the practical problem of overcoming institutional inertia so as to realize in fact an agreed-upon program.

There is, accordingly, no need to justify further discussion of the problem of the relation of education to social change. I shall do what I can, then, to indicate the factors that seem to me to enter into the problem, together with some of the reasons that prove that the schools do have a role—and an important one —in *production* of social change.

SCHOOLS REFLECT THE SOCIAL ORDER

One factor inherent in the situation is that schools *do* follow and reflect the social "order" that exists. I do not make this statement as a grudging admission, nor yet in order to argue that they should *not* do so. I make it rather as a statement of a *conditioning* factor which supports the conclusion that the schools thereby do take part in the determination of a future social order; and that, accordingly, the problem is not whether the schools *should* participate in the production of a future society (since they do so anyway) but whether they should do it blindly and irresponsibly or with the maximum possible of courageous intelligence and responsibility.

The grounds that lead me to make this statement are as follows: The existing state of society, which the schools reflect, is not something fixed and uniform. The idea that such is the case is a self-imposed hallucination. Social conditions are not only in process of change, but the changes going on are in different directions, so different as to produce social confusion and conflict. There is no single and clear-cut pattern that pervades and holds together in a unified way the social conditions and forces that operate. It would be easy to cite highly respectable authorities who have stated, as matter of historic fact and not on account of some doctrinal conclusion to be drawn, that social conditions in all that affects the relations of human beings to one another have changed more in the last one hundred and fifty years than in all previous time, and that the process of change is still going on. It requires a good deal of either ignorance or intellectual naiveté to suppose that these changes have all been tending to one coherent social outcome. The plaint of the conservative about the imperiling of old and time-tried values and truths, and the efforts of reactionaries to stem the tide of changes that occur, are sufficient evidence, if evidence be needed to the contrary.

Of course the schools have mirrored the social changes that take place. The efforts of Horace Mann and others a century ago to establish a public, free, common school system were a reflection primarily of the social conditions that followed the war by the colonies for political independence and the establishment of republican institutions. The evidential force of this outstanding instance would be confirmed in detail if we went through the list of changes that have taken place in (1) the kind of schools that have been established, (2) the new courses that have been introduced, (3) the shifts in subject-matter that have occurred, and (4) the changes in methods of instruction and discipline that have occurred in intervening years. The notion that the educational system has been static is too absurd for notice; it has been and still is in a state of flux.

The fact that it is possible to argue about the desirability of many of the changes that have occurred, and to give valid reasons for deploring aspects of the flux, is not relevant to the main point. For the stronger the arguments brought forth on these points, and the greater the amount of evidence produced to show that the educational system is in a state of disorder and confusion, the greater is the proof that the schools have responded to, and have reflected, social conditions which are themselves in a state of confusion and conflict.

INCONSISTENT CONSERVATISM

Do those who hold the idea that the schools should not attempt to give direction to social change accept complacently the confusion that exists, because the schools *have* followed in the track of one social change after another? They certainly do not, although the logic of their position demands it. For the most part they are severe critics of the existing state of education. They are as a rule opposed to the studies called modern and the methods called progressive. They tend to favor return to older types of studies and to strenuous "disciplinary" methods. What does this attitude mean? Does it not show that its advocates in reality adopt the position that the schools can do something to affect positively and constructively social conditions? For they hold in effect that the school should discriminate with respect to the social forces that play upon it; that instead of accepting the latter *in toto*, education should select and organize in a given direction. The adherents of this view can hardly believe that the effect of selection and organization will stop at the doors of school rooms. They must expect some ordering and healing influence to be exerted sooner or later upon the structure and movement of life outside. What they are really doing when they deny directive social effect to education is to express their opposition to some of the directions social change is actually taking, and their choice of other social forces as those with which education should throw in its lot so as to promote as far as may be their victory in the strife of forces. They are conservatives in education because they are socially conservative and vice-versa.

ALTERNATIVE COURSES

This is as it should be in the interest of clearness and consistency of thought and action. If these conservatives in education were more aware of what is involved in their position, and franker in stating its implications, they would help bring out the real issue. It is not whether the schools shall or shall not influence the course of future social life, but in what direction they shall do so and how. In some fashion or other, the schools will influence social life anyway. But they can exercise such influence in different ways and to different ends, and the important thing is to become conscious of these different ways and ends, so that an intelligent choice may be made, and so that if opposed choices are made, the further conflict may at least be carried on with understanding of what is at stake, and not in the dark.

There are three possible directions of choice. Educators may act so as to perpetuate the present confusion and possibly increase it. That will be the result of drift, and under present conditions to drift is in the end to make a choice. Or they may select the newer scientific, technological, and cultural forces that are producing change in the old order; may estimate the direction in which they are moving and their outcome if they are given freer play, and see what can be done to make the schools their ally. Or, educators may become intelligently conservative and strive to make the schools a force in maintaining the old order intact against the impact of new forces.

If the second course is chosen—as of course I believe it should be—the problem will be other than merely that of accelerating the rate of the change that is going on. The problem will be to develop the insight and understanding that will enable the youth who go forth from the schools to take part in the great work of construction and organization that will have to be done, and to equip them with the attitudes and habits of action that will make their understanding and insight practically effective.

DRIFT OR INTELLIGENT CHOICE?

There is much that can be said for an intelligent conservatism. I do not know anything that can be said for perpetuation of a wavering, uncertain, confused condition of social life and education. Nevertheless, the easiest thing is to refrain from fundamental thinking and let things go on drifting. Upon the basis of any other policy than drift—which after all is a policy, though a blind one—every special issue and problem, whether that of selection and organization of subject-matter of study, or methods of teaching, of school buildings and equipment, of school administration, is a special phase of the inclusive and fundamental problem: What movement of social forces, economic, political, religious, cultural, shall the school take to be controlling in its aims and methods, and with which forces shall the school align itself?

Failure to discuss educational problems from this point of view but intensifies the existing confusion. Apart from this background, and outside of this perspective, educational questions have to be settled *ad hoc* and are speedily unsettled. What is suggested does not mean that the schools shall throw themselves into the political and economic arena and take sides with some party there. I am not talking about parties; I am talking about social forces and their movement. In spite of absolute claims that are made for this party or that, it is altogether probable that existing parties and sects themselves suffer from existing confusions and conflicts, so that the understanding, the ideas, and attitudes that control their policies, need re-education and re-orientation. I know that there are some who think that the implications of what I have said point to abstinence and futility; that they negate the stand first taken. But I am surprised when educators adopt this position, for it shows a profound lack of faith in their own calling. It assumes that education as education has nothing or next to nothing to contribute; that formation of understanding and disposition counts for nothing; that only immediate overt action counts and that it can count equally whether or not it has been modified by education.

NEUTRALITY AIDS REACTION

Before leaving this aspect of the subject, I wish to recur to the utopian nature of the idea that the schools can be completely neutral. This idea sets up an end incapable of accomplishment. So far as it is acted upon, it has a definite social effect, but that effect is, as I have said, perpetuation of disorder and increase of blind because unintelligent conflict. Practically, moreover, the weight of such action falls upon the reactionary side. Perhaps the most effective way of re-inforcing reaction under the name of neutrality, consists in keeping the oncoming generation ignorant of the conditions in which they live and the issues they have to face. This effect is the more pronounced because it is subtle and indirect; because neither teachers nor those taught are aware of what they are doing and what is being done to them. Clarity can develop only in the extent to which there is frank acknowledgment of the basic issue: Where shall the social emphasis of school life and work fall, and what are the educational policies which correspond to this emphasis?

REVOLUTIONARY RADICALS BELIEVE
EDUCATION IMPOTENT

So far I have spoken of those who assert, in terms of the views of a conservative group, the doctrine of complete impotence of education. But it is an old story that politics makes strange bedfellows. There is another group which holds the schools are completely impotent; that they so necessarily reflect the dominant economic and political regime, that they are committed, root and branch, to its support. This conclusion is based upon the belief that the organization of a given society is fixed by the control exercised by a particular economic class, so that the school, like every other social institution, is of necessity the subservient tool of a dominant class. This viewpoint takes literally the doctrine that the school can only reflect the existing social order. Hence the conclusion in effect that it is a waste of energy and time to bother with the schools. The only way, according to advocates of this theory, to change education in any important respect is first to overthrow the existing class-order of society and transfer power to another class. Then the needed change in education will follow automatically and will be genuine and thorough-going.

This point of view serves to call attention to another factor in the general issue being discussed. I shall not here take up in detail the basic premise of this school of social thought, namely the doctrine of domination of social organization by a single rather solidly-unified class; a domination so complete and pervasive that it can be thrown off only by the violent revolutionary action of another distinct unified class. It will be gathered, however, from what has been said that I believe the existing situation is so composite and so marked by conflicting criss-cross tendencies that this premise represents an exaggeration of actual conditions so extreme as to be a caricature. Yet I do recognize that so far as any general characterization of the situation can be made, it is on the basis of a conflict of older and newer forces—forces cultural, religious, scientific, philosophic, economic, and political.

But suppose it is admitted for the sake of argument that a social revolution is going on, and that it will culminate in a transfer of power effected by violent action. The notion that schools are completely impotent under existing conditions then has disastrous consequences. The schools, according to the theory, are engaged in shaping as far as in them lies a mentality, a type of belief, desire, and purpose that is consonant with the present class-capitalist system. It is evident that if such be the case, any revolution that is brought about is going to be badly compromised and even undermined. It will carry with it the seeds, the vital seeds, of counter-revolutions. There is no basis whatever, save doctrinaire absolutism, for the belief that a complete economic change will produce of itself the mental, moral, and cultural changes that are necessary for its enduring success. The fact is practically recognized by the school of thought under discussion in that part of their doctrine which asserts that no genuine revolution can occur until the old system has passed away in everything but external political power, while within its shell a new economic system has grown to maturity. What is ignored is that the new system cannot grow to maturity without an accompanying widespread change of habits of belief, desire, and purpose.

335

John Dewey

IS INDOCTRINATION THE WAY OUT?

It is unrealistic, in my opinion, to suppose that the schools can be a *main* agency in producing the intellectual and moral changes, the changes in attitudes and disposition of thought and purpose, which are necessary for the creation of a new social order. Any such view ignores the constant operation of powerful forces outside the school which shape mind and character. It ignores the fact that school education is but one educational agency out of many, and at the best is in some respects a minor educational force. Nevertheless, while the school is not a sufficient condition, it is a necessary condition of forming the understanding and the dispositions that are required to maintain a genuinely changed social order. No social change is more than external unless it is attended by and rooted in the attitudes of those who bring it about and of those who are affected by it. In a genuine sense, social change is accidental unless it has also a psychological and moral foundation. For it is then at the mercy of currents that veer and shift. The utmost that can be meant by those who hold that schools are impotent is that education in the form of *systematic indoctrination* can only come about when some government is sufficiently established to make schools undertake the task of single-minded inculcation in a single direction.

The discussion has thus reached the point in which it is advisable to say a few words about indoctrination. The word is not free from ambiguity. One definition of the dictionary makes it a synonym for teaching. In order that there may be a definite point to consider, I shall take indoctrination to mean the systematic use of every possible means to impress upon the minds of pupils a particular set of political and economic views to the exclusion of every other. This meaning is suggested by the word "inculcation," whose original signification was "to stamp in with the heel." This signification is too physical to be carried over literally. But the idea of stamping in is involved, and upon occasion does include physical measures. I shall discuss this view only as far as to state, in the first place, that indoctrination so conceived is something very different from education, for the latter involves, as I understand it, the active participation of students in reaching conclusions and forming attributes. Even in the case of something as settled and agreed upon as the multiplication table, I should say if it is taught educatively, and not as a form of animal training, the active participation, the interest, reflection, and understanding of those taught are necessary.

The upholders of indoctrination rest their adherence to the theory in part upon the fact that there is a great deal of indoctrination now going on in the schools, especially with reference to narrow nationalism under the name of patriotism, and with reference to the dominant economic regime. These facts unfortunately *are* facts. But they do not prove that the right course is to seize upon the method of indoctrination and reverse its objective.

DEMOCRACY AS A FRAME OF REFERENCE

A much stronger argument is that unless education has some frame of reference it is bound to be aimless, lacking a unified objective. The necessity for a frame of reference must be admitted. There exists in this country such a unified frame. It is called democracy. I do not claim for a moment that the significance of democracy as a mode of life is so settled that there can be no disagreement as to its significance. The moment we leave glittering generalities and come to concrete details, there is great divergence. I certainly do not mean either that our political institutions as they have come to be, our parties, legislatures, laws, and courts constitute a model upon which a clear idea of democracy can be based. But there is a tradition and an idea which we can put in opposition to the very much that is undemocratic in our institutions. The idea and ideal involve at least the necessity of personal and voluntary participation in reaching decisions and executing them—in so far it is the contrary of the idea of indoctrination. And I, for one, am profoundly sceptical of the notion that because we now have a rather poor embodiment of democracy we can ultimately produce a genuine democracy by sweeping away what we have left of one.

The positive point, however, is that the democratic ideal, in its human significance, provides us with a frame of reference. The frame is not filled in, either in society at large or in its significance for education. I am not implying that it is so clear and definite that we can look at it as a traveler can look at a map and tell where to go from hour to hour. Rather the point I would make is that the *problem* of education in its relation to direction of social change is all one with the *problem* of finding out what democracy means in its total range of concrete applications; economic, domestic, international, religious, cultural, economic, *and* political.

I cannot wish for anything better to happen for, and in, our schools than that this problem should become the chief theme for consideration until we have attained clarity concerning the concrete significance of democracy—which like everything concrete means its application in living action, individual and collective. The trouble, at least one great trouble, is that we have taken democracy for granted; we have thought and acted as if our forefathers had founded it once for all. We have forgotten that it has to be enacted anew in every generation, in every year and day, in the living relations of person to person in all social forms and institutions. Forgetting this, we have allowed our economic and hence our political institutions to drift away from democracy; we have been negligent even in creating a school that should be the constant nurse of democracy.

I conclude by saying that there is at least one thing in which the idea of democracy is not dim, however far short we have come from striving to make it reality. Our public school system was founded in the name of equality of opportunity for all, independent of birth, economic status, race, creed, or color. The school cannot by itself alone create or embody this idea. But the least it can do is to create individuals who understand the concrete meaning of the idea with their minds, who cherish it warmly in their hearts, and who are equipped to battle in its behalf in their actions.

Democracy also means voluntary choice, based on an intelligence that is the outcome of free association and communication with others. It means a way of living together in which mutual and free consultation rule instead of force, and in which cooperation instead of brutal competition is the law of life; a social order in which all the forces that make for friendship, beauty, and knowledge are cherished in order that each individual may become what he, and he alone, is capable of becoming. These things at least give a point of departure for the filling in of the democratic idea and aim as a frame of reference. If a sufficient number of educators devote themselves to striving courageously and with full sincerity to find the answers to the concrete questions which the idea and the aim put to us, I believe that the question of the relation of the schools to direction of social change will cease to be a question, and will become a moving answer in action.

John Dewey

Conflicting Theories of Education

I. L. Kandel (1881–1965), a professor of education, is considered the father of the study of comparative and international education in the United States. He founded the Center for International Studies of Education at Teachers College, Columbia University, in the 1930s and edited more than 20 of the yearbooks on world education published by the center. He published lengthy studies on the educational systems in Germany, France, and several other nations as well as on issues in American education. He wrote one of the first textbooks on comparative education and one of the first critiques of the Nazi educational program in Germany, *The Making of Nazis* (Teachers College Press, 1935).

Kandel saw a threat to democratic nation-states in the 1930s. What he had to say about it is as relevant for our time as it was for his. The selection that follows is from *Conflicting Theories of Education* (Macmillan, 1938). In it, Kandel discusses the role of education in defense of freedom of thought, and he addresses the issue of education and social change. He argues that educational processes do not take place in a social or cultural vacuum; schools are institutions created by societies to achieve certain specific purposes. He maintains that students should be taught to understand the world in which they live. Here he discusses teachers' responsibilities in dealing with social controversies. He says that there is no choice but to bring conflicting social issues into the classroom.

Key Concept: education and social change

*E*ducation does not ... take place in a vacuum. The school is an agency established by society to achieve certain ends. These ends will differ according to the form of each society. Totalitarian states have adopted fixed patterns into which the individual is to be molded. Democracies will fail if they attempt to adopt a type of education which ignores any values but those chosen by each individual to suit the needs of the moment. The mystical, irrational notion that freedom is synonymous with the right to follow inner drives ignores both the history and the meaning of freedom.

That freedom is a conquest has been as true of the progress of humanity as it is of the growth of the individual. The whole history of humanity has been —despite aberrations in recent years—the history of the emancipation from external controls and, at the same time, of the ways in which man has learned to control himself. This history has been one of the emancipation of man from servitude to fears—fears of nature, slavery, political tyranny, and external controls and coercion over life. Man's struggle for personal freedom, freedom of movement, freedom of thought and expression, freedom of worship, justice, tolerance, and equality of opportunity has been painfully slow and is not yet ended. But in emerging successfully from the struggle, man did so by learning that he must accept certain limitations on his freedom, by recognizing his responsibility and duty to others. It was only as man learned to appreciate the moral consequence of his actions that he became free.

What has been true of the history of civilization applies equally to the education of the individual—freedom is not an inherent right (totalitarian states have proved how easily it may be lost) but a privilege to be won. And it is in confusing freedom with noninterference and in failing to stress social and moral obligations adequately that those who have most loudly urged freedom in education have erred. The slogan of self-expression, for example, failed to recognize that the true self can be realized only in and through a social milieu. Hence, the fundamental issue is the extent to which such realization of the self can be free and yet result in a personality enriched through and by a consciousness of social values. Here again the answer will be found in the principle that freedom is a right which, like all other rights, must be won, and that all rights imply a corresponding responsibility in their use, no matter what the field of activity may be.

A free society cannot divest itself of the obligation of handing on to new generations those common traditions, loyalties, and interests which make community life possible, but it can and should avoid that claim to omniscience and infallibility which must in the long run spell stagnation and failure to permit adaptation to changing conditions. If this is accepted, then the only thing that a free society should indoctrinate is faith in freedom and in free inquiry. But the essence of freedom and free inquiry is the recognition of responsibility. Not until the concept of responsibility is incorporated in the discussion of education in a free society, can education be expected to make its rightful contribution to a troubled world. For such a discussion Santayana's description of English liberty may well furnish the text, for in it may be found the answer of a free society to the criticisms of the totalitarian: "It moves by a series of checks, mutual concessions, and limited satisfactions; it counts on chivalry, sportsmanship, brotherly love, and on that rarest and least lucrative of virtues, fair-mindedness; it is a broad-based, stupid, blind adventure, groping towards an unknown goal."

And this, in essence, is the definition of liberal education, which has unfortunately acquired a connotation in terms of familiarity with certain subjects. But a liberal education implies more than a knowledge of classical or modern languages, science and mathematics. It implies breadth of interests, knowledge and information, standards of taste and appreciation, and the possession of certain moral and social qualities. It should result in tolerance and openmindedness, in ability to meet new situations because one has knowledge and insight, and in readiness to co-operate because of a refined sense of responsibility. All these are social values, values which make the existence of a free society possible and which cannot be acquired incidentally as and when the pupil feels the need of them.

... And if a free society is to accept the challenge and meet the charges of totalitarianism it will be only as it realizes that there must be common agreement, common social faith, and common values as a foundation for that freedom upon which it is based. It is upon these common elements, consciously and deliberately recognized and defined, that education can build a free personality. To set up the child as an idol and to worship his inner drives, urges, and impulses is to encourage chaos; to set up the ideal of a free personality implies a vision of social purposes which alone can give meaning to education and save the rising generation from immersion in the destructive element which sees no values in the past, no meaning in the present, and no hope in the future. In this task of defining the meaning of freedom in education the English-speaking peoples can find a field of common endeavor—England with her reverence for traditional values and deliberate and cautious acceptance of change, the United States with her buoyant optimism and preference for change at the cost of traditions, and the Dominions rooted in British traditions but with the vigor and vision of youthful pioneers. Democratic institutions may safely be entrusted to them, but only as these nations become conscious of the significance of these institutions for humanity and the part to be played by education in their preservation....

EDUCATION AND SOCIAL CHANGE

The general social and cultural unrest which can be traced back to the beginnings of the modern scientific movement and the consequent technological changes, an unrest which has grown in intensity since the War, has had its repercussions on educational thought. This has, indeed, been the history of education, for education has been most vigorous and vital in periods of great social changes, as, for example, in Athens, during the Renaissance and the Reformation, at the time of the early scientific movement of the seventeenth century, and at the beginning of the nineteenth century following the Industrial Revolution and the consolidation of nation-states. The period through which the world is passing in the present era is probably one of those nodal periods in which old ideas and ideals, standards and loyalties, are being questioned and modified, if not revolutionized. Science is remaking the world and bringing an economic upheaval in its train; political institutions are being questioned or overturned; a war of ideas is going on in every field that concerns human relationships. The conflicts are more profound and more widespread than those which have always existed between the older and younger generations.

Under these conditions unrest in education is inevitable, but in the discussions on education and social change it is not clear whether a formula is being sought whereby the rising generation shall be acquainted with the social changes going on about it or whether it is proposed that the school itself should be made an instrument for the reconstruction of society. These alternatives can be answered only in the light of the purposes for which society establishes schools.

The earliest and most persistent reason for the establishment of schools as formal agencies of education is the desire on the part of a group, society, or state to conserve and transmit its culture and heritage to the younger generation and to equip this generation with those habits, skills, knowledges, and ideals that will enable it to take its place in a society and contribute to the stability and perpetuation of that society. This purpose is based on faith in the possibilities of formal education during the formative and plastic period of childhood and adolescence. This is the principle in Plato's statement that the effectual functioning of the state depends upon the proper training of the young, and in Aristotle's insistence that the stability of systems of government has its basis in the adaptation of education to the form of government.

Education does not proceed in a vacuum; its character is determined by the group culture, and schools are institutions created by society to attain certain specific ends. These ends began to be defined when the national states at the beginning of the nineteenth century undertook to establish systems of education to initiate their future citizens into the national culture. Stability was to be secured by instructing the pupils in the schools in a common language, common history, common government and political ideals, common economic and social ideas and ideals, and common objects of social allegiance in order that there might emerge a common group, or national, self-consciousness. If the younger generation is to enter into meaningful partnership in and responsibility for its heritage the first function of the school is to initiate it into its common culture. Society is, in fact, prior to the individual, and the school is an agency for promoting stability and adapting the individual to the environment in which he lives. Without entering into other considerations which justify the transmission of the social heritage or the experiences of the race as a basis for understanding the present, it will be generally agreed that the function here described has received wide acceptance from the days of Plato down to modern times.

If, however, the school stops with the performance of this function, then a society either stagnates, as was the case in China, or its progress is determined by the will of the few who lead the rest, trained through the school to habits of duty, discipline, quiescent obedience, and uncritical acceptance of authority. The method of such a school is that of direct indoctrination and education becomes indistinguishable from propaganda. This was already the trend in authoritarian states of the last century; it is the principle definitely accepted in the totalitarian states of the present, in which education is directed by and to a common ideology. The social changes wrought by revolutions have produced patterns which know no compromise and are not open to question or criticism. Education has become adjustment to a fixed and unchanging environment, and national culture is something that is colored by a particular ideology and controlled by organizations created to prevent changes in it.

The situation is different in those countries in which culture is accepted as the spontaneous expression of individuals and the free interplay among individuals or groups. It is at this point that education and social change begin to be clothed with meaning and to challenge traditional practices. The procedure in the past was to impart a body of content, knowledge, and information representing selections from the group culture designed primarily to "train the mind." It tended to become stereotyped and formal and rarely came to grips with the present. The school was a cloistered institution which eschewed any contact with the environment into which the pupil was soon to pass. It must be remembered, however, that even this type of procedure did not ignore the changing environment and was not designed to maintain a static society, but it was conducted with the conviction that a mind trained by "academic" or "scholastic" material would have no difficulty in dealing with the realities of life. Nor was the procedure in the education of the masses differentiated from the procedure in the education of the potential leaders.

These practices were not accepted without protest. Since the days of Seneca educators have urged that education must be for life and not for the school, but it was not until the beginning of the present century that widespread efforts began to be made to bring school and society together. A better understanding of the process of child growth, a new interpretation of the concept of interest, a clearer realization of the meaning of democracy and the part to be played by the individual in it, and the rapid changes in the culture, due in the main to the progress of science—all these forces and many others contributed to the spread of the theory that if education is a social process, it must contribute to an understanding of the society which it serves. The influence of John Dewey's philosophy in bringing about the change of outlook not only in the United States but in other parts of the world is too well known to need further discussion. The vast body of educational literature which has grown up in the United States in the past three decades speaks eloquently of this influence. The educational trend in Germany during the period of the short-lived Republic was rooted in *Bodenständigkeit,* the relation of education to the environment. In England the latest edition of the *Handbook of Suggestions for Teachers* is inspired by the same principle, as is illustrated by a statement in the general introduction that "we feel more deeply the need of relating what is taught in the schools to what is happening in the world outside."

The new theory of education, in insisting that the work of the school must be related to the environment in which and for which its pupils are being educated, contains in its definition the suggestion that discussions of social change are implicit in the curriculum. It means that pupils should be taught to understand the world in which they live. Up to this point the problem is fairly simple. Difficulties arise, however, when it is suggested that change is the characteristic note of the present world—and change not merely in its material but in its ideational aspects. To what extent should or can the school concern itself with political and economic conflicts, with changes in the attitudes to authority, or with the general atmosphere that questions all traditions?

Changes in the material world are facts; political and economic theories are matters of opinion. If the teacher is an agent of the state, to what extent is he free to introduce controversial issues into the classroom? It is not necessary here to state that the issues should be relevant to the stage of development and the maturity of the pupils concerned and to the subject of instruction. But if the function of education is to develop an understanding of the problems of the environment in which the learner lives, the opportunity of discussing controversial issues in the school cannot be ignored. Indeed, one may argue that it is essential to train the pupil in recognizing the importance of accurate knowledge before reaching an opinion.

If the doors of the school are to be closed to the discussion of controversial issues, it might well be asked what the alternative would be; in a period of change the schools would be guilty of turning pupils out into the world ignorant of the problems that will confront them. There is, in fact, no choice but to bring those elements of conflict into the classroom. To adopt an ostrichlike attitude and ignore the existence of such issues, to deny the right to mention even the existence of what may be regarded as subversive ideas, is to follow the old practice of ignoring the existence of sex. Carried to its logical conclusion, such a policy could be used to justify the suppression of a free press and of freedom of opinion, and the arrest of anyone suspected of "harboring dangerous thoughts."

Any reference to the introduction of controversial issues in politics and economics arouses the fear that pupils will be exposed to the bias of the teachers. It may be true that no teacher can successfully conduct a discussion of controversial issues without the pupils' detecting his bias. Nevertheless, pupils pass through the hands of a large number of teachers during their school careers; to suspect that all teachers have the same bias has no justification in fact; nor are teachers the only educational influences that play upon the growing youth. The choice is whether the rising generation is to receive its political and economic education through informal agencies or through methods that are truly educative; whether the young are to be enlightened and trained through the scientific study of facts or whether they are to be exposed to deliberate propaganda without the support of accurate information on both sides of an issue. If the relationship between school and society or education and the environment means anything, then the schools must, at the appropriate stage, impart the realities of society. And if that society is in process of change, then all that the school can do is to place the pupils in possession of full knowledge of the facts in the issues involved and to give them that training which will enable them to make up their own minds on the basis of that knowledge.

The emphasis in this argument is on training in methods of thinking through issues that are real. There is some truth in the objection that solutions cannot be given to contemporary controversial issues; this objection is, however, not a valid argument for their exclusion from the schools. Neither the issues nor the solutions are likely to be the same when pupils now in school take their places in life as adult citizens; the detailed facts of an issue and the knowledge requisite to its solution will inevitably be different, but unless some training is given in the schools in the patterns of thinking with which a problem is to be approached, the intellectual equipment necessary to recognize even the existence of problems will have been withheld. If democracy depends for its survival upon the intelligence and understanding of the ordinary man, it is the function of the school to equip him in advance with the necessary knowledge and powers of clear thinking to discharge his duties as a citizen.

It is only in this sense that education and social change can be discussed. Education must go beyond its task of imparting a knowledge and appreciation of the common interests, or what Dewey has called the objects of that social allegiance which makes common social understanding and consciousness of group membership possible. It must help men and women to think for themselves, unless they are to succumb to the will of an authority which claims omniscience and infallibility.

There has, however, been injected into discussions of education and social change the suggestion that schools should, in a period of change, educate for a new social order, and that teachers should ally themselves with some political group and use their classrooms to propagate certain doctrines. Schools and teachers should, in other words, participate more directly and vitally in projecting particular ideas or patterns of social change and in their execution. The whole history of education emphasizes the impossibility of this idea, for society establishes schools to provide a firm basis for itself and to sustain the common interest. Schools are a part of the environment which they serve; they are not autonomous or insulated against the social forces and influences around them; nor can teachers on the basis of a guess as to the active forces of the day help to build a new social order. Society changes first and schools follow.

It is, however, becoming increasingly important that teachers should be more alive than they have been in the past and better informed about the environment in and for which they are educating their pupils. Only in this way can they give meaning to the subjects for which they are responsible, for subjects, if they are to have any significance, must be saturated with social meaning. To attempt to instill ready-made ideas on controversial issues or to influence pupils to accept one doctrine rather than another is to adopt the methods of totalitarian states and to confuse education with propaganda.

In a democracy the only acceptable aim in bringing the school and society more closely together is to develop the knowledge and understanding that make for enlightened citizenship. But the acquisition of knowledge, facts, and information about the environment in all those aspects that concern the conduct of the citizen is not the sole end of education; such an acquisition must be made the vehicle for training in scientific methods of thinking and for cultivating free and disciplined minds. To educate for a new social order is to close the minds of the pupils, for, in a society in transition, no one can have a final answer concerning the issues that are involved. True education would help to put the pupils in a position to appreciate the urgent necessity of acquiring knowledge, to discriminate between facts and prejudices, to weigh and judge evidence, to reach conclusions warranted by the information secured, and to recognize the issues involved in a period of social transition or crisis. If this end is to be achieved, if the aim of education is to develop free and enlightened citizens, then the teachers who are to be entrusted with carrying out this aim must themselves be enlightened and free. The problem, like all other problems in education, becomes one of teacher preparation and of the status of teachers. In the words of a former president of the English Board of Education, "The standards of the teaching profession itself are the only sure protection" against the abuse of the teachers' positions in discussing educational and social change.

The problem of education and social change solves itself if education is defined as the process of bringing pupils to an understanding of the environment in and for which they are being educated. That environment is a constantly expanding one; to concentrate on change alone is to deal only with the immediate present and to avoid the development of an understanding of the rich heritage which the environment carries with it. But understanding must lead to conduct, and if democracy is to survive, the schools must cultivate in their pupils ideals of freedom, tolerance, and open-mindedness, a critical attitude and intellectual sensitiveness based on ascertained facts and knowledge, a spirit of inquiry and insight, and those emotional qualities in addition which make for a sense of responsibility and cooperation. For democracy, in the words of Santayana, is a blind, groping adventure which implies openmindedness and sensitiveness to the need of flexibility and adaptation of social institutions. These are the qualities which education can cultivate as the basis of social change....

EDUCATION AND THE CHALLENGE TO DEMOCRACY

In the war of ideas which is raging between totalitarianism and democracy the special responsibility which falls on education in a democracy is too frequently ignored. This is in part due to failure to recognize the challenge to democratic ideals; it is due also to the basic difference between the two groups of ideas— totalitarianism because it is built on a set body of doctrines dominated by acceptance of the supremacy of the state has by far the simpler task in education, while democracy as an ideal is a way of life based on the freedom and responsibility of the individual. The democratic state depends upon the collective will of the individuals who make it up and exists to guarantee the rights of individuals and to maintain justice between them; though too frequently the free citizen of a democracy is more conscious of his rights than he is of his duties. The totalitarian state insists upon the co-ordination of all individuals so that all think and behave like all other individuals, and how they may think and behave is determined by a dictator or a party. The essence of democracy is that each individual thinks for himself and behaves as his conscience dictates, provided that he does not encroach on the right of others to do the same. In the one case the individual must be "in the right line"; in the other the individual has a right to his own opinions.

The totalitarian state has recognized more clearly than the democratic the axiom already enunciated by Plato and Aristotle that education and the form of government are closely interdependent, that education, in other words, is an instrument of social control employed to perpetuate society and to advance social progress. Whether education is defined as a process of molding all individuals to the same pattern or of promoting progress through the enlightenment of all individuals depends upon the nature of the state and its form of government. Here is to be found the explanation of the interest shown in the provision of education by the nation states in the nineteenth century as well as the insistence of George Washington on the enlightenment of public opinion through "institutions for the general diffusion of knowledge."

CHAPTER 14 Culture and Education

14.1 HOWARD GARDNER

In a Nutshell

Howard Gardner is a professor of human development in the Harvard Graduate School of Education. His book *Frames of Mind: The Theory of Multiple Intelligences* (Basic Books, 1983), which won the Best Book Award from the American Psychological Association in 1984, has been extremely influential in the ongoing debate about the nature of intelligence. He is also the author of *Multiple Intelligences: The Theory in Practice* (Basic Books, 1993), which is an updated summary of his theory of multiple intelligences.

In the selection that follows, which is from *Multiple Intelligences*, Gardner presents a synthesis of his views on the nature of intelligence and how his pluralistic view of the concept runs counter to the standard, quantifiable, universalistic conception of intelligence developed in the early decades of the twentieth century. He discusses traditional conceptions of the nature of intelligence in terms of a corresponding view of schoolings that he refers to as the "uniform view." In uniform schools, he says, there is a common core curriculum and a set knowledge base that every student is expected to learn. He goes on to explain how his pluralistic view of the nature of intelligence requires a more diversified and personalized conception of how students should experience schooling. He identifies an alternative vision of how teachers should teach: they should individualize their interactions with students to focus on each student's unique strengths and learning styles. In essence, Gardner argues that instruction should be customized to take full advantage of a student's strengths and to optimize his or her academic development. This model of schooling is based on the assumptions that not all persons have the same interests or abilities and that no one person can learn everything there is to learn. He goes on to propose a new set of roles for educators that will relate well to his proposed model of schooling.

Key Concept: a new concept of intelligence

Allow me to transport all of us to the Paris of 1900—La Belle Epoque—when the city fathers of Paris approached a psychologist named Alfred Binet with an unusual request: Could he devise some kind of a measure that would predict which youngsters would succeed and which would fail in the primary grades of Paris schools? As everybody knows, Binet succeeded. In short order, his discovery came to be called the "intelligence test"; his measure, the "IQ." Like other Parisian fashions, the IQ soon made its way to the United States, where it enjoyed a modest success until World War I. Then, it was used to test over one million American recruits, and it had truly arrived. From that day on, the IQ test has looked like psychology's biggest success—a genuinely useful scientific tool.

What is the vision that led to the excitement about IQ? At least in the West, people had always relied on intuitive assessments of how smart other people were. Now intelligence seemed to be quantifiable. You could measure someone's actual or potential height, and now, if seemed, you could also measure someone's actual or potential intelligence. We had one dimension of mental ability along which we could array everyone.

The search for the perfect measure of intelligence has proceeded apace. Here, for example, are some quotations from an ad for a widely used test:

> Need an individual test which quickly provides a stable and reliable estimate of intelligence in four or five minutes per form? Has three forms? Does not depend on verbal production or subjective scoring? Can be used with the severely physically handicapped (even paralyzed) if they can signal yes or no? Handles two-year-olds and superior adults with the same short series of items and the same format? Only $16.00 complete.

Now, that's quite a claim. The American psychologist Arthur Jensen suggests that we could look at reaction time to assess intelligence: a set of lights go on; how quickly can the subject react? The British psychologist Hans Eysenck suggests that investigators of intelligence should look directly at brain waves.

There are also, of course, more sophisticated versions of the IQ test. One of them is called the Scholastic Aptitude Test (SAT). It purports to be a similar kind of measure, and if you add up a person's verbal and math scores, as is often done, you can rate him or her along a single intellectual dimension. Programs for the gifted, for example, often use that kind of measure; if your IQ is in excess of 130, you're admitted to the program.

I want to suggest that along with this one-dimensional view of how to assess people's minds comes a corresponding view of school, which I will call the "uniform view." In the uniform school, there is a core curriculum, a set of facts that everybody should know, and very few electives. The better students, perhaps those with higher IQs, are allowed to take courses that call upon critical reading, calculation, and thinking skills. In the "uniform school," there are regular assessments, using paper and pencil instruments, of the IQ or SAT variety. They yield reliable rankings of people; the best and the brightest get into the better colleges, and perhaps—but only perhaps—they will also get better rankings in life. There is no question but that this approach works well for certain people—schools such as Harvard are eloquent testimony to that. Since this measurement and selection system is clearly meritocratic in certain respects, it has something to recommend it.

But there is an alternative vision that I would like to present—one based on a radically different view of the mind, and one that yields a very different view of school. It is a pluralistic view of mind, recognizing many different and discrete facets of cognition, acknowledging that people have different cognitive strengths and contrasting cognitive styles. I would also like to introduce the concept of an individual-centered school that takes this multifaceted view of intelligence seriously. This model for a school is based in part on findings from sciences that did not even exist in Binet's time: cognitive science (the study of the mind), and neuroscience (the study of the brain). One such approach I have called my "theory of multiple intelligences." Let me tell you something about its sources, its claims, and its educational implications for a possible school of the future.

Dissatisfaction with the concept of IQ and with unitary views of intelligence is fairly widespread—one thinks, for instance, of the work of L. L. Thurstone, J. P. Guilford, and other critics. From my point of view, however, these criticisms do not suffice. The whole concept has to be challenged; in fact, it has to be replaced.

I believe that we should get away altogether from tests and correlations among tests, and look instead at more naturalistic sources of information about how peoples around the world develop skills important to their way of life. Think, for example, of sailors in the South Seas, who find their way around hundreds, or even thousands, of islands by looking at the constellations of stars in the sky, feeling the way a boat passes over the water, and noticing a few scattered landmarks. A word for intelligence in a society of these sailors would probably refer to that kind of navigational ability. Think of surgeons and engineers, hunters and fishermen, dancers and choreographers, athletes and athletic coaches, tribal chiefs and sorcerers. All of these different roles need to be taken into account if we accept the way I define intelligence—that is, as the ability to solve problems, or to fashion products, that are valued in one or more cultural or community settings. For the moment I am saying nothing about whether there is one dimension, or more than one dimension, of intelligence; nothing about whether intelligence is inborn or developed. Instead I emphasize the ability to solve problems and to fashion products. In my work I seek the building blocks of the intelligences used by the aforementioned sailors and surgeons and sorcerers.

The science in this enterprise, to the extent that it exists, involves trying to discover the *right* description of the intelligences. What is an intelligence? To try to answer this question, I have, with my colleagues, surveyed a wide set of sources which, to my knowledge, have never been considered together before. One source is what we already know concerning the development of different kinds of skills in normal children. Another source, and a very important one, is information on the ways that these abilities break down under conditions of brain damage. When one suffers a stroke or some other kind of brain damage, various abilities can be destroyed, or spared, in isolation from other abilities. This research with brain-damaged patients yields a very powerful kind of evidence, because it seems to reflect the way the nervous system has evolved over the millennia to yield certain discrete kinds of intelligence.

My research group looks at other special populations as well: prodigies, idiot savants, autistic children, children with learning disabilities, all of whom exhibit very jagged cognitive profiles—profiles that are extremely difficult to explain in terms of a unitary view of intelligence. We examine cognition in diverse animal species and in dramatically different cultures. Finally, we consider two kinds of psychological evidence: correlations among psychological tests of the sort yielded by a careful statistical analysis of a test battery; and the results of efforts of skill training. When you train a person in skill A, for example, does that training transfer to skill B? So, for example, does training in mathematics enhance one's musical abilities, or vice versa?

Obviously, through looking at all these sources—information on development, on breakdowns, on special populations, and the like—we end up with a cornucopia of information. Optimally, we would perform a statistical factor analysis, feeding all the data into a computer and noting the kinds of factors or intelligences that are extracted. Alas, the kind of material with which I was working didn't exist in a form that is susceptible to computation, and so we had to perform a more subjective factor analysis. In truth, we simply studied the results as best we could, and tried to organize them in a way that made sense to us, and hopefully, to critical readers as well. My resulting list of seven intelligences is a preliminary attempt to organize this mass of information.

I want now to mention briefly the seven intelligences we have located, and to cite one or two examples of each intelligence. Linguistic intelligence is the kind of ability exhibited in its fullest form, perhaps, by poets. Logical-mathematical intelligence, as the name implies, is logical and mathematical ability, as well as scientific ability. Jean Piaget, the great developmental psychologist, thought he was studying *all* intelligence, but I believe he was studying the development of logical-mathematical intelligence. Although I name the linguistic and logical-mathematical intelligences first, it is not because I think they are the most important—in fact, I am convinced that all seven of the intelligences have equal claim to priority. In our society, however, we have put linguistic and logical-mathematical intelligences, figuratively speaking, on a pedestal. Much of our testing is based on this high valuation of verbal and mathematical skills. If you do well in language and logic, you should do well in IQ tests and SATs, and you may well get into a prestigious college, but whether you do well once you leave is probably going to depend as much on the extent to which you possess and use the other intelligences, and it is to those that I want to give equal attention.

Spatial intelligence is the ability to form a mental model of a spatial world and to be able to maneuver and operate using that model. Sailors, engineers, surgeons, sculptors, and painters, to name just a few examples, all have highly developed spatial intelligence. Musical intelligence is the fourth category of ability we have identified: Leonard Bernstein had lots of it; Mozart, presumably, had even more. Bodily-kinesthetic intelligence is the ability to solve problems or to fashion products using one's whole body, or parts of the body. Dancers, athletes, surgeons, and craftspeople all exhibit highly developed bodily-kinesthetic intelligence.

Finally, I propose two forms of personal intelligence—not well understood, elusive to study, but immensely important. Interpersonal intelligence is the ability to understand other people: what motivates them, how they work, how to work cooperatively with them. Successful salespeople, politicians, teachers, clinicians, and religious leaders are all likely to be individuals with high degrees of interpersonal intelligence. Intrapersonal intelligence, a seventh kind of intelligence, is a correlative ability, turned inward. It is a capacity to form an accurate, veridical model of oneself and to be able to use that model to operate effectively in life.

These, then, are the seven intelligences that we have uncovered and described in our research. This is a preliminary list, as I have said; obviously, each form of intelligence can be subdivided, or the list can be rearranged. The real point here is to make the case for the plurality of intellect. Also, we believe that individuals may differ in the particular intelligence profiles with which they are born, and that certainly they differ in the profiles they end up with. I think of the intelligences as raw, biological potentials, which can be seen in pure form only in individuals who are, in the technical sense, freaks. In almost everybody else the intelligences work together to solve problems, to yield various kinds of cultural endstates—vocations, avocations, and the like.

This is my theory of multiple intelligence in capsule form. In my view, the purpose of school should be to develop intelligences and to help people reach vocational and avocational goals that are appropriate to their particular spectrum of intelligences. People who are helped to do so, I believe, feel more engaged and competent, and therefore more inclined to serve the society in a constructive way.

These thoughts, and the critique of a universalistic view of mind with which I began, lead to the notion of an individual-centered school, one geared to optimal understanding and development of each student's cognitive profile. This vision stands in direct contrast to that of the uniform school that I described earlier.

The design of my ideal school of the future is based upon two assumptions. The first is that not all people have the same interests and abilities; not all of us learn in the same way. (And we now have the tools to begin to address these individual differences in school.) The second assumption is one that hurts: it is the assumption that nowadays no one person can learn everything there is to learn. We would all like, as Renaissance men and women, to know everything, or at least to believe in the potential of knowing everything, but that ideal clearly is not possible anymore. Choice is therefore inevitable, and one of the things that I want to argue is that the choices that we make for ourselves, and for the people who are under our charge, might as well be informed choices.

An individual-centered school would be rich in assessment of individual abilities and proclivities. It would seek to match individuals not only to curricular areas, but also to particular ways of teaching those subjects. And after the first few grades, the school would also seek to match individuals with the various kinds of life and work options that are available in their culture.

I want to propose a new set of roles for educators that might make this vision a reality. First of all, we might have what I will call "assessment specialists." The job of these people would be to try to understand as sensitively and comprehensively as possible the abilities and interests of the students in a school. It would be very important, however, that the assessment specialists use "intelligence-fair" instruments. We want to be able to look specifically and directly at spatial abilities, at personal abilities, and the like, and not through the usual lenses of the linguistic and logical-mathematical intelligences. Up until now nearly all assessment has depended indirectly on measurement of those abilities; if students are not strong in those two areas, their abilities in other areas may be obscured. Once we begin to try to assess other kinds of intelligences directly, I am confident that particular students will reveal strengths in quite different areas, and the notion of general brightness will disappear or become greatly attenuated.

In addition to the assessment specialist, the school of the future might have the "student-curriculum broker." It would be his or her job to help match students' profiles, goals, and interests to particular curricula and to particular styles of learning. Incidentally, I think that the new interactive technologies offer considerable promise in this area: it will probably be much easier in the future for "brokers" to match individual students to ways of learning that prove comfortable for them.

There should also be, I think, a "school-community broker," who would match students to learning opportunities in the wider community. It would be this person's job to find situations in the community, particularly options not available in the school, for children who exhibit unusual cognitive profiles. I have in mind apprenticeships, mentorships, internships in organizations, "big brothers," "big sisters"—individuals and organizations with whom these students might work to secure a feeling for different kinds of vocational and avocational roles in the society. I am not worried about those occasional youngsters who are good in everything. They're going to do just fine. I'm concerned about those who don't shine in the standardized tests, and who, therefore, tend to be written off as not having gifts of any kind. It seems to me that the school-community broker could spot these youngsters and find placements in the community that provide chances for them to shine.

There is ample room in this vision for teachers, as well, and also for master teachers. In my view, teachers would be freed to do what they are supposed to do, which is to teach their subject matter, in their preferred style of teaching. The job of master teacher would be very demanding. It would involve, first of all, supervising the novice teachers and guiding them; but the master teacher would also seek to ensure that the complex student-assessment-curriculum-community equation is balanced appropriately. If the equation is seriously imbalanced, master teachers would intervene and suggest ways to make things better.

Clearly, what I am describing is a tall order; it might even be called utopian. And there is a major risk to this program, of which I am well aware. That is the risk of premature billeting—of saying, "Well, Johnny is four, he seems to be musical, so we are going to send him to Juilliard and drop everything else." There is, however, nothing inherent in the approach that I have described that demands this early overdetermination—quite the contrary. It seems to me that early identification of strengths can be very helpful in indicating what kinds of experiences children might profit from; but early identification of weaknesses can be equally important. If a weakness is identified early, there is a chance to attend to it before it is too late, and to come up with alternative ways of teaching or of covering an important skill area.

We now have the technological and the human resources to implement such an individual-centered school. Achieving it is a question of will, including the will to withstand the current enormous pressures toward uniformity and unidimensional assessments. There are strong pressures now, which you read about every day in the newspapers, to compare students, to compare teachers, states, even entire countries, using one dimension or criterion, a kind of a crypto-IQ assessment. Clearly, everything I have described today stands in direct opposition to that particular view of the world. Indeed that is my intent—to provide a ringing indictment of such one-track thinking.

I believe that in our society we suffer from three biases, which I have nicknamed "Westist," "Testist," and "Bestist." "Westist" involves putting certain Western cultural values, which date back to Socrates, on a pedestal. Logical thinking, for example, is important; rationality is important; but they are not the only virtues. "Testist" suggests a bias towards focusing upon those human abilities or approaches that are readily testable. If it can't be tested, it sometimes seems, it is not worth paying attention to. My feeling is that assessment can be much broader, much more humane than it is now, and that psychologists should spend less time ranking people and more time trying to help them.

"Bestist" is a not very veiled reference to a book by David Halberstam called *The best and the brightest.* Halberstam referred ironically to figures such as Harvard faculty members who were brought to Washington to help President John F. Kennedy and in the process launched the Vietnam War. I think that any belief that all the answers to a given problem lie in one certain approach, such as logical-mathematical thinking, can be very dangerous. Current views of intellect need to be leavened with other more comprehensive points of view.

It is of the utmost importance that we recognize and nurture all of the varied human intelligences, and all of the combinations of intelligences. We are all so different largely because we all have different combinations of intelligences. If we recognize this, I think we will have at least a better chance of dealing appropriately with the many problems that we face in the world. If we can mobilize the spectrum of human abilities, not only will people feel better about themselves and more competent; it is even possible that they will also feel more engaged and better able to join the rest of the world community in working for the broader good. Perhaps if we can mobilize the full range of human intelligences and ally them to an ethical sense, we can help to increase the likelihood of our survival on this planet, and perhaps even contribute to our thriving.

14.2 JONATHAN KOZOL

Amazing Grace

The following selection is from *Amazing Grace: The Lives of Children and the Conscience of a Nation* (Crown Publishers, 1995). In that book, Jonathan Kozol powerfully portrays the spirit of young life in the South Bronx in New York City. He paints a portrait of children who live amidst poverty and social chaos yet cling to hope and love. Kozol lived with the children of the impoverished South Bronx for more than a year, and he dedicates *Amazing Grace* to them. Although wounded by the social chaos and poverty amidst which they live, Kozol tells us that the children are not hardened; they are full of hope and love and are open to welcome life. Kozol interviews many children in *Amazing Grace*, along with some of their teachers, psychologists, and clergy. His interviews with the children reveal their hope for the future in the midst of social despair. Kozol asks important questions: Why doesn't America care about the children of the poor? Why are they neglected? Don't they have the right to the same educational opportunities as the children of wealthy suburbs? Why do we shun them? How can the children of the South Bronx still pray? What gives them hope? Kozol makes a powerful appeal to the conscience of the American people. He describes how AIDS has reached almost pandemic proportions in the South Bronx, and he reports that many of the children with whom he talked have lost loved ones to this dread scourge on the neighborhood.

Kozol offers a particularly pertinent observation regarding the social isolation and neglect of the children of the urban poor: "Whatever good things may happen for the children of another generation are, in any case, of little solace to those who are children now and will not have their childhood to live a second time in the next century." He goes on to say that this is particularly true for those children who are losing their loved ones to AIDS.

Key Concept: America's unwanted children

The Number 6 train from Manhattan to the South Bronx makes nine stops in the 18-minute ride between East 59th Street and Brook Avenue. When you enter the train, you are in the seventh richest congressional district in the nation. When you leave, you are in the poorest.

The 600,000 people who live here and the 450,000 people who live in Washington Heights and Harlem, which are separated from the South Bronx by a narrow river, make up one of the largest racially segregated concentrations of poor people in our nation.

Brook Avenue, which is the tenth stop on the local, lies in the center of Mott Haven, whose 48,000 people are the poorest in the South Bronx. Two thirds are Hispanic, one third black. Thirty-five percent are children. In 1991, the median household income of the area, according to the *New York Times,* was $7,600.

St. Ann's Church, on St. Ann's Avenue, is three blocks from the subway station. The children who come to this small Episcopal church for food and comfort and to play, and the mothers and fathers who come here for prayer, are said to be the poorest people in New York. "More than 95 percent are poor," the pastor says—"the poorest of the poor, poor by any standard I can think of."

At the elementary school that serves the neighborhood across the avenue, only seven of 800 children do not qualify for free school lunches. "Five of those seven," says the principal, "get reduced-price lunches, because they are classified as only 'poor,' not 'destitute.'"

In some cities, the public reputation of a ghetto neighborhood bears little connection to the world that you discover when you walk the streets with children and listen to their words. In Mott Haven, this is not the case. By and large, the words of the children in the streets and schools and houses that surround St. Ann's more than justify the grimness in the words of journalists who have described the area.

Crack-cocaine addiction and the intravenous use of heroin, which children I have met here call "the needle drug," are woven into the texture of existence in Mott Haven. Nearly 4,000 heroin injectors, many of whom are HIV-infected, live here. Virtually every child at St. Ann's knows someone, a relative or neighbor, who has died of AIDS, and most children here know many others who are dying now of the disease. One quarter of the women of Mott Haven who are tested in obstetric wards are positive for HIV. Rates of pediatric AIDS, therefore, are high.

Depression is common among children in Mott Haven. Many cry a great deal but cannot explain exactly why.

Fear and anxiety are common. Many cannot sleep.

Asthma is the most common illness among children here. Many have to struggle to take in a good deep breath. Some mothers keep oxygen tanks, which children describe as "breathing machines," next to their children's beds.

The houses in which these children live, two thirds of which are owned by the City of New York, are often as squalid as the houses of the poorest children I have visited in rural Mississippi, but there is none of the greenness and the healing sweetness of the Mississippi countryside outside their windows, which are often barred and bolted as protection against thieves.

Some of these houses are freezing in the winter. In dangerously cold weather, the city sometimes distributes electric blankets and space heaters to its tenants. In emergency conditions, if space heaters can't be used, because substandard wiring is overloaded, the city's practice is to pass out sleeping bags.

"You just cover up . . . and hope you wake up the next morning," says a father of four children, one of them an infant one month old, as they prepare to climb into their sleeping bags in hats and coats on a December night.

In humid summer weather, roaches crawl on virtually every surface of the houses in which many of the children live. Rats emerge from holes in bedroom walls, terrorizing infants in their cribs. In the streets outside, the restlessness and anger that are present in all seasons frequently intensify under the stress of heat.

In speaking of rates of homicide in New York City neighborhoods, the *Times* refers to the streets around St. Ann's as "the deadliest blocks" in "the deadliest precinct" of the city. If there is a deadlier place in the United States, I don't know where it is.

In 1991, 84 people, more than half of whom were 21 or younger, were murdered in the precinct. A year later, ten people were shot dead on a street called Beekman Avenue, where many of the children I have come to know reside. On Valentine's Day of 1993, three more children and three adults were shot dead on the living room floor of an apartment six blocks from the run-down park that serves the area.

In early July of 1993, shortly before the first time that I visited the neighborhood, three more people were shot in 30 minutes in three unrelated murders in the South Bronx, one of them only a block from St. Ann's Avenue. A week later, a mother was murdered and her baby wounded by a bullet in the stomach while they were standing on a South Bronx corner. Three weeks after that, a minister and elderly parishioner were shot outside the front door of their church, while another South Bronx resident was discovered in his bathtub with his head cut off. In subsequent days, a man was shot in both his eyes and a ten-year-old was critically wounded in the brain.

What is it like for children to grow up here? What do they think the world has done to them? Do they believe that they are being shunned or hidden by society? If so, do they think that they deserve this? What is it that enables some of them to pray? When they pray, what do they say to God? . . .

No matter how final a visit seems, I keep on going back to the same places—Beekman Avenue, and St. Ann's Avenue, and Cypress, and East Tremont, and the area around the Hunts Point Market, then to Featherbed Lane and Shakespeare Avenue, and back to St. Ann's Church. Thinking often of a teacher I had met some months before at P.S. 65, who had wondered whether the kinds of questions I was asking could be answered by a teacher and whether they were "better asked to priests or theologians," I go back again and again to talk with ministers and priests in almost every neighborhood, to Gregory Groover in Hunts Point, to the priest of St. Luke's Church, near P.S. 65, in which Bernardo Rodriguez had been baptized and in which a memorial mass was held upon his death, and to the ministers of several of the storefront churches on Brook Avenue. I also talk with a number of the nuns from several different Catholic orders who work at the clinics and food pantries of the area.

Each time, the conversation starts with something quite specific—AIDS or education, welfare rules or housing or lead poison or the flight of jobs—but ends with talk of personal pain, anxiety about the future of the children, the search for faith in almost anyone or anything that offers strength, sometimes with talk of God.

The specifics of each issue—dump-sites, asthma, or waste burners, or whatever else—soon begin to seem almost beside the point. The search for explanations of the sadness heard in many of the voices of the people I have met is not answered by the factual questions one might ask about "environment" or "health care" or "the public schools." The questions that need asking seem to go beyond these concrete matters. One wants instead to know how certain people hold up under terrible ordeal, how many more do not, how human beings devalue other people's lives, how numbness and destructiveness are universalized, how human pity is at length extinguished and the shunning of the vulnerable can come in time to be perceived as natural behavior. "The poor frighten me," a rich lady told St. Vincent. "The poor are frightening," he answered, "as frightening as God's justice." What do we do to those who frighten us? Do we put them off, as far away as possible, and hope, as one of the students said to me during the previous summer, that they'll either die or disappear? How does a nation deal with those whom it has cursed?

One day in the spring, when Reverend Overall is driving with me from Manhattan to the Bronx, she stops her car at 96th Street, then drives one block more to 97th Street, in order to enable me to see the cutoff point between the races in this section of New York.

The sharpness of the demarcation line, which I have never seen before at the street level, is more dramatic and extreme than I anticipated. To the south, along Park Avenue, impressive buildings stand on both sides of the street, pedestrian islands with well-tended grass and flower plantings in the center. In the other direction, to the north, a railroad line, submerged beneath Park Avenue up to this point, appears from under 97th Street and splits the avenue in two. The trains, from this point on, run along the street for several blocks until Park Avenue dips slightly and the tracks are elevated on a large stone viaduct that shadows children playing in the sun of afternoon.

The significance of 96th Street in New York is inescapable and comes up time and again in conversations and in the newspapers. Luxury grocers advertise their willingness to make deliveries only south of 96th Street, and even liberal papers such as the *Observer* print these ads. McDonald's announces "home delivery" from 40 of its outlets in New York, but none of them north of this point on the East Side....

"The next ten years will see a new South Bronx," said South Bronx congressman Herman Badillo in 1972, in reference to... signs of progress.

Visitors to Lincoln Hospital or Beekman Avenue today may have an opportunity to judge to what degree the optimism of those years was justified. The new public schools of the South Bronx, with stilts or without stilts, have proven, with a few remarkable exceptions, to be sad repositories for the disappointed dreams of children of dark skin. The newly built Lincoln Hospital has proven to be another terrifying and chaotic monument to medical apartheid. The wiring in many of those "sparkling new apartment houses" along Beekman Avenue has long since been eaten through by rats. The new plumbing of 22 years ago sprays scalding steam at mothers and their infants. . . .

"If there is one thing more destructive and demoralizing to poor people than to live in desolation," Reverend Overall observes, "it is to have these false hopes reawakened at these routine intervals. Do that to me enough times and I'll never hope again. It's like shooting someone up with drugs. This is how you turn poor people into zombies."

There is another, entirely different issue that is being raised about these promises of reconstruction and renewal. Even if the efforts under way today should prove, unlike those of the past, to be enduring, and even if they ever reach the St. Ann's neighborhood, many of the poorest residents believe that they are not the people who will benefit. They are convinced that those who benefit will be "the least poor of the poor," for whom the city or a nonprofit corporation may provide unusual security and private sanitation, so that the immediate environs may become an island of protected, if ephemeral, wholesomeness within a sea of suffering and sickness. And, if the South Bronx as a whole should ever become a truly pleasant place to live, many here feel certain that the very poor will simply be pushed off into another squalid quarter somewhere else, perhaps one of the deeply troubled, segregated suburbs that are now proliferating on all sides of New York City.

No one in New York, in any case, expects the racial isolation of these neighborhoods to lessen in the years ahead. A demographic forecast by the city's planning agency predicts that the population of the Bronx—both North and South—half of which was white in 1970, and nearly a quarter of which was white in 1990, will be entirely black and Hispanic by the early years of the next century, outside of a handful of de facto segregated enclaves of white people and a few essentially detached communities like parts of Riverdale. By that time, the Bronx and Harlem and Washington Heights will make up a vast and virtually uninterrupted ghetto with a population close to that of Houston, Texas, which is America's fourth-largest city.

Despite these demographic probabilities, the Bronx borough president, Fernando Ferrer, with whom I've talked at length about the health and education problems of the families here, manages to be contagiously enthusiastic. He is a likable person and seems genuinely dedicated to the people whom he represents; it is, of course, his job to be enthusiastic. I have met politicians equally dedicated and enthusiastic in Detroit and East St. Louis, but their energy and dedication could not bring back life-sustaining jobs or first-class schools or anything like modern health care to a population viewed as economically and socially superfluous; nor, of course, could they reverse the flight of most white people from those cities. There are neighborhoods with handsome houses in Detroit and East St. Louis too. Both these cities have their periodic episodes of neighborhood renewal also.

Perhaps something is truly different this time in the Bronx. Perhaps the skepticism of the people I have talked with in Mott Haven is misplaced. Perhaps the predictions of the city's planning agency will prove to be in error too. Perhaps the children of the children who are growing up today in the South Bronx will someday live in attractive houses on the same nice streets as middle-class and working-class homeowners of all races. It is tempting to imagine this, but it is only honest to report that no one I have met here holds such expectations.

Whatever good things may happen for the children of another generation are, in any case, of little solace to those who are children now and will not have their childhood to live a second time in the next century. This is particularly the case for those, especially the very young, who are about to lose, or have already lost, their mothers or their fathers to the epidemic that now stalks the neighborhood.

The rapid emergence in New York of thousands of black and Hispanic children of low income who have lost their parents to the plague of AIDS is, says the director of an organization called the Orphans Project, a catastrophe that has no real analogy within our nation in this century. "Only the great influenza pandemic of 1918... offers a partial analogy from diseases of the twentieth century.... We are only at the beginning of this phenomenon. We do not yet know its duration."

Already in 1993, when I began to visit in the South Bronx, some 10,000 children in New York had lost their mothers to the epidemic. As many as 2,000 of these children were believed to live in the Mott Haven area and in three or four adjacent sections of the Bronx. The Orphans Project estimated that, between then and the year 2000, HIV-infected mothers in New York would "give birth to between 32,000 and 38,000 HIV-infected babies" and more than twice as many babies who would not have been infected. If these projections prove to be correct, and if the city continues with its present policy of channeling its sickest and most troubled families, often addicted and quite frequently infected, into housing in this area, it is likely that entire blocks will soon be home to mourning orphans, many of whom will follow their own parents to an early grave.

"The viral path" of AIDS, says *Newsday*, "has crept through the family tree" in many South Bronx neighborhoods, "breaking branch after branch." By the spring of 1993, 1,381 women in the area and 3,428 men had been diagnosed. But thousands of people in the South Bronx "have no personal physician.... Infected women still go undiagnosed, their lifespans significantly reduced" because they get no early treatment.

A specialist in pediatric AIDS says he's "seeing things medically that I've never seen before and never thought I would ever see." Speaking of people with "rampant TB and three other types of infection at the same time" waiting at hospitals as long as three days for a bed, he says, "It's like the Middle Ages."

"Right now at Bronx-Lebanon," says Mrs. Washington's doctor, "a quarter of all our *general* admissions—not just on obstetric wards—are known to be positive for HIV." The area served by the hospital, according to a study of blood samples tested at the hospital, "apparently has one of the highest AIDS rates in the world."

According to the city's health officials, 91 percent of children in New York who are born with AIDS are black or Hispanic, as are 84 percent of women who have AIDS. So the racial demographics of Mott Haven, as well as the prevalence of intravenous drug use in the area and an apparent increase in the rate of HIV infection among adolescents here, tend to justify the somber language used by doctors in Mott Haven as they look into the future.

At a walk-in center in Mott Haven, run by the Dominican Sisters, which offers medical help and other services to families with AIDS, a social worker who does "anticipatory grieving" with the children of AIDS patients speaks of a 15-year-old girl who is infected "but is afraid to tell her mother, because her mother is already dying." The girl's ten-year-old sister has AIDS also, says the social worker, "presumably because she was infected perinatally," in which case it is remarkable that she has lived this long. But, she says, "with a ten-year-old you can't be sure exactly *how* she was infected."

The incubation period for development of AIDS in infants is, she tells me, generally shorter than in adults—an average of three years. Most subsequently die in 18 months. Only about five percent live to be 12 years old.

In another family in the neighborhood, she says, the father died two years ago and the mother is about to die. The four soon-to-be-orphaned children are being cared for by their 75-year-old grandmother. "One of the children, a nine-year-old, is sick with full-blown AIDS. Another child, seven years old, is less sick but he's been getting IV blood infusions. The six-year-old may be okay. But it's the 13-year-old girl, who *isn't* sick, who's causing the most worries. She's staying out all night, defying her grandmother. She started to do this at 11, when her father died. Recently, this girl had an abortion."

"Thirteen years old?"

"Yes," she replies. "Thirteen years old. You can imagine the risks that child must be taking. . . ."

All of the families she's described, she tells me, live in approximately a 12-block radius of St. Ann's Church, and, she adds, "we're barely scratching the surface of the families in the neighborhood who need our help."

How do children living in this medieval landscape face the losses that they must expect? How do they confront the process of bereavement? . . .

Amazing grace! How sweet the sound
That saved a wretch like me.
I once was lost and now am found
Was blind but now I see.

. . . [T]he organ becomes louder and the congregation rises and the verse that Reverend Groover spoke is turned to music and the whole room sings. They end with the hopeful words of the fourth verse that I have read now several times at home. But reading it in Massachusetts and hearing it sung by people in Hunts Point are not the same.

When the service ends, people turn to those around them and shake hands and say, "God bless you." The woman beside me says, "God bless you" to her baby and then turns and says the same to me, but I am afraid to say it in return.

Reverend Groover invites me to have lunch upstairs with members of the church. After lunch, a couple who grew up here but now live out in the suburbs offer me a ride back to Mott Haven. I sit for the rest of the afternoon in the garden of St. Ann's and think for a long time of the sermon I have heard.

The preacher told the mothers of the church to tell their sons in prison, "I am a woman! One day the God I see, you shall see also!" She told the mothers, "I want you to know there is a song for *you*.... Your children may be drowning in despair today but they will rise in glory!"

I write this question on the back of the church program: "Then where is He? What is He waiting for? Come on, Jehovah! Let's get moving. Where's your sword?"

As soon as I write this down, I feel embarrassed by these thoughts. The words of the gospel songs I heard in church, like a stern reprimand, keep going through my mind.

There are children in the garden. Their playfulness is like a reprimand as well. The sweetness of the hour and the voices of the children soon dispel the feeling of irreverence I had fallen into. Their voices are like summer songs, not songs of pain. Several boys are walking single-file on the top rung of a wooden structure, daring one another to go all the way to a small platform at the end. Precariously balanced, they shout challenges to one another. How long will they be content to stay within this garden?

When it gets dark, I fish in my pocket for two quarters and go out on St. Ann's Avenue and buy an icie and walk up to Beekman Avenue, ... but see no children there and head off finally to Brook Avenue, then to the train and the hotel, then to the Delta terminal, and then the plane. As the plane takes off, I try to get a look at Rikers Island, but I'm on the wrong side of the plane and it climbs fast into the clouds.

I look at my notes as the plane crosses Connecticut. I'm looking forward to getting home and sitting at my desk and trying to make sense of everything I've learned. But I don't really think I will make sense of anything and I don't expect that I'll be able to construct a little list of "answers" and "solutions," as my editor would like. I have done this many times before; so have dozens of other writers; so have hundreds of committees and foundations and commissions. The time for lists like that now seems long past.

Will the people Reverend Groover called "the principalities and powers" look into their hearts one day in church or synagogue and feel the grace of God and, as he put it, "be transformed"? Will they become ashamed of what they've done, or what they have accepted? Will they decide they do not need to quarantine the outcasts of their ingenuity and will they then use all their wisdom and their skills to build a new society and new economy in which no human being will be superfluous? I wish I could believe that, but I don't think it is likely. I think it is more likely that they'll write more stories about "Hope Within the Ashes" and then pile on more ashes and then change the subject to the opening of the ballet or a review of a new restaurant. And the children of disappointment will keep dying.

I think that Mrs. Washington is right to view the years before us with foreboding. I have never lived through a time as cold as this in the United States. Many men and women in the Bronx believe that it is going to get worse. I don't know what can change this.

ACKNOWLEDGMENTS

1.1 From E. D. Hirsch, Jr., *Cultural Literacy: What Every American Needs to Know* (Houghton Mifflin, 1987). Copyright © 1987 by Houghton Mifflin Company. Reprinted by permission. All rights reserved. Notes omitted.

1.2 From Diane Ravitch, *The Troubled Crusade: American Education, 1945–1980* (Basic Books, 1983). Copyright © 1983 by Diane Ravitch. Reprinted by permission of Basic Books, a division of HarperCollins Publishers, Inc. Notes omitted.

1.3 From Mortimer Adler, "The Paideia Proposal: Rediscovering the Essence of Education," *The American School Board Journal* (July 1982). Copyright © 1982 by The National School Boards Association. Reprinted by permission. All rights reserved.

2.1 From John Dewey, *Democracy and Education: An Introduction to the Philosophy of Education* (Macmillan, 1916). Notes omitted.

2.2 From William Heard Kilpatrick, "The Project Method," *Teachers College Record*, vol. 19, no. 4 (September 1918).

3.1 From Henry A. Giroux, "Culture, Power and Transformation in the Work of Paulo Freire: Toward a Politics of Education," in Henry A. Giroux, *Teachers as Intellectuals: Toward a Critical Pedagogy of Learning* (Bergin & Garvey, 1988). Copyright © 1988 by Bergin & Garvey Publishers, Inc. Reprinted by permission of Greenwood Publishing Group, Inc., Westport, CT.

3.2 From Michael W. Apple, *Ideology and Curriculum* (Routledge & Kegan Paul, 1979). Copyright © 1979 by Routledge & Kegan Paul. Reprinted by permission.

3.3 From Paulo Freire, *Pedagogy of the Oppressed*, trans. Myra Bergman Ramos (Seabury Press, 1970). Copyright © 1970 by Paulo Freire. Reprinted by permission.

3.4 From Ivan Illich, *Deschooling Society* (Harper & Row, 1971), pp. 10–12, 25–33. Copyright © 1971 by Ivan Illich and Valentina Borremans. Reprinted by permission.

4.1 From Maria Montessori, *The Montessori Method* (Robert Bentley, 1965). Copyright © 1965 by Robert Bentley, Inc. Reprinted by permission.

4.2 From Katherine Camp Mayhew and Anna Camp Edwards, *The Dewey School: The Laboratory School of the University of Chicago, 1896–1903* (D. Appleton-Century, 1936). Notes omitted.

4.3 From Harold Rugg and Ann Shumaker, *The Child-Centered School: An Appraisal of the New Education* (World Book, 1928). Copyright © 1928 by Harcourt Brace & Company. Reprinted by permission. Some notes omitted.

5.1 From Hilda Taba, *Curriculum Development: Theory and Practice* (Harcourt, Brace & World, 1962), under the general editorship of Willard B. Spalding. Copyright © 1962 by Harcourt Brace & Company. Copyright renewed 1990 by Margaret A. Spalding. Reprinted by permission of the publisher. Notes and references omitted.

5.2 From Theodore R. Sizer, *Horace's Hope: What Works for the American High School* (Houghton Mifflin, 1996). Copyright © 1996 by Theodore R. Sizer. Reprinted by permission of Houghton Mifflin Company. All rights reserved. Notes omitted.

6.1 From Peter McLaren, "Multiculturalism and the Postmodern Critique: Toward a Pedagogy of Resistance and Transformation," in Henry A. Giroux and Peter McLaren, eds., *Between Borders: Pedagogy and the Politics of Cultural Studies* (Routledge, 1994). Copyright © 1994 by Routledge. Reprinted by permission.

6.2 From E. D. Hirsch, Jr., *The Schools We Need and Why We Don't Have Them* (Doubleday, 1996). Copyright © 1996 by E. D. Hirsch, Jr. Reprinted by permission of

Doubleday, a division of Bantam Doubleday Dell Publishing Group, Inc. All rights reserved. Notes omitted.

7.1 From Diane Ravitch, *The Troubled Crusade: American Education, 1945–1980* (Basic Books, 1983). Copyright © 1983 by Diane Ravitch. Reprinted by permission of Basic Books, a division of HarperCollins Publishers, Inc. Notes omitted.

7.2 From Booker T. Washington during the Atlanta Exposition, Atlanta, Georgia, September 18, 1895.

7.3 From W. E. B. Du Bois, *The Souls of Black Folk* (Vintage Books, 1990).

7.4 From James Baldwin, "A Talk to Teachers," *Saturday Review* (December 21, 1963). Copyright © 1963 by S. R. Publications, Ltd. Reprinted by permission.

7.5 From Meyer Weinberg, *A Chance to Learn: The History of Race and Education in the United States* (Cambridge University Press, 1977). Copyright © 1977 by Cambridge University Press. Reprinted by permission. Notes omitted.

8.1 From Paulo Freire and Donaldo Macedo, *Literacy: Reading the Word and the World* (Bergin & Garvey, 1987). Copyright © 1987 by Paulo Freire and Donaldo Macedo. Reprinted by permission of Greenwood Publishing Group, Inc., Westport, CT. Some notes omitted.

8.2 From Benjamin R. Barber, *An Aristocracy of Everyone: The Politics of Education and the Future of America* (Oxford University Press, 1992). Copyright © 1992 by Ballantine Books, a division of Random House, Inc. Reprinted by permission. Notes omitted.

9.1 From Elizabeth Cady Stanton, *Eighty Years and More (1815–1897): Reminiscences of Elizabeth Cady Stanton* (T. Fisher Unwin, 1898).

9.2 From American Association of University Women, *How Schools Shortchange Girls: A Study of Major Findings on Girls and Education* (American Association of University Women, 1992). Copyright © 1992 by The American Association of University Women Educational Foundation, 1111 16th Street, NW, Washington, DC 20036, (202) 785-7700. Reprinted by permission. Notes omitted.

9.3 From bell hooks, *Teaching to Transgress: Education as the Practice of Freedom* (Routledge, 1994). Copyright © 1994 by Gloria Watkins. Reprinted by permission.

10.1 From *Brown v. Board of Education of Topeka, Kansas,* 347 U.S. 483 (1954).

10.2 From Marian Wright Edelman, "Twenty Years After 'Brown': Where Are We Now?" *New York University Education Quarterly,* vol. 4 (Summer 1974). Copyright © 1974 by Marian Wright Edelman. Reprinted by permission.

10.3 From United States Commission on Civil Rights, *A Better Chance to Learn: Bilingual-Bicultural Education* (Clearinghouse Publication 51, May 1975). Notes omitted.

11.1 From Benjamin S. Bloom, Max D. Engelhart, Edward J. Furst, Walker H. Hill, and David R. Krathwohl, *Taxonomy of Educational Objectives, Handbook I: Cognitive Domain* (David McKay, 1956). Copyright © 1956 by Longman, Inc.; renewed 1984 by Benjamin S. Bloom and David R. Krathwohl. Reprinted by permission of Addison-Wesley Educational Publishers, Inc.

11.2 From David R. Krathwohl, Benjamin S. Bloom, and Bertram B. Masia, *Taxonomy of Educational Objectives, Handbook II: Affective Domain* (David McKay, 1964). Copyright © 1964 by Longman, Inc. Reprinted by permission of Addison-Wesley Educational Publishers, Inc. Some notes omitted.

11.3 From Grant P. Wiggins, *Assessing Student Performance: Exploring the Purpose and Limits of Testing* (Jossey-Bass, 1993). Copyright © 1993 by Jossey-Bass Publishers, Inc. Reprinted by permission.

12.1   From Ann L. Brown, John D. Bransford, Roberta A. Ferrara, and Joseph C. Campione, "Learning, Remembering, and Understanding," in Paul H. Mussen, ed., *Handbook of Child Psychology, vol. 3: Cognitive Development*, 4th ed. (John Wiley, 1983). Copyright © 1946, 1954, 1970, and 1983 by John Wiley & Sons, Inc. Reprinted by permission. Notes and references omitted.

12.2   From John Bransford, Robert Sherwood, Nancy Vye, and John Rieser, "Teaching Thinking and Problem Solving," *American Psychologist*, vol. 41, no. 10 (October 1986), pp. 1078, 1083–1086. Copyright © 1986 by The American Psychological Association. Reprinted by permission. References omitted.

12.3   From Howard Gardner and Joseph Walters, "A Rounded Version," in Howard Gardner, *Multiple Intelligences: The Theory in Practice* (Basic Books, 1993). Copyright © 1993 by Howard Gardner. Reprinted by permission of Basic Books, a division of HarperCollins Publishers, Inc. References omitted.

13.1   From John Dewey, "Education and Social Change," *The Social Frontier: A Journal of Educational Criticism and Reconstruction*, vol. 3, no. 26 (May 1937). Copyright © 1937 by The Center for Dewey Studies, Southern Illinois University, Carbondale, IL. Reprinted by permission.

13.2   From I. L. Kandel, *Conflicting Theories of Education* (Macmillan, 1938).

14.1   From Howard Gardner, *Multiple Intelligences: The Theory in Practice* (Basic Books, 1993). Copyright © 1993 by Howard Gardner. Reprinted by permission of Basic Books, a division of HarperCollins Publishers, Inc.

14.2   From Jonathan Kozol, *Amazing Grace: The Lives of Children and the Conscience of a Nation* (Crown Publishers, 1995). Copyright © 1995 by Jonathan Kozol. Reprinted by permission of Crown Publishers, Inc.

Index

academic approach to reading, 196–197

Accelerated Schools Project, 122

active discipline, Montessori's theory of, 81–89

Adler, Mortimer, on the Paideia proposal, 22–28

affective objectives, of instruction and evaluation, Bloom's, 261–270

affirmative action, 249–250

Africa, literacy in, 193–201

Afrocentrism, 208–209

age, grouping students by, 74–75

AIDS, 358–359

Alexander v. Holmes County Board of Education, 242

Alzheimer's disease, 322

America 2000 (U.S. Department of Education), 223

American Association of University Women, on gender inequality in education, 221–228

American Dilemma, An (Myrdal), 13, 154

analysis, as a classification in Bloom's taxonomy of educational objectives, 267–268, 279

aphasia, 323

Apple, Michael W., on the hidden curriculum, 53–62

application, as a classification in Bloom's taxonomy of educational objectives, 267–268, 279

Aristotle, 341, 345

art: in the child-centered school, 107; in the Dewey Laboratory School, 96–97

assembly, weekly general, at the Dewey Laboratory School, 95–96

assessment. *See* testing

Atlanta Exposition Address, Booker T. Washington's, 160–163; reaction to, 164–173

authoritarianism, 198

autism, 323, 349

autonomous regulation, Piaget's theory of, 299–300

Bagley, William, 143, 144

Baldwin, James, on educating black children, 174–180

"banking" method of teaching, vs. problem-posing approach, 63–70

Barber, Benjamin R., on radicals and postmodernism, 202–211

Bayard, Henry, 214–215

behaviorism, 296

"Bestist" bias, in education, 352

Bickel, Alexander, 242, 243

bilingual education, 200, 252–257

bill of rights, student, regarding testing, 286–294

biophily, 67

Black Athena (Bernal), 208

Black Panther, The, 11–12, 13

black studies, 57

blacks. *See* racial issues

Bloom, Benjamin S., on a taxonomy of educational objectives, 261–270, 271–285

bodily-kinesthetic intelligence, 315, 318–319, 350

border pedagogy, 136–137

Bransford, John, on teaching thinking and problem solving, 308–314

Broca's area, of the brain, 320

Brown, Ann L., 309–310; on metacognition, 295–307

Brown v. Board of Education of Topeka, Kansas, 186–188, 191, 235–239, 240–251, 252, 253

busing, of school children, to achieve racial equality, 248

cafeteria-style education, 10

Carter, Robert, 186, 189

characterization by a value or value complex, as a classification in Bloom's taxonomy of educational objectives, 273–275, 278

checking outcomes, metacognition and, 298

child-centered schooling, 100–109

choice, school reform and, 125, 126

Choosing Life (Soelle), 47

Christmas, Florence, 20, 151–152

civil rights: and bilingual education, 252–257; and racism in education, 151–159. *See also Brown v. Board of Education of Topeka, Kansas*

Civil Rights Act of 1964, 191, 242, 243, 253

classification device, Bloom's taxonomy of educational objectives as, 262–264

Coalition of Essential Schools, 122, 124, 126

cognition: multiple intelligences and, 315–325; problem-solving and, 308–314. *See also* metacognition

cognitive development approach to reading, 198

cognitive objectives, of instruction and evaluation, Bloom's, 261–270, 276–285

cold cognition, 304–305

college, 27

common core curriculum, Hirsch's, 142–148

common school, 116

community colleges, 27

comprehension, as a classification in Bloom's taxonomy of educational objectives, 267–268, 279

computers, 126
conflict, nature of, hidden curriculum and, 53–62
Congress of Industrial Organizations, 157
conscious regulation, Piaget's theory of, 300
conservatism: cultural literacy and, 3–13; and education from 1945 to 1980, 14–21; and the Paideia proposal, 22–28; social change and, 331–332
Constitution, U.S. *See* individual amendments; Supreme Court
content knowledge, 148
core knowledge curriculum, Hirsch's, 122, 126
creative self-expression, in the child-centered school, 106–107
critical pedagogy, literacy and, 193–201; postmodernism and, 202–211
cultural literacy, 3–13
cultural politics, education and, 43–52
culture: education and, 110–120; multiple intelligences and, 346–352; and poverty and social inequality, 353–360; role of, in the work of Paulo Freire, 43–52
Cummings v. County Board of Education, 185
curriculum reform: Afrocentrism and, 208–209; common core as, 142–148; cultural literacy and, 3–13; culture and, 110–120; at the Dewey Laboratory School, 90–99; Paideia proposal and; 22–28; progressive education and, 29–34; and the project method, 35–42
custodian, teacher as, 77

Dawn (Nietzsche), 288
De Funis v. Odegaard, 250
de jure/de facto segregation, and *Brown v. Board of Education of Topeka, Kansas*, 240–251
deconstructionism, postmodernism and, 202–211
democracy, and education, 29–34, 336–337, 345
demographic changes, in education from 1945 to 1980, 14–21
Depression, 154, 177
Derrida, Jacques, 202, 204
deschooling society, Illich's theory of, 71–78
Dewey, John, 9, 35, 42, 100–101, 102, 116–117, 198, 343–344; on democracy and education, 29–34; on education and social change, 329–337; laboratory school founded by, 90–99
discipline, Maria Montessori on, 81–89
discovery learning, 26, 284
domination, education and, 68
dropouts, female high school, 227–228
drug abuse, in the schools, 20
Du Bois, W. E. B., 160, 182, 187; on Washington's Atlanta Compromise, 164–173
due process clause, of the Fourteenth Amendment, 239

Edelman, Marian Wright, on *Brown v. Board of Education of Topeka, Kansas*, 240–251
Educational Frontier, The (Counts), 119
Edwards, Anna Camp, on the Dewey Laboratory School at the University of Chicago, 90–99
electives, course, elimination of, in Paideia proposal, 23
Elementary and Secondary Education Act of 1965, 242
engaged pedagogy, 229–232
English as a Second Language (ESL) programs, bilingual education and, 252–257
English, standard written, 5
Enlightenment, 145, 146
equality, educational. *See* civil rights
"evaded" curriculum, 225
evaluation, as a classification in Bloom's taxonomy of educational objectives, 267–268, 279–280
executive processes, specific knowledge and, 310–313
experience-based education, project method and, 35–42

Fair Employment Practices Committee, 182
faith, in the work of Paulo Freire, 48
feminism, 140. *See also* women
financial issues, school reform and, 125, 126, 183–184
First Amendment, to the U.S. Constitution, 145
Foucault, Michel, 202, 206, 287–288, 289
Fourteenth Amendment, to the U.S. Constitution, 186, 236, 239
Frames of Mind (Gardner), 316
Frankfurt school, 53
Frankfurter, Felix, 188–189
freedom: vs. control, in the child-centered school, 102–103; education as the practice of, 63–70
Freire, Paulo: Henry A. Giroux on, 43–52; on literacy and critical pedagogy, 193–201; on the pedagogy of the oppressed, 63–70
frontal lobes, of the brain, personality and, 323

Gaines v. Canada, 185, 237
Gallwey, Tim, 318–319
Gardner, Howard, on multiple intelligences, 315–325, 346–352
gender equity, in education, 212–220, 221–228
Giroux, Henry A., 131, 136, 197–198, 199; on Paulo Freire, 43–52
Gittelsohn, Roland B., 156–157
Great Books curriculum, 22
Green v. County School Board, 242, 248
Guided Design program (Wales and Stager), 312

Harvard Project Zero, 122
hidden curriculum, 46–47, 53–62, 78

hierarchy: problem of, in Bloom's taxonomy of educational objectives, 266–269; of subjects, in education, 114–115

Hirsch, E. D., Jr., 122, 126; on a common core curriculum, 142–148; on cultural literacy, 3–13

Hispanics. *See* racial issues

history, study of, at the Dewey Laboratory School, 91, 92

homework, future of, 125–126

hooks, bell, on engaged pedagogy, 229–232

humanism, of "banking" method of education, 66

idiot savants, 349

Illich, Ivan, on deschooling society, 71–78

in loco parentis, 20

Instrumental Enrichment program, Feuerstein's, 312

intelligences, Gardner's theory of multiple, 315–325, 346–352

intercultural understanding, Washington's theory of, 160–163

interest span, project method and, 41

internalization, of affective educational objectives, 261–263

interpersonal intelligence, 315, 321–322, 350

intrapersonal intelligence, 315, 322–323, 350

James, William, 101, 276, 281

Jefferson, Thomas, 12, 144, 145

Job Corps, 21

junior colleges, 27

Kandel, I. L., on conflicting theories of education, 338–345

Keller, Helen, 321–322

Kett, Joseph F., 3, 4

Kilpatrick, William Heard, 100, 101–102, 329; on the project method, 35–42

knowledge, as a classification in Bloom's taxonomy of educational objectives, 267–268, 278

Kozol, Jonathan, on poverty and social inequality, 353–360

Krathwohl, David R., on a taxonomy of educational objectives, 271–285

language: and bilingual education, 252–257; role of, in literacy, 199–201; study of, at the Dewey Laboratory School, 92–93. *See also* linguistic intelligence

language of critique, in the work of Paulo Freire, 44, 46–47

language of possibility, liberation theology and, 47–48

Lau v. Nichols, 253, 256–257

learning disabilities, 349

learning, metacognition and, 295–307

liberal arts education, 19, 23

liberation theology, 47–48; critical pedagogy and, 193–201

liberty, Montessori's theory of discipline through, 81–89

limited English proficiency (LEP) students, bilingual education and, 252–257

linguistic intelligence, 315, 320, 349, 351

literacy: critical pedagogy and, 193–201; cultural, 3–13

logical-mathematical intelligence, 315, 319–320, 349, 351

Logo, 311

ludic postmodernism, 135

Macedo, Donaldo, on literacy and critical pedagogy, 193–201

Mann, Horace, 116, 144, 145, 331

manual skills, in the Paideia proposal, 25

Marshall, Thurgood, 183, 184, 188–189

Marxism, 44, 45, 57

Masia, Bertram B., on a taxonomy of educational objectives, 271–285

math: girls and, 226–227; study of, at the Dewey Laboratory School, 91, 92, 93–94. *See also* logical-mathematical intelligence

Mayhew, Katherine Camp, on the Dewey Laboratory School at the University of Chicago, 90–99

McClintock, Barbara, 319–320

McKee, Alice, 221–222

McLaren, Peter, on multiculturalism and postmodernism, 131–141

McLaurin v. Oklahoma State Regents, 195, 237, 238

measurement. *See* testing

memory, metacognition and, 295–307

Menuhin, Yehudi, 317–318

metacognition, 295–307, 309–310, 311–312

Mismeasure of Man, The (Gould), 289

mobility, in the United States, and lack of common core curriculum, 142–148

monitoring activities, metacognition and, 298

Montessori, Maria, on discipline, 81–89

moral education, 40

moral issues, testing and, 286–294

moralist, teacher as, 77

multicultural education, 8, 146, 208, 252–257; postmodernism and, 131–141

multiple intelligences, Gardner's theory of, 315–325, 346–352

music, study of, at the Dewey Laboratory School, 96

musical intelligence, 315, 317–318

My Millionaire Uncle (Notari), 83–84

Myrdal, Gunnar, 13, 154

National Assessment of Educational Progress (NAEP), 6

National Association for the Advancement of
Colored People (NAACP), 154, 156, 157, 158,
164, 182, 183, 184, 185, 186
National Education Goals (National Governors
Association), 223
Native Americans. *See* racial issues
navigation, spatial intelligence and, 320–321
Netherlands, lack of common core curriculum
in, 143
neutral, schools as, 333
New York City, poverty and social inequality
in, 353–360
New Zealand, principles for assessment
adopted by, 292–293
nineteenth century, education of girls in,
212–220
Nixon, Richard, 72, 248

objectives, Bloom's taxonomy of educational,
261–270, 271–285
oppressed, pedagogy of the, 63–70
organization, as a classification in Bloom's
taxonomy of educational objectives,
273–275, 278

Paideia proposal, Adler's, 22–28
pattern recognition, 313
Patterson, Orlando, 7–8, 11, 145–146
perceptual learning, 313
personality, in the child-centered school,
107–108
Philosophy for Children program, Lipman's,
312
physical training, in the Paideia proposal, 25
Piaget, Jean, 198, 349; regulation theory of,
299–300, 302
planning activities, metacognition and, 298
Plato, 205, 309, 341, 345
Plessy v. Ferguson, 186, 235, 236, 237–238
political issues, education and, 14–21, 43–52
postmodernism: deconstructionism and,
202–211; multiculturalism and, 131–141
poverty, social inequality and, 353–360
power: gender and, 225; role of, in the work of
Paulo Freire, 43–52; testing and, 286–294
practical education, for blacks, Washington's
theory of, 160–163
problem-posing approach to education,
Freire's, 63–70
problem-solving skills, teaching of, 308–314
procedural knowledge, 148
prodigies, 349
progressive education: child-centered schooling
and, 100–109; John Dewey on, 29–34;
postmodernism and, 202–211; and the
project method, 35–42
project method, 35–42, 101–102

racial issues, education and, 14–21, 57, 208–209;
James Baldwin on, 174–180; bilingual
education and, 252–257; W. E. B. Du Bois on,
164–173; and education from 1945 to 1980,
151–159; and equality of education, 181–192;
and literacy of Africa, 193–201; poverty and
social inequality and, 353–360; school
achievement and, 226; Booker T.
Washington on, 160–163. *See also* civil rights
radicalism, education and, 334–335
Ravitch, Diane: on education from 1945 to 1980,
14–21; on racial issues in education, 151–159
reading, 4. *See also* literacy
receiving, as a classification in Bloom's
taxonomy of educational objectives,
273–275, 278, 279
Reconstruction, 168, 177
reconstruction of experience, education as,
29–34, 119
reductionism, 208
religion, education and, 17–18, 47–48
Republic, The (Socrates), 205
resistance postmodernism, 135, 137
responding, as a classification in Bloom's
taxonomy of educational objectives,
273–275, 278, 279, 280, 284
Romantic approach to reading, 198–199
Romanticism, core curriculum and, 148
Roosevelt, Franklin Delano, 154, 182
Rugg, Harold, 329; on child-centered schooling,
100–109
Ruth, Babe, 318–319

Scholastic Aptitude Test (SAT), 18, 227, 347
School Development Project, Comer's, 122
science: girls and, 226–227; study of, at the
Dewey Laboratory School, 91, 94
segregation, school, 151–159, 181–192. *See also
Brown v. Board of Education of Topeka, Kansas*
self-discipline, Montessori's theory of, 81–89
self-regulation, metacognition and, 295–307
"separate but equal," *Plessy v. Ferguson* and,
235, 236, 238–239
services curriculum, 10
"set," learning process and, 38–39
sexual harassment, 224
"shopping mall school," vs. cultural literacy,
10–11
shop-work, at the Dewey Laboratory School, 92
Shumaker, Ann, on child-centered schooling,
100–109
Sipeul v. Oklahoma, 185, 237
Sizer, Theodore R., on the future of American
public education, 121–130
Smith, Horace, Sizer's fictional American
teacher, 121–130
social adjustment, in the child-centered school,
107–108
social change, education and, 329–337, 338–345

social issues, education and, 32–34, 110–120, 353–360

socioeconomic status, school achievement and, 226

Sophism, 205

spatial intelligence, 320–321, 325, 349–350

specialization, in education, 27

standard written English, 5

Stanton, Elizabeth Cady, on educational rights of women, 212–220

Sullivan, Anne, 321–322

Supreme Court, 127, 185–186, 241, 252; on *Brown v. Board of Education of Topeka, Kansas,* 235–239. *See also* individual cases

Swann v. Charlotte-Mecklenburg Board of Education, 242, 248–249

Sweatt v. Painter, 185, 237, 238

Switzerland, lack of common core curriculum in, 143

synthesis, as a classification in Bloom's taxonomy of educational objectives, 267–268, 279

Taba, Hilda, on schools and society, 110–120

taxonomy of educational objectives, Bloom's, 261–270, 271–285

television, education and, 10, 19

testing: and Bloom's taxonomy of educational objectives, 261–270, 271–285; morality of, 286–294

"Testist" bias, in education, 352

Theory and Resistance (Giroux), 197

theory-practice relationship, in the work of Paulo Freire, 51–52

therapist, teacher as, 77

Torrey, Rowan, 20–21

transformation, role of, in the work of Paulo Freire, 43–52

Trefil, James, 3, 4

Truman, Harry, 17; and racial issues in education, 151–159

Turner, Nat, 167, 170

understanding, metacognition and, 295–307

United States Commission on Civil Rights, on bilingual education, 252–257

utilitarian approach to reading, 197–198

utilitarianism, 208

values, consensus, hidden curriculum and, 53–62

valuing, as classification in Bloom's taxonomy of educational objectives, 273–275, 278

voice, literacy and, 201

voting rights, 155, 170

Walters, Joseph, on multiple intelligences, 315–325

Warren, Earl, 189, 236

Washington, Booker T., on interracial relations, 160–163

WASP (White Anglo-Saxon Protestant) culture, cultural literacy and, 7

Weinberg, Meyer, on racial equality in education, 181–192

"Westist" bias, in education, 352

Wiggins, Grant P., on the morality of testing, 286–294

women, and education: and autobiography of Elizabeth Cady Stanton, 212–220; engaged pedagogy and, 229–232; gender inequality and, 221–228

women's studies, 57

Woolf, Virginia, 322–323

work, in the Paideia proposal, 25

world knowledge, 4

World War II, 182